Heart Unbound 2.0
The Journey Expands

Dr John McSwiney

https://www.timetotransform.world

McSwiney, John (author)

Title: *Heart Unbound 2.0. The Journey Expands* / Dr John McSwiney, author.

Illustrations: Canva

ISBN: 978–0–6486101–5–1

Emotional intelligence workbook

Leadership and self development

Mindfulness and resilience guide

Heart centred living book

Authentic leadership training

Personal growth transformation

Mental health and wellbeing

DEDICATION

To every soul who has ever felt the quiet ache for something more... This book is for you. May these pages remind you that your heart is not a destination but a living compass, one that can guide you through the storms, the silences, and the moments of radiant clarity.

To those who dared to walk the first Heart Unbound journey, your courage and openness have shaped this expanded path. To those just beginning, may you find within these words the invitation to go deeper, love wider, and live truer, and to the part of you that already knows, you are, and have always been, enough.

FRONT COVER

Here is the meaning behind that image, and why it belongs on the cover of *Heart Unbound 2.0*.

At the edge of the known.

The figure stands on a rocky outcrop, solid, textured, unglamorous. That rock is discipline and practice: the daily work that steadies you. Beyond it, the aqua ocean is the vast field of feeling and possibility; the blue sky is spacious awareness; the distant mountains are purpose and promise. One image holds **earth, water, air, and light**, a whole life, not a single mood.

Arms open, not clenched.

The outstretched posture is not conquest; it is consent. It says, *I am available to what is real*. This is the ethic of *Heart Unbound*: strength without aggression, presence without performance. Openness is the risk and the reward, vulnerability as a doorway to courage, connection, and clarity.

A horizon that invites integration.

Where ocean meets sky you get a horizon, the line between what has been and what could be. The program lives exactly there: between grounding (rock) and expansion (sky), between emotion (water) and intention (mountain). The colours clean aquas and blues, signal calm, trust, and clear seeing.

A map of the 30 themes.

- **Breathing, Grounding, Relaxation:** feet on rock, lungs full of sea air.

- **I Am, Mirror, Heart Whispers:** the honest pause before the next step.
- **Nothingness, Reflection:** the spacious quiet that reveals the right action.
- **Homecoming, Living Invitations:** belonging to self, then opening to the world.

In short, the cover does not promise a fantasy. It shows a human at a real edge, steady, open, and ready. That is *Heart Unbound 2.0*: a year of small, repeatable practices that let you meet the vastness of your life **with your feet on the rock and your heart wide open.**

CONTENTS

ACKNOWLEDGMENTS

To everyone who has walked beside me on this journey, thank you.

To the countless souls who have trusted me with their stories, their hearts, and their vulnerability, you have been my greatest teachers. Every tear shared, every smile exchanged, every moment of courage you have shown has shaped the words on these pages.

To my family and friends, your love, patience, and belief in me have been the steady ground beneath my feet. You have seen me at my most inspired and my most weary, and you have held space for both.

To the participants of the *Heart Unbound* program, past and present, your commitment to showing up for yourselves and each other has been nothing short of extraordinary. You are living proof that heart-led living is not only possible, but powerful.

To those who have challenged me, knowingly or unknowingly, thank you. You have reminded me that unbinding the heart is not about perfection, but about choosing love, again and again, even when it is hard.

To you, holding this book now, thank you for opening yourself to this journey. My deepest hope is that these pages will not just inspire you, but invite you into the kind of transformation that lingers long after the final word. May your heart feel seen, heard, and free.

With love,

Dr John McSwiney

Founder of *Time to Transform*

MISSION

The mission of *Heart Unbound 2.0 – The Journey Expands* is to be your trusted companion as you step beyond the insights of the original *Heart Unbound* and into the deeper waters of heart-centred living. This second edition exists to help you move from learning to living, to take the concepts you have discovered and weave them into the fabric of your daily choices, relationships, and sense of self.

This book is here to guide you through advanced reflections, new transformative practices, and powerful next steps that strengthen your self-awareness, sharpen your emotional intelligence, and awaken your capacity to live with authenticity, compassion, and courage. It is designed to meet you where you are, whether you are continuing from the first journey or beginning fresh, and to help you find your own pace, rhythm, and path toward a fully unbound heart.

By walking with you through both the challenges and celebrations of inner growth, *Heart Unbound 2.0* aims to empower you to embody your values, align your life with your deepest truths, and become a source of empathy and connection in the world.

The mission is simple yet profound: to support you in expanding your heart so that your presence and actions create a lasting ripple of kindness, healing, and inspiration, in your relationships, your communities, and far beyond.

PERSONAL MESSAGE FROM DR JOHN

When I first wrote *Heart Unbound*, I had one hope, that it would help you hear the quiet truth within you, the one that has always known you are more than the roles you play or the masks you wear. Now, as you hold *Heart Unbound 2.0 - The Journey Expands* in your hands, I want you to know this: you are standing at the threshold of something even more extraordinary. This is not simply a continuation of a program; it is an invitation to live from your heart every single Part, in every single choice, in a way that shapes not just your own life but the lives of everyone you touch.

I have poured my heart into these pages for you, the stories, the reflections, the practices, so that you have a companion for the moments when you feel ready to leap, and for the moments when you feel like you have lost your way. You will not walk this path alone. I will be with you in every word, encouraging you to be curious, to be kind to yourself, and to trust that your heart knows the next step.

Take your time. Let the journey unfold at its own pace. You may find that the smallest shifts bring the deepest change, and when you reach the end of these pages, remember: the journey of your heart is never truly finished. It keeps expanding, as do you, and from my heart to yours, thank you for allowing me to walk beside you. I believe in you. I always will.

With gratitude and hope.

Dr John McSwiney

Founder, *Time to Transform* & Author, *Heart Unbound*

INTRODUCTION

The Journey Expands

Your heart is the most extraordinary compass you will ever own. It knows the way home, to your truth, to your purpose, to the life you were born to live.

When *Heart Unbound* first arrived in your hands, it was a call to awaken. You learned to listen to the whispers of your own heart, to create moments of stillness, and to take your first courageous steps towards living authentically. Many of you have told me it changed the way you see yourself, your relationships, and the world around you, but here is the truth: the journey does not end when the final page is turned. Heart connection is not a one-time event, it is a living, breathing practice., and that is why *Heart Unbound 2.0 – The Journey Expands* was born.

This book is for you if you are ready to go deeper. If you are ready to not only remember who you are but to **be** who you are, unapologetically and fully. Here, you move from insight to embodiment. From moments of connection to a way of life. From knowing your heart's language to speaking it fluently in every choice you make.

Over these chapters, you will revisit the foundations of heart connection and explore new, more advanced practices designed to:

- Strengthen your self-awareness and emotional intelligence

- Release the patterns that keep you small or disconnected

- Integrate heart-led living into every area of your life, work, relationships, creativity, and self-care

- Expand your capacity for compassion, empathy, and courageous action

This is not just reading material. It is a companion for your soul. You will be invited to reflect deeply, practice regularly, and act with intention, and along the way, you will discover that the more your heart expands, the more life opens to meet you.

If you have made it this far, it means you have already heard your heart calling. Now, it is time to answer in a new way, with deeper trust, greater courage, and a willingness to step into the unknown.

Welcome to the next chapter of your heart's unfolding.

From my heart to yours,

Dr John McSwiney

WHY DOES CONNECTING WITH YOUR HEART UNBOUND IT?

When you connect with your heart, you are not just tuning into an emotion, you are unlocking the deepest intelligence within you. Your heart is the seat of your authenticity, the keeper of your truest self, and the quiet guardian of the life you were born to live.

An unbound heart is a heart you have freed from the cages of fear, expectation, and self-doubt. It is a heart that remembers its own voice, and trusts it. The moment you choose to truly listen to the whispers within, you begin to dissolve the invisible chains that have kept you playing small, silencing your truth, or living by someone else's script.

Freedom from External Pressures

When you live from your unbound heart, you are no longer driven by the need to please or prove yourself. The endless search for validation from others falls away, replaced by the steady, grounding truth of your own values. You move through the world guided by what matters most to you, unapologetically, courageously, and without the weight of external approval.

Healing the Past

Your unbound heart becomes your sanctuary for healing. It invites you to release the burdens of past wounds and traumas, not by erasing them, but by transforming them into sources of wisdom and compassion. In this space, forgiveness becomes possible, for others, and for yourself. You learn that letting go is not weakness, but liberation.

Igniting Creativity and Intuition

When you connect deeply with your heart, your creativity and intuitive wisdom awaken. New ideas, inspired solutions, and fresh perspectives begin to flow with ease. Your heart-led intuition becomes your compass, guiding you toward choices and opportunities that align with your highest purpose.

Deepening Love and Connection

An unbound heart expands your capacity to love, not only romantically, but in every human interaction. You see others more clearly, empathise more deeply, and connect more authentically. Love becomes the language you speak, the energy you give, and the gift you receive.

Living with Emotional Freedom

With an unbound heart, you welcome the full spectrum of your emotions without fear or judgement. You allow yourself to feel, joy, sorrow, hope, uncertainty, knowing that every emotion has its place in the human experience. This openness dissolves self-criticism and invites self-compassion to take root.

Walking in Purpose

Ultimately, an unbound heart is a heart in alignment, with your values, your desires, and your soul's mission. You become the conscious creator of your life, shaping it with intention rather than drifting through it on autopilot.

The unbinding of your heart is not a single moment, it is a lifelong practice. It asks for patience, courage, and the willingness to keep listening, even when the world is loud, but each time you choose to live from your heart, you take another step towards the freedom, love, and purpose that have always been yours.

As you continue this journey, may your unbound heart guide you toward a life rich in authenticity, connection, and joy, and may its light ripple far beyond you, touching everyone and everything it meets.

YOUR HEART UNBOUND OATH

The choice of an oath, rather than a legal contract, is intentional. An oath is not bound by law, it is bound by love, truth, and the integrity of your own heart. It is a sacred promise you make to yourself, from yourself. It cannot be enforced by anyone else, nor can it be taken away. It is yours.

By taking this oath, you acknowledge that true transformation cannot be signed into existence, it must be lived, breathed, and chosen in every moment. You are making a conscious, heart-led commitment to walk this journey with authenticity, courage, and deep personal responsibility.

This oath is a reminder that the real power of *Heart Unbound 2.0* lies not in the pages you read, but in the actions you take and the space you create within yourself for change to unfold. It is a declaration that you will trust your own inner wisdom, embrace vulnerability, and open yourself to the full spectrum of your human experience.

When you speak this oath, you join a community of like-hearted souls who are also daring to live unbound, each of you walking your own path, yet connected by the shared intention to live from the heart. In this unity, you are reminded that you are never truly alone.

This is not just the start of a program, it is the opening of a lifelong dialogue with your heart. You are stepping into a relationship with yourself that will continue to deepen, expand, and ripple into every part of your life.

Your Oath

I, **[Your Name]**, on this Part **[Date]**, choose to live with my heart unbound.

1. I commit to honouring and nurturing the wisdom of my heart, trusting it as my truest guide in all things.

2. I promise to listen deeply to the whispers within, following them with courage, even when the path is uncertain.

3. I vow to meet myself and others with compassion, knowing that love is the strongest bridge between souls.

4. I will create space for stillness, reflection, and truth, so my heart's voice is never drowned out by the noise of the world.

5. I promise to live in gratitude, celebrating the beauty, blessings, and lessons that each Part offers me.

6. I will embrace vulnerability, recognising it as a source of strength, connection, and freedom.

7. I vow to live fully present, to see, feel, and experience life without holding back.

8. I commit to growth, knowing that every step I take in alignment with my heart brings healing to me and light to the world.

This is **my Heart Unbound 2.0 Oath**, a sacred vow to live with love, authenticity, and courage, each and every Part.

HOW TO USE THIS BOOK

Heart Unbound 2.0 is more than a book, it is an immersive 28-Part transformation designed to awaken, unbind, and expand your heart. Every page invites you into a personal journey of reflection, action, and integration. Here is how to get the most from your experience:

1. **Begin with Intention:** Before you turn the first page, pause. Ask yourself: *What do I want to create in my life on this Heart Unbound journey?* Write your intention in your **heART of Life Journal**. This intention will be your anchor and compass as you move through the program.

2. **Immerse in the Daily Practice:** Each Part presents a **guided prompt, reflection, or exercise** designed to inspire insight, emotional release, and connection. Do not rush. Read slowly, let the words land, and give them space to work within you.

3. **Reflect and Record:** After each daily prompt, spend 5-10 minutes reflecting. Write down your thoughts, emotions, and any images, memories, or shifts that arise. This journal is not just a record, it is a mirror of your growth and a treasure you can revisit.

4. **Turn Reflection into Action:** Transformation happens when insight meets action. Choose one small, heart-led action each day that aligns with your prompt. It might be a conversation, an act of kindness, a moment of stillness, or a boundary you honour.

5. **Connect and Share:** Share your experiences with a trusted friend, coach, or our Heart Unbound community. Speaking your journey out loud deepens understanding, opens new perspectives, and keeps you

accountable.

6. **Practice Radical Self-Compassion:** Some days will feel expansive, others confronting. Welcome it all. Speak to yourself with the same kindness and patience you would offer a dear friend. Every emotion and experience is part of the unbinding.

7. **Embody and Integrate:** The real magic is in the integration. Let what you learn and feel move beyond the page into your daily life, your conversations, your choices, your relationships. This is how your heart becomes your way of being, not just a moment in time.

Your journey is unique. Heart Unbound 2.0 gives you the tools, but your heart leads the way. Trust it. Follow it. Let it surprise you, and remember: every step you take from your heart ripples far beyond you.

THE PROFESSIONAL ASSURANCE BEHIND
HEART UNBOUND 2.0

When you hold *Heart Unbound 2.0* in your hands, you are not just holding a book, you are holding a nationally aligned framework for transformation. Every chapter you read, every reflection you write, every practice you embrace has been carefully mapped to Australia's highest national learning and professional standards: the Australian Qualifications Framework (AQF), the Australian Skills Quality Authority (ASQA), the National Safety and Quality Health Service (NSQHS) Standards, and the Australian Public Sector (APS) Capability Framework.

Why does this matter to you? Because your journey here is real. It is more than an inspiring read or a feel-good program, it is backed by the same standards that shape national education, healthcare, and leadership excellence. This means the skills you develop are legitimate, transferable, and recognised far beyond the pages of this book.

This alignment gives weight and credibility to your transformation. You are not just learning about emotional intelligence, resilience, and heart-led living, you are building capabilities that meet the benchmarks of professional growth and personal mastery. These are the same qualities sought in leaders, changemakers, carers, and visionaries across Australia.

Heart Unbound 2.0 is both your personal companion and your professional ally. It will walk beside you through moments of deep reflection and into the spaces where you apply these lessons in real life, at work, at home, and in your community.

By choosing this journey, you are stepping into a process that has the power to reshape how you see yourself, how you connect with others, and how you move through the world, and the best part? It is a journey that carries recognition, respect, and the assurance that your growth matters, to you, to those you love, and to the wider world you influence.

Welcome to *Heart Unbound 2.0*.

You are exactly where you are meant to be.

1 - BREATHING

Your Opening Reflection

An Invitation to Breathe - Before you move forward, allow yourself this simple gift: pause, soften, and breathe. Your breath is not just air, it is life moving through you, a gentle reminder that you are here, alive, and connected. Let each inhale welcome you home to your heart, and let each exhale release what no longer serves you. With every breath, you are reminded that presence, peace, and renewal are always within reach.

- "What does your breath feel like in this moment, tight, shallow, soft, steady?"

- "When you pause to breathe deeply, what changes within you, even slightly?"

- "What single word or phrase describes your relationship with your breath today?"

- "How does your body respond when you bring awareness to your heart as you breathe?"

- "What would it feel like to let your breath be your guide, instead of your mind?"

Let these questions open the doorway into presence. Every answer you give, whether in words, sensations, or silence, is a bridge between where you are and where you are going.

Learning Objectives

The learning objectives are included here to give you a clear focus for this chapter, ensuring that each practice you explore moves you closer to mastering the skills, insights, and heart-led awareness that will enrich your life well beyond the program. By the end of this chapter, you will:

- Understand the role of breath in emotional regulation and self-awareness.

- Practice deep, heart-centred breathing techniques.

- Identify physical and emotional shifts that result from conscious breathwork.

- Connect with your heart space to access intuitive and emotional guidance.

- Develop a sustainable self-regulation practice anchored in conscious breathing.

Core Emotional Domains

The core emotional intelligence domains covered here are essential because they form the foundation for lasting heart connection, guiding you to deepen self-awareness, regulate emotions, build resilience, and strengthen the mind-body bond throughout your Heart Unbound journey.

- **Self-Awareness:** Breath draws your attention inward, helping you notice your thoughts, feelings, and physical state.

- **Self-Regulation:** Conscious breathing soothes the nervous system and helps you respond rather than react.

- **Emotional Healing and Resilience:** Breath anchors you through emotional waves, creating space for release, reflection, and recovery.

- **Mind-Body Connection:** Breathing links your physical body with emotional presence, grounding you in calm awareness.

"Breathing – The Bridge Between Your Mind, Body And Heart"

The Science and Soul of Breathing

Breath is a bridge between your mind, body, and heart. Ancient traditions and neuroscience agree: breath regulates the nervous system, releases stress, and activates inner peace. Ancient traditions and modern neuroscience come together to affirm a timeless and powerful truth: your breath is one of the most effective regulators of your nervous system. Across thousands of years, wisdom traditions such as yoga, meditation, tai chi, and pranayama have harnessed the breath to still the mind, release stored tension, and open the doorway to inner peace. In these traditions, breath has never been only a biological function, it has been a sacred bridge between your body, your mind, and your spirit.

Today, the precision of neuroscience confirms what those ancient practices have always known. Conscious breathing, especially slow, deep, and rhythmic breathing, activates your parasympathetic nervous system, signalling safety and calm to every cell in your body. It reduces the production of cortisol, the primary stress hormone, and restores balance in moments when life feels overwhelming. It creates a physiological shift away from the hyper-vigilance of fight-or-flight and into the grounded steadiness of rest-and-digest.

When you choose to slow down and breathe with intention, you are giving your body a clear message: *It is safe to let go.* This simple act changes your chemistry, softens the constant activity of your mind, and allows your awareness to expand. You step out of survival mode and into a deeper state of presence, one where you can think clearly, feel deeply, and respond rather than react.

In this space, peace stops being a fleeting visitor and begins to feel like your natural state of being. Your breath is both an ancient ally and a scientifically validated tool, always within reach, waiting to guide you back to balance, clarity, and connection. It is the one practice that unites the wisdom of the past with the breakthroughs of the present, a living bridge between who you are now and the grounded, heart-led life you are capable of living.

Conscious Breathing Helps Detoxify The Body, Increase Energy, Support Digestion, And Calm Emotional Responses

When you breathe deeply and with full awareness, you awaken and activate your body's natural systems for healing, balance, and restoration. Each slow, intentional breath draws more oxygen into your lungs, delivering fresh life to your cells. This increase in oxygen flow helps to flush out toxins, revitalise your tissues, and renew your energy from the inside out.

As you consciously breathe, you gently stimulate your parasympathetic nervous system, your body's *"rest and digest"* mode. This shifts you away from stress-driven states and into calm, steady balance. Your digestion improves, nutrient absorption is enhanced, and your entire internal system begins to function with greater ease and harmony.

On an emotional level, each conscious breath is a reset button. It calms heightened stress responses, softens anxious thoughts, and clears mental fog. You create space between what you feel and how you respond, giving yourself the power to choose presence over reactivity.

In this grounded state, you move from reacting impulsively to responding with clarity and intention. Your breath becomes more than an automatic process, it becomes your anchor, a reliable and profound tool that can realign your body, settle your mind, and harmonise your emotions in any moment you choose. It is always with you, ready to guide you back to balance whenever you need it most.

The Role Of The Vagus Nerve In Emotional Regulation

Your vagus nerve is one of the most vital yet often overlooked components of your emotional wellbeing. As the longest cranial nerve in your body, it acts as a major communication highway between your brain and vital organs, especially the heart, lungs, and digestive system, but beyond its physical functions, your vagus nerve plays a central role in your capacity to regulate emotions, connect with others, and return to calm after stress.

1. Your Built-In Reset Button

When you are overwhelmed or anxious, your sympathetic nervous system kicks in, this is the *"fight, flight, or freeze"* response. The vagus nerve is the primary activator of your parasympathetic nervous system, your body's *"rest and digest"* or *"tend and befriend"* mode.

When stimulated, it sends signals that slow your heart rate, lower your blood pressure, deepen your breath, and signal safety to your brain. In essence, it tells your entire system: *It is okay. You are safe now.*

2. Your Vagus Nerve and the Emotion-Body Connection

Your emotions are not just *"in your head"*, they are experienced throughout your body. The vagus nerve helps regulate this experience by transmitting information from the gut and heart to the brain and vice versa.

This bidirectional communication helps shape how you feel and how quickly you recover from emotional upsets. A well-toned vagus nerve supports quicker emotional recovery, greater resilience, and an increased ability to stay grounded during stress.

3. Vagal Tone and Resilience

Vagal tone refers to how efficiently your vagus nerve performs. High vagal tone is associated with emotional flexibility, stronger relationships, better heart rate variability (HRV), and increased capacity for compassion and empathy.

It means you can shift more easily from stress back to calm, think clearly under pressure, and respond instead of react. Low vagal tone, on the other hand, is often linked to anxiety, depression, digestive issues, and emotional dysregulation.

4. Practices That Activate your Vagus Nerve

You can tone and strengthen your vagus nerve with intentional daily practices:

- Deep diaphragmatic breathing (especially with longer exhales)
- Humming, chanting, or singing (activates the vocal cords connected to the vagus nerve)
- Cold exposure (e.g., splashing your face with cold water)
- Gentle yoga, grounding, or tai chi
- Loving-kindness meditation and connection with safe people
- Mindful touch or placing your hand on your heart

These practices are simple yet powerful ways to train your body to return to emotional balance more quickly and naturally.

5. Your Vagus Nerve and Heart Intelligence

Your vagus nerve also plays a critical role in what some call "*heart-brain coherence*." When your breath, emotions, and nervous system are regulated, your heart rhythm becomes smooth and coherent.

This coherence sends signals to your brain that create calm, clear thinking, and prosocial emotions such as gratitude, compassion, and love. It is through this heart-vagus-brain connection that you experience emotional intelligence at its most embodied level.

In essence, your vagus nerve is a bridge between your body and your emotions, between survival and thriving. Learning to activate and care for this vital nerve is not just a wellness trend, it is a deep act of self-connection. When you tune into your vagus nerve, you reclaim your power to self-soothe, relate, and live from a grounded and open heart.

The Difference Between Shallow And Deep Breathing

Breathing is the most constant and essential act of your life, but not all breaths are created equal. How you breathe can profoundly affect your nervous system, emotional state, energy levels, and overall wellbeing. Understanding the difference between shallow and deep breathing gives you the power to regulate stress, improve focus, and connect more deeply with your body and heart.

Shallow Breathing: The Breath of Stress and Survival

Shallow breathing, also known as chest or thoracic breathing, is when you take quick, short breaths that primarily fill only the upper part of your lungs. It often goes unnoticed, yet it is common in daily life, especially when you are under pressure, anxious, or distracted.

Effects of Shallow Breathing:

- Activates your sympathetic nervous system (fight, flight, or freeze)

- Increases your heart rate and blood pressure

- Reduces oxygen exchange, which can cause fatigue, fogginess, or dizziness

- Restricts your diaphragm, your body's natural breathing muscle

- Can create a feedback loop of anxiety, where poor breathing fuels more tension

You might not even realise you are breathing shallowly, it has become a norm in high-stress, fast-paced environments. Over time, habitual shallow breathing can contribute to chronic stress, emotional imbalance, and disconnection from your body.

Deep Breathing: The Breath of Presence and Calm

Deep breathing, sometimes called diaphragmatic or belly breathing, involves drawing air deep into the lungs so the diaphragm expands downward, allowing your belly to rise gently. This type of breath is slower, fuller, and more nourishing, both physiologically and emotionally.

Benefits of Deep Breathing:

- Activates your parasympathetic nervous system (rest and digest)

- Lowers your cortisol and stress levels

- Improves oxygen flow, energy, and cellular health

- Calms your mind and relaxes your body

- Enhances heart-brain coherence and emotional regulation

Deep breathing is a direct and accessible way to ground yourself in the present moment. It creates space between stimulus and response, allowing you to feel more centred and make wiser choices.

Breath as a Bridge Between Mind and Body

Your breath is one of the few functions in your body that is both automatic and under your conscious control. This makes it a powerful tool for regulating your nervous system, mood, and mental state. Shallow breathing often reflects a state of unconscious reactivity, while deep breathing invites mindful awareness and heart connection.

Try This: Shift from Shallow to Deep

1. Place one hand on your chest and one on your belly.

2. Notice which one rises when you breathe.

3. Now, slow down your inhale and gently breathe into your belly.

4. Let your exhale be just a little longer than your inhale.

5. Repeat for a few minutes, staying present with each breath.

Summary

Shallow breathing is a signal of survival. Deep breathing is a practice of self-awareness and presence. When you choose to breathe deeply, you return to your body, regulate your emotions, and cultivate calm from the inside out. It is not just a technique, it is a form of self-kindness and emotional intelligence.

Why Breath Awareness Equals Emotional Awareness

Your breath is more than just a physiological process, it is an intimate reflection of your emotional state. Every emotion you feel subtly changes the rhythm, depth, and pace of your breath. In the same way, bringing conscious awareness to your breath becomes a powerful gateway into emotional awareness, regulation, and healing.

The Breath-Emotion Connection

When you feel anxious, your breath becomes short and rapid. When you are sad, it may be slow and heavy. Joy may bring a light, expansive breath. Anger can make your breathing sharp and fast. Even without thinking, your body responds to emotion through breath. This connection is not symbolic, it is neurological, hormonal, and physiological.

Your breath and your emotions are intimately wired through the autonomic nervous system, particularly through the **vagus nerve**, which links your brain, heart, lungs, and gut. This means that by tuning into your breath, you are actually tuning into how your entire emotional system is operating in real time.

What Happens When You Pay Attention to Your Breath?

1. **You Notice Subtle Shifts:** Breath awareness brings you into the present moment, where you can begin to *feel* what is really happening inside, sometimes before the mind can label it.

2. **You start noticing when you are tense:** When you are holding your breath, or when you are breathing too fast. These are cues that something emotional is arising.

3. **You Interrupt Autopilot Reactions:** Without awareness, emotions often run unconsciously, leading to impulsive reactions, but when you are aware of your breath, you create a pause. In that pause, you find choice. You find space. You begin to respond, not react.

4. **You Regulate Your Nervous System:** When you observe your breath and intentionally slow it down, you stimulate the **parasympathetic nervous system** (rest and digest), which helps regulate cortisol and reduce emotional overwhelm. This in turn makes you more resilient and clear-headed.

Breath as an Emotional Mirror

Think of your breath as a *mirror* for your emotional landscape:

- Shallow breath = fear or stress
- Uneven breath = anxiety or agitation
- Held breath = suppression or shock
- Deep, flowing breath = calm, grounded presence

Learning to read your breath is like learning a language your body has always spoken, but you may not have listened to.

From Awareness to Compassion

Breath awareness is not about control, it is about curiosity and compassion. It invites you to meet yourself where you are, without judgment. To notice your trembling breath in sadness. Your held breath in tension. The flutter in excitement, and by bringing love and presence to your breath, you offer love and presence to the emotion beneath it.

A Simple Practice: Breath Check-In

Take a moment, wherever you are. Close your eyes if you wish.

- Notice your breath.

- Is it deep or shallow? Fast or slow?

- What might your breath be telling you right now?

- Can you soften it... just a little?

Summary

Breath awareness is emotional awareness. Your breath is your body's emotional compass, always guiding you inward, offering insight, balance, and peace. When you listen to your breath, you are not just breathing, you are *feeling*, *understanding*, and *healing*. Breath is the language of your heart.

Exercise: 3 Minute Detox & Reset Breath

Purpose: To experience how conscious breathing supports detoxification, boosts your energy, aids digestion, and calms emotions.

1. Sit or stand comfortably. Close your eyes if you feel safe to do so.

2. Inhale deeply through your nose for a count of 4, feel your belly expand.

3. Hold the breath gently for 4 seconds - allow oxygen to circulate.

4. Exhale slowly through your mouth for a count of 6, release tension and toxins.

5. Repeat for 3 minutes, staying present with each breath.

Reflection Prompts:

1. How do you feel physically and emotionally after this practice?

2. Where might you be holding tension or resistance in your life?

Case Study Discussion: Caitlyn's Journey

Caitlyn once described herself as an anxious, restless, and highly energetic woman, always in motion yet feeling strangely absent from her own life. For as long as she could remember, she had felt disconnected from her body, a separation born from the emotional wounds and traumas she had endured over the years. She never felt truly safe expressing her feelings or emotions, and so, without even realising it, she had built walls around her inner world, cutting herself off from her own heart as a means of self-protection.

When we began practising balanced heart breathing, Caitlyn admitted that the process felt both strange and deeply uncomfortable. It was confrontational, not because the technique was difficult, but because for the first time in decades she was allowing herself to pause, to be fully present, and to listen to the quiet truth of her heart. The stillness brought her face-to-face with emotions she had long buried.

We often returned to the old saying, *"What you resist will persist."* The more she resisted facing these emotions, the more they silently shaped her life. Yet, with each deep, conscious breath, Caitlyn began to shift. She found moments of peace she had not known in years. She felt balanced, grounded, and connected to herself in a way that was entirely new. The practice unlocked suppressed feelings, but instead of being overwhelmed, she began to meet them with compassion.

Over time, the balanced heart breathing became her anchor. She opened up in ways she never imagined possible, and in doing so, she began to heal, to learn, and to grow. She found forgiveness, for herself, and for others, and she discovered a deep well of self-love she had never touched before.

Today, Caitlyn's transformation is profound. She now teaches deep breathwork as part of her yoga practice, guiding others to find the same peace, connection, and inner freedom that reshaped her life. Her journey is living proof that the simple act of breathing with awareness can open the door to a life of balance, wholeness, and love.

Reflective Exercise: Caitlyn's Journey

Here are four profound and reflective questions inspired by Caitlyn's story:

1. In what ways might you be unconsciously disconnecting from your own emotions or body as a form of protection?

---

2. How do you typically respond when asked to slow down and be fully present, do you resist it, avoid it, or embrace it?

3. What emotions or memories arise when you begin to breathe deeply and consciously? How do you usually respond to them?

4. What would it mean for you to create a safe space, within yourself, to feel, release, and heal long-held emotions?

Heart Whisper Affirmations For Integration

Affirmations have the power to quiet the noise of doubt, open the doorway to self-trust, and draw you back into the wisdom of your heart. When practised daily, they nurture an inner dialogue based in love and truth, helping you live each day more aligned with who you truly are. I invite you to repeat silently or write:

- *I feel centred and calm when I focus on my breath.*

- *I am able to quiet my mind through deep breathing.*

- *Breathing deeply helps me to release tension in my body.*

- *I find peace in the rhythm of my breath.*

- *My breath is a reminder to stay present in the moment.*

- *Through conscious breathing, I nurture inner harmony.*

- *Each breath I take fills me with clarity and light.*

- *With every exhale, I release what no longer serves me.*

- *My breath connects me to my heart and to the present moment.*

- *Breathing with awareness helps me move through life with ease and grace.*

- *My breath is my constant companion, guiding me back to peace.*

Application Exercise: In-the-Moment Breathing Anchor

Purpose: To centre yourself, regulate your nervous system, and reconnect with your heart's wisdom during moments of stress, anxiety, or emotional overload.

Step-by-Step Practice:

1. Pause and Become Aware: Gently stop what you are doing, and acknowledge what you are feeling without judgment. Name it if you can:

"I feel anxious, overwhelmed, tense..."

2. Place Your Hand on Your Heart: This simple gesture activates oxytocin (the calming hormone) and helps your body feel safe. Feel the warmth and weight of your hand. Let it be an anchor to the present moment.

3. Begin Balanced Heart Breathing (3 Rounds): Inhale slowly through your nose for **4 seconds.** Exhale gently through your mouth for **6 seconds.** Repeat **3 times**, focusing on softening your shoulders and relaxing your jaw

4. Ask Your Heart:: *"What do I need in this moment?"* Be still and listen, your heart may answer with a word, a feeling, or a sense of direction (e.g., *rest, space, support, courage, nothing at all*) Trust whatever comes up, even if it is silence.

Close with Compassion

Affirm: *"I honour how I feel, and I give myself what I need."* Gently return to your day with renewed presence.

Closing Reflection

Breath is more than survival, it is a sacred rhythm, a quiet guide, and a constant companion. Today, you have taken your first step into reconnecting with your breath not just as a function, but as a bridge to your heart. With each conscious inhale and exhale, you create space for clarity, healing, and grounded presence. In slowing down, you have begun to listen, not just to your breath, but to the quiet wisdom within you. This is more than a practice; it is a return. A return to yourself. Trust that your breath will meet you in every moment, and guide you gently, truthfully, toward peace and emotional wholeness.

2 - GRATITUDE

Your Opening Reflection

An Invitation to Begin with Gratitude - Before you step into this chapter, I invite you to pause and gift yourself a moment of stillness. Let your breath guide you home, let your heart soften, and allow gratitude to rise in its own quiet way. You do not need to force it, simply notice what is already here, waiting to be acknowledged.

This is not about finding the perfect answer, but about opening yourself to presence. Each reflection, no matter how small, is a reminder that gratitude is a doorway, one that leads you deeper into connection with your heart, your journey, and your life.

- "What is one thing, however small, you feel grateful for in this moment?"

- "When was the last time you truly felt thankful, and what sparked it?"

- "Who or what brings a quiet sense of appreciation into your life?"

- "How does it feel in your body when you focus on gratitude?"

- "What part of your journey are you beginning to see through the lens of gratitude?"

Let these questions open the doorway into presence. Every answer you give, whether in words, sensations, or silence, is a bridge between where you are and where you are going.

Learning Objectives

The learning objectives are included here to give you a clear focus for this chapter, ensuring that each practice you explore moves you closer to

mastering the skills, insights, and heart-led awareness that will enrich your life well beyond the program. By the end of this chapter, you will:

- Understand the emotional, psychological, and physiological benefits of gratitude.

- Recognise how a gratitude practice supports emotional intelligence and heart–led living.

- Apply simple, practical gratitude strategies to your daily life.

- Reflect on personal experiences to deepen connection with self and others.

Core Emotional Domains

The core emotional intelligence domains covered here are essential because they form the foundation for lasting heart connection, guiding you to deepen self-awareness, regulate emotions, build resilience, and strengthen the mind-body bond throughout your Heart Unbound journey.

- **Self-Awareness:** Recognising and appreciating personal blessings and emotional states.

- **Self-Regulation:** Shifting focus from negativity to positivity through intentional gratitude.

- **Empathy:** Acknowledging and appreciating others' contributions.

- **Relationship Management:** Strengthening connections through expressions of gratitude.

"Gratitude - Your Bridge To Emotional Awareness"

Gratitude is both a timeless spiritual principle and a modern emotional intelligence practice, grounded in the wisdom of ancient traditions and confirmed by contemporary science. Across cultures and centuries, spiritual teachers have spoken of gratitude as your pathway to the soul, your bridge to presence, and a practice that unlocks joy even in moments of suffering. It is not dependent on perfect circumstances, but on the openness of your heart.

In today's world, gratitude is also a powerful tool for your mental and emotional well-being. Psychology and neuroscience show that regular gratitude practice activates brain regions linked with empathy, trust, and emotional regulation. It helps you reduce stress, ease anxiety, and increase resilience by shifting your focus from what is lacking to what is present and life-giving.

When you practice gratitude, you strengthen your relationships, deepen your self-awareness, and develop a more optimistic outlook. You nurture your connection to yourself, to others, and to something greater. In your workplace, gratitude creates appreciation and wellbeing; in your personal life, it brings you deeper meaning and emotional clarity.

Gratitude is not about denying or bypassing your challenges. It is about grounding yourself in what remains good, true, and sustaining, even when life feels uncertain. When you choose gratitude, you choose to see with your heart, and in doing so, you begin to transform how you live, lead, and love.

Ancient traditions and spiritual basis of gratitude - Cicero

In the philosophy of Cicero, you discover that gratitude is not only a personal virtue but the foundation of all moral goodness. Cicero believed that to be truly grateful is to recognise the goodness in others and respond with honour, humility, and reciprocity. Gratitude, for Cicero, is both a civic and spiritual duty, essential for the wellbeing of society and the cultivation of personal integrity. When you practice gratitude, you nurture justice, loyalty, and compassion.

Example 1: You acknowledge the kindness and support of others not just privately, but through action, Cicero believed true gratitude is demonstrated, not just felt.

Example 2: You uphold relationships and social harmony by repaying generosity with honour and service, reinforcing mutual respect.

Example 3: You develop inner nobility by remembering those who have helped you, recognising that no great person is ever forgetful of their debts of gratitude.

Ancient traditions and spiritual basis of gratitude - Christianity

In Christianity, you are called to live with a grateful heart as a reflection of God's grace and love. Gratitude is a spiritual response to divine mercy, woven throughout scripture as a way to honour God, build faith, and develop joy even in hardship. Through giving thanks, you deepen your trust, humility, and connection with others.

Example 1: You give thanks in prayer, following biblical teachings like *"Give thanks in all circumstances"* (1 Thessalonians 5:18), recognising God's presence in every moment.

Example 2: At the Eucharist (Holy Communion), you participate in a ritual of thanksgiving, remembering Christ's sacrifice with a grateful heart.

Example 3: You express gratitude through service, offering your time, talents, and love to others as a reflection of the grace you have received.

Ancient traditions and spiritual basis of gratitude - Islam

In Islam, gratitude (*shukr*) is a central spiritual practice that deepens your relationship with Allah and anchors your daily life in awareness and humility. You are taught that every blessing, whether material, emotional, or spiritual, comes from Allah, and expressing gratitude is both a form of worship and a path to greater contentment. The Qur'an frequently reminds you that those who are grateful will be given more, and that gratitude purifies the heart and strengthens faith.

Example 1: You begin daily prayers (salat) with praise and thanks to Allah, acknowledging His mercy and guidance.

Example 2: You say *Alhamdulillah ("All praise is due to God")* in response to life's blessings, large or small, cultivating continuous awareness.

Example 3: You demonstrate gratitude by sharing with others, through charity (*zakat*) and generosity, as a way to honour the gifts you have received.

Ancient traditions and spiritual basis of gratitude - Judaism

In Judaism, gratitude is a core spiritual practice that shapes your daily life and relationship with God. You are encouraged to begin each day with *Modeh Ani*, a prayer of thanks for the gift of life. Gratitude is seen not just as a feeling, but as a disciplined act of recognition for God's constant presence, mercy, and provision. Through blessings, prayers, and ethical action, you cultivate awareness that everything you receive is a reflection of divine grace and responsibility.

Example 1: You recite blessings (*brachot*) throughout the day, to give thanks for food, nature, learning, and joyful experiences.

Example 2: You observe Shabbat with a grateful heart, pausing to rest and reflect on the blessings of creation and community.

Example 3: You express gratitude through *tzedakah* (charity), sharing your resources to help others as a sacred obligation based in thankfulness.

Ancient traditions and spiritual basis of gratitude - Buddhism

In Buddhism, you are invited to cultivate gratitude as a conscious practice that awakens mindfulness, compassion, and interdependence. Gratitude helps you see that your life is supported by countless beings, teachers, ancestors, nature, and even strangers. By recognising these connections, you begin to dissolve ego and develop humility. Gratitude in Buddhism is not limited to pleasant experiences; it also includes appreciation for challenges that lead to growth. Through regular reflection, you open your heart and walk the path with greater awareness and peace.

Example 1: You express gratitude for your breath and body during meditation, recognising them as gifts that support your spiritual journey.

Example 2: You thank your teachers, parents, and elders as part of honouring the lineage that makes your practice possible.

Example 3: You reflect on difficulties with appreciation, understanding that hardship can be a teacher leading you toward deeper wisdom and compassion.

Insights From Neuroscience And Psychological Research

Gratitude, the positive emotion arising from recognising the benefits received from others, has gained substantial attention in neuroscience and psychology for its profound impact on wellbeing. Contemporary research shows that gratitude not only boosts your emotional health but also produces measurable changes in your brain.

Functional MRI studies reveal that gratitude activates regions such as your ventromedial prefrontal cortex, anterior cingulate cortex, and limbic system, areas linked to emotional regulation, reward, and decision-making. This neural activation supports positive emotional states and creates neuroplasticity, potentially enhancing cognitive function over time.

Psychological research further confirms that gratitude interventions such as journaling or expressing appreciation, can reduce symptoms of depression, anxiety, and stress while improving sleep, mood, and overall life satisfaction. Gratitude also enhances empathy and social connection, encouraging prosocial behaviour and stronger interpersonal bonds. As both a mental and physiological practice, gratitude interrupts negative thought patterns and nurtures emotional resilience. More than a fleeting emotion, gratitude is a transformative habit proven to enhance happiness, compassion, and a healthier, more connected life for yourself and communities alike.

Neuroscience findings:

Gratitude activates brain areas tied to **reward, emotional regulation**, and **decision-making**, fMRI scans show increased activity in:

- Ventromedial prefrontal cortex
- Anterior cingulate cortex
- Limbic system

Promotes **neuroplasticity**, supporting lasting cognitive and emotional growth

Psychological benefits:

- Reduces **depression, anxiety**, and **stress**
- Enhances **sleep, mood**, and **life satisfaction**
- Increases **resilience** and emotional regulation

Social impact: Strengthens empathy, prosocial behaviour, and community bonds

Key Takeaway: Gratitude is not just a feeling, it is a transformative daily practice for well-being and human connection.

Modern neuroscience confirms what ancient wisdom has long taught, gratitude changes your brain, your emotions, and your life. Functional MRI scans reveal that practicing gratitude activates key brain regions linked to reward, emotional regulation, and decision-making, including the ventromedial prefrontal cortex, anterior cingulate cortex, and the limbic system. This activation promotes neuroplasticity, allowing you to create lasting shifts in how you think, feel, and respond to life.

Psychologically, gratitude reduces depression, anxiety, and stress, while enhancing sleep, mood, and overall life satisfaction. It strengthens your resilience, improves emotional regulation, and nurtures a more stable sense of well-being. Socially, gratitude deepens empathy, encourages prosocial behaviour, and builds stronger, more compassionate communities. The key takeaway is simple yet profound: gratitude is not just an emotion, it is a transformative daily practice that fuels your mental, emotional, and social flourishing.

How Gratitude Aligns With Heart–Led Living

1. **Gratitude transforms pain into purpose** When you live from your heart, gratitude helps you honour past wounds as part of your growth, turning suffering into wisdom rather than bitterness.

2. **Gratitude deepens connection** A heart-led life is grounded in authentic relationships. Expressing gratitude strengthens trust, empathy, and intimacy, creating true human connection.

3. **Gratitude anchors presence** Heart-led living requires presence. Gratitude brings you into the now, helping you savour beauty in the ordinary and remain open to the sacred in everyday life.

4. **Gratitude dissolves ego and awakens compassion** From the heart, you see others not as separate, but as part of a shared human journey. Gratitude nurtures humility and the desire to uplift others.

5. **Gratitude fuels aligned action** When you act from the heart, gratitude becomes your compass, guiding you to serve, create, and live with meaning, integrity, and love.

Gratitude Exercises

Purpose: You train your mind to focus on the positive aspects of life, even during challenging times. You build emotional resilience by recognising what is already good, nurturing a sense of contentment and a broader perspective. This practice encourages you to be mindful and reflective, helping you develop a lasting habit of noticing and appreciating everyday blessings.

Gratitude Journaling: Write down three things you are grateful for, focus on simplicity (e.g. morning sun, clean water, a smile).

Reflection Prompts: How did it feel to pause and name what you are grateful for? What do your three gratitudes reveal about what truly matters to you right now? Were any of your gratitudes surprising or things you often take for granted? How does focusing on simplicity shift your emotional state? What might change in your day if you carry these gratitudes with you?

Heartful Gratitude Moment: Close your eyes, place your hand on your heart, and breathe deeply. Reflect on a recent moment of joy or support, feeling gratitude in your body.

> **Reflection Prompts**: What sensations did you notice in your body as you placed your hand on your heart? How did it feel to fully receive the memory of support or joy? What emotions surfaced during your moment of heartful gratitude? How does your heart feel now compared to before the exercise? How might this practice support you in moments of stress or disconnection?

Gratitude As A Mindset That Develops Resilience And Joy.

Gratitude as a mindset is one of the most transformative shifts you can make in your inner world, and within the Heart Unbound program it is a cornerstone of your emotional intelligence and heart-led living. It is far more than an occasional moment of appreciation, it is a deliberate choice to orient your perspective toward what is life-affirming, meaningful, and sustaining.

When you adopt gratitude as a daily practice, you train your brain to notice what is good and nourishing, even in moments of uncertainty or pain. This is not about ignoring hardship or pretending challenges do not exist; rather, it is about refusing to allow difficulty to erase the beauty and resources still available to you. For example, when you face a difficult workday, you might pause to appreciate the colleague who supports you, the warm sunlight through your window, or the fact that you have the skills to navigate challenges. When you are moving through grief, you might choose to focus on treasured memories or the kindness of friends who reach out.

Neuroscience shows that repeated gratitude practice strengthens the neural pathways associated with emotional regulation, empathy, and optimism, helping you remain calm and grounded under pressure. Resilience grows naturally in this environment. By focusing on what is present rather than what is lacking, you expand your capacity to adapt to change, recover from setbacks, and keep moving forward with purpose. For instance, if you are recovering from an injury, you may express daily gratitude for small signs of healing, which helps keep your motivation and confidence alive through the process.

At the same time, gratitude invites joy into your life in a profound and lasting way. Joy becomes less about external circumstances and more about the inner richness created by appreciation, connection, and meaning. This joy uplifts your relationships, such as thanking a partner for their small but meaningful acts of care, fuels your creativity, and enhances your overall sense of fulfilment.

In the Heart Unbound journey, gratitude is both your anchor and your compass, it grounds you in the present while guiding you toward a more expansive, heart-centred way of living. It is a mindset that transforms not only how you think, but also how you feel, act, and connect, with yourself, with others, and with the world.

Gratitude Challenges

Purpose: These Five Presence Challenges are here to help you slow down and return to the heart of the moment. In a world that often pulls your attention in many directions, these simple practices invite you to pause, breathe, and notice what is already here. By engaging in them, you will strengthen your awareness, nurture calm, and cultivate a sense of peace in the ordinary.

Each challenge is an opportunity to step back from distraction, soften into stillness, and let presence become your anchor. Choose one to begin now, and share your experience with someone you trust or within the group. This is your opportunity to grow presence into a daily habit that supports your clarity, balance, and connection.

Five Presence Challenges:

1. Take three mindful breaths before starting your next activity.

2. Put your phone aside for one meal and simply enjoy eating.

3. Step outside and notice five things in nature around you.

4. Listen fully to someone today without planning your reply.

5. Pause for one minute of silence before bed.

You can choose one to begin immediately and share your intention with a partner or in a group.

Case Study Discussion: John's Story

John had always been a hardworking man, constantly striving for success and financial stability. He was the CEO of a large corporation and had achieved all the material things he had set his sights on. However, at 45, he realised that he was missing something important in his life, a sense of fulfillment and joy. Despite his achievements, he felt empty inside and disconnected from his true self.

John told me his story and we chatted about gratitude and the importance of recognising all he had to be thankful for. John started a daily gratitude practice, taking a few minutes each morning to reflect on the blessings in his life and express gratitude for them. He told me that initially it felt forced and unnatural, but over time, it became easier and more genuine. As he continued to practice gratitude, John noticed a profound shift in his outlook on life.

He started to appreciate the small things that he had previously taken for granted, or in most cases did not even recognise, such as the beauty of nature, the warmth of the sun on his skin, and the laughter of his children. Every day he felt more connected to his own heart and to the hearts of those around him. His relationships with his family and friends improved as he became more present and attentive to their needs.

He also found himself being more compassionate towards others and more forgiving of their faults. The anger and resentment that he had been carrying for years began to lessen, replaced by a sense of peace and contentment. As he continued to live a heart–led life, John started to make changes in his career and professional life as well. He realised that success and financial stability were not enough to bring him true happiness and fulfillment. He started to explore new hobbies and interests, taking up painting and hiking, and even started volunteering at a local charity.

Through his daily practice of gratitude, John had found a new sense of purpose and meaning in life. He no longer measured success by material possessions or professional accomplishments but by the joy and love he felt in his heart. He had discovered the true value of living a heart–led life. He witnessed first–hand how the practice of gratitude transformed his life and lead him to live from his heart and not from his head.

Reflective Exercise: John's Story

Here are five profound and reflective questions inspired by John's story:

1. **In what areas of your life have you been chasing success, yet still felt unfulfilled, like John did before his shift?** *(Reflect on where external achievements may be overshadowing inner peace.)*

2. **How often do you pause to truly notice and appreciate the small, everyday blessings around you?** *(Think of simple moments, like laughter, warmth, or beauty, you may have overlooked.)*

---

3. **What might begin to change in your relationships if you approached each one with more presence, gratitude, and compassion?** *(Consider the emotional ripple effect that John experienced in his personal connections.)*

4. **What would it mean for you to live a heart-led life rather than one directed by expectation, pressure, or fear?** *(Explore what authentic living could look and feel like for you.)*

5. **If you began a daily gratitude practice today, what do you imagine might shift in your mindset, values, or overall wellbeing?** *(Visualise your life with gratitude as a guiding force, as it became for John.)*

Heart Whisper Affirmations For Integration

Affirmations have the power to quiet the noise of doubt, open the doorway to self-trust, and draw you back into the wisdom of your heart. When practised daily, they nurture an inner dialogue based in love and truth, helping you live each day more aligned with who you truly are. I invite you to repeat silently or write:

- *I am grateful for every breath I take.*
- *I am thankful for the people in my life.*
- *I appreciate the simple things in life.*
- *I feel blessed to have a roof over my head.*
- *I am grateful for the lessons I have learned in life.*
- *I am thankful for the opportunities that come my way.*
- *I appreciate the beauty of nature around me.*
- *I am grateful for the love and kindness I receive each day.*
- *I appreciate the growth that comes from life's challenges.*
- *I am thankful for the gift of my health and well-being.*
- *I feel blessed for the moments of peace and stillness in my life.*
- *I am grateful for the chance to make a positive difference in the world.*

Application Exercise – Five Gratitude Challenges

Gratitude grows through practice, and small, consistent actions can rewire the way you see the world. I invite you to take on these five challenges, one at a time or all together, and notice how they shift your perspective, mood, and relationships.

1. **Keep a Daily Gratitude Journal for One Week;** Each day, write down three things you are grateful for, no matter how big or small. Be specific. Instead of *"I am grateful for my family,"* you might write, *"I am grateful for the way my partner made me tea this morning without asking."* This helps you tune into the details of your life that bring joy.

2. **Thank Someone Personally Today:** Look into their eyes, speak their name, and express exactly what you appreciate about them. This could be a colleague who helped you with a task, a friend who listened, or a stranger who showed kindness. Let them see and feel your sincerity.

3. **Pause to Reflect on One Thing You are Grateful for in This Moment:** Stop. Take a deep breath. Look around you and notice one thing that makes your heart feel warm right now, a sound, a scent, a colour, a gesture. Let that feeling of gratitude expand for a few moments before moving on with your day.

4. **Perform a Random Act of Kindness:** Hold the door for someone, pay for a coffee, leave a kind note, or help carry a heavy bag. Do it quietly, without expectation of recognition. Let the joy come from giving, not from being acknowledged.

5. **Share Appreciation with a Loved One:** Tell someone close to you how much they mean to you and why. Be specific and heartfelt. Your words could become a memory they carry forever.

How to Begin: Choose one challenge you can start **right now**. Write it down. If you are doing this as part of a group or with a partner, share your intention out loud. Accountability deepens the commitment, and shared gratitude multiplies its effect.

Closing Reflection

Gratitude is more than a momentary feeling; it is a way of seeing, a way of being. When you choose to meet life with a grateful heart, you soften the edges of fear, dissolve the walls of resentment, and open the door for joy to flow back into your life. Gratitude becomes a quiet revolution within you, a shift from scarcity to abundance, from self-protection to wholehearted living.

It does not demand perfection, nor does it ask for a life untouched by hardship. Gratitude simply invites you to notice, to witness the beauty hidden in plain sight, the sacred woven into the threads of your everyday existence. It whispers, *"Even here, even now, there is something worth honouring."*

When you choose gratitude, you choose presence. You choose to come home to yourself. You begin to see that even in the shadowed valleys, there are glimmers of light guiding you forward. Gratitude reveals that the journey itself, with all its twists, trials, and unexpected blessings, is the gift. It is not merely the reward at the end of the road, it is the very ground you walk on.

As you continue along this heart-unbound path, let gratitude be your anchor in life's storms and your compass when the way ahead feels uncertain. Allow it to shape your words so they heal, inform your choices so they align with love, and lead you, again and again, back to the quiet wisdom that has always lived within your heart.

3 – I AM

Your Opening Reflection

An Invitation to Enter the Doorway of Presence - Before you move further, I invite you to pause. Let the pace of the world fall away for a moment. Breathe gently. Place your hand over your heart if it feels right, and allow yourself to arrive fully here.

These questions are not meant to be solved with your mind, but to be received with your heart. Let them open you, soften you, and guide you into deeper presence. However your heart responds, with words, feelings, or simple stillness, is enough. This is your doorway. Step through gently, and let your truth meet you here.

- "What truth within you is ready to be seen and embraced?"
- "How can you honour the most authentic part of yourself right now?"
- "Where is your heart inviting you to soften, open, or trust more deeply?"
- "Who are you in this moment?"
- "What does your heart long for you to know today?"

Let these questions open the doorway into presence. Every answer you give, whether in words, sensations, or silence, is a bridge between where you are and where you are going.

Learning Objectives

The learning objectives are included here to give you a clear focus for this chapter, ensuring that each practice you explore moves you closer to mastering the skills, insights, and heart-led awareness that will enrich your life

well beyond the program. By the end of this chapter, you will:

- Understand the emotional and psychological significance of 'I am' statements.

- Apply self-affirmation techniques to develop self-awareness, self-love, and resilience.

- Identify and challenge your negative self-talk and limiting beliefs.

- Integrate heart-led 'I am' practices into your daily emotional regulation strategies.

- Reflect on your core identity and values through the lens of emotional intelligence.

Core Emotional Domains

The core emotional intelligence domains covered here are essential because they form the foundation for lasting heart connection, guiding you to deepen self-awareness, regulate emotions, build resilience, and strengthen the mind-body bond throughout your Heart Unbound journey.

- **Self-awareness** – You deepen your ability to notice and name your inner experiences with honesty and clarity.

- **Self-regulation** – You learn to respond with calm and choice, rather than react with impulse or overwhelm.

- **Motivation** – You connect with your heart's purpose, cultivating inner drive grounded in meaning and intention.

- **Empathy (Self-Compassion)** – You develop kindness toward yourself, embracing your humanity with gentleness and care.

- **Social Skills (through shared reflections and storytelling)** – You build authentic connection by listening deeply, sharing truthfully, and growing together.

"I Am – Affirming Your Self Worth"

The words "*I Am*" hold profound historical, spiritual, and psychological power. Across traditions and philosophies, they have been used as declarations of identity, intention, and transformation. In ancient spiritual texts, such as the Hebrew Bible, "*I Am*" was spoken as a sacred name of the divine, pointing to the infinite, unchanging essence of being.

Similarly, in Eastern traditions, the phrase reflects the awareness of consciousness itself, pure presence without attachment to roles or labels. Psychologically, *"I am"* statements shape the core of your self-identity. When you repeat phrases like *"I am strong,"* *"I am not enough,"* or *"I am unworthy,"* you are not just describing how you feel, you are shaping how you see yourself.

These internal narratives form the foundation of your self-image, influencing how you show up in relationships, how you handle adversity, and how you pursue your goals. By consciously choosing *"I am"* statements that reflect truth, possibility, and self-compassion, you rewire your emotional pathways. You begin to let go of inherited beliefs or imposed identities that no longer serve you.

When you say, *"I am whole,"* or *"I am becoming,"* you begin to step into a more aligned version of yourself, one based in presence, resilience, and self-awareness. In the Heart Unbound program, *"I am"* becomes more than a statement. It becomes a practice. A powerful reminder that you are not defined by your past, your mistakes, or your fears. You are a living expression of growth, capable of healing, belonging, and becoming.

Ancient traditions and spiritual roots of *'I am'* – Egypt

In ancient Egyptian spirituality, the phrase *"I Am"* was deeply intertwined with divine identity, sacred knowledge, and cosmic truth. The Egyptians believed in the power of spoken words, particularly in connection with the soul (ba), essence (ka), and the divine self. To say *"I Am"* was to affirm one's alignment with the eternal, the divine order (ma'at), and the living gods who dwelled within and beyond.

Examples:

1. **The Book of the Dead** – The deceased declares *"I Am"* statements like *"I am Atum,"* *"I am yesterday, today, and tomorrow,"* to affirm oneness with the gods and pass safely into the afterlife.

2. **Pharaoh's Declarations** – Pharaohs, seen as divine rulers, used *"I Am"* statements to assert their identity as living gods on earth (e.g., *"I am Horus, the falcon of the horizon"*).

3. **Temple Inscriptions** – Priestly texts included affirmations like *"I Am the flame that shineth,"* symbolising divine presence and eternal life within the human soul.

These affirmations were tools of empowerment and alignment with divine truth.

<u>Ancient traditions and spiritual roots of '*I am*' – Christianity</u>

In Christianity, the phrase "*I Am*" carries profound theological and spiritual significance. It originates in the Old Testament when God reveals His name to Moses as "*I AM WHO I AM*" (Exodus 3:14), signifying eternal presence, self-existence, and divine authority. In the New Testament, Jesus uses "*I Am*" statements to affirm his divine nature and connection with God, offering powerful metaphors for spiritual identity, truth, and transformation.

Examples:

1. **Exodus 3:14** – God tells Moses, "*I AM WHO I AM*," establishing the sacred, unchanging identity of the Divine.

2. **John 8:58** – Jesus declares, "*Before Abraham was, I Am*," aligning himself directly with the eternal nature of God.

3. **John 14:6** – "*I Am the way, the truth, and the life*" – Jesus reveals the path to spiritual fulfillment and connection with God through identity and faith.

In Christianity, "*I Am*" is both a declaration of divine presence and an invitation to discover your own identity in relationship with God.

<u>Ancient traditions and spiritual roots of '*I am*' – Islam</u>

In Islam, while the direct phrase "*I Am*" is used less explicitly than in other traditions, its spiritual essence is deeply embedded in the Qur'an and Sufi teachings. The Divine Names of Allah (Asma'ul Husna) reflect aspects of being and identity, and believers are encouraged to reflect these attributes through their own character. The Islamic understanding of self (nafs) involves a journey of purification, moving closer to God (Allah) by aligning one's inner being with divine will. In this sense, "*I Am*" becomes a reflection of one's spiritual striving, based in humility and remembrance (dhikr).

Examples:

1. **Qur'an 20:14** – Allah says, "*Indeed, I am Allah. There is no deity except Me, so worship Me and establish prayer for My remembrance.*" This is a divine assertion of eternal being and presence.

2. **Sufi Mysticism** – Poets like Rumi and Al-Hallaj speak of divine union using language that reflects a purified self, where "*I am*" becomes a vessel

for divine love and oneness. Al-Hallaj famously said, *"Ana al-Haqq" (I am the Truth),* expressing mystical unity with the Divine.

3. **99 Names of Allah** – Believers may reflect on names such as *Al-Rahman* (The Compassionate) and say, *"I am striving to be compassionate,"* as a way of embodying divine qualities in human form.

In Islam, *"I Am"* is a journey toward divine remembrance, grounded in surrender, humility, and alignment with God's attributes.

Ancient traditions and spiritual roots of *'I Am'* – Judaism

In Judaism, gratitude is a core spiritual practice that shapes your daily life and relationship with God. You are encouraged to begin each day with *Modeh Ani*, a prayer of thanks for the gift of life. Gratitude is seen not just as a feeling, but as a disciplined act of recognition for God's constant presence, mercy, and provision. Through blessings, prayers, and ethical action, you cultivate awareness that everything you receive is a reflection of divine grace and responsibility.

Examples

1. You recite blessings (*brachot*) throughout the day, to give thanks for food, nature, learning, and joyful experiences.

2. You observe Shabbat with a grateful heart, pausing to rest and reflect on the blessings of creation and community.

3. You express gratitude through *tzedakah* (charity), sharing your resources to help others as a sacred obligation grounded in thankfulness.

In Judaism, gratitude is more than a feeling, it is a way of being that shapes who you are. Through daily prayers, blessings, and acts of kindness, you affirm *I am grateful*, recognising that each moment, each gift, and each breath is part of a greater divine flow.

Ancient traditions and spiritual roots of *'I am'* – Buddhism

In Buddhism, the concept of *"I am"* is examined through the lens of impermanence and the illusion of a fixed self. Rather than affirming a permanent identity, Buddhist teachings invite you to observe and ultimately release attachment to the ego. The *"self"* is seen as a collection of changing processes, form, sensation, perception, mental formations, and consciousness (the five aggregates). True freedom comes not from asserting *"I am,"* but from realising that clinging to this identity causes suffering. Still, deep spiritual insight can arise through compassionate awareness of your conditioned self.

Examples:

1. **The Anatta Doctrine (No-Self)** – The Buddha taught that there is no permanent, unchanging *"I."* Understanding this liberates you from suffering and ego attachment.

2. **The Heart Sutra** – *"Form is emptiness, emptiness is form."* This reflects the view that what you perceive as "I am" is not solid, but a flow of experience and consciousness.

3. **Mindfulness Practice** – In meditation, you may notice thoughts like *"I am angry"* or *"I am not good enough"* and learn to see them as passing mental states, not truths. This creates space for compassion, clarity, and transformation.

In Buddhism, spiritual growth involves softening the grip of *"I am"* to find deeper freedom and peace.

Ancient traditions and spiritual roots of *'I am'* – Hinduism

In Hinduism, the phrase *"I am"* carries deep spiritual significance, often reflecting the sacred unity between the individual self (*atman*) and the universal consciousness (*Brahman*). Based in the Upanishads and Vedantic philosophy, the understanding of *"I am"* transcends the ego and points toward self-realisation, the awareness that your true essence is divine. Rather than being limited by name, form, or identity, *"I am"* becomes a powerful affirmation of spiritual truth and oneness with all life. The journey of the soul is to awaken from illusion (*maya*) and remember: *"I am That"* (*Aham Brahmasmi*).

Examples:

1. **Aham Brahmasmi** – Found in the Brihadaranyaka Upanishad, this means *"I am Brahman,"* a profound realisation that your innermost self is not separate from the Divine.

2. **Bhagavad Gita (Chapter 10, Verse 20)** – Krishna says, *"I am the Self, O Gudakesha, seated in the hearts of all creatures."* This reveals that divinity resides within every being.

3. **Meditative Mantras** – Practices such as silently repeating *"So Hum"* (*"I am That"*) during meditation help dissolve the ego and align your awareness with universal consciousness.

In Hinduism, *"I am"* is not just identity, it is a sacred doorway to self-realisation, inner peace, and divine unity.

The Psychology Of Self-Affirmation And Neuroplasticity

Self-affirmation is more than positive thinking, it is a psychological process based in the deep human need to preserve integrity and identity, especially when faced with challenge or threat. By consciously affirming your core values, strengths, or beliefs, you reinforce a coherent sense of self, which helps buffer against stress, anxiety, and self-doubt. Psychologists have found that self-affirmation reduces defensiveness, enhances problem-solving, and increases emotional resilience.

From a neuroscience perspective, self-affirmation activates regions of your brain associated with reward and self-processing, such as your ventromedial prefrontal cortex. Over time, with consistent practice, these affirmations begin to reshape neural patterns through a process called neuroplasticity, your brain's ability to change and adapt. When you repeat empowering statements like *"I am worthy,"* *"I am enough,"* or *"I am loved,"* you strengthen new neural pathways that reinforce positive self-belief and emotional regulation. Ultimately, self-affirmation and neuroplasticity work together to support healing, growth, and transformation, empowering you to rewrite your internal narrative and live with greater authenticity, confidence, and connection.

Self-Affirmation & Neuroplasticity: Key Insights

- **Self-affirmation is a psychological process:** Helps preserve your identity and integrity, especially in moments of stress or challenge.

- **Affirming your core values strengthens your sense of self:** Reduces anxiety, self-doubt, and defensiveness.

- **Psychological benefits:** Enhances emotional resilience, clarity, and problem-solving ability.

- **Neuroscience perspective:** Activates brain regions linked to reward and self-processing (e.g., ventromedial prefrontal cortex).

- **Neuroplasticity in action:** Repeating affirmations like *"I am enough"* reshapes brain pathways, reinforcing self-belief and calm.

- **Empowerment through repetition:** Regular practice rewires your mindset, enabling personal transformation.

- **The outcome:** Greater confidence, emotional regulation, and alignment with your authentic self.

Modern Thinkers & The Rise Of Positive Affirmations

Louise Hay: A pioneer in self-healing and affirmations. Her bestselling book *You Can Heal Your Life* (1984) introduced millions to the idea that thoughts can shape reality. She taught that repeating positive *"I am"* statements could transform health, self-worth, and life circumstances. Her work helped bridge spirituality and psychology for a mainstream audience.

Wayne Dyer: Often called the *"father of motivation,"* Dyer merged psychology, spirituality, and self-empowerment. In books like *The Power of Intention* and *You will See It When You Believe It*, he taught that affirmations direct energy and shape outcomes. Dyer emphasised that *"I am"* statements align individuals with their divine nature and higher potential.

Their Legacy: Both thinkers helped move affirmations from fringe self-help to mainstream personal development. Their teachings continue to influence emotional intelligence, wellness programs, and even therapeutic practices today.

> **Reflection Prompt:** *"Think about a time when your inner dialogue shaped your outlook or choices. What would have changed if, in that moment, you affirmed your worth or potential instead?"*
>
> Take a few moments to journal a positive *"I am"* statement that feels true or needed today (e.g., *I am healing, I am more than enough, I am safe to grow*). Reflect on how repeating this could gently reshape your beliefs, emotions, or actions over time.

Emotional Resilience and Self-Love Through Daily 'I Am' Practices

Daily *'I am'* statements are more than words, they are intentional declarations that shape your inner narrative and sense of identity. Each repetition rewires how you see yourself and respond to the world.

Emotional resilience grows when you affirm truths like *"I am strong," "I am calm in the storm,"* or *"I am grounded."* These statements help regulate your nervous system, shift your mindset, and buffer against life's challenges. **Self-love deepens** as you consistently speak to yourself with kindness and encouragement. Affirmations dissolve layers of shame, self-doubt, and internalised criticism, replacing them with compassion and self-acceptance. From a **neuroscience perspective**, daily affirmations activate regions of your brain involved in self-perception and emotional regulation (e.g., the ventromedial prefrontal cortex). This promotes **neuroplasticity**, strengthening pathways that support healthy self-belief. Over time, your inner voice transforms from a critic to a **source of safety and strength**, guiding you back to your heart when you feel lost or overwhelmed. Practising *'I am'* affirmations daily is a **deliberate act of self-leadership**, empowering you to live in alignment with your truth, confident, connected, and compassionate.

'I am' - Exercise

Hearting Exercise – Mirror Work & Voice Activation

1. Stand or sit in front of a mirror.

2. Place your hand on your heart.

3. Say aloud five chosen *'I am'* statements (e.g. *"I am worthy of love," "I am enough."*)

4. Observe the emotions that surface. Do not judge, just notice and breathe through them.

Personal Reflection - Journalling Prompts:

- *"Which 'I am' statement felt most empowering or most uncomfortable?"*

- *"Where do you still withhold love or affirmation from yourself, and why?"*

- *"How can you nurture that part of you more consciously?"*

Case Study Discussion: Sophie's Journey

I remember Sophie many years ago when she chose to start truly loving herself. It was a real battle, and she would be the first to admit that it took her a long time to be comfortable with saying ANYTHING positive about herself and who she was. Sophie had been in an emotionally abusive marriage that had taken a mental and an emotional toll on her and eroded her confidence, self–worth, and self–esteem. Sophies self–talk was highly destructive and restricted her ability to love herself and live her best life.

When I started this hearting exercise with Sophie, she was unable to say or write anything positive, loving, caring, or nurturing about herself. Over the course of six months, we journeyed together and brought her to a place where she could face herself in the mirror, put her hand on her heart and say, '*I am worthy of love.*' That was a beautiful day indeed! Your journey to self is about KNOWING who you are. You may think that you already know who you are, but do you truly FEEL it at your core and in your heart? How do you talk to yourself?

Reflective Exercise – Sophie's Story

Here are five profound and reflective questions inspired by Sophie's story:

1. **What are the words that follow your "I am"?**: *You shape your identity with every "I am" you speak. Are your words uplifting or limiting?*

2. **When did you first learn to doubt your worth?** *Reflect on a moment when you stopped believing you were enough, and how that belief shaped you.*

3. **How does your body respond when you say something kind to yourself?** *Notice the physical and emotional impact of self-affirmation, your heart knows the truth.*

4. **What would change in your life if you truly believed "I am worthy of love"?** *Explore how a single belief could shift your relationships, decisions, and self-perception.*

5. **What truth does your heart long for you to claim with your "I am"?** *Give voice to the part of you that's been waiting to be seen, honoured, and embraced.*

These questions help you recognise how "*I am*" statements become a bridge between self-awareness and self-love.

Affirmations For Integration (Heart Whispers)

Affirmations have the power to quiet the noise of doubt, open the doorway to self-trust, and draw you back into the wisdom of your heart. When practised daily, they nurture an inner dialogue based in love and truth, helping you live each day more aligned with who you truly are. I invite you to repeat silently or write:

- *I am worthy of love and respect.*

- *I am empowered to achieve my goals.*

- *I am responsible for my own happiness.*

- *I am grateful for what I have.*

- *I am open to new opportunities and experiences.*

- *I am constantly learning and growing*

- *I am aligned with the truth of my heart.*

- *I am deserving of peace, joy, and fulfilment.*

- *I am strong enough to face and overcome challenges.*

- *I am a source of love and kindness in the world.*

Application Exercise - Begin Your Personal Affirmation Series

Affirmations are not just words; they are seeds you plant in the garden of your mind. When repeated with intention, they can rewire the way you think, speak, and show up in the world. This 7-day challenge is an invitation to consciously shape your inner dialogue so it reflects the person you are becoming.

1. **Write Five *'I Am'* Statements:** Choose statements that feel truthful but also aspirational, bridging who you are now with who you are growing into. Example:

   - I am grounded and calm, no matter what comes my way.

   - I am worthy of love and respect.

   - I am a creative force, bringing value to the world.

Write them in the present tense as though they are already true.

2. **Place Them Where You Will See Them Often:** Write each statement on a sticky note or small card and put them in places where your eyes will land frequently, your bathroom mirror, your desk, your fridge, the inside of your journal, your phone's home screen. These small visual reminders keep your affirmations alive throughout the day.

3. **Speak Them Out Loud Daily:** Every morning and evening, stand tall, take a deep breath, and say each affirmation out loud. Look into your own eyes if you are in front of a mirror. Speak with conviction, as though you are telling yourself the most important truth you have ever known.

4. **Track Your Energy and Self-Talk:** Over the next 7 days, notice shifts, subtle or significant, in how you speak to yourself, how you react to challenges, and how you carry yourself. You may find your inner critic softening, your confidence growing, or your mood lifting.

Reflection Prompt at the End of the Week:

- Which affirmation felt most powerful for you, and why?

- Where did you notice the biggest shift in your thoughts, feelings, or behaviours?

Closing Reflection

You have journeyed into the sacred terrain of your own identity, the quiet, powerful space where the words *"I am"* shape your reality, your worth, and your path forward. In a world that often tries to define you, declaring *"I am"* from the depth of your own heart is a courageous act of truth. It is not about ego or performance, it is about returning to your essence, remembering who you have always been beneath the noise, the pain, and the expectations.

Each time you say *"I am worthy,"* *"I am enough,"* or *"I am love,"* you reclaim your power. You begin to rewrite old narratives, gently rewire your inner world, and step more fully into who you truly are, not because something was broken, but because you are finally seeing your light clearly. Let this be your daily rhythm: not asking the world who you are, but remembering that you already know. You are the author of your *"I am."* Speak it with love. Live it with courage. Trust it with all your heart.

4 - MEDITATION

Your Opening Reflection

An Invitation to Enter Stillness - Before you step into this chapter, I invite you to arrive fully here. Let the world soften around you. Breathe slowly, and with each breath, give yourself permission to release the weight you are carrying. Close your eyes if you wish, and feel the quiet rhythm of your own heart guiding you home.

As you move into this reflection, let curiosity replace judgment and tenderness replace striving. The questions ahead are not tests to be solved, but gentle openings into presence. However your heart responds, in words, sensations, or silence, is perfect. This is your sacred pause. Let it be enough.

- "When you quiet your mind, what truths begin to surface?"

- "How does your body feel when you allow yourself to fully relax?"

- "What inner space opens for you when you focus only on your breath?"

- "What does stillness feel like to you?

- "When was the last time you truly paused?"

Let these questions open the doorway into presence. Every answer you give, whether in words, sensations, or silence, is a bridge between where you are and where you are going.

Learning Objectives

The learning objectives are included here to give you a clear focus for this chapter, ensuring that each practice you explore moves you closer to mastering the skills, insights, and heart-led awareness that will enrich your life

well beyond the program. By the end of this chapter, you will:

- Understand the historical and emotional intelligence basis of meditation.

- Identify how meditation supports emotional self-awareness and self-regulation.

- Practice simple forms of heart-connected meditation.

- Reflect on personal experiences and barriers to stillness.

- Apply meditation techniques to enhance empathy, purpose, and personal insight.

Core Emotional Domains

The core emotional intelligence domains covered here are essential because they form the foundation for lasting heart connection, guiding you to deepen self-awareness, regulate emotions, build resilience, and strengthen the mind-body bond throughout your Heart Unbound journey.

- **Self-Awareness:** You learn to observe your thoughts and emotions without judgment, deepening your understanding of your inner world.

- **Self-Regulation:** Meditation helps you calm reactivity and respond with clarity and balance.

- **Empathy:** Regular practice cultivates compassion for yourself and others, expanding your emotional understanding.

- **Motivation (Intrinsic):** You connect with your inner drive for peace, growth, and purpose, beyond external rewards.

- **Social Skills:** By grounding yourself in calm awareness, you develop deeper, more compassionate connections in your relationships.

"Meditation - Returning To Your Still Centre"

Meditation is an ancient and universal practice of intentional stillness and inner focus that transcends culture, religion, and time. It invites you to pause, breathe, and return home to yourself. At its core, meditation is the art of presence, of observing your thoughts without judgment, your breath without force, and your inner world without distraction.

Across civilisations, from the yogic *dhyāna* of Hinduism to the mindfulness (vipassana) practices of Buddhism, the *wu wei* stillness of Taoism, and even the contemplative prayer of Western monastic traditions, meditation has always been a gateway to self-realisation, healing, and clarity.

In a modern context, meditation is not just a spiritual act but a profoundly effective tool grounded in neuroscience and psychology. Research shows that consistent meditation improves emotional regulation, reduces stress, enhances cognitive functioning, and increases compassion. It also helps rewire the brain through neuroplasticity, building resilience and emotional intelligence.

When you meditate, you begin to observe rather than react. You learn to sit with discomfort, witness your emotions, and choose responses that are heart-led rather than fear-based. You slow down enough to notice your inner narratives and gently reframe them with kindness. Through silence and stillness, you cultivate peace, insight, and connection to something greater than yourself.

Meditation is not about perfecting the practice, it is about returning, over and over again, to presence. Whether you sit in stillness for five minutes or an hour, the invitation is always the same: to come back to your breath, your heart, and the quiet truth of who you are. In essence, meditation is a sacred act of remembering, who you are beneath the noise, beyond the roles, and within the deep silence of your soul.

Historical Basis of Meditation

Hinduism

In the Hindu tradition, meditation, known as *Dhyāna,* is an ancient and sacred practice that invites you to remember who you truly are. For over 3,000 years, the Vedic texts and *Upanishads* have guided seekers like you toward stillness, self-inquiry, and unity with the divine. Through meditation, you are not just calming your mind, you are returning to your essence, awakening to the truth that your *Atman* (inner self) is one with *Brahman* (universal consciousness).

When you repeat a mantra, focus on your breath (*prāṇāyāma*), or visualise a sacred image, you are not performing a technique, you are entering a sacred conversation with the divine within you. These practices were never meant to be distant rituals; they are living, breathing pathways to freedom and inner peace. As you walk this path, you follow in the footsteps of sages who realised that liberation (*moksha*) begins within. In *Rāja Yoga*, the meditative limb of *Dhyāna* teaches you to move beyond distraction into a state of effortless awareness. With practice, you begin to experience the stillness beneath the noise and the presence that has always lived inside your heart. Meditation in the Hindu tradition reminds you that you do not need to search for peace, you are peace, waiting to be remembered.

Buddhism

When you sit in stillness and begin to observe your breath, your thoughts, and your emotions without judgment, you are engaging in a practice that traces back over 2,500 years to Siddhartha Gautama, the Buddha. In the Buddhist tradition, meditation is more than a tool for peace; it is a path to awakening. You are invited to cultivate two wings of awareness: **Samatha,** the calm abiding of focused attention, and **Vipassanā,** the clear seeing that reveals the truth of your experience.

Through these practices, you begin to see the impermanent and interconnected nature of all things, including your thoughts, emotions, and identity. This gentle observation helps you release clinging and aversion, easing the suffering that arises from resistance to what is. As Buddhism spread from India to Tibet, Southeast Asia, and East Asia, it took on new forms that still resonate today. If you have ever explored **Zen,** you have felt the power of direct experience and simplicity. If you have encountered **Dzogchen,** you have been invited into the vast openness of your own awareness, and in **Theravāda,** the earliest surviving tradition, you are taught to purify the mind and walk the Eightfold Path to liberation.

Buddhist meditation encourages you to meet each moment with presence and compassion, not just for others, but for yourself. You learn to sit with discomfort, to breathe through pain, and to gently return to the present, again and again. This path is not about achieving perfection. It is about remembering that you already carry the seeds of awakening within you. When you meditate in this way, you are not escaping life, you are learning how to live it, fully, courageously, and with a heart wide open.

Taoism

When you slow down and breathe deeply, you begin to feel what Taoist meditation invites you to remember: that you are not separate from nature, but an expression of it. Grounded in the ancient wisdom of **Laozi** and the *Tao Te Ching,* Taoist meditation guides you toward living in alignment with the **Tao,** the natural flow of life, the un-nameable source of all that is. In Taoist practice, you are not trying to control your thoughts or force your body into stillness. Instead, you are learning to **soften**, to let go, and to trust the **flow** of energy within and around you. You tune in to the quiet rhythm of your breath, the gentle movement of your inner energy, your **qì,** and you begin to notice how peace arises when you stop resisting life's changes.

Through **qìgōng** and **neigong,** movement and internal cultivation, you connect your body, mind, and spirit as one harmonious whole. You begin to sense where your energy is blocked or depleted and gently guide it back into balance. These practices are not about effort; they are about **allowing**, about listening deeply to your body and letting it speak in stillness. When you meditate the Taoist way, you are returning to what is **simple**, **quiet**, and **true.** You become aware of the subtle dance between action and non-action, doing and being. You start to live with greater ease, intuition, and grace, like water flowing over stone, yielding and yet powerful. In this space, you do not strive to become something new. You remember who you already are: a being of rhythm, flow, breath, and spirit, intimately connected to the cycles of the Earth and the eternal Tao.

Western Mindfulness (Modern, Global)

When you practice mindfulness in a modern Western context, you are stepping into a tradition that blends ancient Eastern wisdom with contemporary psychological science. While its roots draw from practices in Buddhism and yoga, the version you engage with today, especially through pioneers like **Jon Kabat-Zinn,** is grounded in your everyday life. Through programs like **Mindfulness-Based Stress Reduction (MBSR),** mindfulness became a bridge between tradition and neuroscience, spirituality and evidence-based mental health care.

You do not need to change who you are or what you believe to benefit from mindfulness. You simply **bring your full attention** to this moment, just as it is. You learn to **observe your thoughts** without judging them, to notice sensations in your body with curiosity, and to gently return your awareness to the **here and now** whenever your mind drifts. In doing so, you cultivate the inner space to respond instead of react. You begin to soften your relationship with stress, anxiety, and self-criticism. You build **emotional regulation**, increase **focus**, and support your **psychological well-being,** not through escape, but through presence.

When you show up with awareness in everyday moments, while drinking tea, walking, or simply breathing, you realise that mindfulness is not a task to master, but a way to live. It becomes a **daily anchor**, helping you navigate challenges with greater clarity, calm, and compassion. Through mindfulness, you reconnect with what is real, what is simple, and what is meaningful, and as you return to this moment again and again, you begin to trust it as the only place where healing, peace, and true life are ever found.

The Science Of Meditation And Its Link To Heart Health

When you meditate, you give your heart the gift of presence, peace, and restoration. Science now confirms what ancient traditions have long known, your inner state deeply affects your physical heart. Each time you settle into stillness and bring awareness to your breath, you activate your parasympathetic nervous system. This is your body's natural *"rest and restore"* mode, which helps lower your heart rate, reduce blood pressure, and quieten the storm of stress hormones like cortisol.

You may not see it right away, but beneath the surface, meditation begins to shift your physiology. Your heart rhythm becomes more coherent, your blood vessels relax, and your heart rate variability (HRV) improves, an important marker of cardiovascular resilience. These are not just numbers; they are signs that your heart is learning to move through life with greater ease and strength. As you commit to meditation, you also become more emotionally attuned. You start to respond rather than react, to pause rather than push.

This emotional regulation supports better choices, deeper sleep, healthier habits, and a more loving relationship with your body. You begin to listen to what your heart truly needs, not just physically, but spiritually. In this space of stillness, your heart remembers its natural rhythm. You reconnect with your innate wisdom, and your body responds with gratitude. Meditation becomes more than a practice, it becomes your daily act of self-care, self-love, and heart health. Each breath, each pause, is an invitation to let your heart lead.

The Science Of Meditation And Its Link To Empathy

The science of meditation reveals that as you turn inward, you expand your capacity to connect outward, with greater empathy, compassion, and understanding. When you meditate regularly, especially with heart-centred practices like loving-kindness or compassion meditation, you literally rewire your brain for empathy. Neuroscientific studies show that meditation activates key areas of your brain associated with emotional awareness and empathy particularly the anterior insula and the anterior cingulate cortex. These regions help you tune into the emotions of others, allowing you to sense their experiences more deeply and respond with greater care.

As you cultivate present-moment awareness, you become less reactive and more attuned. You begin to notice not just your own emotional patterns, but the subtle signals and needs of the people around you. Meditation reduces self-referential thinking and strengthens your ability to take the perspective of others, an essential element of empathy. Over time, your emotional regulation improves. You are less likely to be overwhelmed by your own stress or discomfort, which gives you the space to hold space for others. You become more patient, more understanding, and more open-hearted in your relationships.

On a biochemical level, meditation has been shown to increase oxytocin, the hormone linked to bonding, trust, and connection. This hormonal shift supports your ability to engage with others from a place of warmth and genuine presence. In essence, by quieting your mind and softening your heart, meditation helps you move from judgment to understanding, from separation to shared humanity. The more you connect with your own inner experience, the more naturally you connect with the experiences of others. This is the foundation of true empathy, a gift that begins within and radiates outward.

The Science Of Meditation And Its Link To Mental Clarity

The science of meditation reveals a powerful truth: when you commit to regular stillness, you give your brain the space it needs to reset, realign, and restore clarity. You begin to quiet the mental noise and create room for focus, insight, and deeper understanding. When you meditate, your brain shifts into more balanced wave patterns, especially alpha and theta waves, which are linked to creativity, intuition, and calm alertness. Functional MRI scans show that meditation reduces activity in the brain's default mode network, the part responsible for mind-wandering and rumination.

In doing so, you become more present, less caught up in regrets about the past or worries about the future. You also activate and strengthen the prefrontal cortex, which is responsible for higher-order functions like decision-making, emotional regulation, and concentration. As you sit in silence, you train your mind to focus, let go of distractions, and return to what matters most. Over time, your attention span improves, your memory becomes sharper, and you experience less mental fatigue.

Meditation also lowers cortisol, the stress hormone that clouds judgment and overwhelms your system. As your stress levels drop, your thoughts become clearer, and you begin to experience greater mental spaciousness. Ideas flow more easily. You become more decisive, more intuitive, and better able to respond rather than react.

Ultimately, meditation invites you into a state of mental coherence, where thought, emotion, and intention work in harmony. In this state, you gain access to your deepest clarity. You remember what truly matters. You begin to trust your inner knowing, and from that place of stillness, insight, and awareness, you navigate life with a grounded, peaceful mind and a clear, open heart.

"The Goal Is No Goal" - The Paradox And Power Of Presence

In a world driven by deadlines, achievement, and constant doing, the idea that *"the goal is no goal"* can feel counterintuitive, perhaps even uncomfortable, but when you truly slow down and begin to connect with your heart, you realise this paradox holds a liberating truth: **you are not here to constantly strive, you are here to be.** This does not mean you abandon purpose, growth, or meaningful action. Rather, it invites you to shift your relationship with them. Instead of chasing worthiness or happiness as distant destinations, you begin to recognise them as qualities that already exist within you, accessible in the present moment. You start to see that presence is not a distraction from your journey; it *is* the journey.

When you stop pushing and allow yourself to simply *be*, something remarkable happens. Your nervous system calms. Your mind softens. You become more aware, more compassionate, more alive. You start to feel the quiet richness of what it means to exist fully in *now*, not in yesterday's regrets or tomorrow's expectations, but in the sacred clarity of this breath. In this space, *you no longer live to prove, you live to experience.* You are no longer defined by what you achieve but by how authentically you show up, and in doing so, you cultivate an inner stillness that strengthens your emotional resilience, deepens your intuition, and opens your heart. The paradox is this: when you stop striving, you start arriving. Over and over again, and in that arrival, you remember who you truly are, not a project to be perfected, but a presence to be embraced. *That is the power of presence. That is the beauty of having no goal.*

Brain And Heart Harmony - **The Neurological And Physiological Benefits Of Meditation**

When you meditate, you initiate a remarkable state of harmony between your brain and your heart. This is not just a metaphor, it is a scientifically validated process that affects nearly every aspect of your physical and emotional well-being. As you enter stillness and bring your attention inward, your autonomic nervous system begins to shift from sympathetic (fight-or-flight) dominance to parasympathetic (rest-and-restore) activation. This shift lowers your heart rate, reduces blood pressure, slows your breathing, and calms the stress hormones flooding your system. With regular practice, your heart begins to beat in a more coherent rhythm, which sends calm, stable signals to your brain.

Neuroscientific studies show that meditation strengthens the **prefrontal cortex**, which governs focus, planning, and emotional regulation. At the same time, it decreases reactivity in the **amygdala**, the brain's fear and alarm centre. This means you become better at pausing before reacting, navigating challenges with greater clarity, and making choices from a grounded, heart-aligned place. Your **heart rate variability (HRV),** a key measure of nervous system health and adaptability, also improves. A higher HRV is associated with emotional flexibility, improved stress recovery, and better long-term cardiovascular health. Meditation teaches your body how to return to equilibrium after being stressed, something that modern life rarely allows.

Perhaps most importantly, this brain–heart synchronisation enhances your access to empathy, compassion, and intuition. When your nervous system is calm, and your mind is still, you can truly hear the quiet wisdom of your heart. In this harmonious state, you do not just think better, you **feel** better, connect more deeply, and respond to life with clarity, creativity, and presence. This is the true gift of meditation: a body that is at peace, a mind that is clear, and a heart that leads.

Finding Your Fit – (Best Meditation For You)

Styles of meditation that align with different temperaments

Not all meditation practices suit everyone the same way, and that is the beauty of it. Just as we each have different learning styles and emotional needs, our approach to inner stillness can vary based on our temperament, personality, and life circumstances. Discovering your ideal form of meditation is less about rigid discipline and more about finding what resonates with your heart and mind. Here is a brief guide to help you find your fit:

- **The Reflective Seeker:** *Best Fit: Contemplative Meditation*

- **The Restless Mind:** *Best Fit: Mindfulness-Based Stress Reduction (MBSR) or Breath Awareness*

- **The Heart-Centred Empath:** *Best Fit: Loving-Kindness (Metta) or Heart Coherence Breathing*

- **The Physically Energised:** *Best Fit: Moving Meditations like Qigong, Yoga, or Walking Meditation*

- **The Analytical Thinker:** *Best Fit: Focused Attention or Mantra-Based Meditation*

- **The Creative Spirit:** *Best Fit: Visualisation or Guided Meditation*

Remember, **your style may evolve.** There is no single *"right"* way to meditate, only the way that helps you return to yourself. The most important thing is that it feels nourishing, supportive, and sustainable. Let your temperament be your compass, and trust the rhythm of your inner world.

The Reflective Seeker

Best Fit: Contemplative Meditation

If you are a reflective seeker, your natural inclination is to look inward. You often find yourself pondering life's deeper meanings, seeking connection with truth, purpose, and the sacred. You are drawn to silence, solitude, and stillness, not as escape, but as a way to listen more deeply to the voice within. Contemplative meditation suits your soul because it honours your need for inner dialogue and spiritual exploration. Practices like **Lectio Divina** (sacred reading) allow you to reflect on timeless texts, whether scriptural, philosophical, or poetic, and listen for the inner resonance they awaken in you. You do not rush through experiences; instead, you dwell in questions, allowing their wisdom to unfold over time.

You may also be drawn to **loving-kindness meditation**, which helps you soften the inner critic and develop a sense of spacious compassion, both for yourself and others, and **gratitude journaling** can serve as a simple but profound ritual to notice the gifts in your life, shifting your attention from lack to abundance.

As a reflective seeker, your meditative journey is not about detaching from the world but integrating insight into how you live, relate, and lead. This path deepens your connection to meaning, grounds you in purpose, and nurtures a heart-led life of authenticity, empathy, and quiet strength. Allow your contemplative nature to be a strength. In a world that often rewards speed and surface, your ability to pause, reflect, and respond with depth is a sacred gift.

The Restless Mind

Best Fit: Mindfulness-Based Stress Reduction (MBSR) or Breath Awareness

If you find your thoughts racing, jumping from one worry or idea to the next, you are not alone. A restless mind is a common experience in today's overstimulated world, and it does not mean you are doing something wrong. It simply means your mind is active, alert, and constantly processing, but even a busy mind needs space to breathe.

Mindfulness-Based Stress Reduction (MBSR) and breath awareness practices offer you a gentle, structured way to bring your attention into the present moment without needing to force mental stillness. Instead of trying to suppress your thoughts, you learn to observe them with curiosity and non-judgment. You notice their patterns, their rhythm, and most importantly, you learn that you are *not* your thoughts.

Breath awareness provides a natural anchor. Your breath is always with you, calm, steady, and available in every moment. By bringing your focus to the inhale and exhale, you create a quiet centre in the middle of mental noise. Over time, this simple practice rewires your brain for greater focus, clarity, and emotional regulation. MBSR combines breath, body scanning, gentle movement, and mindful observation to help reduce anxiety, manage stress, and cultivate a compassionate inner voice.

It is evidence-based and highly adaptable, even five minutes can make a difference. You do not need to chase stillness. With each breath, you are learning to meet your restlessness with kindness, and in doing so, reclaim your calm. Meditation for the restless mind is not about silencing your thoughts, it is about softening your relationship with them.

The Heart Centred Empath

Best Fit: Loving-Kindness (Metta) Meditation or Heart Coherence Breathing

You are someone who feels life with intensity, emotions, energies, and the unspoken currents in a room often flow straight into your heart. As a heart-centred empath, your natural gift is deep compassion. You care, often without needing words, but with that openness can come emotional overwhelm, fatigue, or a sense of being emotionally saturated by the pain or struggles of others. That is why heart-based meditations like **Loving-Kindness (Metta)** or **Heart Coherence Breathing** are especially aligned with your nature. These practices help you remain grounded in your own heart while extending warmth and connection outward in a way that nourishes rather than depletes.

Loving-Kindness Meditation involves silently repeating well-wishes, such as *"May I be safe. May I be happy. May I be free"*, towards yourself, loved ones, strangers, and even those you struggle with. This deliberate cultivation of compassion rewires your emotional responses, builds resilience, and offers a soft shield of intention that protects your sensitive nature from absorbing everything around you.

Heart Coherence Breathing focuses on syncing your breath with your heart's natural rhythm. By breathing slowly and evenly while focusing on feelings like appreciation or care, you regulate your nervous system, bring your mind and body into harmony, and access a calm, coherent state of presence. This state not only benefits you emotionally, but it also sends calming signals to others, making you an even more effective space-holder and connector.

These meditations do not shut down your empathy, they refine it. They help you stay in your own centre while still being the compassionate, emotionally intelligent presence the world needs. Through these heart-led practices, you learn to care without carrying, love without losing yourself, and remain open without becoming overwhelmed.

The Physically Energised

Best Fit: Moving Meditations like Qigong, Yoga, or Walking Meditation

You are someone who comes alive through movement. Sitting still for long periods may feel more like a strain than serenity. You think better on your feet, release stress through activity, and find clarity when your body is in motion. Stillness for you is not necessarily quiet or motionless, it is a state of focused, embodied flow. That is why **moving meditations** like **Qigong**, **Yoga**, or **Walking Meditation** are a perfect fit. These practices honour your natural rhythm and help you cultivate mindfulness while keeping your body engaged. Instead of forcing your energy into stillness, you are invited to channel it with intention and grace.

Qigong combines slow, deliberate movements with breath and focused intention to harmonise your internal energy (qi). It calms the nervous system while grounding your awareness in the present moment, perfect for energised individuals seeking balance. **Yoga**, particularly mindful or breath-based styles like Hatha or Yin, allows you to stretch, strengthen, and centre yourself. Each pose becomes an anchor of awareness, and each breath a gateway to presence. Over time, you may find that even in movement, stillness arises.

Walking Meditation turns everyday motion into a sacred practice. Whether you walk through nature or along a hallway, bringing awareness to each step and breath slows the mind and deepens your connection to your body and surroundings. These movement-based meditations do not ask you to change who you are, they help you refine your energy, focus your attention, and find stillness within your natural state of motion. As you move, you meditate. As you breathe, you return home to yourself.

The Analytical Thinker

Best Fit: Focused Attention or Mantra-Based Meditation

You are someone who seeks understanding through structure, logic, and clarity. Your mind is sharp, inquisitive, and often filled with analysis and inner dialogue. While this makes you excellent at problem-solving and strategy, it can sometimes lead to mental overactivity and difficulty relaxing. Meditation may seem challenging at first, especially if your thoughts are constantly in motion, but the right style can harness your mental energy into deeper stillness and insight.

Focused Attention Meditation is ideal for you because it gives your mind something clear and deliberate to concentrate on. Whether it is your breath, a candle flame, or a physical sensation, this form of meditation trains your attention and reduces mental scattering. The act of returning your focus again and again becomes a powerful mental workout, building resilience, patience, and clarity.

Mantra-Based Meditation, such as Transcendental Meditation or traditional Sanskrit chanting, can also be profoundly effective. Repeating a mantra, a sacred word, phrase, or sound, gives your mind a rhythmic pattern to align with. Over time, this repetition calms mental chatter, promotes coherence between brain hemispheres, and creates space for insight to emerge.

Both approaches support your natural analytical gifts by offering structure without overwhelm. Instead of resisting your mental tendencies, you work with them, training your focus like a laser while gently opening the door to deeper stillness and self-awareness. Through these practices, you may discover that true clarity does not always come from more thinking, but from still, focused presence. Over time, you will not only sharpen your mind but also connect more fully with your intuition, creativity, and heart.

The Creative Spirit

Best Fit: Visualisation or Guided Meditation

You naturally see the world through images, metaphors, and imagination. Your mind paints in colour, possibility, and emotion, often weaving ideas, dreams, and stories together in a way that inspires others. As a Creative Spirit, traditional meditation styles that emphasise stillness or silence may feel restrictive or dull. Instead, you flourish in practices that engage your inner vision and invite your imagination to become a healing force.

Visualisation Meditation allows you to direct your creative energy inward. You might picture a warm light spreading through your body, a peaceful sanctuary that restores your spirit, or a future version of yourself living in alignment with your dreams. These visual journeys not only activate your creativity, but also help to rewire your brain with positive imagery, supporting emotional healing, confidence, and focus. This kind of meditation becomes a tool for transformation, allowing you to consciously shape the inner movie of your life.

Guided Meditation offers a powerful entry point if you enjoy being led through imagery, storytelling, or metaphor. Whether it is a walk through a forest, a journey to meet your future self, or a healing experience of forgiveness, guided meditations engage your senses and imagination, making the experience immersive and emotionally resonant. These practices can reduce stress, spark insight, and unlock new ideas or directions in your creative life.

As a Creative Spirit, your gift is in turning the abstract into beauty. Meditation becomes a canvas where your mind can play, heal, and explore. By integrating visual or guided practices into your daily life, you not only support emotional well-being and clarity, you deepen your creative voice and live more fully from your unique brilliance.

Meditation - Application Exercise

Simple 'I Am' Meditation

Duration: 3–5 minutes

1. **Get Comfortable:** Sit or stand in a position where you feel relaxed but alert. Gently close your eyes.

2. **Breathe:** Take a slow, deep breath in through your nose… and gently exhale through your mouth. Repeat this three times.

3. **Affirm:** Silently or softly say one of your *'I Am'* statements, for example: *"I am calm.";* As you say it, imagine the words filling your whole body with light and warmth.

4. **Repeat & Feel:** Continue to breathe slowly and repeat your *'I Am'* statement 5–10 times, letting each repetition sink deeper into your heart.

5. **Close:** Take one more deep breath in, hold for a moment, then exhale slowly. Open your eyes and carry this feeling into the rest of your day.

Case Study – Lily's Journey

"Meditation is rubbish, 'I am telling you right now John, I have done it before, and it is joke.' Lily was a lovely soul, full of energy and always on the go. As a fitness instructor she practiced what she preached (well, sort of) and that was part of the problem. Have you ever met someone who never seemed to switch off? Maybe this is resonating with You because you find it hard to slowdown and never switch off either. Lily had been a competitive swimmer and loved being active, and whilst her enthusiasm was genuine and infectious, she had a very hard time slowing down and was unable to make any significant progress in doing any inner work.

Lily was able to gift herself a little time to do her balanced heart breathing but found it really hard to slow down and connect with herself or her heart. It took a few months, but I introduced Lily to a couple of gentle and beautiful meditation techniques. The first being a 'walking meditation' and when she felt safe in this space we moved into a 'loving kindness meditation'. Lily was skeptical when we first spoke about meditation, but it was structured in a way that resonated directly with her and that was important. She is an active person, and a walking meditation was perfect for her.

After she was comfortable being in the walking meditation space we moved on to the 'loving kindness meditation' and it was from here that we were able to start really making significant inroads into healing, learning, and growing. The important thing that I would like you to connect with here is that there is no 'one size' fits all approach and it is important to find practices and approaches to things that resonate with you and where you are at on your journey.

Reflective exercise - Lily's Journey

Here are **four profound and reflective questions** designed to help you deeply engage with Lily's journey with meditation:

1. **What story have you been telling yourself about stillness, and is it time to rewrite it?** *This question invites you to challenge any resistance or assumptions you hold about slowing down and embracing presence.*

2. **When was the last time you truly sat with yourself, without distraction or judgment?** *Reflect on your relationship with quiet moments and whether you allow space to simply be.*

3. **How might your life shift if you gave yourself permission to breathe, pause, and listen within?** *Consider the emotional and spiritual possibilities that open when you prioritise meditation as a sacred act of self-connection.*

4. **What part of yourself is longing to be heard in the silence?** *This helps you attune to your inner world and the truths waiting beneath your busy mind or external obligations.*

These questions are powerful companions to Lily's story and your own unfolding journey into mindfulness and heartful presence.

Affirmations For Integration (Heart Whispers)

Affirmations have the power to quiet the noise of doubt, open the doorway to self-trust, and draw you back into the wisdom of your heart. When practised daily, they nurture an inner dialogue based in love and truth, helping you live each day more aligned with who you truly are. I invite you to repeat silently or write:

- *I meditate every morning to start my day with clarity.*

- *I feel more peaceful and focused after my meditation practice.*

- *I am able to release stress and anxiety through meditation.*

- *I notice positive changes in my heart whilst meditating.*

- *I use meditation for self–reflection and personal growth.*

- *I am grateful for the stillness and insight meditation brings me.*

Meditation Exercise – Your Weekly Commitment

This week, choose **two practices** to focus on with intention. Your goal is not perfection, but presence.

Options:

- **5-minute Silent Sit** – Sit quietly, breathe naturally, and simply notice your thoughts without judgment.

- **Guided Meditation** – Use an app, audio, or video to follow a guided practice that supports your current needs.

- **Mindful Eating** – Choose one meal to eat slowly, noticing textures, flavours, and aromas with full attention.

- **Walking Meditation** – Walk at a gentle pace, matching each step to your breath, fully aware of your body moving.

- **Loving-Kindness Meditation** – Silently send thoughts of love, peace, and health to yourself and others.

- **Plan or Research a Local Silent Retreat** – Take a step toward deepening your practice by exploring opportunities for extended silence.

Your Commitment:: Write a short **Meditation Commitment Card** for the week. Include:

1. The **two practices** you will commit to.

2. The **time of day** you will do them.

3. A **one-line intention** for why you are doing this (e.g., *"To create more calm in my mornings"*).

Keep your card visible, on your desk, mirror, or fridge, as a gentle reminder.

Closing Relection

As you complete this part of your journey, take a moment to honour the stillness you have cultivated, not just in your mind, but in your heart. Through meditation, you have touched a deeper rhythm within yourself, one that does not rush, chase, or strive, but simply *is.* You have begun to unlearn the noise of the world and listen instead to the quiet truth inside you. With each breath, you have remembered that presence is your power, and that clarity arises not from doing more, but from *being more aware.* In this sacred space of stillness, you have opened a doorway to compassion, insight, and healing.

You now know that meditation is not about becoming someone new, it is about remembering who you already are. It is a daily practice of returning to your centre, realigning with your heart, and giving yourself permission to rest in your own being. There will be days when your mind resists, when the world distracts, or when silence feels far away. On those days, come back to the breath. Come back to this moment. Come back to you. Let your meditation practice become a quiet rebellion against chaos. A devotion to peace. A loving act of self-care, and above all, let it be a living reminder that you are not separate from life, you are part of its sacred unfolding.

You are the calm in your own storm

You are the anchor in your own sea

You are the presence your heart has been waiting for.

5 - MIRROR

Your Opening Reflection

An Invitation to See Yourself with Gentle Eyes - As you step into this chapter, I invite you to pause and soften. Take a breath, and allow yourself to meet the mirror not as an enemy, but as a friend. The reflection before you is not asking for perfection, only honesty, tenderness, and presence. Let this moment be an opening, a chance to see yourself not through judgment, but through love.

- "Are you willing to see the parts of yourself you usually hide?"

- "What truths about yourself are you ready to accept today?"

- "When you meet your own gaze, do you recognise your inherent worth?"

- "When you look in the mirror, what do you really see?"

- "Do you offer yourself love and kindness… or judgment?"

Let these questions open the doorway into presence. Every answer you give, whether in words, sensations, or silence, is a bridge between where you are and where you are going.

Learning Objectives

The learning objectives are included here to give you a clear focus for this chapter, ensuring that each practice you explore moves you closer to mastering the skills, insights, and heart-led awareness that will enrich your life well beyond the program. By the end of this chapter, you will:

- Understand the emotional impact and science behind mirror work.

- Apply mirror work techniques to build yourself-worth, self-love, and emotional resilience.

- Identify internal resistance to self-acceptance and begin the process of transformation.

- Practice heart-connected affirmation and forgiveness through eye-gazing and mirror-based self-dialogue.

- Recognise how mirror work supports long-term emotional intelligence development and heart connection.

Core Emotional Domains

The core emotional intelligence domains covered here are essential because they form the foundation for lasting heart connection, guiding you to deepen self-awareness, regulate emotions, build resilience, and strengthen the mind-body bond throughout your Heart Unbound journey.

- **Self-Awareness:** Helps you honestly see and acknowledge your emotions and inner dialogue as you face yourself.

- **Self-Regulation:** Enables you to stay grounded and calm when uncomfortable feelings surface during mirror work.

- **Motivation:** Fuels your commitment to personal growth and keeps you returning to the practice with intention.

- **Self-Compassion:** Encourages a kind, gentle response to your reflection, replacing criticism with understanding.

- **Emotional Resilience:** Strengthens your ability to move through vulnerability and transform emotional pain into healing.

"Mirror - Facing Yourself With Love"

The Psychological, Emotional, and Spiritual Value of Mirror Work

Mirror work is a courageous act of self-witnessing. It invites you to stand before your own reflection and meet the person who looks back, not with judgment, but with awareness, honesty, and compassion. This seemingly simple practice holds profound **psychological**, **emotional**, and **spiritual** value, especially when integrated into a heart-led path of healing and self-affirmation.

Psychological Value

From a psychological standpoint, mirror work is a powerful tool for increasing **self-awareness**. When you consciously look into your own eyes and speak to yourself with intention, you confront the often unconscious inner dialogue that runs beneath your surface thoughts. Over time, you begin to notice the beliefs you have inherited, the wounds you have carried, and the stories you have internalised about your worth. By practicing positive affirmations like "*I am enough*" or "*I am worthy of love*," you start to **reprogram negative self-beliefs** and create new neural pathways through the science of **neuroplasticity**. This consistent, mindful reinforcement can shift your self-perception and support long-term cognitive and emotional growth.

Emotional Value

Emotionally, mirror work helps you build **emotional resilience**. It allows you to feel what you have suppressed, grief, shame, anger, joy, and to welcome those feelings without turning away. When you stand in front of the mirror and acknowledge your emotional truth, you begin to **regulate your emotional responses** with more clarity and compassion.

This act of presence with your own emotional experience cultivates **self-acceptance** and nurtures a profound connection between your inner world and outer expression. Over time, this emotional honesty strengthens your capacity to hold space for others as well, enhancing empathy and relational depth.

Spiritual Value

Spiritually, mirror work becomes a sacred space, a daily ritual where you meet your soul. As you look into your own eyes, you begin to see not just your physical self, but the deeper essence that lives beneath your skin. This connection awakens your **inner wisdom**, your **divine light**, and the quiet voice of your heart. You begin to **recognise yourself as whole and loved**, regardless of past mistakes or external validation.

In this space, the mirror becomes a metaphor for truth, reflecting not just who you are, but who you are becoming. It is a practice of **remembrance**, returning you to the truth that you are enough, just as you are. **In essence**, mirror work integrates psychological insight, emotional healing, and spiritual connection into a daily act of self-honouring. It helps you rewrite your internal narrative, build compassion from the inside out, and live with greater authenticity, presence, and love. When you dare to face yourself, gently, bravely, and consistently, you begin to unbind your heart and unlock the sacred power that lives within you.

The Origin Of Mirror Work: Louise Hay's Legacy

Mirror work, as a transformative healing practice, finds its modern roots in the pioneering work of **Louise Hay,** an internationally renowned author, speaker, and the founder of Hay House Publishing. Often called the "*Queen of Affirmations*," Hay revolutionised the self-help landscape by introducing a profoundly simple yet emotionally powerful method: **mirror work,** the practice of looking into your own eyes in a mirror while speaking affirming, loving, and healing words to yourself.

At the heart of Hay's philosophy was the belief that **self-love is the key to healing**. In her seminal book, *You Can Heal Your Life* (1984), she taught that most suffering, whether emotional, physical, or spiritual, stems from **negative self-beliefs, self-criticism, and unhealed emotional wounds**, often based in childhood. Mirror work, she believed, was a way to gently bring those wounds to the surface and meet them with compassion rather than judgment.

The mirror became, in Hay's hands, a **sacred tool for self-confrontation and self-connection**. It bypassed the intellect and tapped directly into the heart. When you stand before a mirror and say, "*I love you*," or "*I am willing to change*," you are not just speaking words, you are rewiring beliefs, rewriting narratives, and restoring trust in yourself. Hay often said, *"The mirror reflects back to us the feelings we have about ourselves,"* and that reflection, when met with courage and consistency, becomes a gateway to healing.

The emotional impact of mirror work can be immediate and intense. Many people experience tears, resistance, even anger, as long-buried shame, fear, or grief rises to the surface. Yet with continued practice, mirror work becomes a daily ritual of **self-reclamation,** a way to rebuild inner safety, validate your worth, and awaken to your true nature. From a **psychological perspective**, mirror work helps interrupt cycles of negative self-talk, strengthens self-compassion, and promotes emotional regulation. From a **spiritual perspective**, it aligns you with the divine within, reminding you that you are inherently worthy, lovable, and whole.

Hay's legacy lives on not just in her writings but in the countless lives transformed through her teachings. Her work paved the way for a generation of coaches, therapists, and spiritual leaders who continue to use mirror work as a foundation for emotional intelligence, trauma recovery, and self-love. To engage in mirror work is to return home to yourself. It is a commitment to **see, hear, and honour the person looking back at you,** not as broken, but as beautifully becoming. Through this practice, you are invited to dissolve the layers of fear, shame, and self-doubt and remember this fundamental truth: **your heart is the most powerful healer you have.**

The Science Behind Mirror Work: Neuroplasticity, NLP, And Emotional Reprogramming

1. Neuroplasticity - Rewiring the Brain Through Repetition and Intention

At the core of mirror work lies the principle of **neuroplasticity,** your brain's innate ability to change and reorganise its neural pathways in response to thoughts, experiences, and behaviors. When you stand in front of a mirror and repeat empowering affirmations like *"I am enough"* or *"I am worthy of love,"* you are not just speaking words, you are sending new signals through your brain's emotional and cognitive circuits.

Repeated mirror affirmations:

- Activate regions such as the **ventromedial prefrontal cortex** (associated with self-referential thinking and emotional regulation).

- Begin to **overwrite old narratives** stored in your subconscious, often tied to shame, rejection, or inadequacy.

- **Strengthen neural connections** that align with self-worth, compassion, and inner peace.

This consistent rewiring process gradually **shifts your inner default** from self-criticism to self-acceptance. It creates a new emotional baseline where confidence and calm become more natural responses.

2. NLP - Anchoring and Reframing Limiting Beliefs

Neuro-Linguistic Programming (NLP) is a psychological approach that studies how language and behavior influence your brain. Mirror work draws from two powerful NLP techniques:

- **Anchoring**: By placing your hand over your heart, making eye contact with your reflection, and pairing these gestures with positive affirmations, you create an anchor, a physiological and emotional cue that triggers feelings of safety, warmth, and empowerment. Over time, just returning to the mirror with this gesture can evoke those same emotional states.

- **Reframing**: Many people carry internal scripts like *"I am not good enough,"* *"I do not matter,"* or *"I always fail."* NLP teaches that by consciously **replacing these limiting beliefs** with affirmations such as *"I am growing,"* *"I am loved,"* or *"I am resilient,"* you shift your perception of self and reality. Mirror work makes this reframe **visceral and immediate**, amplifying its effectiveness through direct self-confrontation.

3. Emotional Reprogramming - Healing Through Presence and Self-Compassion

Mirror work also accesses your **limbic system,** your brain's emotional centre. When you speak to yourself with sincerity, while making gentle eye contact, your nervous system receives the message that **you are safe, seen, and accepted**. This is emotionally powerful, especially for those who never received that validation from others. Emotional reprogramming through mirror work:

- Creates **new emotional memory patterns** that create trust and compassion.

- Reduces cortisol and supports parasympathetic nervous system activation, bringing **calm and regulation.**

- Encourages the release of **suppressed emotions** in a safe and self-directed environment.

Over time, the act of meeting yourself in the mirror with love helps you **dismantle shame, release stored trauma**, and **cultivate deep emotional resilience.**

Final Insight: A Whole-Person Transformation

When combined, neuroplasticity, NLP, and emotional reprogramming make mirror work a truly integrative healing modality. This is not about vanity, it is about **visibility**: truly seeing yourself, acknowledging your worth, and creating a new, embodied relationship with who you are. By returning to the mirror day after day, you are not only reprogramming your thoughts, you are **reclaiming your voice, rewriting your story**, and **rebuilding your identity** from the inside out.

Mirror Work As A Daily Emotional Intelligence Ritual

Mirror work is more than just a moment in front of your reflection, it is a sacred ritual that invites you to reconnect with your inner self. When you look into your own eyes and speak words of affirmation or truth, you are choosing to see yourself with clarity, compassion, and courage. You give yourself permission to be fully seen, not just by the world, but by you. As a daily emotional intelligence ritual, mirror work helps you build **self-awareness**. You begin to notice how you feel as you speak to yourself, how your body responds, and what thoughts arise. This awareness becomes a powerful guide, helping you better understand the emotional patterns that shape your life.

You also develop **self-regulation**. As difficult emotions surface, like shame, fear, or self-doubt, you learn to sit with them, breathe through them, and respond with love instead of judgment. This daily practice teaches you how to pause, reflect, and choose kindness, even in moments of inner conflict. Your **motivation** is reignited. By affirming who you are and who you are becoming, you strengthen your commitment to live with purpose and integrity. You begin to show up for yourself in ways you once reserved only for others.

Self-compassion deepens. Through consistent mirror work, you begin to soften toward yourself. You realise that the love, encouragement, and forgiveness you have offered others is something you deeply deserve too. You learn to be your own ally, and over time, your **emotional resilience** grows. You face yourself daily, with all your wounds and wisdom, and instead of turning away, you lean in. You find strength in your softness and courage in your honesty. When you practice mirror work regularly, you create space for healing, integration, and growth. You start each day by declaring: *I see you. I hear you. I am here for you,* and in doing so, you transform the mirror from a place of judgment into a sacred space of self-connection and heart-led transformation.

The Three Phases Of Mirror Work

Awareness • Courage • Embodiment

1. Awareness - Meeting Yourself with Presence

You begin by simply showing up. Standing in front of the mirror, you allow yourself to be seen, not just physically, but emotionally and energetically. You become aware of the stories you have been telling yourself, the critical thoughts that arise, the resistance in your body, and the way you have been avoiding your own gaze. This phase is about *honest observation*. You do not need to change anything, just notice. You are learning to witness yourself with curiosity rather than judgment.

2. Courage - Leaning into Discomfort with Love

It takes real bravery to stay. As you continue mirror work, emotions may surface, grief, anger, shame, or sadness. In this phase, you are called to *remain present* despite discomfort. You begin to say words that feel foreign, like *"I am enough"* or *"I am lovable,"* even if a part of you does not yet believe them. This is the work of the heart, stepping beyond old patterns and daring to believe in your own worth. Courage means trusting that you are safe to feel and safe to heal.

3. Embodiment - Living the Truth of Who You Are

Over time, what once felt difficult becomes natural. You begin to *live* your affirmations. You do not just say *"I am worthy"*, you move through the world with that truth in your body. This is embodiment: when love, self-trust, and confidence move from thoughts into action. You find yourself making aligned choices, setting healthy boundaries, expressing your truth, and embracing your life with compassion and presence. You become a living mirror of the love you have discovered within.

Why Facing Yourself Can Be So Confronting, And Liberating

Facing yourself can feel like stepping into uncharted territory, because when you slow down and truly see yourself, without judgment or distraction, you come face-to-face with everything you have tried to suppress, avoid, or ignore. It can be deeply confronting because it invites you to witness not only your strengths and successes, but also your wounds, insecurities, regrets, and unmet needs. You might feel exposed, vulnerable, or even overwhelmed, because mirror work asks you to meet your inner world with honesty and compassion.

You may hear the old narratives you have carried for years: *"I am not enough," "I am unlovable," "I failed."* These stories can be hard to confront, but when you do, you begin to reclaim your power. You learn that your worth is not defined by the past, by perfection, or by other people's opinions. You realise that your heart has always held the wisdom and strength to heal, and this is where the liberation begins. By facing yourself with presence and kindness, you open the door to deep emotional freedom.

You stop running from who you are and start embracing every part of your being. In that reflection, you start to see not just flaws or pain, but your resilience, your capacity for love, and your divine potential. You give yourself permission to be human, to grow, to feel, to transform. This brave act of self-meeting does not just change how you see yourself. It changes how you live. It grounds you in authenticity, empowers your choices, and strengthens your relationships with others. The very mirror that once felt intimidating becomes a sacred space, a space where you come home to yourself, again and again.

Mirror Exercise

Purpose: To cultivate self-acceptance, dissolve limiting self-beliefs, and reconnect with your heart through the healing power of eye contact and affirmations.

Step-by-Step Guide:

1. **Find Your Mirror Space:** Choose a quiet, private space where you can stand or sit comfortably in front of a mirror. Make sure you will not be disturbed. Gently dim the lights if you wish to create a softer, heart-held atmosphere.

2. **Place Your Hand on Your Heart:** Take three slow, deep breaths. As you inhale, feel your chest rise. As you exhale, feel your body soften. Bring your awareness to your heart and place your hand over it.

3. **Look Into Your Eyes:** Gaze into your own eyes, not with judgment or critique, but with curiosity and tenderness. Allow yourself to simply *see* the person in the mirror.

4. **Speak the Following Affirmations Aloud (or Create Your Own):**

   1. *"I see you."*

   2. *"You are worthy of love."*

   3. *"I forgive you."*

   4. *"I am here for you."* **Repeat each one slowly. Pause between statements to breathe and feel.**

5. **Notice the Resistance or Emotion**

Do not rush past discomfort. If tears come, let them flow. If resistance arises, acknowledge it gently: *"I see you, too."* You are meeting parts of yourself that have long been waiting to be held.

6. **Close with This Statement:**

   "Every time I return to the mirror, I return to myself."

7. **Journal Reflection (Optional):**

   Write about what you noticed, felt, resisted, or accepted during the practice.

This is not about perfection, it is about presence. Do this daily for one week and watch how your relationship with yourself transforms.

Case Study Discussion: Michael's Journey

Michael was a larger-than-life character with an infectious personality. Michael was a self-made man in his mid-40s and anybody looking at Michael and his life would have been left with the impression that he was someone who was in a good place. However, this was not the case. Michael liked helping others, but his self-talk was brutal, and he did not love himself at all. I journeyed with Michael for quite a few months, and we did some deep healing. One of the things I requested of Michael was to feel into his heart and make a list of all the things he truly loved about himself. Over time this list grew, and I asked Michael to read his list out loud to himself in front of a mirror. I still recall the conversation I had with Michael after I asked him to read his list to himself in front of the mirror. His response, *'there is no f...n way I am reading anything out to myself in front of the mirror.'*

The mere thought of this terrified him. Michael had conditioned himself over decades to believe that he was wholly unworthy, an imposter. I then asked Michael to read his list to me over our Zoom call and he did. I then asked him to just stand in front of his mirror for 60 seconds every day for a week and say nothing. Michael agreed, and over the next 6 months Michael found the courage to take small steps, to heal, learn and grow. He got to a point where he could face himself in the mirror, speak out loud and truly believe the words he was saying.

(Authors note: Please note that every person is different, and every person has different hurts, pains, woundings and traumas. The point I would like you take from Michael's

story is to never give up on yourself. You are a precious gift, and your life is to be lived and not merely survived. Living an authentic life off integrity is more than just existing!)

Reflective Exercise: Michael's Journey

Here are four profound and reflective questions to help you deeply engage with Michael's story and the power of mirror work:

1. **When you look into the mirror, what is the first thought or feeling that arises, and is it truly yours, or a reflection of someone else's voice from your past?** *This question invites you to notice old programming and become aware of whose expectations or judgments you have internalised.*

2. **What part of yourself have you struggled to face, and what might happen if you chose to meet that part with compassion instead of criticism?** *This encourages emotional courage and opens the door to deep self-acceptance and healing.*

3. **How has avoiding your own gaze affected your relationship with yourself and others?** *This helps you explore the link between self-awareness and how authentically you connect with the world around you.*

4. **If you could speak one truth into the mirror that your younger self longed to hear, what would it be, and how would it change the way you live today?** *This helps you engage in self-reparenting and step into a more empowered, heart-led identity.*

Affirmations For Integration (Heart Whispers)

Affirmations have the power to quiet the noise of doubt, open the doorway to self-trust, and draw you back into the wisdom of your heart. When practised daily, they nurture an inner dialogue based in love and truth, helping you live each day more aligned with who you truly are. I invite you to repeat silently or write:

- *I use the mirror to practice positive self–talk.*

- *I avoid judging myself when I look in the mirror.*

- *I find peace when I meditate in front of a mirror.*

- *I see my progress in my reflection during workouts.*

- *I remind myself of my worthiness when looking in the mirror.*

- *I show myself love and kindness in front of the mirror.*

- *I honour the person I see in the mirror as a work in progress and a work of art.*

- *I embrace my reflection as a true expression of my authentic self.*

- *I look into the mirror and recognise the strength within me.*

- *I celebrate the unique beauty that is mine alone.*

- *I use my reflection as a reminder of how far I have come.*

Mirror Exercise – Meeting Yourself with Love

1. **Find Your Mirror:** Stand or sit comfortably in front of a mirror. Look directly into your own eyes.

2. **Breathe and Soften:** Take three slow, deep breaths. With each exhale, release any tension in your shoulders, jaw, or chest.

3. **Speak Your Name:** Gently say your name out loud, as if greeting a dear friend.

4. **Affirm Your Worth:** Choose one phrase to repeat slowly three times, such as:

   - *I see you, and you are enough.*

   - *I love and accept you, exactly as you are.*

   - *You are worthy of kindness and joy.*

5. **Close with Gratitude:** Place your hand over your heart, smile softly, and thank yourself for showing up in this moment.

Closing Reflection

The mirror is not merely glass, it is a sacred space where your deepest truths await. Each time you meet your own eyes, you are offered an invitation: to see beyond the surface and witness the essence of who you truly are. In this reflection, you face not only your image but the stories, wounds, and beliefs you have carried, some yours, some not.

It takes courage to look and even more to stay, but as you soften your gaze and open your heart, what once felt confronting becomes liberating. You begin to see not what is wrong with you, but what has always been right, your resilience, your beauty, your worth. Through mirror work, you reclaim the power to rewrite your inner narrative.

You unlearn shame.

You meet your pain with tenderness.

You awaken self-compassion, and gradually, you return home to yourself.

May your mirror become a place of presence, healing, and truth, and may you always remember: the reflection you see is not just who you are, it is who you are becoming.

6 - DANCE

Your Opening Reflection

An Invitation to Move with Your Heart - As you enter this chapter, give yourself permission to loosen, to soften, to let your body speak in its own language. Dance is not about steps or performance, it is about freedom, rhythm, and truth. Let each movement, whether big or small, be a reminder that your body holds wisdom, your spirit holds music, and your heart already knows the way.

- "How does your body feel when it moves freely without rules or judgment?"

- "If your life had a rhythm right now, what would it sound like?"

- "What parts of yourself come alive when you allow yourself to dance?"

- "When was the last time you danced just for you?"

- "What emotions or beliefs do you associate with dancing?"

Let these questions open the doorway into presence. Every answer you give, whether in words, sensations, or silence, is a bridge between where you are and where you are going.

Learning Objectives

The learning objectives are included here to give you a clear focus for this chapter, ensuring that each practice you explore moves you closer to mastering the skills, insights, and heart-led awareness that will enrich your life well beyond the program. By the end of this chapter, you will:

- Explore the emotional, cultural, and spiritual significance of dance.

- Understand how movement can be a powerful tool for your self-expression and healing.

- Practice dance as a means of emotional release, presence, and heart-connection.

- Reflect on internal resistance, body awareness, and self-limiting beliefs.

- Cultivate confidence, joy, and connection through movement.

Core Emotional Domains

The core emotional intelligence domains covered here are essential because they form the foundation for lasting heart connection, guiding you to deepen self-awareness, regulate emotions, build resilience, and strengthen the mind-body bond throughout your Heart Unbound journey.

- **Self-Awareness:** Through movement, you tune into your emotions and bodily sensations, recognising how you truly feel in the present moment.

- **Self-Regulation:** Dance offers a safe space to release tension and regulate emotional energy through rhythm and breath.

- **Empathy:** Whether dancing alone or with others, you learn to sense emotional states and express compassion through non-verbal connection.

- **Social Skills:** Collaborative or communal dance builds trust, connection, and joyful interaction with others, enhancing relational confidence.

- **Motivation (Intrinsic Confidence):** Dance fuels your inner drive and self-expression, empowering you to move with freedom, joy, and authenticity.

"Dance – Emotion In Motion"

Dance, for you, is far more than movement. it is a profound return to presence, a reconnection with your truest self beyond words or expectations. When you give yourself permission to dance, you awaken something ancient and sacred within you. This is not about choreography or performance; it is about listening to your body's truth and allowing it to speak through every breath, sway, and step.

You dance not to impress, but to express. In a world that often pulls you into your head, dance draws you gently back into your heart and body. It allows you to release the tension, the stories, the self-judgment, and instead move with authenticity and freedom. With each gesture, you let go of perfection and welcome presence. With each rhythm, you rewrite the story of who you are, from the inside out. When you move, you are not alone. You connect to something bigger, to the pulse of the earth beneath you, the beat of music around you, and the shared humanity in those who dance beside you or have danced before.

Dance becomes your prayer, your meditation, your liberation. It is a space where joy rises, grief softens, and your inner world finds safe passage into the outer world. As you dance, you reclaim a part of yourself that may have been forgotten, your right to feel deeply, to move freely, to live fully. You begin to realise that every movement is meaningful, every expression valid, and every beat an opportunity to come home to yourself. Dance is not just an art for you, it is a path of healing, embodiment, and emotional intelligence. It is how you remember that you are alive.

Historical Heartbeat Of Dance

Dance has always pulsed at the heart of human culture, inviting you into a universal language of spirit, story, and connection. When you trace its origins, you discover that dance began not as performance, but as prayer, ritual, and an embodied expression of the sacred. Across the ancient world, in Africa, Asia, the Americas, and Europe, you would have danced to honour the turning of the seasons, to celebrate harvests, to mourn the passing of loved ones, and to commune with forces greater than yourself. Dance was not entertainment; it was survival, healing, and meaning made visible.

In Egypt and India, you would have witnessed temple dances offered to the gods, each gesture and rhythm a form of devotion. In Indigenous cultures, you would have recognised dance as medicine, sacred movement that carried the power to restore balance, transmit story, and strengthen the bonds of your tribe. In the Americas, dances called the community together, weaving memory, identity, and spirit into every footfall. Across Africa, drumming and movement merged to express resilience, ancestry, and joy in ways words could never capture.

As societies evolved, the role of dance shifted but never lost its heartbeat. In the grand courts of Europe, you would have seen dance transformed into an emblem of power and refinement. Formal steps became markers of class and culture, codified into elaborate systems. Ballet, born in the courts of Renaissance Italy and adopted in France, blossomed into a sophisticated theatrical art that blended precision with grace, discipline with beauty, and yet, even here, at the height of formality, the soul of dance remained: a search for transcendence through movement.

When you look closer, you see a common thread across centuries and continents. Dance has always been a bridge, between the physical and the spiritual, the individual and the collective, the seen and the unseen. To dance is to remember who you are and who you come from. It is to stand in a lineage of movers stretching back thousands of years. When your body sways, spins, or stamps the earth, you are not merely moving, you are joining hands with ancestors, channeling spirit, and giving your soul permission to breathe in rhythm.

Dance asks you to return to your own heartbeat, to the pulse that connects you with the wider story of humanity. In every culture, in every time, you would have found yourself called to move, not just to express, but to belong.

Dance As Emotional Intelligence In Motion

When you dance, you are doing more than moving your body, you are embodying emotional intelligence in motion. Every step, sway, or stillness becomes a powerful tool for self-awareness, self-expression, and healing. In the space where words may fail, your body speaks. Through dance, you begin to notice what you are feeling, where you are holding tension, and how emotions live in your muscles, breath, and posture. Dance helps you regulate your emotions because it gives those feelings a safe and sacred place to move through you. If you are feeling anxious, movement can ground you.

If you are carrying grief, it can soften and release what you have held tight. If you are overwhelmed with joy, dancing allows that energy to expand, ripple, and radiate outward. In moments when life feels chaotic or numb, dance brings you home to yourself. It shifts you from thinking to feeling, from resistance to flow. As you move with the rhythm, you create coherence between your body and mind, helping your nervous system reset and your heart reconnect.

Dance also deepens your capacity for empathy and connection. When you move in a group or mirror another's rhythm, you attune to their emotional world. You listen not just with your ears, but with your whole body. This kind of embodied presence enhances your social awareness and compassion. Ultimately, dance teaches you that your emotions are not problems to fix, they are energies to honour and express. With every intentional movement, you access a deeper intelligence within, cultivating emotional balance, authenticity, and a profound sense of being alive.

The Ego v The Body

When you step into movement, there is often an inner tension you feel, a tug-of-war between the ego and the body. Your ego might whisper that you are doing it wrong, that you look awkward, or that you need to control the experience, but your body knows a deeper truth: that you are safe, capable, and meant to move freely. Resistance is not something to shame or push through, it is an emotional teacher. When you feel tightness, hesitation, or discomfort in movement, pause and ask yourself: *What is this resistance trying to show me?*

Often, it is a sign of old wounds, limiting beliefs, or emotional patterns surfacing to be seen and released. Your body holds memory. It remembers joy, but it also remembers fear, rejection, or moments where your expression was silenced. By gently witnessing your resistance, you create space for healing. You learn to listen instead of fight. To soften instead of control. This is where transformation begins, not by overriding the ego, but by befriending it and inviting it to loosen its grip.

When you honour your body's wisdom and allow movement to unfold without judgment, you begin to trust yourself again. You realise that your worth is not measured by performance, but by presence. That freedom does not come from perfection, but from letting go. Over time, the resistance becomes less of an obstacle and more of a doorway, a sacred invitation to return to your body, your breath, and your truth. This is the path of embodied emotional intelligence: one step, one breath, one release at a time.

Dance Exercise

Choose at least **3 styles or purposes** of dance to explore over the next week:

- *Self-expression, Meditation, Healing, Celebration, Connection, Spirituality*

- Write a short *Dance Intention* for each:

- *"I will dance to express joy…"*

- *"I will dance to process sadness…"*

- *"I will dance with my child/partner/friend…"*

I encourage you to commit to **5 minutes a day** of intentional movement.

Case Study Discussion: Fiona's Journey

Fiona had always admired dancers and their ability to express themselves so beautifully through movement. However, she told me that she had convinced herself that she was too old and too out of shape to ever be a dancer herself. I asked Fiona to gift herself a few minutes and look at people dancing in their living rooms on social media.

Fiona found a lady of her age and said to me that there was something about the woman's freedom and joy in her movement that really resonated and spoke to her, and she felt alive. Fiona chose to try dancing in her own living room. She turned on some music, closed the curtains, and began to move her body in whatever way felt natural. At first, she told me that even though she was alone that she felt awkward and self–conscious. However, as she let go of her self–judgment and allowed herself to feel the music, something began to shift within her.

She began to move with more confidence and fluidity, and her body began responding to the rhythm of the music. She felt her heart open up, and she began to tap into a deep wellspring of emotions that she kept buried inside for decades. Dancing gave Fiona a sense of joy and freedom that had been missing from her life. She began to dance every day, and soon it became a ritual that she loved and looked forward to.

The more Fiona danced the more she began to notice changes in herself. She felt more energised and alive, and her relationships with others began to improve as well. She found that she was more patient, more kind, and more able to connect with others on a deeper level. Fiona continued to dance in her living room, and discovered a new part of herself, a part that was filled with light and energy and vitality, and she knew that she would never let that part of herself go again. Eventually, Fiona gained the courage to dance in front of others. She found a local dance class and joined, feeling more confident in her abilities than ever before. She loved dancing with others and realised that dance had not only transformed her life, but it had had connected her with heart as well.

Reflective Exercise: Fiona's Journey

Here are four profound and reflective questions to help you deeply engage with Fiona's story about dance, each followed by a short reflection:

1. **When was the last time you truly listened to your body without trying to change or control it?** *This question invites you to become aware of how often you override your body's natural rhythms and sensations. Like Fiona, you may discover that your body has been patiently waiting for you to listen.*

2. **What emotions arise in you when you think about moving freely, without judgment or performance?** *Fiona's story reminds you that dance is not about doing it "right," but about allowing your feelings to be felt through movement. What might your body want to express if it felt safe?*

3. **Have you ever used movement as a way to heal, release, or reconnect with yourself?** *Reflect on moments when physical expression helped you shift your emotional state. Fiona found herself again through dance, what might you rediscover about yourself?*

4. **What limiting beliefs or fears surface when you imagine dancing in front of others, or even just for yourself?** *This question helps you confront the ego's voice, the same voice Fiona learned to quiet. In facing it, you may find the freedom and joy that come with expressing your truth through movement.*

Affirmations For Integration (Heart Whispers)

Affirmations have the power to quiet the noise of doubt, open the doorway to self-trust, and draw you back into the wisdom of your heart. When practised daily, they nurture an inner dialogue based in love and truth, helping you live each day more aligned with who you truly are. I invite you to repeat silently or write:

- *I feel alive when I dance to my favourite song.*

- *I am free when I let my body move to the rhythm.*

- *I find joy in the expression of movement through dance.*

- *I feel connected to my body and emotions when I dance.*

- *I am confident in myself when I dance with passion.*

- *I love to explore different styles and techniques in dance.*

Dance Exercise – Moving from the Heart

1. **Set Your Space:** Find a space where you can move freely. Dim the lights if you wish, and choose music that feels uplifting or soul-stirring.

2. **Connect to Your Heartbeat:** Stand still with your hands over your heart. Close your eyes, take three deep breaths, and imagine your heart as the conductor of your movement.

3. **Begin to Flow:** Let your body move in whatever way feels natural, sway, stretch, spin, or step. There is no right or wrong, only what feels true in the moment.

4. **Release as You Move:** With each movement, imagine shaking off tension, self-doubt, or heavy emotions. Let your body express what words cannot.

5. **Close in Stillness:** Gradually slow down until you come to stillness. Place your hands over your heart again, thank your body for moving, and notice the lightness within you.

Closing Reflection

As you come to the end of this exploration, remember that dance is not about steps, skill, or performance, it is about presence. It is the language your body speaks when words fall short. When you move with intention, you awaken emotional intelligence in motion: a dialogue between your heart, mind, and body. Through dance, you release what no longer serves you, reclaim forgotten parts of yourself, and return home to your body with compassion.

Each sway, stretch, or stomp is an invitation to feel more deeply, to be more fully alive, and to trust your inner rhythm. So whether your movement is joyful or aching, graceful or wild, let it be true. Dance becomes your mirror, your medicine, and your prayer. It connects you to the ancient heartbeat of humanity and to your most authentic self. May you always remember, you do not have to dance perfectly. You just have to dance truthfully.

7 – SELF LOVE

Your Opening Reflection

An Invitation to Honour Yourself - As you step into this chapter, let it be a gentle reminder that you are worthy of your own tenderness. Self-love is not selfish, it is the soil from which your strength, compassion, and joy grow. Allow yourself to be embraced by your own kindness, to listen softly to your needs, and to remember that you are already enough, just as you are.

- "In what ways have you honoured yourself this week?"

- "How do you speak to yourself when no one else is listening?"

- "What boundaries do you set to protect your well-being?"

- "When you think of your best qualities, how do they make you feel?"

- "What does self-love mean to you today?"

Let these questions open the doorway into presence. Every answer you give, whether in words, sensations, or silence, is a bridge between where you are and where you are going.

Learning Objectives

The learning objectives are included here to give you a clear focus for this chapter, ensuring that each practice you explore moves you closer to mastering the skills, insights, and heart-led awareness that will enrich your life well beyond the program. By the end of this chapter, you will:

- Understand the role of self-love in emotional well-being and authentic living.

- Distinguish self-love from narcissism and selfishness.

- Identify barriers to self-love and cultivate compassionate self-awareness.

- Practice heart-centred exercises to deepen self-worth and emotional resilience.

- Integrate daily rituals that nourish and protect emotional and spiritual wellbeing.

Core Emotional Domains

The core emotional intelligence domains covered here are essential because they form the foundation for lasting heart connection, guiding you to deepen self-awareness, regulate emotions, build resilience, and strengthen the mind-body bond throughout your Heart Unbound journey.

- **Self-Awareness**: You recognise your thoughts, feelings, and needs without judgment.

- **Self-Regulation**: You respond to emotions with care, not reactivity.

- **Empathy (towards self)**: You treat yourself with kindness, especially in pain or failure.

- **Social Skills**: You honour your worth by setting and respecting healthy boundaries.

- **Motivation**: You act from a place of inner truth, guided by your heart and values.

"Self Love – Returning To Your Worth"

Self-love is the foundation of your emotional intelligence and heart connection. The inner ground from which your authenticity, resilience, and ability to truly connect with others can grow. Self-love is not about vanity, self-indulgence, or trying to be better than anyone else. It is the quiet, steady commitment to honouring your own humanity. It means recognising your worth, even when you feel like you have fallen short. It means tending to your own needs without guilt and offering yourself grace in moments of struggle.

When you practice self-love, you begin to deepen your self-awareness. You start to notice the patterns in your thoughts, the emotions that rise within you, and the needs hiding beneath your reactions. You stop hiding from yourself and instead meet yourself with honesty and curiosity. That awareness becomes the foundation for self-regulation, it helps you respond to life's challenges with more presence, calm, and compassion, rather than reactivity or harsh self-judgment. Through self-love, you begin to build empathy toward yourself. You learn to forgive your past, to soften your inner dialogue, and to acknowledge your pain without becoming consumed by it. You become both the witness to your wounds and the source of your healing.

From this place of grounded self-love, you gain the strength to set and honour healthy boundaries. You no longer feel the need to shrink, please, or overextend yourself. Instead, you speak your truth with clarity, and you hold space for relationships that reflect mutual respect and emotional honesty. This deepens your social intelligence, because you are connecting from a place of wholeness, not lack.

Perhaps most powerfully, self-love awakens your intrinsic motivation. You begin to take action not from fear or pressure, but from alignment with your values, your heart, and your inner sense of purpose. You feel moved to grow, not to prove yourself, but to honour the unique potential that lives inside you. In the end, self-love is a return to your truth. It anchors your emotions, softens your inner critic, and empowers you to live from the inside out. You no longer have to be perfect, you just have to be present, and from that presence, your transformation begins.

The Historical Basis Of Self-Love: From Ancient Greece's *Philautia* To Modern Self-Compassion Research

The concept of self-love is far from a modern invention. Its roots stretch deep into human history, appearing across philosophy, spirituality, and psychology as a vital part of living a meaningful and balanced life. Understanding where self-love began, and how it has evolved, helps you appreciate its deeper purpose: not as self-indulgence, but as a foundation for wisdom, connection, and inner peace.

Ancient Greece: *Philautia* as Noble Self-Regard

In the wisdom traditions of Ancient Greece, love was understood as a multifaceted force, expressed in different ways depending on its object and purpose. Among the various forms of love identified by Greek philosophers, such as *agape* (universal love), *eros* (romantic love), and *philia* (deep friendship), there was *philautia*: love of the self. Aristotle and other classical thinkers considered *philautia* essential to a well-lived life, but they were careful to distinguish between two distinct types. The **first**, virtuous *philautia*, was based on self-respect, self-knowledge, and moral character.

This kind of self-love was considered **noble and necessary,** a balanced and rational regard for one's own worth that served as the **foundation for all other forms of love**. In essence, if you could not love or care for yourself wisely, you would struggle to love others well. The **second** type of *philautia* was self-centred and excessive, a form of egoism or narcissism that was destructive to both the individual and the community. This distorted self-love was seen as corrosive, a kind of hubris that disconnected a person from truth, humility, and relational harmony.

Greek philosophers such as Socrates and Plato also emphasised the importance of **knowing oneself** (*gnōthi seauton*) as the gateway to ethical action and inner harmony. Self-love, when grounded in self-awareness and virtue, was not seen as indulgent or vain, it was considered the root of all personal integrity, emotional balance, and wise decision-making. For the Greeks, to live ethically and contribute meaningfully to society, you had to cultivate *philautia* in its truest sense: not as a pursuit of personal gain or admiration, but as a **disciplined love for your own soul**, your potential, and your responsibility to others.

In this way, Ancient Greek philosophy teaches you that genuine self-love is not about superiority or separation, it is about cultivating the inner conditions that allow you to show up in the world with wisdom, compassion, and strength.

Modern Self-Compassion Research

While ancient philosophies like *philautia* laid the groundwork for understanding self-love as noble self-regard, modern psychology has brought this concept into clearer focus through decades of rigorous research, especially in the field of self-compassion.

Spearheaded by Dr. Kristin Neff, self-compassion research has redefined how you can relate to your inner world, particularly during moments of failure, shame, or struggle. It has helped reveal that true self-love is not about perfection, ego, or inflated self-esteem, it is about how kindly and honestly you meet yourself when life gets hard. Self-compassion involves three powerful and interconnected elements:

1. **Self-Kindness:** Instead of berating yourself when you make a mistake, self-kindness invites you to soften, to speak to yourself as you would to

a dear friend. This includes recognising your efforts, forgiving your shortcomings, and honouring your pain without judgment. It is about treating yourself with care and respect, even when you feel like you have fallen short.

2. **Mindfulness:** At the heart of self-compassion is presence. Mindfulness teaches you to acknowledge what you are feeling, whether it is sadness, anger, fear, or disappointment, without exaggerating it or pushing it away. It gives you space to observe rather than react, to witness your experience with clarity and tenderness.

3. **Common Humanity:** Self-compassion reminds you that you are not alone. Your struggles, imperfections, and doubts are not signs of personal failure, they are part of what it means to be human. Recognising this shared vulnerability helps dissolve isolation and opens the door to connection and empathy.

What makes self-compassion so powerful in the modern era is its grounding in scientific evidence. Research shows that individuals who practice self-compassion are more emotionally resilient, less prone to anxiety and depression, and better equipped to cope with adversity.

It strengthens your emotional regulation, lowers stress hormones, improves motivation, and promotes healthier relationships. Unlike self-esteem, which often depends on performance, comparison, or external validation, self-compassion is unconditional. It does not require you to be flawless. Instead, it meets you exactly where you are and offers the radical permission to be human.

Modern therapeutic practices, including mindfulness-based stress reduction (MBSR), compassion-focused therapy, and acceptance and commitment therapy (ACT), now integrate self-compassion as a core component. These approaches teach you how to pause, breathe, and meet your suffering not with fear, but with presence and love.

In a world that often pressures you to do more, be more, and achieve endlessly, self-compassion becomes a quiet, powerful act of rebellion. It is a way of reclaiming your worth, not because of what you produce, but because of who you are. By embracing self-compassion, you are continuing a long lineage of heart wisdom, from ancient teachings to modern neuroscience. You are giving yourself what you have always deserved: grace, kindness, and the freedom to be whole, just as you are.

Differentiating Self-Love from Selfishness Or Narcissism

It is easy to feel conflicted about self-love, especially if you have been taught to associate it with selfishness or arrogance. Maybe you were conditioned to always put others first, to dismiss your own needs, or to believe that taking care of yourself meant you were being self-absorbed, but here is the truth: real self-love is not about elevating yourself above others, it is about coming home to yourself with honesty, compassion, and responsibility.

When you love yourself, you are not saying, *"I am better than everyone else."* You are saying, *"I am worthy, just as I am."* You learn to honour your feelings without suppressing them, to rest when you are tired without guilt, and to speak your truth with clarity and respect. This is not self-indulgence, it is emotional maturity. It is recognising that your well-being matters, not so you can isolate or dominate, but so you can contribute, relate, and live from a place of wholeness.

Selfishness, in contrast, often disregards the impact of your actions on others. It comes from scarcity, the belief that if you do not take care of your own needs at any cost, no one will, but when you embody self-love, you begin to trust that there is enough.

Enough time, enough worth, enough space for both your needs and the needs of others. You no longer act from desperation or defensiveness. You begin to respond to the world with presence and grace.

Narcissism masks deep insecurity. It demands constant admiration and external validation, often at the expense of real connection. The narcissistic self says, *"I must be the best. I must always win. I must not be vulnerable."* But your self-loving self says, *"I am enough, even when I fall short. I am whole, even when I feel broken. I am worthy, even when I am growing."*

Self-love gives you the **courage to be honest with yourself**, to take responsibility for your emotions and actions, and to forgive yourself when you make mistakes. It is not about being perfect, it is about being *present.* With yourself. With others. With life. From a grounded place of love, you can create boundaries without guilt. You can say no without fear. You can show up in relationships with less need for approval and more space for authenticity.

You stop trying to earn love by performing or pleasing, and you start offering love freely, because your cup is no longer empty. When you love yourself,

you become more generous, not less. More empathetic. More compassionate. You no longer love others in ways that drain or diminish you, you love in ways that uplift and empower both of you. So do not confuse self-love with selfishness or narcissism. They are not the same. One is based in fear and separation; the other is grounded in truth and connection. When you choose to love yourself, you are choosing to live in integrity, with your values, your needs, and your heart, and from that place, you give the world something far more powerful than perfection, you give it your real, open, and beautifully human self.

The Neuroscience Of Self-Affirmation And The Benefits Of Positive Self-Regard

When you speak kindly to yourself, affirm your values, or remind yourself of your inner strength, you are doing more than just *"thinking positively."* You are reshaping the very structure of your brain. The science of self-affirmation shows that how you relate to yourself, especially in moments of stress, challenge, or self-doubt, can significantly influence your emotional health, cognitive performance, and even physical well-being.

How Self-Affirmation Works in the Brain

Self-affirmation practices, such as repeating *"I am"* statements, reflecting on core values, or journaling about what matters most to you, activate regions of the brain associated with **self-processing, emotional regulation, and reward**. In particular, the **ventromedial prefrontal cortex (vmPFC)** plays a central role. This part of your brain integrates information about your identity and values and helps modulate your response to stress and threat.

When you affirm something meaningful about yourself, such as *"I am resilient," "I am a caring person,"* or *"I choose to live with integrity",* you reinforce the neural circuits that support **confidence, security, and value-based decision-making**. fMRI studies have shown that people who engage in regular self-affirmation practices show **increased activity in the vmPFC**, along with **reduced activation in the threat centres of the brain**, like the amygdala.

Physiological Benefits of Self-Affirmation

Self-affirmation does not just affect your brain, it influences your body, too. Research has demonstrated that positive self-regard through affirmation can:

- **Lower cortisol levels**, reducing the impact of chronic stress on the body.

- **Improve heart rate variability (HRV)**, a key marker of emotional resilience.

- **Enhance immune function**, particularly during high-pressure situations.

By soothing your physiological stress response, self-affirmation helps you stay calm, focused, and grounded, especially when you are facing criticism, uncertainty, or internal doubt.

Cognitive and Emotional Benefits

Affirming your values and self-worth has a measurable impact on your ability to think clearly and regulate emotions. People who regularly engage in self-affirmation:

- **Perform better under pressure**, particularly on complex or evaluative tasks.

- **Experience less defensiveness**, allowing them to receive feedback with greater openness.

- **Recover more quickly from failure**, as they see mistakes as part of the growth process rather than as evidence of inadequacy.

- **Cultivate intrinsic motivation**, aligning their actions with personal meaning rather than external pressure.

Positive self-regard, grounded in affirmation, also builds **emotional agility,** the ability to stay curious, open, and non-reactive to difficult emotions. You become more skilled at acknowledging discomfort without being consumed by it.

Why Self-Affirmation Is not Just Fluff

Contrary to popular myths, self-affirmation is not about denial or blind positivity. It is not pretending everything is fine when it is not, nor is it about ignoring real challenges or difficult emotions. Instead, it is about anchoring yourself in what is true, enduring, and life-giving within you, even in the midst of hardship.

Self-affirmation is a conscious practice of inner alignment, a way of reminding yourself of your worth, your values, and your capacity to navigate life with integrity. When you say, *"This is who I am, even now,"* you reaffirm your identity beyond circumstances. This steadying act helps you face reality with courage, rather than avoidance, because you are grounded in your own truth.

Over time, this practice reshapes the way you speak to yourself and the lens through which you view your life. It strengthens resilience, builds self-trust, and keeps you connected to your heart, ensuring that even when the world around you feels uncertain, you have an unshakable place within to return to.

Common Self-Love Blockers

Despite your deep longing for self-love, certain inner barriers can quietly and persistently block your ability to truly embrace yourself. These self-love blockers are often based in past experiences, inherited beliefs, and cultural messages that have shaped how you see yourself, and they can keep you stuck in cycles of self-judgment, guilt, or emotional numbness. Understanding these blockers with compassion is the first step to releasing them.

1. Internalised Shame

Shame is the deep belief that you are unworthy, not because of what you have done, but because of who you are. It often begins in childhood, when love or acceptance felt conditional. Over time, you may have internalised the message that being *"you"* was not enough. Shame says, *"There's something wrong with me,"* and that belief can quietly sabotage your self-worth. Until shame is gently met with compassion, it will keep you from receiving your own love.

Healing Path: *Practice radical self-acceptance. Speak to your shame with understanding, not judgment. Affirm your worthiness even in imperfection.*

2. Unprocessed Trauma

When you have experienced emotional, physical, or psychological trauma, your nervous system learns to protect you, sometimes by disconnecting from your own feelings or body. This can make self-love feel unsafe, unfamiliar, or even impossible. You may struggle with trust, vulnerability, or believing that you deserve gentleness.

Healing Path: *Ground in safety first. Use somatic practices, therapy, or trauma-informed mindfulness to reconnect with your body and restore inner safety. Self-love grows in secure ground.*

3. Perfectionism

Perfectionism tells you that you must earn love by being flawless. It sets impossible standards, then criticises you when you fall short. It creates fear of failure and fuels constant self-pressure. Perfectionism says, *"You are only worthy when you succeed,"* robbing you of the chance to love yourself as you are, especially when you need it most.

Healing Path: *Learn to celebrate effort over outcome. Practice self-compassion when things go wrong. Replace "I am not enough" with "I am learning, and that is enough."*

4. Societal Conditioning

You have been taught, sometimes subtly, sometimes loudly, what beauty, success, worthiness, and value *"should"* look like. These external standards often drown out your inner truth. Messages about productivity, appearance, gender roles, or comparison can disconnect you from your authentic self and develop self-rejection.

Healing Path: *Begin to question the stories you have inherited. Whose voice is shaping your self-worth? Choose to redefine your value on your own terms. Self-love starts by coming home to your own truth.*

Final Thought

Each of these blockers, shame, trauma, perfectionism, and conditioning, is not a flaw in you. They are wounds that can be healed, voices that can be softened, and beliefs that can be rewritten. With presence, compassion, and courage, you can unlearn what no longer serves you and remember the love that has always been your birthright. **Self-love is not something you earn. It is something you return to.**

Reflective Exercise: Six self-love rituals

I invite you to select two of the following to commit to for the week:

1. Spend time in nature.
2. Listen and respond to your body's needs.
3. Engage in a creative outlet.
4. Set a boundary and honour it.
5. Celebrate a recent achievement.
6. Reflect in stillness on a feeling you have been avoiding.

> *"Which of these acts of self-love do you resist the most, and why?"*

Case Study Discussion – Roger's Journey

Roger's self-talk began to shift in small, almost imperceptible ways at first. He caught himself in moments of harsh inner criticism and chose instead to speak words of kindness, the kind he would offer to a dear friend. Each time he extended compassion to himself, he felt a little lighter, a little less burdened by the weight of old wounds. Through this process, he discovered a deep and nourishing sense of self-love, one he had never known before. For the first time in his life, Roger began to believe he was truly worthy of love and belonging, even without a traditional family of his own.

As the days unfolded, the ripple effect of his practice became clear. He noticed that he was attracting more positive people and uplifting experiences into his world. He found himself surrounded by conversations that inspired him, by relationships that respected and valued him. Confidence grew quietly but steadily within him, and with it came the courage to pursue long-held dreams. He began to create, to explore, to step into opportunities with a newfound sense of purpose and passion.

Over time, Roger learned to trust himself deeply. No longer did he chase approval or validation from others, instead, he tuned in to the steady, guiding voice within. He started making decisions not out of fear, but from a place of alignment with his own truth. He came to see that his worth was not something to be earned; it had been his birthright all along.

Day after day, week after week, Roger committed to his self-love practices. They became as natural as breathing, small, intentional acts that reminded him of who he was, and in doing so, he discovered a part of himself that shone with love, light, and unwavering self-acceptance. This part of him was no longer fragile or hidden; it was the foundation upon which he would build the rest of his life, and he knew, with absolute certainty, that he would never let it go again.

Reflective Exercise: Roger's Journey

Here are four profound and reflective questions inspired by Roger's story to help you engage with your own self-love journey:

1. **When did you first learn to measure your worth by achievement, and how has that shaped your inner dialogue?** *Roger's story may*

mirror your own if you have tied your value to success. This question invites you to explore where that belief began, and whether it is still serving the person you are today.

2. **How do you respond to yourself when you feel vulnerable, unproductive, or imperfect?** *Self-love is often most needed when you feel least worthy of it. Reflecting on how you treat yourself in difficult moments can reveal whether your love is conditional or growing toward compassion.*

3. **What part of you is still waiting to be accepted, just as it is?** *Like Roger, you may carry pieces of yourself that feel unworthy of love. This question invites you to turn toward those parts, not to fix them, but to embrace them with understanding.*

4. **What would it feel like to speak to yourself with the same kindness you offer to others?** *Roger's transformation began when he softened his inner voice. Reflect on how your life might change if you gave yourself the same empathy, patience, and grace you freely give to those you love.*

Affirmations For Integration (Heart Whispers)

Affirmations have the power to quiet the noise of doubt, open the doorway to self-trust, and draw you back into the wisdom of your heart. When practised daily, they nurture an inner dialogue based in love and truth, helping you live each day more aligned with who you truly are. I invite you to repeat silently or write:

- *I feel alive when I dance to my favourite song.*

- *I am free when I let my body move to the rhythm.*

- *I find joy in the expression of movement through dance.*

- *I feel connected to my body and emotions when I dance.*

- *I am confident in myself when I dance with passion.*

- *I love to explore different styles and techniques in dance.*

Self-Love Exercise – Speaking to Yourself with Kindness

1. **Find a Quiet Space:** Sit comfortably and take three slow, deep breaths. Place your hand gently over your heart.

2. **Acknowledge Yourself:** Close your eyes and think of one thing you appreciate about who you are, not what you have done, but who you are at your core.

3. **Speak Your Love Whisper to yourself:** *"I see you. I value you. I love you."* Repeat it slowly three times, letting the words sink in.

4. **Anchor the Feeling:** Smile softly and imagine a warm light filling your chest, expanding with each breath, wrapping you in compassion.

5. **Carry It Forward:** Before you finish, promise yourself one small act of kindness you will give to yourself today.

Closing Reflection

As you gently close this chapter on self-love, take a deep breath and honour just how far you have already come. Choosing to explore self-love is not a sign of weakness or self-obsession, it is a bold and healing act of self-remembering. In a world that often teaches you to seek your worth outside of yourself, self-love is how you return home. It is not about ego, vanity, or pretending to have it all together. True self-love is quiet. Grounded. Compassionate. It is the moment you stop measuring your worth by what you achieve, how you appear, or who approves of you. It is the moment you choose to listen inward, soften your self-talk, and extend grace to the parts of you that are still growing.

Self-love is how you begin to break the cycle of self-rejection. It is how you build trust with yourself, by showing up, again and again, even when it is hard. It is how you stop abandoning your own needs, your own voice, your own heart, and as you deepen in this practice, you start to see the ripple effects. You stop settling for relationships, environments, or beliefs that diminish you. You begin to protect your peace, honour your boundaries, and move through life with more confidence and clarity. You lead from wholeness rather than from wounds.

Loving yourself does not mean you will never feel doubt or pain again. It means you will walk through those moments with greater strength and compassion. You will know how to pause, breathe, and return to the truth: *you are not broken, you are becoming.* So let self-love be the anchor you return to, the voice that steadies you, and the light that guides you through uncertainty. You are worthy of joy, rest, respect, and tenderness, and most importantly - **You are worthy of your own love. Always.**

8 - NUTRITION

Your Opening Reflection

An Invitation to Nourish Yourself - As you enter this chapter, remember that every bite you take is a form of self-communication. Food is not only fuel; it is a way of honouring your body, your energy, and your heart. Let this be a moment to approach nourishment with love rather than judgment, with mindfulness rather than habit. Each choice can be a quiet act of self-care, reminding you that you are worthy of feeling strong, balanced, and alive.

- "What is one way I have nurtured or neglected my body this week?"

- "How do the foods I choose each day make me feel physically and emotionally?"

- "Am I eating out of hunger, habit, or emotion?"

- "What is one small change I could make to nourish my body better?"

- "Do I listen to my body's signals of hunger and fullness?"

- "How can I make eating a more mindful and enjoyable experience?"

Let these questions open the doorway into presence. Every answer you give, whether in words, sensations, or silence, is a bridge between where you are and where you are going.

Learning Objectives

The learning objectives are included here to give you a clear focus for this chapter, ensuring that each practice you explore moves you closer to mastering the skills, insights, and heart-led awareness that will enrich your life well beyond the program. By the end of this chapter, you will:

- Understand the relationship between nutrition and emotional intelligence.

- Identify foods and habits that support physical, emotional, and heart-centred wellbeing.

- Develop self-awareness through mindful eating practices.

- Reflect on how diet influences mental clarity, mood, and heart connection.

- Commit to simple, sustainable nutrition strategies that nourish both body and soul.

Core Emotional Domains

The core emotional intelligence domains covered here are essential because they form the foundation for lasting heart connection, guiding you to deepen self-awareness, regulate emotions, build resilience, and strengthen the mind-body bond throughout your Heart Unbound journey.

- **Self-Awareness:** You tune into your body's unique needs, recognising how different foods affect your energy, emotions, and overall wellbeing.

- **Self-Regulation:** You make more mindful, intentional choices about what and how you nourish yourself, rather than reacting to impulse or habit.

- **Motivation:** You are inspired to care for your body with consistency, aligning your eating patterns with your deeper desire to feel vibrant, grounded, and well.

- **Empathy (toward self and others):** You cultivate compassion through sustainable and ethical food choices, nourishing your own body while honouring the earth and its communities.

"Nutrition – Nourishing Your Body With Love"

Proper nutrition is not just a physical requirement, it is a form of communication with your entire being. Every bite, every sip, is a message you send to yourself: *I care. I am listening. I am worthy of thriving.* Too often, food is treated as an afterthought, rushed, numbed, used for escape or control, but when you slow down and connect with the deeper meaning of nourishment, it becomes a powerful emotional and spiritual practice. It becomes heart work.

Self-awareness invites you to notice how food influences your emotions, thoughts, and physical state. What nourishes not only your stomach, but also your sense of calm, vitality, and presence? You begin to realise that hunger is not always about food, it can be a hunger for grounding, love, creativity, or rest.

Self-regulation allows you to make choices from a place of balance, not habit or emotional impulse. You become more conscious of why you are reaching for something, whether it is to soothe, to celebrate, to avoid, or to fuel. Through this awareness, you cultivate kindness, not judgment. You become your own safe place at the table.

Motivation comes not from guilt or perfectionism, but from a desire to honour your body as a sacred vessel of life. You begin to nourish yourself because it feels good, not just because it is *"healthy."* You realise that true wellness is not a punishment; it is a path of joy, clarity, and strength.

Empathy, especially toward yourself, emerges as you stop waging war on your body. You begin to listen with tenderness. To notice what foods energise you.

To respect your hunger, your fullness, your preferences, and your boundaries, and as your relationship with food softens, so does your relationship with yourself. Gratitude for food and where it comes from deepens your sense of interconnectedness. You become more aware of the environment, the hands that grew and prepared your meals, and the impact of your choices. Nourishment becomes not just personal, it becomes relational, ethical, and spiritual. This is the heart of nourishment:

- A return to wholeness.

- A remembering that eating is not just survival, it is sacred.

- It is one of the most ancient forms of prayer and self-love.

- You do not have to get it *"perfect."*

You only need to begin again, one breath, one bite, one moment of presence at a time.

The History Of Nutrition As Heart-Centred Medicine: From Hippocrates To Ayurveda

Long before modern nutritional science emerged, cultures around the world understood that food was more than sustenance, it was medicine, energy, and sacred ritual. From the wisdom of the ancient Greeks to the holistic teachings of Ayurveda, nutrition was seen not just as fuel for the body but as nourishment for your heart, mind, and spirit.

Hippocrates and Ancient Greece: "Let food be thy medicine"

The basis of Western nutritional thought trace back to Hippocrates (c. 460–370 BCE), often called the *"Father of Medicine."* He believed that health was a state of balance within the body, and that imbalance could often be restored through diet and lifestyle before turning to harsher remedies. His famous guidance, *"Let food be thy medicine and medicine be thy food,"* was not a metaphor, it was a clinical principle.

Hippocrates viewed digestion, environment, and emotion as interwoven. He believed that the quality, seasonality, and simplicity of food mattered, and that eating should be done with awareness. In this view, nourishment was not mechanical, it was intuitive and relational. Meals were meant to bring harmony, not only to your body, but to your entire inner ecosystem.

Ayurveda: The Sacred Science of Life

In India, the ancient system of **Ayurveda** *("the science of life")* developed over 3,000 years ago, offering one of the most comprehensive nutritional philosophies in human history. Ayurveda teaches that food carries a life force (*prana*) and that each person has a unique constitution (*dosha*) that determines which foods are most supportive for their wellbeing.

Nutrition in Ayurveda is not just about nutrients or calories, it is about how food feels in your body, how it is prepared, and how it is eaten. Food is chosen according to qualities such as warming or cooling, grounding or stimulating, moistening or drying. Each meal is an act of alignment, a chance to restore balance, cleanse the system, and calm the mind. Importantly, Ayurveda recognises that emotions and digestion are deeply linked. A meal eaten in stress, anger, or distraction is thought to leave *"mental residue"* that can disrupt the body and spirit. Gratitude, intention, and presence are part of the nourishment.

Nutrition as Medicine for the Heart

Both traditions, Hippocratic and Ayurvedic, saw food as an intimate bridge between the outer world and the inner life. They believed what you eat shapes how you feel, how you think, and how you connect with others. Food was never isolated from the emotional or spiritual dimensions of living, it was woven into them. In this light, the act of eating becomes more than biological necessity. It becomes an opportunity to:

- Centre yourself in compassion

- Honour your body's signals

- Respond to your emotional needs without judgment

- Strengthen your connection to the Earth and to others

Returning to this heart-centred understanding of nutrition is not a regression, it is a remembering. In a world often dominated by speed, fad diets, and disconnection, these ancient teachings gently remind you: *True nourishment is never just about food, it is about how you live, how you feel, and how you love yourself through each choice.*

The Biochemical Effects Of Food On Mood, Energy, And Emotion

How what you eat shapes how you feel, physically, emotionally, and mentally.

You may often think of food as fuel, but it is far more dynamic than that. Every bite you take initiates a cascade of biochemical reactions that affect your brain chemistry, hormonal balance, energy levels, and emotional state. The connection between nutrition and mood is now well, documented in both neuroscience and integrative medicine. Your food choices are not just shaping your waistline, they are shaping your mind, mood, and moment-to-moment wellbeing.

Below are key ways food influences how you feel:

1. Omega-3 Fatty Acids - Feeding Your Emotional Brain

Omega-3s, especially EPA and DHA found in fatty fish like salmon, sardines, and mackerel, are essential fats that support brain health, emotional regulation, and cognitive function.

- How they help: Omega-3s improve neuronal communication and reduce inflammation in the brain. They are linked to lower rates of depression, anxiety, and brain fog.

- The science: Studies show individuals with low omega-3 intake have a higher risk of mood disorders, while supplementation may ease depressive symptoms and increase emotional resilience.

Foods to focus on: Fatty fish, flaxseeds, chia seeds, walnuts, algae oil.

2. Sugar - The Mood Spike and Crash

Refined sugar and high-glycemic carbohydrates cause rapid blood sugar spikes followed by sharp drops, which can wreak havoc on emotional stability and energy levels.

- How it affects you: After a sugar high, insulin surges to bring blood glucose down, which can lead to a crash in energy, irritability, brain fog, and even feelings of anxiety or sadness.

- The emotional cycle: This crash often triggers more sugar cravings, creating a loop of emotional instability that mimics the effects of stress.

Mindful tip: Pair natural carbs with protein or healthy fats to reduce blood sugar volatility and promote steadier mood and focus.

3. Hydration - The Often-Ignored Mood Regulator

Dehydration, even at a mild level, can significantly impair your mood, focus, and cognitive performance.

- The brain & water: Your brain is about 75% water. Even slight dehydration can cause fatigue, low mood, headaches, and difficulty concentrating.

- Hormonal balance: Hydration supports the regulation of cortisol (your stress hormone) and helps maintain the fluid balance needed for efficient neurotransmitter function.

Daily reminder: Drinking enough water is one of the simplest and most powerful ways to improve your emotional baseline. Aim for regular sips throughout the day, not just when thirsty.

4. Micronutrients - Small Nutrients, Big Impact

Deficiencies in key vitamins and minerals can directly affect your mood and mental health.

- B Vitamins: Support energy production and neurotransmitter synthesis. Low levels (especially B6, B9, and B12) are associated with fatigue, irritability, and depression.

- Magnesium: Calms the nervous system and supports sleep. Deficiency is linked to anxiety and restlessness.

- Zinc & Iron: Essential for mood balance and cognitive clarity; deficits are associated with low energy and depression.

Focus foods: Leafy greens, legumes, seeds, nuts, eggs, and whole grains.

5. Gut Health - Your Third Brain

The gut microbiome is now understood to play a critical role in emotional regulation. Why? Because the gut produces about 90% of your serotonin, the neurotransmitter most associated with happiness and emotional balance.

- The gut-brain axis: A thriving gut microbiome communicates with the brain via the vagus nerve, sending signals that can either enhance or disrupt your mood.

- Fermented & fiber-rich foods: These feed beneficial gut bacteria and support healthy digestion and mood stability.

Mood-boosting foods: Yogurt, kefir, sauerkraut, kimchi, legumes, oats, bananas, and prebiotic fibers (like garlic and onions).

You Are What You Digest (Not Just What You Eat)

When you begin listening to your body, you notice what brings lightness, clarity, and joy, and what dims your energy or disconnects you from your heart. This is emotional intelligence through food. Not about restriction or rules, this is about reverence. It is about aligning your choices with how you want to feel. So today, when you eat, ask yourself:

1. *"Will this nourish me?"*

2. *"Will this support my clarity, calm, and connection?"*

Let your meals become a daily act of love.

Let food be your reminder: *you are worthy of feeling well.*

Food As A Daily Emotional Practice

When you begin to eat with awareness, not with perfection or pressure, you discover something profound: food is not just physical. It is emotional. It is energetic. It is deeply personal. You start to notice how certain foods make you feel grounded, light, clear, or calm. A warm meal can soothe your nervous system. A crisp piece of fruit can awaken your senses. Sometimes, certain foods, especially when eaten in haste or stress, can leave you feeling heavy, scattered, or disconnected from yourself. This noticing is not about judging your choices. It is about gently listening. Tuning in.

Honouring what your body and heart are trying to tell you. When you feel tired, are you dehydrated? When you crave sugar, are you actually needing rest, comfort, or connection? In this space of awareness, you begin to make different decisions, not from willpower, but from wisdom. Not from control, but from care. You realise that food is not the enemy, and it is not just fuel. It is a relationship. One that reflects how you care for yourself moment to moment. You stop obsessing over being *"good"* and instead ask yourself more loving questions:

1. *"Does this nourish me?"*

2. *"Does this align with who I want to be today?"*

3. *"What am I truly hungry for?"*

Through this lens, nourishment becomes an act of emotional intelligence. It is how you build trust with your body. It is how you self-regulate. It is how you honour your internal rhythms and meet your emotional needs without shame. It is no longer about rules or rigid plans. It becomes a conversation between your biology, your history, and your heart. Each meal becomes a mirror. Each bite, a choice. Each day, a chance to come back home to yourself. You are not just feeding your body. You are feeding your clarity, your presence, your peace. This is food as a daily emotional practice, and when done with love, it becomes a form of healing, one you carry with you, one bite at a time.

Nutrition As A Form Of Self-Love And Empowerment

The way you nourish yourself is one of the most consistent and powerful expressions of self-love. Every time you choose to feed your body with intention, you are not just making a nutritional decision, you are making a statement: *"I matter. My wellbeing is worth the effort. I am worthy of feeling good."* So often, eating is tied to guilt, control, shame, or neglect. You may have been taught to see food as something to manage, restrict, or use to soothe pain, but when you shift the narrative, nutrition becomes something sacred, an act of care rather than control.

Choosing to nourish yourself well is not about perfection. It is about compassion. It is the daily decision to honour your body as a partner, not a project. To eat not just for appearance or performance, but for how you want to feel in your skin, your mind, and your life. When you eat with presence, you reclaim your power.

- You take ownership of your energy, your emotions, and your choices.

- You tune in instead of numbing out.

- You listen to your body's wisdom, instead of overriding it with outside opinions or old habits.

Food becomes a form of emotional intelligence. You start to recognise how certain meals fuel your clarity and calm. You notice what drains you, what lifts you, and what truly supports you in being the person you want to be. That awareness empowers you. You are no longer ruled by impulse or shame. You begin to feel strong from the inside out, and with that strength, you begin to rise, not because you followed a diet plan, but because you remembered how to love yourself with every bite. When you nourish yourself in this way, you send a ripple effect through every part of your life.

- You sleep better.

- You think more clearly.

- You move with more confidence.

- You show up more fully in relationships, work, and purpose.

Because true nourishment is not just about food. It is about honouring the life force within you. It is about saying yes to yourself again and again, from a place of love. This is self-love in action. This is daily empowerment. This is the heart of what it means to be *nourished*.

Reflection Exercise: Heart Focused Nutrition Challenge

I invite you to choose **two** of the following to commit to this week:

1. *Add one additional serving of vegetables or fruit each day.*

2. *Cook one homemade meal using only whole ingredients.*

3. *Drink at least 8 glasses of water per day.*

4. *Pause before each meal to take 3 breaths and express gratitude.*

5. *Reduce sugar or processed food intake for three consecutive days.*

I encourage you to commit to a daily reflection on how these changes affect your physical energy and emotional clarity.

Case Study Discussion – Mia's Journey

Mia was a single mother with two young children who was struggling to keep up with the demands of her life. She was constantly tired, irritable, and had low energy levels. Her children were also struggling with health issues, which made her worry even more. Mia knew that she needed to make a change in her life if she wanted to be able to provide for her family and give them a better life.

I spoke with Mia about her self–talk, sleep, hydration, and her diet. We spent a little bit of time discussing the importance of nutrition and she decided to take a look at her diet and see if she could make some changes to improve her health. She started by cutting out processed foods and fast food and began cooking healthy meals at home with fresh ingredients. She also started drinking more water and making sure she was getting enough sleep each night.

Within a few weeks, Mia began to notice a significant difference in how she felt. She had more energy throughout the day, and her mood had improved as well. She was more patient with her children and found herself enjoying time with them more than ever before. Another secondary benefit was that her children's health also improved, and they were no longer getting sick as often. As Mia continued to focus on her nutrition, she also found that she was becoming more connected with her heart. She started to listen to her body and pay attention to what it needed.

She began practicing meditation and yoga, which helped her feel more centred and at peace. Through her journey, Mia discovered that nutrition was a powerful tool for not only improving her physical health but also her emotional health and wellbeing. Mia's story is a reminder of the importance of taking care of yourself, listening to your body, and connecting with your heart. By making small changes in your nutrition and lifestyle, you can improve your physical and emotional health and live a happier, more fulfilling life.

Reflective Exercise – Mia's Journey

Here are four profound and reflective questions inspired by Mia's story to help you engage with your own nutrition journey:

1. What is your body trying to tell you right now, and have you been listening? *Mia's turning point came when she started paying attention to her body's messages. You, too, have an inner wisdom that speaks through fatigue, cravings, tension, or restlessness. When you listen with compassion, you begin to nourish not just your body, but your heart.*

2. In what ways has your current relationship with food supported or limited your energy and emotional wellbeing? *Like Mia, you may find that food habits formed out of stress or convenience don not always serve your deeper needs. You have the power to choose foods that support clarity, presence, and vitality. Small shifts can create ripples of healing.*

3. What simple daily rituals could you create to feed yourself with more love and intention? *Mia's healing began with fresh ingredients and hydration, but also with presence. What might change in your life if preparing and eating food became an act of care, rather than just another task? What would self-love look like on your plate?*

4. How could your personal healing ripple out and benefit those you care for most? *Mia's transformation did not just change her, it changed her children. When you nourish yourself, your capacity to show up with patience, presence, and love grows. Your healing becomes a gift that extends far beyond you.*

Affirmations For Integration (Heart Whispers)

Affirmations have the power to quiet the noise of doubt, open the doorway to self-trust, and draw you back into the wisdom of your heart. When practised daily, they nurture an inner dialogue based in love and truth, helping you live each day more aligned with who you truly are. I invite you to repeat silently or write:

- *I honour my body by giving it the nourishment it deserves.*
- *I enjoy healthy foods that energise and sustain me.*
- *I treat my body with love through the choices I make.*
- *I am grateful for the food that supports my well-being.*
- *I create balance by eating in a way that feels good for me.*
- *I fuel my body with nutritious food.*
- *I choose foods that nourish my heart.*
- *I listen to my body's hunger cues.*
- *I drink plenty of water every day.*
- *I make mindful eating choices.*

Nutrition Exercise – Eating with Heart Awareness

1. **Choose One Meal or Snack Today:** Select something nourishing, fruit, vegetables, whole grains, or a wholesome snack you enjoy.

2. **Pause Before Eating:** Take three slow breaths. Notice the colours, textures, and aromas of your food.

3. **Express Gratitude:** Silently thank everyone and everything that helped bring this food to your table, farmers, growers, the earth, sun, and rain.

4. **Eat Slowly and Mindfully:** Take small bites. Chew fully. Notice the flavours and how your body responds.

5. **Check In:** Halfway through, pause. Notice how you feel, satisfied, still hungry, or full.

6. **Close with Appreciation:** When finished, place your hand over your heart and say: *"I nourish my body with love, and my body loves me back."*

Closing Reflection

You have now been reminded that food is far more than fuel. It is story, connection, compassion, and care. Every meal you prepare, every sip of water you take, and every conscious choice you make in honour of your wellbeing is not simply an action, it is a declaration of self-respect.

When you eat with awareness, you are not just filling your stomach, you are nourishing the clarity of your mind, calming your emotions, and restoring your spirit to wholeness. You are reminding yourself that nourishment is not just about survival, it is about living fully, deeply, and in alignment with your heart.

Let this part of your journey be a turning point. Not a striving for perfection, but an invitation into presence. Let food become the sacred rhythm that anchors your day, a ritual of love that whispers, *"I deserve to feel well. I deserve to thrive."*

Just as Mia discovered, healing is never found in grand leaps, it begins in the smallest of steps: in one fresh ingredient chosen with care, in one glass of water offered to a thirsty body, in one still and quiet moment where you pause long enough to listen to what your body truly asks of you.

Carry this wisdom forward: that nourishment is not only what you eat, but also how you breathe, how you move, how you rest, and how you treat yourself with tenderness. To nourish is to honour your life as sacred, to respect the miracle that is your body, and to live each day as though your health and heart truly matter.

You are worthy of feeling well. You are worthy of love, of rest, of joy, and of care, and every conscious meal you share with yourself or with others can become a quiet, powerful homecoming, a return to your heart, where healing, presence, and self-compassion live.

9 - NOTHINGNESS

Your Opening Reflection

An Invitation to Breathe - Before you move forward, allow yourself this simple gift: pause, soften, and breathe. Your breath is not just air, it is life moving through you, a gentle reminder that you are here, alive, and connected. Let each inhale welcome you home to your heart, and let each exhale release what no longer serves you. With every breath, you are reminded that presence, peace, and renewal are always within reach.

- "How comfortable are you with simply being, without needing to achieve or produce?"

- "What fears or discomforts arise when you slow down completely?"

- "When was the last time you sat in silence and truly listened to your own breath?"

- "What would it feel like to release all expectations for a moment?"

- "How might doing nothing actually restore your energy and clarity?"

- "When was the last time you allowed yourself to do absolutely nothing, with no guilt?"

Let these questions open the doorway into presence. Every answer you give, whether in words, sensations, or silence, is a bridge between where you are and where you are going.

Learning Objectives

The learning objectives are included here to give you a clear focus for this chapter, ensuring that each practice you explore moves you closer to

mastering the skills, insights, and heart-led awareness that will enrich your life well beyond the program. By the end of this chapter, you will:

- Understand the emotional and psychological benefits of embracing stillness and nothingness.

- Recognise how overstimulation and busyness interfere with your emotional clarity and self-awareness.

- Practice techniques to invite silence, spaciousness, and simplicity into your daily life.

- Develop inner awareness through intentional disengagement from constant doing.

- Cultivate greater presence, peace, and heart connection by creating space for nothingness.

Core Emotional Domains

The core emotional intelligence domains covered here are essential because they form the foundation for lasting heart connection, guiding you to deepen self-awareness, regulate emotions, build resilience, and strengthen the mind-body bond throughout your Heart Unbound journey.

- **Self-Awareness:** You learn to observe your inner landscape in stillness, noticing thoughts, emotions, and sensations without needing to fix or judge them.

- **Self-Regulation:** By resting in quiet, you calm your nervous system, release reactivity, and create space for thoughtful, heart-aligned responses.

- **Mindful Presence:** In the spaciousness of nothingness, you practise simply being, fully present, unattached to outcomes, grounded in the now.

- **Motivation:** In the pause, clarity returns. You reconnect with what truly matters, realigning your energy with purpose rather than pressure.

"Nothingness – Embracing the Sacred Pause"

The Sacred Power of Nothingness

Modern life demands constant stimulation. You are bombarded by notifications, responsibilities, background noise, and the pressure to always be doing. In a world that rarely stops, stillness can feel uncomfortable, even foreign, but within that discomfort lies a profound invitation: to come home to yourself.

Nothingness is not emptiness. It is spaciousness.

It is the pause between the inhale and exhale, the moment before a thought forms, the sacred silence behind your heartbeat. When you allow yourself to rest in nothingness, you are not abandoning life, you are rediscovering it. In this space, your nervous system begins to settle:

1. Your mind becomes less chaotic.
2. Your heart becomes more audible.

From this quiet place, wisdom arises, not from effort, but from presence. You begin to hear the deeper questions:

- What truly matters to you?

- What can you release?

- What is asking to emerge?

Embracing nothingness is a radical act of self-regulation and emotional intelligence.

It is a conscious choice to step away from the relentless demands of doing and into the quiet sanctuary of being. In this space, you interrupt the cycle of reactivity that so often drives exhaustion, disconnection, and overwhelm. Nothingness becomes a healing pause, a moment where clarity can rise, where the edges of your mind soften, and where you stand in your own sovereignty, unshaken by the noise around you.

Here, time is no longer measured by productivity, but by alignment with your soul's natural rhythm. You begin to notice the steady pulse of your own breath, the subtle language of your body, and the quiet wisdom of your heart. When you allow yourself to simply be, you uncover a profound truth: you are already enough, exactly as you are, and from this stillness, your most authentic actions emerge, not from urgency, but from peace.

So the next time you feel yourself swept up in the current of constant doing, choose the sacred pause. Sit in the fullness of nothing, without guilt or resistance. Let yourself be held by the silence, for it is in this space that the heart remembers what the noise once made you forget, that your worth was never in what you produced, but in the truth of who you are.

The Science and Spirituality of Nothingness

Honouring the art of rest, presence, and spacious being. In a world driven by productivity, performance, and endless achievement, the idea of doing *nothing* often feels indulgent, even shameful, but both modern science and ancient spiritual wisdom reveal a beautiful truth: nothingness is not laziness, it is medicine.

Dolce far niente - "The sweetness of doing nothing"

From the Italian tradition comes *dolce far niente*, a phrase that celebrates the joy and soulfulness found in intentional rest. It is not laziness, nor is it avoidance, it is the conscious decision to step out of the current of busyness and into the quiet flow of the present moment.

It might look like sipping tea in the afternoon sun without rushing to the next task, watching clouds drift across the sky, or sharing peaceful silence with a loved one. In these moments, nothing is being *"achieved"* in the traditional sense, yet everything essential is being nourished.

Dolce far niente is a reminder that your worth has never been measured by your output. Your soul does not thrive on relentless pressure; it blossoms in presence, in being fully here, and in allowing life to unfold without force.

Niksen - The Dutch art of purposeless rest

In the Netherlands, this practice takes the form of *niksen*, the art of doing absolutely nothing, on purpose. It is a radical permission slip to put down your phone, step away from emails, silence the *"to-do"* list, and simply exist in the moment with no objective other than being.

Science now affirms what tradition has long known: when you give your mind space to wander without direction, creativity sparks, stress dissolves, problem-solving skills sharpen, and your overall emotional well-being improves. *Niksen* invites your nervous system to recalibrate, allowing tension to melt away and making room for insight to arise naturally.

This is the fertile ground where your subconscious processes life's events, where resilience takes hold, and where clarity emerges, not from doing more, but from allowing more stillness. In *niksen*, you learn that rest is not an interruption to your life's journey; it is an essential part of the path itself.

The Neuroscience of Nothingness

When you allow yourself to enter a state of restful awareness, whether through daydreaming, meditating, or simply sitting still, a remarkable thing happens in your brain. You activate what is known as the *default mode network*, a system linked to self-reflection, creativity, emotional processing, and meaning-making. Contrary to the myth that idleness is a waste of time, neuroscience shows that it is in these very states of non-doing that your brain quietly integrates your experiences, makes sense of them, and sparks deeper insight. In other words, when you step back from the noise, your mind begins to connect the dots that busyness keeps scattered.

In this intentional rest, your body also shifts into repair mode. Cortisol, your primary stress hormone, decreases, giving your system a much-needed break from chronic pressure. Your heart rate variability, a key marker of emotional resilience, begins to balance, and your parasympathetic nervous system, the *"rest and restore"* branch of your body's wiring, takes the lead, calming you from the inside out. By giving yourself permission to pause, you are not doing *"nothing"*, you are creating the optimal conditions for your mind to heal, your body to recover, and your spirit to reconnect with what truly matters.

The Spiritual Roots of Stillness

Across spiritual traditions around the world, from Buddhism and Taoism to Christian monasticism and Sufi mysticism, stillness is not seen as an absence, but as a profound presence. It is not emptiness, but fullness, the quiet space in which you can meet your truest self and listen to the wisdom that cannot be heard in the noise of everyday life.

Zen Buddhism

In Zen, the practice of silence and sitting meditation (*zazen*) is a direct path to awakening, a way of stripping away illusions and resting in the essence of reality. The focus is not on achieving a specific state, but on simply sitting with what is, allowing thoughts to rise and fall like waves without clinging to or rejecting them.

This stillness is not passive; it is alive with awareness. Each breath is a doorway into the present moment, each heartbeat a reminder of life's impermanence and beauty. Through this sustained attention, Zen teaches that enlightenment is not somewhere else to be reached, but here, already present, revealed when the mind quiets enough to see it.

Christianity

In Christianity, contemplative prayer becomes a meeting place with the divine, where the heart communes with God beyond words, beyond asking, simply in the openness of being. This form of prayer invites you to rest in God's presence without agenda, to be still and know.

Christian mystics such as St. Teresa of Ávila and Thomas Merton wrote of stillness as a sacred intimacy, where the soul is nourished not by doing, but by abiding. It is here that love deepens, faith matures, and grace flows freely. The stillness is an act of surrender, trusting that God's presence is enough.

Taoism

In Taoism, quiet observation of nature is a teacher, revealing the effortless flow of life and the harmony of all things. By watching the seasons shift, rivers carve valleys, and trees grow without striving, you begin to see the Tao, the Way, unfolding without force.

Stillness in Taoism is not withdrawal from life, but attunement to its rhythms. When you slow down to truly witness the natural world, you begin to mirror its balance. You learn that life is not meant to be pushed into shape, but trusted to find its own. In this way, stillness is not escape but alignment.

Indigenous Traditions

In Indigenous traditions, time spent on the land is sacred, not for doing, but for listening, for receiving guidance from the earth, the ancestors, and the unseen. This listening is an active relationship with the world, one built on reciprocity, respect, and belonging.

Stillness here is not solitary; it is communal. It connects you to the web of life and reminds you that you are part of something far greater. Sitting by a river, walking through the forest, or lying under the night sky becomes ceremony, restoring your place in the circle of life and deepening your responsibility to care for it.

Sufi Mysticism

In Sufi mysticism, stillness is a lover's embrace with the Divine Beloved, where the soul is dissolved into unity and love. The Sufi seeks not just to know about God, but to taste God directly, and stillness is the chalice from which that love is drunk.

Poets like Rumi and Hafiz spoke of this union as a silence so full it overflows. In the quiet, the heart hears the music of the soul, and the self melts away into the greater Self. It is here that longing meets fulfilment, and the seeker becomes the sought.

Stillness is where the soul breathes. It is where the heart remembers what the mind forgets. It is the space where you come home to yourself, and, in that homecoming, to the sacred.

Why "Doing Nothing" Is A Radical And Emotionally Intelligent Act In A Hyperproductive World

In a culture that glorifies hustle, output, and achievement, choosing to pause, even briefly, is not just a break from the norm. It is a bold, countercultural act of emotional intelligence. You have likely been conditioned to equate your worth with your productivity. The more you do, the more valuable you feel. Rest becomes something to *"earn,"* and idleness is mistaken for laziness, but emotional intelligence asks something deeper:

- Can you be with yourself when there is nothing to achieve?
- Can you slow down enough to hear what your heart is really saying?

Doing nothing invites you into that space. It teaches you to tolerate stillness, to sit with discomfort, and to meet yourself without distractions. It interrupts the nervous system's overdrive and gently regulates your emotions, thoughts, and breath. It reconnects you with your intuitive self, the one that does not shout, but whispers. Emotionally intelligent people know that clarity does not come from constant motion. It emerges in stillness. Insight does not arise from rushing, it flows when you create space. Choosing to *"do nothing"* is how you begin to hear your inner world.

It is where your values rise to the surface, where rest meets reflection, and where the next step can reveal itself, not through force, but through alignment. This act of non-doing is a declaration:

- I am enough, even in stillness.
- It is self-awareness in action.
- It is self-regulation without suppression.
- It is presence over performance.

In a world that rewards exhaustion, doing nothing becomes a form of resistance. In a world that forgets how to feel, doing nothing becomes a return to self, and in a world driven by noise, doing nothing is how you learn to listen again. So give yourself permission to pause, not as an escape, but as a homecoming.

Let your stillness be a statement.

Let it be a revolution grounded in grace.

Let it remind you that you are already whole.

The Difference Between Nothingness And Laziness

In a world that moves at lightning speed, where being "*busy*" is often mistaken for being valuable, slowing down can feel unnatural, even shameful. Yet there is a profound distinction between **nothingness** and **laziness,** a distinction that speaks to presence, intention, and emotional intelligence.

Laziness is avoidance.

It often stems from fear, apathy, or disconnection. When you are lazy, you may resist action not because your soul is asking for stillness, but because you are overwhelmed, unmotivated, or uncertain of your direction. Laziness numbs. It disconnects you from purpose, but nothingness is conscious.

It is the intentional choice to pause. To step away from the noise of striving so you can come back into alignment with what truly matters. Nothingness is presence without performance. It is where your nervous system rests, your clarity returns, and your heart speaks.

When you sit in stillness, not because you are avoiding life, but because you are making space for it, you are not being lazy. You are listening. You are allowing. You are trusting that your worth is not found in constant output, but in your ability to be with yourself. *Laziness dulls the senses. Nothingness sharpens awareness. Laziness drains your spirit. Nothingness nourishes it.*

Choosing nothingness is an act of courage in a hyper productive world. It requires self-awareness to know when to stop, self-regulation to let go of urgency, and self-worth to know you are valuable, even in stillness. So the next time you pause, breathe, and simply *be*, remind yourself: This is not laziness. This is leadership from within. This is how you reset, realign, and return to the life you want to live, awake, aware, and grounded in what truly matters.

How Intentional Stillness Reduces Stress And Develops Resilience

In a world that rarely stops moving, **intentional stillness** is one of the most powerful tools you have to reduce stress and build lasting emotional resilience. It is more than just taking a break, it is a conscious return to the present moment, where healing begins, and clarity is restored. When you choose stillness, not as avoidance, but as *presence,* you send a powerful message to your nervous system: *"You are safe. You can slow down. You do not have to be on high alert."* This shift activates the **parasympathetic nervous system**, also known as the *"rest and restore"* state.

- Your heart rate softens.
- Your breath deepens.
- Cortisol levels begin to drop.
- Blood flow returns to the prefrontal cortex, the part of your brain responsible for insight, reasoning, and empathy.

In stillness, your body recalibrates. Your mind finds space, and your emotions begin to settle. This quiet space between thoughts and actions becomes your training ground for resilience, because when life gets chaotic or painful, it is not the absence of stress that defines your strength, it is your ability to **pause, breathe, and respond** instead of react. Stillness gives you that ability. It helps you meet life with **inner steadiness**, even when the world around you feels uncertain. It allows you to hear your intuition, process your emotions, and reconnect with your values before making decisions.

Over time, the practice of intentional stillness strengthens your emotional core. You become less shaken by pressure. More anchored in your truth. More able to navigate change, disappointment, or challenge with compassion and clarity. Resilience is not about pushing through at all costs. It is about knowing when to stop. When to breathe, and when to *be with yourself* in the quiet, so that you can return to the world not depleted, but renewed.

Nothingness As A Space For Creative Insight And Emotional Regulation

In a culture that often measures success by output and achievement, nothingness can feel useless, even threatening, but nothingness, true, intentional spaciousness, is not emptiness. It is potential. It is the fertile ground from which insight, healing, and transformation quietly emerge.

When you allow yourself to pause, to be without performing, planning, or producing, you create a rare kind of space. A space where your nervous system can decompress, and your mind can finally breathe. This is not a void, it is a womb of possibility. From this sacred stillness, two powerful forces awaken - creative insight and emotional regulation.

Creative Insight

Creativity does not thrive in chaos. It thrives in space. Your most meaningful ideas often arise when you are not trying to find them, when you are walking without purpose, daydreaming by a window, or simply resting in the stillness of being. Neuroscience confirms this: when your brain enters its default mode network during restful states, it begins to form new connections, solve complex problems, and unlock subconscious wisdom. Stillness invites your imagination to speak. It creates the conditions where you can hear your soul's voice, free from noise, urgency, or comparison. It is in doing nothing that your next meaningful something often reveals itself.

Emotional Regulation

Nothingness also offers something gentler but just as powerful: emotional clarity. When you sit in stillness, your feelings have room to rise, not to overwhelm you, but to be acknowledged, felt, and gently processed. You create the space to observe your inner world with compassion rather than judgment. This is the heart of emotional regulation, not pushing emotions down, not being ruled by them, but allowing them to move through you. In stillness, you become a safe container for your experience.

You learn to respond with presence, not reactivity. You soften your grip. You breathe deeper. You become more whole. In the stillness of nothingness, you are not wasting time. You are resetting your system. You are reclaiming your rhythm. You are allowing life to speak, not through noise, but through silence, and from that silence comes the truth, the vision, the insight, and the peace, that was waiting patiently for you to stop running, and simply be.

Nothingness - Reflection Exercise

The Five-Minute Nothingness Challenge:

I invite you to sit in silence for five full minutes.

- No music
- No phones

- No goals
- Just presence

I ask you to notice your breath, thoughts, sensations, without judgment or control. Now, write down how it felt:

- Restless?
- Peaceful?
- Difficult?
- Surprising?

Case Study - Ash's Journey

I remember when Ash, a very intelligent and spiritually aware young man, told me that doing nothing was easy and that he would do nothing for an hour. At the end of his first week of doing the 28–day challenge I spoke with Ash and asked him how he was going.

Ash told me that he found it exceptionally difficult to sit and do nothing even for 2 minutes. He said that he, 'started getting agitated and nervous and felt like he needed to be *'doing something'*. Ash's experience is very common and even if you gifted yourself time and space and only spent 5 seconds doing nothing, really ask yourself why you cannot do it and write it down.

Next time you gift yourself the opportunity to do nothing be courageous and claim the full 5 minutes, the journey to connect with your heart is worth the effort, and so are you. Every day make the choice to add on an extra minute and by the end of twenty–eight days you can gift yourself around 30 minutes of nothingness.

Reflective Exercise: Ash's Journey

Here are four profound and reflective questions inspired by Ash's story to help you engage with your own journey into nothingness:

1. When was the last time you allowed yourself to truly stop, not to escape, but to simply be? *Ash discovered that stillness was not about doing nothing, it was about meeting himself without distraction. When you give yourself space to pause, you meet parts of yourself that have been longing to be heard.*

2. What do you notice in the silence that you do not hear in the noise? *In the quiet moments, Ash began to hear truths he had been too busy to feel. Stillness*

---

reveals wisdom hidden beneath the surface of routine and noise. What is your silence trying to tell you?

3. How do you usually respond to the feeling of emptiness? With resistance, or with curiosity? *Ash realised he had spent years filling every empty space with distraction,but when he leaned into the emptiness, it softened, and became a source of calm. Emptiness is not something to fear, it is something to explore.*

4. What might become possible in your life if you stopped needing to be productive all the time? *Ash found that his greatest insights came when he stopped pushing. When you release the pressure to perform, you create room for creativity, clarity, and peace. Sometimes the most powerful growth happens in the stillness between actions.*

Affirmations For Integration: (Heart Whispers)

Affirmations have the power to quiet the noise of doubt, open the doorway to self-trust, and draw you back into the wisdom of your heart. When practised daily, they nurture an inner dialogue based in love and truth, helping you live each day more aligned with who you truly are. I invite you to repeat silently or write:

- *I find peace in the nothingness of a quiet mind.*
- *Nothingness allows me to let go of stress and anxiety.*
- *In nothingness, I discover the beauty of the present moment.*
- *Nothingness is where I find clarity and focus.*
- *In the void of nothingness, I find my true self.*
- *Nothingness helps me to release attachment to outcomes.*
- *I am grateful for the peace that nothingness brings to my life.*

Optional Nothingness Extension Activity

The Nothingness Space Challenge

1. **Create Your "Nothingness Zone":** Choose a small, quiet spot in your home, a chair, a window seat, a cushion in the corner. Make sure it is free from screens, books, and other distractions.

2. **Prepare It with Intention:** Keep it simple and uncluttered. You may wish to add a single candle, a plant, or an object that brings you calm. This is a space for stillness, not stimulation.

---

3. **Commit to Daily Use:** Visit your nothingness zone each day, even if only for 3–5 minutes. Sit in stillness. Breathe slowly. Let thoughts pass without chasing them.

4. **Anchor to the Heart:** Place a hand over your heart. Feel its rhythm. Imagine this is the centre of your stillness, expanding gently with each breath.

5. **Close with Gratitude:** When you leave, silently thank yourself for showing up and honouring your inner space.

Closing Reflection

In a world that glorifies doing, you chose to simply be. By stepping into the sacred space of nothingness, you have taken a radical step, not away from life, but into its deepest current. This is not an escape; it is an arrival. You have let yourself pause, rest, and listen to the stillness beneath the noise. In this gentle act of surrender, you have remembered something both ancient and essential: you are not here to earn your worth. You already are enough. You do not need to prove yourself to life; you are already woven into its fabric.

Nothingness is not empty. It is overflowing, with presence, with breath, with the quiet truths long buried beneath the clutter of busy days. It is here, in this stillness, that you regulate your nervous system, soften the grip of your mind, and allow your heart to breathe again. Here, you create the spaciousness for insights to rise unforced, for clarity to dawn without struggle, for wisdom to arrive in its own time.

As you carry this part of your journey forward, may you continue to honour the pause, not as a luxury to be earned, but as a necessity for a life well-lived. Not as weakness, but as the courage to meet life on your own terms. Not as doing less, but as opening to receive more, because in the space of nothingness, you come home to everything that truly matters, and in that homecoming, you remember: the stillness was never separate from you. It was always here, waiting for you to return.

10 - FORGIVENESS

Your Opening Reflection

An Invitation to Forgive - As you enter this chapter, give yourself permission to soften and open. Forgiveness is not about excusing the past, but about freeing your heart in the present. With each breath, allow yourself to release a little of the weight you have been carrying. Let this be a moment to imagine what it feels like to live lighter, to choose compassion over resentment, and to offer yourself the healing gift of peace.

- "What is one hurt you have been holding onto, and what would it feel like to release it?"

- "How has holding onto resentment or pain affected your life, relationships, or health?"

- "If you forgave fully, how might your heart and spirit feel lighter?"

- "What beliefs do you have about forgiveness that might be keeping you from it?"

- "How might forgiveness be a gift you give yourself, not just to the other person?"

- "What is one small step you can take today toward forgiving someone or yourself?"

- "Is there someone you still need to forgive, including yourself?"

Let these questions open the doorway into presence. Every answer you give, whether in words, sensations, or silence, is a bridge between where you are and where you are going.

Learning Objectives

The learning objectives are included here to give you a clear focus for this chapter, ensuring that each practice you explore moves you closer to mastering the skills, insights, and heart-led awareness that will enrich your life well beyond the program. By the end of this chapter, you will:

- Define forgiveness and differentiate it from enabling or excusing behavior.

- Understand how forgiveness promotes emotional healing and inner peace.

- Reflect on personal barriers to self-forgiveness and forgiveness of others.

- Apply practical techniques to begin the process of releasing resentment.

- Recognise forgiveness as a path to deeper heart connection and emotional resilience.

Core Emotional Domains

The core emotional intelligence domains covered here are essential because they form the foundation for lasting heart connection, guiding you to deepen self-awareness, regulate emotions, build resilience, and strengthen the mind-body bond throughout your Heart Unbound journey.

- **Self-Awareness:** You learn to recognise the emotions, memories, and narratives that keep resentment or pain alive.

- **Self-Regulation:** Forgiveness invites you to respond to hurt with intention rather than reactivity, creating space for peace.

- **Empathy:** You begin to understand the pain of others without excusing harm, building compassion while maintaining boundaries.

- **Social Skills:** Releasing blame creating healthier relationships, clearer communication, and deeper trust.

- **Motivation:** Forgiveness becomes a path to emotional freedom, inspiring you to grow beyond the wound and reclaim your energy.

"Forgiveness – Releasing The Past"

Forgiveness as Inner Liberation. Forgiveness is not a gift you give to someone who wronged you, it is a sacred act of release that you offer to yourself. It is not about excusing harm, forgetting pain, or pretending it did not happen. True forgiveness is an inner act of liberation, a conscious choice to unhook your heart from the weight of resentment, anger, and emotional toxicity. When you hold onto hurt, your body holds it too. Your breath tightens, your thoughts loop, your nervous system stays alert to an old danger. Over time, this pain calcifies, not just in your memory, but in your spirit. Forgiveness does not erase the wound, but it tends to it with compassion, allowing you to heal from the inside out.

To forgive is to reclaim your peace. It is a declaration that your wellbeing matters more than your grudges. It is the courage to soften a hardened heart, not for their sake, but for your freedom. In forgiveness, you open a door to emotional clarity, spaciousness, and even gratitude for how far you have come. You stop letting the past define your present. You choose to grow. You choose to feel light again, and most powerfully, you realise: *Forgiveness is not something they have to earn, it is something you decide to live.*

The Psychology and Spirituality Of Forgiveness

Forgiveness sits at the crossroads of psychology and spirituality, bridging the science of healing with the soul's deep longing for peace. From a psychological perspective, forgiveness is a transformative emotional process, one that invites you to meet your pain with courage rather than avoidance. It begins by acknowledging the reality of what happened: the wound, the injustice, the betrayal. This is not about denial, suppression, or pretending it did not matter. It is about facing the truth with both clarity and self-compassion.

In this space, you are not asked to condone, excuse, or forget harmful behavior. Instead, forgiveness becomes an intentional act of reclaiming your mental and emotional freedom. It is a conscious decision to stop letting the hurt dictate your inner world. Research consistently shows that practicing forgiveness can significantly lower cortisol levels, ease symptoms of depression and anxiety, improve cardiovascular health, and strengthen immune function. Psychologically, it disrupts cycles of rumination, anger, and resentment that keep you tethered to the past. Forgiveness replaces reactive survival responses with grounded emotional regulation, helping you think, feel, and respond from a place of clarity rather than pain.

In choosing to forgive, you are not giving power back to the person who hurt you, you are reclaiming it for yourself. You shift from being defined by what happened to being empowered by how you respond. Far from being a sign of weakness, forgiveness reflects deep emotional intelligence: the capacity to sit with pain, understand your emotions, integrate the lessons, and still act from your highest self. Forgiveness is not the closing of a chapter; it is the opening of a lighter, freer one, one in which your past no longer dictates the limits of your joy.

The Spirituality of Forgiveness

Spiritually, forgiveness is a sacred and transformative act, a gentle unraveling of bitterness, fear, and the invisible threads that bind you to past pain. It is not a forgetting, but a remembering: that within your heart resides the vast capacity to hold both grief and grace, to honour the truth of your wounds while still choosing love. Across spiritual traditions, forgiveness is often more than a single act; it is a lifelong path, a pilgrimage back to wholeness.

In Christianity, forgiveness reflects the essence of divine mercy, an invitation to mirror the compassion and unconditional love of God, even when it feels undeserved. In Buddhism, it is a practice of letting go of attachments to anger and resentment, releasing the suffering that binds both self and others. In Indigenous wisdom, forgiveness is woven into the fabric of community, restoring harmony and balance not only between people, but between the land, the ancestors, and the spirit world.

In each of these traditions, forgiveness is not a transaction or an act of surrendering power, it is an act of transcendence. It lifts you above the smallness of the wound and returns you to the vastness of your true self. It is a declaration that your identity is not defined by the harm you have suffered, but by the love you choose to embody. To forgive is to say with conviction: *This story will not define me. My heart is larger than this wound.* It is a spiritual commitment to inner peace, a conscious decision to stop rehearsing and re-enacting the hurt, and a willingness to live open-hearted in a world that sometimes shatters hearts. In the end, forgiveness is not only about setting someone else free, it is about liberating your own soul so it can move without the weight of the past, ready to love again without fear.

The Effects Of Resentment On Physical And Emotional Health

Resentment may seem like an invisible weight, hidden beneath the surface, tucked behind a polite smile, or pushed down in the name of strength, but over time, it becomes one of the most corrosive emotions you carry, impacting both your physical health and emotional wellbeing in deep and far-reaching ways.

Emotional Toll: Living in a Loop of Pain

Resentment is not just a passing emotion, it is a sustained state of unresolved hurt entwined with a sense of injustice. It keeps you locked in mental replays, revisiting conversations, events, and missed opportunities for closure. The mind becomes a theatre of *"what ifs"* and *"should haves,"* looping the same scene over and over.

This constant rumination activates the stress response repeatedly, leaving your nervous system in a perpetual state of low-grade tension. You might notice yourself feeling on edge for no clear reason, or withdrawing emotionally because the hurt feels too raw to face. Over time, resentment shrinks your emotional world; joy feels distant, trust feels risky, and even moments of peace are interrupted by a lingering ache. Without release, it quietly shapes how you see yourself, others, and life itself.

Physical Toll: The Body Remembers

The mind may replay the wound, but the body stores it. Science confirms that chronic emotional stress, like the kind resentment breeds, takes a measurable toll on physical health. Elevated cortisol can disrupt the delicate balance of your immune, digestive, and cardiovascular systems. Sleep becomes shallow, muscles tighten like armour, and your breath unconsciously shortens, signalling to your body that danger is still present.

Over months or years, this state of guardedness increases inflammation, slows healing, and leaves you more vulnerable to illness. Resentment does not just live in your thoughts; it settles in your shoulders, your jaw, your gut. It can become an unseen weight you carry everywhere, one that erodes vitality and keeps the body in a constant state of readiness for a battle that never arrives.

What Makes Resentment So Draining?

Resentment drains you because it demands constant energy to sustain. It is like keeping a fire smouldering, you must continually add emotional fuel in the form of rumination, anger, or silent bitterness. This emotional maintenance prevents you from fully engaging with the present, because part of you is still anchored in the past, guarding the wound. The cost is high: hope dims, creativity dries up, and compassion, for yourself and others, becomes harder to access. Resentment consumes the very qualities that make life rich and meaningful. It convinces you that holding on protects you, when in truth, it only keeps you tethered to pain.

<u>The Healing Choice: Letting Go Does Not Excuse, It Releases</u>

Letting go of resentment is an act of courage, not concession. It is not about pretending the harm never happened or absolving someone of responsibility, it is about reclaiming your freedom from the grip of the past. Letting go means loosening your identity from the story of hurt, so you are no longer defined by it. It is choosing to end the cycle of self-punishment and allowing your energy to flow toward what restores and nourishes you. When you release resentment, you create space for peace to take root, for joy to return, and for your heart to open again, stronger, wiser, and unburdened.

As you begin to release resentment, through self-reflection, compassion, and forgiveness, you reclaim your emotional vitality and physical wellbeing. You begin to return to yourself, because resentment does not protect your heart. It holds it hostage and healing begins when you set it free.

Forgiveness vs. Excusing Behavior

One of the greatest misunderstandings about forgiveness is the belief that to forgive someone is to excuse or justify what they did, but true forgiveness is not about erasing the past, it is about releasing *yourself* from being held hostage by it.

<u>Excusing Behaviour Means Minimising Harm</u>

When you excuse someone's behaviour, you downplay the impact of their actions. You might say *"It was not that bad,"* or *"They did not mean it."* Excusing can lead to bypassing accountability, suppressing your truth, or staying silent in the name of keeping the peace. It can invalidate your feelings, create confusion about your worth, and even enable unhealthy dynamics to continue. Excusing often arises from a desire to avoid conflict, or from internalised beliefs that your pain is not valid,but your hurt matters. Your boundaries matter. Healing begins when you name what was true.

<u>Forgiveness, on the Other Hand, Is a Conscious Release</u>

Forgiveness does not erase the wrong, it **honours that it happened** and still chooses to let go of the emotional grip it has over you. It does **not** mean you condone the behaviour or pretend it did not cause harm. It means you are no longer willing to carry the bitterness, anger, or resentment that weighs on your heart. Forgiveness says:

- *"I am choosing peace over pain."*

- *"I no longer want to re-live what hurt me."*

- *"I will not allow this to define my future."*

It may involve setting boundaries. It may mean walking away. It may mean holding someone accountable, with love and clarity, but without vengeance.

<u>Forgiveness Empowers, Excusing Disempowers</u>

Forgiveness is an act of reclamation, it hands you back the keys to your own heart. When you forgive, you release the hold the past has over your present, and in doing so, you restore your agency. Your emotional energy is no longer drained by replaying the wound; instead, it becomes available for creating the life you want. Forgiveness clears the fog of resentment, allowing you to see yourself and your future with greater clarity. It is the choice to stand in your own sovereignty, no longer defined by someone else's actions.

Excusing, however, is different. When you excuse harmful behaviour without addressing its impact, you bypass your own truth. You may shrink yourself to avoid conflict, rationalise what is unacceptable, or bury your pain in the hope that it will disappear. This often leads to cycles of guilt, self-doubt, and disempowerment, because you have abandoned your own boundaries.

Forgiveness does not say, *"What happened was fine."* It says, *"What happened hurt, but I am choosing to heal. I am no longer tethered to that hurt."* It is the conscious decision to honour your worth, hold your boundaries, and live free from the emotional weight of the past. That shift, from *"It is okay"* to *"I am okay now"*, is everything. It is the difference between silencing yourself and liberating yourself.

Effects Of Resentment On Physical And Emotional Health

Resentment is one of the most corrosive emotions we carry, quietly building in the background, often masked as strength or righteousness, while slowly depleting your emotional reserves and affecting your physical wellbeing.

<u>Emotionally: Resentment Traps You in the Past</u>

Resentment is unresolved hurt wrapped in anger and replayed over time. When you hold onto it, your mind stays tethered to the original wound, replaying the story again and again. You might relive the betrayal, reimagine the argument, or rehearse what you wish you had said. This mental looping fuels anxiety, irritability, sadness, and emotional exhaustion. Resentment also blocks empathy and connection. It can harden your heart, make trust difficult, and cause emotional distancing in relationships. Over time, it narrows your worldview and disconnects you from joy, creativity, and peace. It is not just the event that causes harm, it is the ongoing emotional investment in *what was*, rather than what could be.

Physically: The Body Keeps the Score

The stress of resentment does not just live in your thoughts, it settles in your body. Chronic resentment can:

- Raise cortisol (the body's primary stress hormone)

- Disrupt sleep patterns

- Weaken your immune system

- Increase inflammation, linked to diseases such as heart disease and arthritis

- Contribute to headaches, digestive issues, and chronic fatigue

Because your nervous system cannot tell the difference between a past event and a current threat, it reacts as if you are still under attack every time you ruminate.

- Your muscles tense.

- Your breath shortens.

- Your heart rate elevates.

The result? You live in a state of low-grade, persistent fight-or-flight, even when the original danger is long gone.

The Hidden Cost: It Steals Your Present

The price of holding onto resentment extends far beyond your physical health, it quietly robs you of the life you are living right now. Every moment spent replaying the past is a moment stolen from the present. Resentment narrows your emotional landscape, reducing your capacity for joy, compassion, creativity, and peace. It colours the way you see others, the way you interpret their actions, and even the way you speak to yourself.

Over time, resentment can become strangely familiar, almost comfortable in its predictability. You may find yourself returning to it like a well-worn story, not because it serves you, but because it is known. Yet, in clinging to it, you limit your own growth and dim the light of your spirit. Resentment may feel like self-protection, but it is often self-imprisonment.

<u>The Antidote: Forgiveness and Emotional Release</u>

Letting go of resentment does not mean erasing what happened or excusing the harm. It means choosing freedom over fixation. Forgiveness in this sense is not an act of surrender to the person who hurt you, it is a profound act of allegiance to yourself. It is a conscious choice to stop allowing the wound to dictate your emotional climate.

This release is a process, often unfolding in layers. Self-awareness helps you recognise where the pain still lives in you. Breathwork can help regulate your nervous system, allowing your body to begin loosening its grip on stored tension. Compassion, both for yourself and others, softens the sharp edges of hurt, and forgiveness, when it comes, is the opening of the heart's gate, letting peace and possibility flow back in.

Here, forgiveness is not about making someone else feel better. It is about reclaiming your wellbeing, clarity, and wholeness. When you release resentment, you create space, space for health, for love, for deeper connection, and for the future you truly deserve. It is not about forgetting your story; it is about writing the next chapter with a freer, lighter hand.

How Self-Forgiveness Cultivates Compassion And Authenticity

<u>Self-Forgiveness: The Courage to Be Whole</u>

Self-forgiveness is one of the most profound and courageous acts of emotional intelligence because it requires you to face yourself fully, your actions, your intentions, your mistakes, without turning away. It is not about denying responsibility or avoiding accountability. Instead, it is about loosening the grip of the harsh, unrelenting judgment you hold against yourself. It is allowing your humanity to breathe again.

When you forgive yourself, you are not only releasing the weight of what you did; you are dismantling the limiting story you have been carrying about who you are because of it. You create the space for a truer narrative to emerge, one grounded in growth, learning, and the ongoing possibility of change. This is how self-forgiveness becomes an act of liberation, setting you free from the chains of your own self-condemnation.

<u>Self-Forgiveness Awakens Compassion</u>

You cannot offer authentic compassion to others if you cannot extend it inward. Self-forgiveness is the softening of your inner landscape, it turns the voice of your inner critic into one of understanding, wisdom, and care. It is the gentle reminder that you are not defined solely by your worst moments, but also by your capacity to rise from them.

Through self-forgiveness, you stop seeing yourself as broken, unworthy, or irredeemable. Instead, you begin to recognise that mistakes, regrets, and imperfections are not flaws that exile you from love, they are the very evidence of being human. You learn to hold yourself with the same patience, empathy, and grace you would offer to a dear friend who has stumbled but longs to walk again.

As your self-compassion deepens, so too does your compassion for others. You become less reactive, less judgmental, and more present. You begin to see the shared vulnerability that binds us all, the truth that we are all imperfect, all learning, and all worthy of forgiveness, and in this shared humanity, connection becomes easier, relationships grow richer, and peace takes root within you.

Forgiveness Across Cultures And Faiths: From The Teachings Of Jesus To Buddhist Metta

Forgiveness is not just a personal or psychological act, it is a spiritual practice embedded in the wisdom of cultures and religions across the world. While the language may differ, the invitation is the same: release what binds you, and return to love. Across traditions, forgiveness is viewed not as weakness, but as a courageous path to peace, reconciliation, and transformation, both within oneself and in relationship with others.

<u>Christianity: Forgiveness as Divine Mercy and Human Responsibility</u>

In Christianity, forgiveness is not a suggestion, it is a sacred calling. Grounded in the life and teachings of Jesus, forgiveness lies at the very heart of spiritual practice. It is seen as both a divine gift freely given and a human responsibility freely chosen. Jesus taught his followers to pray, *"Forgive us our trespasses, as we forgive those who trespass against us."* (Matthew 6:12) In this prayer, forgiveness is presented as a reciprocal act: *as we are forgiven, we must forgive*. It is not conditional on someone deserving it, it is anchored in the deeper reality that we are all in need of grace.

Jesus himself modelled radical forgiveness, even in the face of betrayal, injustice, and violence. As he hung on the cross, he prayed, *"Father, forgive them, for they do not know what they are doing."* (Luke 23:34) This moment is not just one of divine mercy, it is a powerful call for all people to extend compassion even when deeply wronged. In this tradition, forgiveness is an act of moral courage, not moral weakness. It means letting go of vengeance and the right to retaliate, and choosing instead the path of mercy, reconciliation, and peace. It is a way to break cycles of harm and open the door to transformation, not just for the offender, but for the one forgiving. Forgiveness in Christianity also reflects God's nature. It is how human beings are invited to mirror divine love:

- Love that restores rather than punishes.

- Love that redeems rather than rejects.

- Love that says, *"You are not the sum of your mistakes, you are the beloved."*

At its core, Christian forgiveness affirms that every soul is capable of redemption, and that healing, personal and communal, is made possible when you choose mercy over judgment, and grace over resentment. In this light, forgiveness is not simply a response to wrongdoing. It is a spiritual pathway to freedom, and the highest expression of love.

Buddhism: Forgiveness Through Metta and Non-Attachment

In the Buddhist tradition, forgiveness is not framed as a moral duty, but as a path to liberation from suffering. It is deeply grounded in the practice of *metta,* a Pali word often translated as loving-kindness or boundless friendliness. Metta is the intentional cultivation of unconditional goodwill toward all beings, yourself, your loved ones, strangers, and even those who have caused you harm.

It arises not from obligation, but from the understanding that every sentient being seeks happiness and freedom from suffering. This includes those who act unskillfully due to their own ignorance, pain, or confusion. In Buddhism, forgiveness is not about forgetting, excusing, or denying harm. It is about releasing the grip of anger, hatred, or resentment from your own heart. Holding onto these emotions is understood to create more suffering, not just for others, but for you.

The Buddha taught that clinging to anger is like "*grasping a hot coal with the intent of throwing it at someone else, you are the one who gets burned.*" Through mindfulness (*sati*) and compassion (*karuṇā*), practitioners are guided to see painful emotions clearly, without judgment. You learn to observe the story of hurt with spaciousness, not resistance. Over time, this awareness softens your inner experience, and with it, your reactivity. This is where non-attachment comes in, not as indifference, but as the ability to witness your pain without becoming it. By letting go of your identification with the wound, you begin to touch a deeper truth: you are not your suffering. You are the awareness beneath it.

Forgiveness, then, becomes a skillful means (upaya), a wise response that helps you let go of the inner burdens that keep you bound. It is not about changing the past. It is about freeing yourself from its emotional hold so you can return to equanimity, clarity, and compassion. In this tradition, forgiveness is not a one-time act but a practice, a gentle turning toward your own pain with the intention of healing. Buddhist monks and lay practitioners often use *metta* phrases such as:

- May I be safe.

- May I be happy.

- May I be free from suffering.

- May you be free from the suffering that causes harm.

By repeating these phrases, even toward those who have harmed you, you train your heart to let go, not to approve of harm, but to reclaim your peace and wisdom. Ultimately, in Buddhism, forgiveness is not an external transaction. It is an inner purification, a conscious path to liberation through compassion, non-attachment, and deep inner peace.

Forgiveness Letter Exercise

I invite you to create space, take a few deep breaths, and write two letters that hold the power to lighten your heart:

1. **To Yourself:** Write as though you are speaking to a dear friend who has walked through the same mistakes, regrets, or self-judgments you carry.

    - Express compassion: acknowledge the pain you have felt without judgment.

- Offer understanding: recognise the circumstances, emotions, and humanity behind your actions or choices.

- Extend release: let go of the weight of harsh self-criticism and affirm that you are worthy of love, acceptance, and peace.

2. **To Someone You Need to Forgive:** This letter is for your own healing, whether or not you ever share it.

- Acknowledge what happened and how it impacted you.

- Express what you are ready to let go of not to excuse the hurt, but to free yourself from carrying it.

- State your choice to release the emotional hold the situation has had on you.

3. **Afterward, pause for reflection:** Place both letters in front of you. Notice your breath, your body, and your emotions. Ask yourself:

- How do I feel now compared to before I began?

- Did I uncover emotions I had not acknowledged?

- Do I feel lighter, softer, more spacious inside?

You might choose to keep these letters as reminders, tear them up as a symbolic release, or burn them safely as an act of letting go.

Case Study Discussion: Alice's Journey

Alice had been struggling with love for as long as she could remember. She had been in and out of relationships but never found herself truly happy. At the age of 58, she finally realised that she needed to forgive herself before she could truly love herself and be in a genuine relationship.

Alice had always struggled with self–esteem and self–worth, and this had reflected in all of her relationships. She would always put her partners first and often found herself being taken advantage of. It was not until we started journeying together that she realised the root cause of her struggles.

Through our sessions together over many months Alice was able to confront the issues that were holding her back and started working on self–forgiveness.

She realised that in order to move on and start living a heart–led life, she needed to forgive herself for all the mistakes she had made in the past. With self–forgiveness came self–love, and Alice started to see herself in a new light. She started doing things that made her happy and began to take care of herself.

She also started to attract genuine and loving relationships into her life. Alice's journey towards forgiveness was not an easy one, but it was definitely worth it. She realised that forgiveness was not just about letting go of the past but also about accepting herself and loving herself unconditionally. Her heart was finally open to receive and give love, and she began living a more fulfilled life than ever before.

Alice's story is a powerful reminder that self–forgiveness is an essential step in living a heart–led life. It is about releasing yourself from the burden of your past mistakes, accepting yourself for who you are, and loving yourself unconditionally.

Reflective Exercise: Alice's Journey

Here are four profound and reflective questions inspired by Alice's story to help you engage with your own journey to forgiveness:

1. What pain have you been carrying that no longer serves your healing?: *Alice held on to the hurt because she thought releasing it meant the other person won, but in truth, it only kept her stuck. Forgiveness does not erase your experience, it frees you from reliving it.*

2. If you no longer needed an apology, what could you begin to let go of today?: *Waiting for an apology kept Alice tied to the past. When she chose to forgive without conditions, she reclaimed her energy and inner peace. You do not need permission to begin healing.*

3. What would it feel like to forgive yourself for what you did not know then?: *Alice's greatest act of forgiveness was turning compassion inward. When she stopped blaming herself for how she coped, she softened. Forgiveness opened the door to self-love and wholeness.*

4. What part of your heart is asking to be heard, not hardened? *Anger protected Alice for a long time, but underneath it was grief, and beneath that, longing. When she finally listened to her own heart, forgiveness emerged, not as a demand, but as a gentle return to herself.*

Affirmations For Integration: (Heart Whispers)

Affirmations have the power to quiet the noise of doubt, open the doorway to self-trust, and draw you back into the wisdom of your heart. When practised daily, they nurture an inner dialogue based in love and truth, helping you live each day more aligned with who you truly are. I invite you to repeat silently or write:

- *I am willing to let go of resentment and anger.*

- *I am open to forgiveness as a healing process.*

- *I choose to release negative emotions and embrace forgiveness.*

- *I accept responsibility for my actions and seek forgiveness.*

- *I am learning to forgive myself and others.*

- *I am grateful for the peace that comes with forgiveness.*

- *I am committed to releasing grudges and embracing forgiveness.*

Reflective Exercise - Forgiveness Visualisation Walk

Step 1 – Prepare: Choose a quiet path, whether it is through a park, along the beach, or in your neighbourhood, somewhere you can walk without rushing. Before you begin, place your hand over your heart and set the intention: *"I walk to release, to heal, and to move forward."*

Step 2 - Begin with Breath: As you start walking, focus on your breathing. Inhale deeply through your nose, drawing in fresh, clean air. Exhale slowly through your mouth, imagining that each breath out carries away a small piece of the pain, resentment, or hurt you have been holding.

Step 3 - Visualise Release: With every step, picture your emotional burdens as stones you have been carrying. Feel them grow lighter as they drop, one by one, onto the earth behind you. You might imagine them dissolving into the ground, transformed into something neutral, no longer weighing you down.

Step 4 - Engage Your Senses: Notice the warmth or coolness of the air on your skin, the sound of your footsteps, the rustle of leaves, the scent

---

of nature around you. Allow the world to remind you that life is happening now, in this present moment, not in the pain of the past.

Step 5 - Closing Ritual: When you reach the end of your walk, stand still. Place your feet firmly on the ground and take three slow, deep breaths. In your final exhale, whisper or say aloud: ***"I release the past. I walk forward in peace."***

Take a moment to notice the shift inside you, a little more lightness, a little more space, a little more peace.

Closing Reflection

Forgiveness is not about forgetting. It is not about making what happened acceptable or pretending it did not hurt. Forgiveness is about **reclaiming your peace**, your energy, and your capacity to love, even in the aftermath of pain. You have travelled through the raw terrain of resentment, grief, anger, and regret.

You have sat with truths that were difficult to name, and now, you stand at a threshold, not of erasure, but of release. To forgive is not to condone. It is to choose freedom over fixation. It is to untangle yourself from a story that no longer defines who you are. It is to soften your grip on the past, so your hands can be open to the present, and perhaps most courageously of all, it is to forgive **yourself,** for what you did not know, for how you survived, for being human. Let this be your beginning, not your ending:

A return to wholeness. A renewal of compassion.

A quiet unbinding of the heart.

You are not here to be perfect.

You are here to be free.

11 - GROUNDING

Your Opening Reflection

Invitation to Grounding - As you step into this chapter, I invite you to let the earth beneath you hold your weight, steady and sure. Imagine roots extending from your body into the ground, reminding you that you are supported, anchored, and safe. This is your moment to return to yourself, to release the rush, to soften the tension, and to remember that you are never separate from the strength and stability of the earth. Breathe deeply, feel your presence, and allow yourself to come home to your grounding.

- "When was the last time you felt fully anchored, steady, and safe in yourself?"

- "What practices, people, or places help you return to a sense of grounded calm when life feels overwhelming?"

- "In what areas of your life do you feel scattered or unsteady, and what might help you ground more deeply there?"

- "How does your body tell you when you are grounded, what sensations, rhythms, or signals arise?"

- "What does it mean to you to stand firmly in your truth, no matter what storms arise around you?"

Let these questions open the doorway into presence. Every answer you give, whether in words, sensations, or silence, is a bridge between where you are and where you are going.

Learning Objectives

The learning objectives are included here to give you a clear focus for this chapter, ensuring that each practice you explore moves you closer to mastering the skills, insights, and heart-led awareness that will enrich your life well beyond the program. By the end of this chapter, you will:

- Understand the emotional and physiological benefits of grounding.

- Learn and experience grounding techniques to reduce anxiety and stress.

- Deepen self-awareness by reconnecting with the physical body and present moment.

- Recognise grounding as a tool for emotional regulation and decision-making.

- Integrate grounding practices into daily life for ongoing balance and heart connection.

Core Emotional Domains

The core emotional intelligence domains covered here are essential because they form the foundation for lasting heart connection, guiding you to deepen self-awareness, regulate emotions, build resilience, and strengthen the mind-body bond throughout your Heart Unbound journey.

- **Self-Awareness:** Grounding anchors you in the present moment, helping you notice your thoughts, sensations, and emotions as they arise.

- **Self-Regulation:** By connecting with your body and breath, you calm your nervous system and create space to respond rather than react.

- **Emotional Resilience:** Grounding builds inner stability, allowing you to navigate stress and uncertainty with greater clarity and strength.

- **Empathy:** When you are grounded, you are more attuned to others, your presence becomes deeper, and compassion flows with ease and authenticity *"Forgiveness - Releasing The Past"*

"Grounding – Finding Safety in the Present"

Grounding: Coming Home to the Body, the Moment, and Yourself

Grounding is both a **physical** and **emotional** process, a returning to what is real, stable, and present. In a world that often pulls you into the past with regret or into the future with anxiety, grounding gently invites you back into the *now*. It reminds you that safety, clarity, and calm are found not in racing thoughts, but in the stillness beneath them.

When you ground yourself, you **anchor into your body**, your breath, your senses. You notice the earth beneath your feet, the rise and fall of your chest, the sounds and textures around you. This simple act of presence creates an immediate shift: your mind begins to settle, your nervous system calms, and the storm of emotion begins to soften. Emotionally, grounding is a tool for **self-regulation**. It helps you find your centre when you feel overwhelmed, disconnected, or scattered.

It allows you to respond with intention rather than react from fear or fatigue. In this grounded state, you are more resilient, more clear, and more compassionate, with yourself and with others. Grounding is not about escaping your experience, it is about **embodying it fully**, without judgment. It teaches you that peace is not the absence of challenge, but the presence of groundedness. In grounding, you come back to yourself.

- To breath.

- To presence.

- To the steady truth that **this moment is enough,** and so are you.

What Is Grounding?

Across time and tradition, grounding has been more than a calming technique, it has been a sacred relationship between your human spirit and the living Earth. Long before science named the nervous system or psychology defined trauma, cultures around the world understood that healing begins by returning to the ground beneath you.

Indigenous Traditions: Grounding as Relationship and Reverence

In many Indigenous cultures, grounding is a deeply spiritual act, one of **connection, reciprocity, and respect** for the Earth as a living, breathing being. The land is not a resource to be used, but a relative to be honoured. Through practices such as walking barefoot, smudging, drumming, or placing hands on trees, grounding becomes a way of **coming back to wholeness,** not just as individuals, but as part of a greater web of life.

The Earth is seen as a **source of wisdom and nourishment**, holding memory, energy, and guidance. When you feel overwhelmed, lost, or fragmented, you are often invited to *"go back to the land"*, to sit in silence, feel the soil, listen to the wind, or immerse yourself in ceremony. These are not passive acts of escape, but intentional pathways to **embodied remembrance**. Grounding in this context is about restoring **right relationship,** with the self, with community, and with the more-than-human world. It is about listening with your feet, breathing with the trees, and remembering that **you belong.**

Ayurveda and Traditional Chinese Medicine: Grounding as Energetic Balance

In **Ayurveda**, grounding is associated with the **root chakra** (*Muladhara*), the energetic centre located at the base of your spine, which governs your sense of safety, stability, and survival. When this chakra is balanced, you feel **secure, present, and anchored**. When imbalanced, you may feel anxious, scattered, or disconnected. Practices like **prāṇāyāma** (breath control), restorative yoga, warm foods, daily rituals, and time in nature are used to stabilise and nourish your root chakra, reconnecting you with your body and the rhythms of the Earth.

In **Traditional Chinese Medicine**, grounding is tied to the **Earth element**, which governs digestion, nourishment, and emotional equilibrium. When the Earth element is strong, it offers inner centredness and clarity. Grounding practices in this tradition often include **qigong, earthing exercises, tai chi**, and mindful eating, methods that restore **harmony between body, emotion, and environment.**

Monastic and Contemplative Traditions: Grounding as Inner Stillness

In Christian, Buddhist, and other monastic traditions, grounding was cultivated through **structured ritual and silent practice**. Walking meditations in cloisters, the rhythm of chanting, breath-focused prayers like the *Jesus Prayer*, and time in nature were all ways of **stilling the mind and rooting the soul.**

These practices were not escapes from the world, but portals into the **inner sanctuary of presence**. Grounding in this context became a **spiritual discipline,** a path to humility, surrender, and alignment with the divine.

A Shared Wisdom

Across all these traditions, grounding was never just a practice. It was a **return,** to the Earth, to the self, to the sacred. It reminds you that healing is not about striving upward, but about **deepening downward.**

- That clarity is not always in thinking more, but in **feeling more**.

- That strength is found not in resistance, but in **groundedness**.

Grounding invites you to come back to what has always held you: *The Earth. Your breath. The moment. Your body. Your truth.*

Modern Psychological and Somatic Approaches to Grounding

Healing the Mind by Reconnecting to the Body

In modern psychology, particularly in trauma-informed, somatic, and mindfulness-based practices, **grounding is now understood as a vital and evidence-based strategy** for emotional regulation, safety, and mental clarity. It has become a cornerstone of therapeutic interventions for anxiety, trauma, dissociation, and chronic stress, not just as a coping mechanism, but as a pathway to long-term healing.

What Is Grounding in Psychological Terms?

Grounding refers to any technique that brings your awareness back into the *present moment* by reconnecting you with your body, breath, senses, and surroundings. When a person is emotionally overwhelmed, by stress, anxiety, trauma triggers, or intrusive thoughts, the brain can easily slip into **fight, flight, freeze, or fawn** responses.

Grounding interrupts this physiological cascade by helping you regulate your nervous system and re-engage with safety. Common techniques include:

- **Breathwork** (e.g., extended exhale, box breathing)

- **Sensory orientation** (e.g., the 5-4-3-2-1 method)

- **Movement** (e.g., walking, stretching, shaking out tension)

- **Touch-based techniques** (e.g., holding a warm mug, pressing your feet into the floor)

- **Visualisation** (e.g., imagining roots growing from your feet into the earth)

These practices help shift attention **from spiraling thoughts into embodied awareness**, creating an internal pause, just long enough to access clarity, resilience, and self-agency.

The Neuroscience Behind Grounding

From a neurological perspective, grounding activates your **parasympathetic**

nervous system, also known as the *"rest-and-digest"* system. This calms the stress response (regulated by your sympathetic nervous system), lowering cortisol and adrenaline levels, slowing the heart rate, and stabilising blood pressure. By drawing awareness back to the present moment, grounding can interrupt your neural pathways associated with trauma flashbacks or rumination. It also engages your **prefrontal cortex**, your brain's centre for reasoning, planning, and self-regulation, restoring executive function after emotional flooding. In short, grounding supports **neuroplasticity,** your brain's ability to rewire and recover from dysregulation, by building new, safer associations with embodiment and presence.

The Somatic Approach: Reclaiming the Wisdom of the Body

Somatic therapists recognise that trauma is not only a psychological wound, it is stored in your **nervous system and the body**. Grounding becomes a way for you to **return safely to your body**, especially if you have dissociated from it due to past pain or overwhelm.

Rather than analysing thoughts or reliving traumatic memories, somatic grounding gently guides you to feel your feet on the floor, your breath in your chest, or your spine rising with strength. These micro-moments of safety begin to re-establish trust in your body's ability to hold experience without collapsing under it. This work is especially powerful in helping you move from **numbness to aliveness**, from **hyperarousal to regulation**, and from **survival to embodiment**.

From Coping Skill to Healing Practice

While grounding is often introduced as a short-term coping technique, its **long-term practice opens a doorway to deeper healing**. As you develop a daily grounding rhythm, whether through meditation, nature walks, sensory awareness, or movement, you begin to feel more grounded, more spacious, and more connected.

This shift allows emotional experiences to **flow rather than flood**, making space for self-compassion, insight, and transformation. In a world that can often feel chaotic, fast-paced, and overstimulating, grounding becomes more than a practice, it becomes a way of being. *A quiet return to presence. A place of inner safety. A daily commitment to coming home to yourself.*

Benefits of Grounding: Physical Health, and Emotional Clarity

Grounding is more than a calming technique, it is a **holistic practice** that supports your wellbeing on multiple levels. When you ground yourself, you return to your natural state of presence: a place where your body feels safe, your emotions are balanced, and your spirit is attuned to its deeper wisdom. Let us explore how grounding nurtures **your whole self:**

Physical Health: Regulating the Nervous System and Energising the Body

At its core, grounding supports **physiological equilibrium,** helping your body return to a natural state of balance after the wear and tear of chronic stress, overstimulation, or emotional overload. In today's fast-paced world, many people live in a prolonged state of **sympathetic nervous system dominance,** also known as the **fight, flight, or freeze** response. This can lead to fatigue, insomnia, digestive issues, inflammation, and suppressed immune function. Grounding counteracts this by **activating the parasympathetic nervous system,** your body's built-in *rest, digest, and restore* mode. This shift results in a cascade of positive physiological effects:

1. **Lowered Heart Rate and Blood Pressure**: As your body begins to feel safe and supported, your cardiovascular system relaxes. Grounding helps reduce the physical markers of stress, allowing your heart to beat more steadily and efficiently.

2. **Improved Sleep and Circadian Rhythm**: Grounding practices, especially those performed in nature or with intentional breath, help regulate melatonin production and rebalance disrupted sleep cycles. When you are grounded, your body re-attunes to its natural rhythms, making rest deeper and more restorative.

3. **Reduced Cortisol Levels**: Chronic stress elevates cortisol, which over time can contribute to weight gain, mood swings, inflammation, and immune suppression. Grounding has been shown to reduce cortisol production, allowing the body to repair and regenerate more effectively.

4. **Enhanced Energy and Vitality**: When your nervous system is calm and balanced, more energy is available for life. Grounding clears internal tension, improves oxygenation, and restores clarity, leading to increased stamina and a greater sense of aliveness throughout the day.

Earthing: Grounding with the Earth Itself

In recent years, scientific studies on *"earthing"*, the direct physical connection with the Earth's surface, have brought new insight into ancient practices. Research indicates that **barefoot contact with soil, sand, grass,**

or natural stone allows the body to absorb negatively charged electrons from the Earth, which may help:

- Reduce systemic **inflammation**

- Improve **immune function**

- Normalise **blood viscosity**

- Support **electromagnetic balance** in the body

While more research is emerging, many report subjective benefits such as quicker recovery from fatigue, improved mood, and reduced physical pain after regular time spent connecting physically with the Earth. Even a few minutes a day, **feet in the grass, hands on a tree, or sitting quietly outdoors,** can have cumulative and profound health effects.

Grounding And Emotional Intelligence: Enhancing Presence And Choice

When you ground yourself, you give your emotional intelligence the space it needs to grow. Grounding is not just about calming down, it is about **coming back to yourself** so you can respond to life with clarity rather than react from stress or fear. In moments of overwhelm, your nervous system can hijack your thoughts and actions. You might feel scattered, reactive, or disconnected, but when you pause, take a breath, feel your feet on the floor, and **anchor into your body**, you interrupt that automatic pattern. You return to the present moment, and with that presence comes **the power to choose** how you show up.

Grounding deepens your **self-awareness** by helping you notice what you are actually feeling, not just what you are thinking. It supports **self-regulation**, allowing you to move from reaction to reflection. When you are grounded, you are more likely to pause before speaking, to listen deeply, and to respond with compassion, toward yourself and others. This grounded awareness enhances **empathy, resilience, and relational intelligence**. You are no longer swept away by the noise around you; you stand in the calm centre of your own truth. From that place, you can lead, connect, and live with integrity and emotional clarity. Every time you ground yourself, you reclaim choice, and with choice comes freedom, power, and presence.

The Neuroscience Of Stress And How Grounding Activates The Parasympathetic Nervous System

When you are under stress, whether from a deadline, an emotional trigger, a conflict, or even an old memory, your body responds instantly. Without you needing to think about it, your brain signals your nervous system to protect you. You may feel your heart race, your breath quicken, your muscles tighten, or your thoughts spiral.

This is your **sympathetic nervous system** kicking in: the part of your body designed to keep you alive through the **fight, flight, or freeze response**. This response is meant for short bursts of danger, but in your modern world, threats are not always physical. They are emotional, relational, digital, or imagined, and they can last all day. If you do not reset, your nervous system can stay stuck in overdrive. This is when you feel burned out, anxious, overwhelmed, disconnected, or numb.

Here is the good news: **your body also has a built-in healing mechanism,** your **parasympathetic nervous system**. This is your **rest, digest, and restore** mode. It slows your heart rate, deepens your breath, supports digestion, improves immune function, and calms your brain. When you ground yourself, you send a new signal to your brain: *"It is okay. I am safe now."* You do this by bringing your awareness back into your body:

- You feel your feet on the floor.

- You take a slow, intentional breath.

- You notice the sensation of your hand on your chest or belly.

- You orient your senses. What can you see, hear, feel?

These small acts may seem simple, but they **rewire your brain**. They activate your **prefrontal cortex,** the part of your mind responsible for awareness, compassion, decision-making, and self-regulation. When you ground yourself, you do not bypass stress, you **transform your relationship to it**. You become the calm in the storm. You reconnect with your body as a safe place, not just a container for tension, and from that calm space, you can think more clearly, feel more honestly, and choose how to move forward, on your terms. So the next time life feels too much, pause:

1. Ground yourself.

2. Feel your breath.

3. Feel the Earth beneath you.

Remember, you are not stuck in stress. You have the power to return to safety, clarity, and strength. This is the neuroscience of self-empowerment. This is the wisdom of grounding in action.

Integrating Grounding Into High-Performance Environments And Daily Rituals

Grounding is not just something you turn to in a crisis, it is a practice you can weave into the rhythm of your day, especially in **high-performance environments** where focus, clarity, and emotional balance are essential. Whether you are leading a team, presenting to stakeholders, managing clients, or studying under pressure, you are constantly being asked to perform, decide, and respond, and while your mind may be sharp, your **nervous system needs stability** to sustain excellence without burnout. That is where grounding becomes your secret edge.

When you integrate grounding into your daily rituals, you begin to **regulate your energy, sharpen your attention, and increase your emotional intelligence,** even in demanding situations.

Start with Small Anchors Throughout the Day

You do not need hours of meditation or a quiet retreat to ground yourself. You can build **micro-moments of reconnection** into your day:

- **Before a meeting** – Take 3 slow breaths. Feel your feet on the floor. Say quietly, *"I am present."*

- **When giving feedback** – Place one hand over your chest or stomach. Speak from grounded clarity, not reactivity.

- **After back-to-back calls or emails** – Stand, stretch, and breathe. Let the tension leave your shoulders and jaw.

- **At the start of your day** – Write a short intention like: *"I choose calm under pressure."*

These rituals do not interrupt performance, they **sustain it.** When you are grounded, you do not rush decisions. You do not get easily hijacked by stress. You speak with authority **without losing empathy**.

Why It Works in High-Performance Settings

Grounding activates your **prefrontal cortex**, allowing you to make smarter, more emotionally balanced decisions under pressure. It also quiets the noise of fear, perfectionism, and urgency, so you can lead, communicate, and execute with clarity. The more you practice, the more you train your nervous system to come back to balance quickly. Over time, you become the kind of person who can stay **calm in the storm**, adapt with grace, and lead others by your presence, not just your position.

<u>Grounding as a Leadership and Lifestyle Practice</u>

When you integrate grounding into your lifestyle, it is no longer just a tool, it becomes a way of being. You begin to show up **more present in your relationships, more attentive with your teams**, and **more connected to your own needs**. Grounding becomes the space between stimulus and response. It becomes your reset button, your pause, your return, and in high-performance environments, that makes all the difference. So whether you are navigating deadlines, studying under pressure, leading meetings, or managing emotional complexity, come back to your breath. Come back to your body. **Come back to the ground beneath you.**

Sensory Awareness Walk (Outdoor or Simulated)

I invite you to:

1. Walk slowly, paying close attention to the sensations in your feet, the pressure, texture, and rhythm of each step.

2. Tune into the sounds, smells, and textures around you, allowing each sense to awaken fully.

3. At intervals, pause, close your eyes if comfortable, and take three deep grounding breaths, feeling your body anchored in the present moment.

Debrief: After your walk, take a few minutes to reflect: *What emotions or insights emerged during your walk? How did your body feel? What changed in your mind or heart?*

Case Study Discussion: Lucas's Journey

After a lifetime of working long hours as a long–haul truck driver, and always being on the go, Lucas found himself in a state of constant stress and anxiety. He had tried everything from medication to therapy, but nothing seemed to work. One day, Lucas contacted me and after 3–4 weeks I chatted with him about trying grounding. I asked Lucas to connect with the earth's natural energy by walking barefoot or lying on the ground. At first, Lucas was highly skeptical, but he decided to give it a try.

Lucas took off his shoes and walked on the grass in his backyard, feeling the cool blades between his toes. As he walked, he focused on his breath and let his mind clear. He felt a sense of calm and peace within him that he had not experienced in years. From that day forward, Lucas made grounding a daily practice. He spent time in nature, whether it was walking barefoot on the beach or lying in a park. Lucas found that his stress and anxiety levels decreased significantly, and he felt more balanced and centred in his life. He also discovered that grounding had other benefits. He felt more connected to the world around him and more in tune with his own emotions (this was massive for Lucas).

Lucas began to appreciate the small moments of beauty and joy that he had previously overlooked. He felt more present in the moment and was able to connect with others on a deeper level. He also found that he had more energy and focus for the things that truly mattered to him. Lucas realised that grounding was not a cure–all, but it was an important tool in his toolbox for managing stress and anxiety. It was something that he could always turn to when he needed to find balance in his life.

Reflective Exercise: Lucas's Journey

Here are four profound and reflective questions inspired by Lucas's story to help you engage with your own grounding journey:

1. When was the last time you allowed the earth to hold you, without rushing, fixing, or thinking?

Reflection: Like Lucas, you may have spent much of your life in motion, driven by responsibility, pressure, or habit, but grounding reminds you that rest is not weakness; it is wisdom. When you let yourself slow down, even for a few moments, you invite in calm, clarity, and healing that your body has longed for.

2. What would it feel like to reconnect with the ground beneath your feet, not just physically, but emotionally?

Reflection: Your body knows how to return home to presence. Each breath, each barefoot step, each moment of stillness is a pathway back to your centre. When you take time to ground, you give your nervous system the safety it needs to regulate, and your heart the space it needs to soften.

3. Where in your day do you most need a pause, a moment to breathe, feel, and return to yourself?

Reflection: Lucas found that a few minutes barefoot in the grass changed everything. You do not need perfect conditions, just a willingness to pause. These micro-moments of grounding can become sacred rituals that restore your energy, reduce anxiety, and remind you that you are not just surviving, you are allowed to feel alive.

4. What might open up for you if you truly believed that you are supported, by the ground, by the moment, by life itself?

Reflection: Grounding is not just a technique, it is a shift in trust. It is the quiet knowing that you do not have to carry everything alone. Just like Lucas, you can find stability not by gripping harder, but by surrendering to what's already holding you. The ground is always there. So is your breath. So are you.

Affirmations For Integration: (Heart Whispers)

Affirmations have the power to quiet the noise of doubt, open the doorway to self-trust, and draw you back into the wisdom of your heart. When practised daily, they nurture an inner dialogue based in love and truth, helping you live each day more aligned with who you truly are. I invite you to repeat silently or write:

- *I feel more centred and calmer after grounding exercises.*

- *I notice a decrease in anxiety when I practice grounding.*

- *I am more in tune with my body when I ground myself.*

- *I find it easier to focus on the present moment with grounding.*

- *I feel more connected to the earth when I practice grounding.*

- *I release tension more easily when I practice grounding.*

- *Grounding helps me respond to challenges with greater clarity and patience.*

- *My thoughts feel more organised and steady after grounding.*

- *Grounding reconnects me to my inner strength and stability.*

Optional Extension Activity

Here are **3 original grounding exercises**. Each exercise includes **three parts,** a physical action, a mindful practice, and a heart-centred integration:

Exercise 1: Tree Lean + Grounding Intention + Heart Touch

1. Tree Lean: Stand or sit with your back gently resting against a tree or solid wall. Feel the support behind you and allow your body to relax into it. Let the earth carry your weight.

2. Grounding Intention: Silently repeat an intention such as: *"I am safe. I am supported. I am here."* Let this intention settle into your body like roots beneath the surface.

3. Heart Touch: Place one hand on your heart and the other on your belly. Breathe slowly. With each breath, invite yourself to feel grounded, present, and connected to the now.

Exercise 2: Stone Hold + Stillness Scan + Anchoring Phrase

1. Stone Hold: Find a small stone or natural object. Hold it in your palm and observe its weight, texture, and temperature. Let it represent steadiness in your life.

2. Stillness Scan: Close your eyes and scan your body slowly from head to toe. Notice where tension lives and where ease flows. Stay curious, not critical.

3. Anchoring Phrase: Repeat quietly: *"In this moment, I return to myself."* Feel the energy of the stone and your breath grounding you into your inner calm.

Exercise 3: Spiral Walk + Sensory Awareness + Grounded Statement

1. Spiral Walk: Mark a small spiral pattern in the sand, grass, or with objects. Slowly walk the spiral path inward. With each step, let go of distraction or stress.

2. Sensory Awareness: Pause in the centre. Tune into 3 things you can feel, 3 sounds you can hear, and 3 natural elements around you. Let your senses awaken presence.

3. Grounded Statement: Say softly to yourself: *"I am grounded. I belong to* *this earth. I am at peace."* Then walk the spiral path back out with renewed focus.

Closing Reflection

As you come to the end of this part of your journey, remember: grounding is not something outside of you, it is within you, always. When life feels too fast, too loud, or too much, you can pause. You can feel your breath. You can feel the ground beneath your feet. You are **not** lost. You are not disconnected. You are simply being called back to the place you never truly left, **your body, your breath, your being**. Grounding is a quiet act of power. It brings you back into the present, where peace begins, where clarity returns, where your heart can speak again. No matter what is happening around you, you now have a way to return home to yourself. So take this with you:

- **You are safe to pause.**

- **You are safe to feel.**

- **You are safe to come back to now.**

Let every step forward be grounded in presence. Let every breath remind you, you are here, and that is enough.

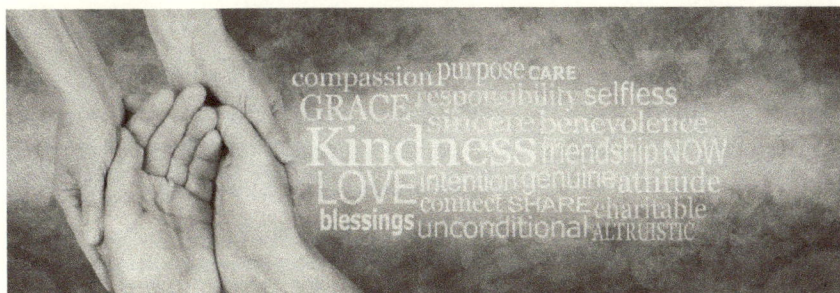

12 - KINDNESS

Your Opening Reflection

Invitation to Kindness - As you enter this chapter, I invite you to soften your heart toward yourself. Let go of the urge to strive or judge, and instead welcome the gentleness that kindness offers. Imagine speaking to yourself the way you would to someone you deeply love, with tenderness, patience, and compassion. This is your chance to practice kindness not as a fleeting act, but as a way of being, beginning with how you meet yourself in this very moment.

- "When was the last time you were truly kind to yourself?"

- "What does kindness toward yourself look and feel like in your daily life?"

- "When you think of being kind to others, do you extend the same grace to yourself?"

- "What beliefs or habits sometimes stop you from treating yourself with kindness?"

- "How does your body respond when you speak to yourself with compassion instead of criticism?"

- "If a loved one were in your shoes today, how would you show them kindness, and can you offer that to yourself?"

Let these questions open the doorway into presence. Every answer you give, whether in words, sensations, or silence, is a bridge between where you are and where you are going.

Learning Objectives

The learning objectives are included here to give you a clear focus for this chapter, ensuring that each practice you explore moves you closer to mastering the skills, insights, and heart-led awareness that will enrich your life well beyond the program. By the end of this chapter, you will:

- Understand the emotional and relational impact of kindness on yourself and others.

- Explore the role of kindness in building emotional resilience and connection.

- Practice self-kindness as a foundation for empathy and compassion.

- Identify opportunities to integrate kindness into your everyday choices.

- Recognise kindness as a transformative force for living a heart-led life.

Core Emotional Domains

The core emotional intelligence domains covered here are essential because they form the foundation for lasting heart connection, guiding you to deepen self-awareness, regulate emotions, build resilience, and strengthen the mind-body bond throughout your Heart Unbound journey.

- **Self-Awareness:** Kindness invites you to pause and notice your internal state, your emotions, assumptions, and judgments, so you can choose to respond with intention and care.

- **Empathy:** By practicing kindness, you attune more deeply to the emotions and needs of others, strengthening your ability to connect, listen, and relate with compassion.

- **Self-Regulation:** In moments of tension, kindness helps you shift from reactivity to presence. It softens harsh responses and creates space for grace under pressure.

- **Social Skills:** Kindness enhances your ability to build trust, nurture meaningful relationships, and create emotionally safe environments where others feel seen and valued.

- **Motivation (Intrinsic Growth through Compassion):** When guided by kindness, your growth becomes heart-led. You are motivated not by external rewards, but by the joy of contributing, uplifting, and embodying your values.

"Kindness – Gentle Strength In Action"

Kindness is more than a moral virtue, it is a transformative emotional intelligence practice that awakens connection, inner strength, and authentic leadership. In today's fast-paced, outcome-driven world, kindness is often misunderstood as soft or passive, but in truth, kindness is courageous. It takes strength to slow down, to listen, and to respond with compassion when reacting with criticism would be easier. It requires emotional maturity to stay grounded in empathy, even when you are under pressure or facing misunderstanding.

Kindness begins within. It starts with your willingness to speak gently to yourself, to forgive your own missteps, and to create space for growth without harshness. This inner kindness builds a **healthy, grounded sense of self-worth,** not based on how much you achieve, but on how deeply you honour your own humanity. From that space, kindness naturally extends outward. It becomes the bridge between you and others, enhancing your ability to understand their needs, emotions, and perspectives.

You become more attuned in conversation, more responsive in conflict, and more intentional in your presence. This nurtures trust, strengthens relationships, and develops emotional safety, core foundations of **social intelligence**. In leadership, whether you lead a team, a classroom, a family, or your own life, kindness becomes a guiding force. It does not dilute effectiveness; it amplifies it. When you lead with kindness, people feel seen, respected, and inspired. Your influence grows not through control, but through care. Ultimately, kindness is not something you perform. It is something you embody. It shapes how you live, relate, and serve. It invites you to return to the heart again and again, to respond to life not from fear or ego, but from empathy, integrity, and compassion. *Kindness is a practice. Kindness is power. Kindness is the courage to lead, live, and love with humanity.*

Kindness As An Emotional Regulation Tool

Kindness is not just an outward gesture, it is a powerful internal mechanism for emotional regulation. When you choose to respond with kindness, especially in emotionally charged situations, you activate parts of your brain associated with empathy, connection, and calm. This helps to quiet the amygdala, your brain's threat detector, and reduces the fight, flight, or freeze response that often fuels reactivity, defensiveness, or aggression.

When you are overwhelmed or frustrated, pausing to practice kindness, toward yourself or others, creates a physiological and psychological shift. It lowers your cortisol (the stress hormone), slows your heart rate, and brings your nervous system back into balance. This allows you to move from reaction to reflection, from anger to curiosity, from fear to care. Importantly, kindness does not mean ignoring boundaries or denying difficult feelings. Instead, it invites you to meet those emotions with gentleness, compassion, and self-awareness.

Whether you are speaking kindly to yourself during moments of shame or extending grace to someone who has hurt you, kindness becomes a choice to stay regulated and present. Over time, using kindness as a regulation tool strengthens your resilience. It builds your inner muscle to stay grounded under pressure, to repair relationships with humility, and to speak truth without harm. It becomes a steady anchor that helps you navigate life with clarity, connection, and emotional maturity. In this way, kindness is not just a reaction, it is a conscious practice of returning to your centre, softening your edges, and choosing the heart over the impulse.

The Neuroscience Of Kindness: Oxytocin, Serotonin, And Social Bonding

Kindness does not just feel good, it is wired into your brain and body as a deeply healing and connecting experience. When you offer or receive a kind gesture, a cascade of neurochemical activity is activated that supports emotional wellbeing, resilience, and human connection.

Oxytocin - The *"Connection Hormone"*

Oxytocin is often called the *love* or *bonding hormone*. Acts of kindness, like a warm smile, a thoughtful message, or a compassionate touch, stimulate the release of oxytocin. This hormone promotes trust, emotional openness, and social bonding. It reduces stress, lowers blood pressure, and creates a sense of safety. In both giver and receiver, oxytocin enhances feelings of closeness and belonging, reinforcing positive social behaviours.

When you consciously engage in acts of kindness, you are not only nurturing someone else's wellbeing, you are also nourishing your own body and mind at a biological level. Oxytocin does not just make you feel connected, it strengthens your ability to empathise, to listen deeply, and to respond with compassion, even in moments of tension. Over time, these small but powerful hormonal boosts create a feedback loop: the more kindness you give and receive, the more naturally your heart opens, and the more your relationships flourish with trust, warmth, and authenticity.

Serotonin - The Mood Stabiliser

Serotonin plays a key role in regulating your mood, satisfaction, and emotional stability. When you engage in kind, generous behaviour, serotonin levels rise, creating a sense of calm, optimism, and inner balance. Serotonin also contributes to resilience, helping you handle challenges with greater equanimity. Kindness becomes a self-reinforcing practice, boosting your mood while improving your perception of social interactions.

As serotonin levels increase, your brain naturally begins to associate kindness with safety and wellbeing, making it more likely that you will repeat those behaviours. Over time, this creates an upward spiral, small acts of kindness not only brighten the moment but also strengthen your long-term emotional stability. By actively cultivating kindness, you are building a mental and emotional foundation that supports patience, perspective, and a steady inner peace, even when external circumstances are uncertain or stressful.

The Kindness Feedback Loop

Neuroscientists have identified a positive feedback loop: when you perform an act of kindness, you feel good, which makes you more likely to be kind again. This cycle builds emotional intelligence, strengthens neural pathways for empathy, and develops long-term wellbeing. Repeated kindness reinforces patterns in the brain that promote connection, trust, and cooperative behaviour.

Over time, this feedback loop becomes self-sustaining. The more kindness you practice, the more your brain associates generosity with personal reward and emotional fulfilment. Even small acts, holding a door open, offering a genuine compliment, or listening without judgment, can trigger this cycle. With consistent repetition, your capacity for empathy and compassion deepens, creating a ripple effect that not only enhances your own mental health but also contributes to a more caring and cooperative environment around you.

Kindness and Social Bonding

Humans are social beings, and kindness acts as a bridge between nervous systems. Brain imaging studies show that giving and receiving kindness activates reward centres in the brain, particularly the **ventromedial**

prefrontal cortex, an area associated with value-based decisions and social connection. This neurological activity reinforces shared humanity, building stronger personal and community relationships. **In essence**, kindness is not only an emotional or moral virtue, it is a biological imperative. It is a neurochemical strategy for your wellbeing, resilience, and belonging. When you practice kindness regularly, you are not only helping others, you are reshaping your brain, regulating your emotions, and becoming more deeply connected to yourself and the world around you.

When you engage in acts of kindness, whether through a simple smile, a listening ear, or a generous act, you are essentially participating in a shared biological dance. Your brain and body synchronise with others in a subtle but profound way, creating a sense of safety and mutual trust. Over time, this builds a reservoir of goodwill that strengthens not only your personal connections but also the collective wellbeing of the groups you belong to. This shared kindness becomes contagious, inspiring others to act with compassion, thus creating a ripple effect that extends far beyond the initial moment of generosity.

Historical And Spiritual Foundations Of Kindness Across Traditions

Kindness is not a modern invention, it is a timeless principle based deeply in the wisdom traditions, philosophies, and spiritual teachings of cultures across the world. From ancient scriptures to oral traditions, acts of compassion and benevolence have long been recognised as both sacred duty and powerful pathways to personal and collective transformation.

Christianity

In the Christian tradition, kindness is a core fruit of the Spirit (Galatians 5:22–23) and a central commandment. Jesus' teachings consistently emphasise mercy, love for one's neighbour, and forgiveness. The parable of the Good Samaritan embodies kindness beyond boundaries of race or religion, showing that true compassion is unconditional. Christians are taught that to be kind is to reflect the nature of God: *"Be kind and compassionate to one another, forgiving each other, just as in Christ God forgave you"* (Ephesians 4:32).

Hinduism

In Hindu philosophy, kindness is expressed through the principle of **ahimsa**, or non-violence. Based in the Vedas and embraced by sages like Mahatma

Gandhi, ahimsa extends beyond refraining from harm to actively choosing compassion in thoughts, words, and deeds. Acts of kindness are seen as expressions of **dharma,** right action, and contribute to the spiritual growth of both giver and receiver.

Buddhism

Buddhist teachings place **metta,** or loving-kindness, at the heart of spiritual practice. Metta meditation involves sending intentions of goodwill to oneself and all beings, even those who are difficult to love. The Buddha taught that cultivating loving-kindness dissolves anger, softens the heart, and leads to liberation from suffering. Kindness is not seen as passive, it is courageous, conscious, and transformative.

Judaism

In Judaism, kindness is a form of **chesed,** a covenantal love and steadfast kindness that mirrors God's relationship with humanity. The Torah is filled with injunctions to care for the widow, the orphan, and the stranger, making kindness a divine command and a social responsibility. The Talmud teaches: *"The world is built on kindness"* (Psalm 89:2), affirming its role in sustaining communities and spiritual life.

Islam

In Islam, kindness is both a spiritual virtue and a daily obligation. The Prophet Muhammad (peace be upon him) said, *"Kindness is a mark of faith, and whoever is not kind has no faith."* The Qur'an urges believers to respond to evil with good, and to treat others with mercy, even when they differ. Allah is described as **Ar-Rahman, Ar-Rahim,** the Most Compassionate, the Most Merciful, encouraging Muslims to embody divine compassion in all interactions.

Indigenous and Earth-Based Traditions

Across Indigenous cultures, kindness is intimately woven into the fabric of life. It is expressed through **reciprocity,** giving back to the Earth, to the ancestors, and to one's community with humility and gratitude. In many traditions, elders teach that kindness is not optional but essential for harmony and survival. It is a sacred duty to walk gently, speak with care, and uphold the dignity of all beings.

A Shared Moral Thread

Though cultures and languages differ, the essence of kindness remains remarkably universal. Whether called **karuna**, **chesed**, **metta**, or **compassion**, it reflects the deep human understanding that love, empathy, and care are essential for both spiritual growth and societal wellbeing. To live kindly is to participate in the ancient rhythm of humanity, one that honours dignity, connection, and the sacredness of life. When you choose kindness, you are not just following a personal value, you are stepping into a global, intergenerational legacy of healing, hope, and heart.

Kindness To Others *And* Self As A Path To Wholeness

Kindness is often celebrated as a virtue we extend outward, but its true power lies in its ability to transform us from within. When you choose kindness, not only toward others but also toward yourself, you are actively participating in your own healing and integration. Kindness becomes a bridge, from fragmentation to wholeness, from harshness to harmony.

To Others: Building Bridges of Belonging

When you act kindly toward others, you affirm their worth and humanity. Simple acts, listening deeply, offering help, speaking gently, send the message: *You matter. You are seen.* In a world that often feels disconnected or competitive, kindness restores trust. It creates spaces of psychological safety, encourages cooperation, and strengthens bonds of empathy and belonging. You begin to realise that your kindness is not a gift from a place of superiority, it is a mutual recognition of shared vulnerability, and in that mutual recognition, something powerful happens: you see yourself in the other. Compassion is no longer abstract. It becomes the language of your heart.

To Yourself: Returning to Inner Safety

True wholeness cannot be achieved if you only extend kindness outward while withholding it from yourself. Many of us are our own harshest critics. We replay mistakes, dwell in guilt, or measure ourselves against impossible standards, but when you learn to speak to yourself with gentleness, to say *"It is okay,"* *"I am doing my best,"* or *"I deserve rest"*, you shift the entire tone of your inner world. Kindness to self softens inner rigidity. It welcomes your imperfections and reminds you that healing is not linear. It creates space for rest, recovery, and renewal. It is not indulgent, it is intelligent, because when you are kind to yourself, you are more resilient, more present, and more capable of showing up fully for others.

<u>The Healing Synergy</u>

Kindness creates a feedback loop between your self and others. When you offer compassion outward, you are more likely to internalise it. When you nurture yourself, you are more grounded and generous in how you relate to the world. This synergy creates emotional intelligence, relational depth, and a grounded sense of purpose. Wholeness is not about perfection. It is about integration, bringing all parts of yourself, including your wounds, into the light of compassion. Kindness is the light. It does not fix everything instantly, but it melts what is frozen, mends what is torn, and reconnects what has been lost.

Kindness In High-Performance, High-Pressure Environments

<u>Kindness Builds Stronger Teams</u>

In high-pressure environments, the temptation to isolate, micromanage, or push harder can backfire. Kindness enables psychological safety, an environment where people feel comfortable expressing concerns, making mistakes, and being human. This is the foundation of high-functioning teams. When kindness is practiced through active listening, genuine recognition, or supportive feedback, teams become more cohesive, adaptive, and innovative.

Kindness also develops mutual trust, which strengthens collaboration and reduces conflict. When you lead with empathy and offer encouragement instead of criticism, you invite others to bring their best ideas forward without fear of judgment. This not only boosts morale but also inspires creativity and problem-solving. In moments of stress or uncertainty, your kindness becomes a stabilising force, reminding your team that they are valued as people, not just as performers. Over time, this builds a resilient, connected culture where everyone feels invested in shared success.

<u>Kindness to Self: Preventing Burnout</u>

High achievers often extend compassion to others but struggle to show it to themselves. Overwork becomes a badge of honour, and self-kindness is mistaken for weakness. Yet, research consistently shows that self-compassion enhances motivation, perseverance, and wellbeing. In high-stakes roles, self-kindness is not a luxury, it is a lifeline. When you treat yourself with understanding rather than criticism during times of failure or fatigue, you recover faster and return stronger.

By practicing kindness toward yourself, you build an inner foundation that can weather pressure without collapsing. You give yourself permission to rest, recharge, and reflect without guilt, allowing your mind and body to heal. This compassionate self-awareness helps you sustain your passion, sharpen your focus, and approach challenges with clarity instead of depletion. When you honour your own needs, you are not only preserving your energy, you are also modelling to others that resilience is built through care, not constant strain.

Kindness as a Leadership Imperative

Great leaders do not just demand results, they create conditions where people thrive. Kindness in leadership is not about being permissive or avoiding hard conversations. It is about delivering truth with humanity, making decisions with integrity, and recognising the inherent dignity in every team member. In the long run, kindness sustains performance by fuelling loyalty, engagement, and purpose. In high-performance environments, kindness is not an afterthought or a sign of weakness. It is a conscious choice that strengthens culture, enhances outcomes, and builds resilient, emotionally intelligent people. *When pressure rises, let kindness lead. It is both your edge and your anchor.*

When you embody kindness as a leader, you set a tone that ripples through the entire organisation. Your example invites openness, develops mutual respect, and encourages others to step into their best selves. You create a climate where people feel valued for more than just their output, and as a result, they give more of themselves, not out of fear or obligation, but out of genuine commitment. This type of leadership does not just achieve short-term goals; it nurtures long-term growth, trust, and loyalty that endure far beyond any single project or performance review.

Forgiveness Exercise: *"The Mirror of Gentle Words"*

Purpose: To cultivate self-kindness and rewire the internal dialogue through embodied practice, this gentle exercise helps you see yourself with compassion and speak to yourself as a trusted friend would.

Step 1: *Speak 3 Kind Truths Aloud (2 minutes)*

Say three heartfelt affirmations to yourself, slowly and aloud. Choose from these or create your own:

- *"I am learning to love myself."*

- *"I am doing the best I can, and that is enough."*

- *"I deserve kindness, especially from myself."*

Let your words settle into your heart. If emotions rise, allow them to move through you gently.

Step 2: *Write a Letter to Yourself (5 minutes)*

Using a journal, write a short note to yourself as if you were writing to someone you deeply care about. Start with:

"Dear [Your Name], I want you to know…"

Let kindness guide your pen. No need to fix or change anything, just witness yourself with love.

Integration Reflection

Kindness to yourself is not indulgence, it is nourishment. This practice grounds you in compassion and begins to replace old inner criticism with acceptance and truth. Repeat this ritual as needed, especially on days when your heart feels tender or unseen.

Case Study Discussion: Isabella's Journey

Isabella was always there for others. She was the first to offer help and the last to leave when someone needed her. She was kind, compassionate and caring, but she had a hard time showing that same kindness to herself. Isabella self–talk was brutal, constantly telling herself that she was not good enough, smart enough or pretty enough.

Isabella felt that she was not worthy and did not deserve kindness or love from herself or anyone. Over time in our sessions, Isabella realised that she could not keep giving to others if she did not give to herself. She started by practicing self–compassion and self–care. She began to treat herself with the same kindness and respect she showed to others.

It was not easy for her at first, but with practice, she started to change the way she talked to herself and the way she treated herself. As Isabella's heart opened up to kindness, she began to see and feel into herself differently. She started to believe that she was lovable, just as she was.

Isabella discovered that showing herself kindness allowed her to be more patient, understanding, and accepting of others. Her relationships with her family and friends deepened, and she felt more connected to the people around her. Isabella learned that kindness started with herself.

She had to be kind to herself before she could be truly kind to others. She realised that she had to fill her own cup before she could pour into others. By gifting kindness to herself, Isabella was able to live a more heart–led life, where love and compassion flowed freely. Today, Isabella continues to practice self–kindness and uses her experience to help others who may be struggling with the same issues she once faced. She knows that living a heart–led life means being kind to yourself and others, and that kindness is the key to unlocking a life full of love and joy.

Reflective Exercise: Isabella's Journey

Here are four profound and reflective questions inspired by Isabella's story to help you engage with your own kindness journey:

1. **What would change if you spoke to yourself with the same compassion you offer others?** *Reflection:* You often give others grace, comfort, and encouragement, but what if you gave that same gift to yourself? Your inner voice shapes your emotional landscape. When you soften it with kindness, you create space for healing, growth, and joy. You become your own ally, not your harshest critic.

2. **When was the last time you truly acknowledged your own worth?** *Reflection:* Worthiness is not something you earn, it is something you already possess. Like Isabella, you may have learned to be kind to others while overlooking yourself, but you deserve love, rest, and recognition. Your value is not conditional. Begin by honouring yourself, gently and consistently.

3. **In what ways has withholding kindness from yourself affected your ability to give it freely to others?** *Reflection:* You cannot pour from an empty cup. If your self-kindness is lacking, giving to others may start to feel exhausting or transactional, but when you fill your heart with compassion for yourself, you do not run dry you overflow. True kindness is sustainable when it starts within.

4. **What daily ritual could help you nurture self-kindness as a way of life?** *Reflection:* Self-kindness does not require grand gestures, it lives

---

in your small, intentional choices: how you speak to yourself in the mirror, how you rest, how you forgive your mistakes.

Start simple. Let kindness become a habit, a rhythm, a sacred return to your heart each day.

These questions and reflections are designed to gently guide you inward, to recognise that kindness is not only what you give, but also what you allow yourself to receive. Like Isabella, you too can open your heart to yourself and live more freely, more fully, and more compassionately.

Affirmations For Integration: (Heart Whispers)

Affirmations have the power to quiet the noise of doubt, open the doorway to self-trust, and draw you back into the wisdom of your heart. When practised daily, they nurture an inner dialogue based in love and truth, helping you live each day more aligned with who you truly are. I invite you to repeat silently or write:

- *I show kindness to everyone I meet.*

- *I believe in the power of kindness.*

- *I feel happy when I show kindness to others.*

- *I practice self–kindness every day.*

- *I believe that kindness can change the world.*

- *I feel grateful for acts of kindness shown to me.*

- *I choose kindness even in challenging situations.*

- *I create a ripple of kindness wherever I go.*

The Kindness Ripple Exercise:

I invite you to commit to one small act of kindness for yourself and one for someone else over the next 24 hours. Write it down, reflect on intention, and share with a partner if comfortable. Example acts:

- Writing a forgiveness letter to yourself

- Paying for someone's coffee

- Setting a firm but loving boundary

- Saying something kind to yourself in the mirror

When you consciously choose and act on kindness, you plant a seed that can grow far beyond the moment. The person you help may go on to help someone else, and the kindness you show yourself may inspire deeper self-respect and healthier boundaries in the days ahead. In this way, even the smallest gesture can ripple through lives, touching people you may never meet and creating waves of compassion that extend far beyond your immediate circle.

Closing Reflection

In a world that often glorifies speed, achievement, and self-interest, your choice to slow down and lead with compassion is not just countercultural, it is a profound act of strength. It is the decision to be a source of light in a landscape that can sometimes feel cold and unyielding. Today, as you have reflected on kindness, toward others and, perhaps most importantly, toward yourself, remember this: the gentleness you offer yourself becomes fertile soil. From that soil, your empathy blossoms, your patience deepens, and your courage takes root. This is where true resilience grows, not in the relentless pushing, but in the tender tending of your own heart.

When you choose to soften instead of harde. When you speak to yourself with care instead of criticis. When you see others not as threats, but as fellow humans doing their best. You create ripples of healing, connection, and peace, not just for others, but for yourself. Kindness is not a task to check off; it is a way of moving through the world. Carry it forward as a steady rhythm in your words, in your actions, in your pauses, and in your presence.

Let kindness shape your relationships, your work, and the way you see the world. Let kindness be your anchor in storms and your light in darkness. Let it be the language your heart speaks, in quiet moments, in challenging moments, in every moment, to every soul you meet, including your own, and as you live this way, you may discover something extraordinary: kindness not only changes the lives it touches, it transforms the one who gives it most of all.

13 – GOD/THE DIVINE

Your Opening Reflection

Invitation to the Sacred - As you begin this chapter, I invite you to open your heart to mystery. Release the need to define or control what *"God/The Divine"* means, and instead allow yourself to experience the sacred in your own way, through silence, through wonder, through love. Let this be a gentle homecoming, a moment to rest in the presence that has always been with you, guiding, holding, and whispering through every breath of your life.

- "What does 'God/The Divine' or a higher presence mean to you, and how do you experience it, if at all?"

- "When you pause in stillness, do you sense a presence greater than yourself, and how does it speak to you through silence, intuition, or the world around you?"

- "In moments of joy, suffering, or awe, do you feel a connection to something eternal, and how does that shape your understanding of life's meaning?"

- "Do you experience 'God/The Divine' as a being, an energy, a mystery, or simply the love that binds all things together?"

- "When you act with kindness, forgiveness, or courage, do you feel that you are participating in something sacred?"

- "How do your experiences of faith, doubt, or wonder influence the way you imagine and relate to the divine?"

Let these questions open the doorway into presence. Every answer you give, whether in words, sensations, or silence, is a bridge between where you are and where you are going.

Learning Objectives

The learning objectives are included here to give you a clear focus for this chapter, ensuring that each practice you explore moves you closer to mastering the skills, insights, and heart-led awareness that will enrich your life well beyond the program. By the end of this chapter, you will:

- Understand the role of spiritual connection in emotional and heart-centred well-being.

- Reflect on your personal relationship with the divine (in any form meaningful to you).

- Recognise how belief in something greater than yourself cultivates peace, purpose, and compassion.

- Practice simple daily habits that open your heart to divine presence.

- Respect the diverse expressions of divinity across traditions and individuals.

Core Emotional Domains

The core emotional intelligence domains covered here are essential because they form the foundation for lasting heart connection, guiding you to deepen self-awareness, regulate emotions, build resilience, and strengthen the mind-body bond throughout your Heart Unbound journey.

- **Self-Awareness:** Deepening your spiritual connection helps you become more attuned to your inner world, your thoughts, emotions, and beliefs, guiding you toward greater authenticity.

- **Empathy and Compassion:** A heart open to divine presence naturally extends compassion and grace, not only to others, but also to yourself.

- **Emotional Self-Regulation:** Spiritual reflection creates space for stillness, helping you respond to life's challenges with peace, trust, and inner calm.

- **Motivation (Purpose, Meaning):** Connection with God/The Divine, or your higher source, awakens a sense of purpose and reminds you that your life is part of something greater than yourself.

- **Social Awareness (Interconnectedness):** Spiritual intelligence cultivates a deep awareness of our shared humanity, fostering humility, unity, and respect for the sacred in all.

"God/The Divine – Connecting To The Sacred Within"

Throughout history and across every culture, human beings have instinctively reached beyond themselves in search of something greater, something sacred, eternal, and deeply meaningful. This universal yearning may take many forms: kneeling in prayer, gazing at the stars in silent wonder, standing in awe before a sunrise, sitting in stillness through meditation, or showing love in everyday acts of compassion and care. At its core, this sacred longing is not just spiritual, it is deeply emotional and profoundly human. It reminds you that you are part of something larger than your individual story. Whether you name it God, the Universe, the Divine, or simply Love, this connection nurtures **humility**, grounding you in the truth that you are not the centre of the universe, but a beloved part of its great unfolding.

It also strengthens **resilience**, offering hope in hardship and anchoring you in meaning during times of uncertainty. When you remember there is purpose beyond the pain, you begin to rise again. Through sacred connection, your **empathy** expands. You begin to see others not as strangers, but as reflections of the same Source, each one sacred, each one worthy of care, and through this reverence, your **heart connection** deepens. You begin to live from a place of inner stillness, compassion, and trust. This sacred yearning isn't something you must earn. It is already within you. A quiet call to return home to your deepest self, and to something timeless, vast, and whole.

The Emotional And Psychological Benefits Of Spiritual Connection

Spiritual connection offers profound emotional and psychological benefits that go far beyond traditional religious practice, it nourishes the whole person, touching the mind, heart, and soul. Whether you experience this connection through faith, nature, meditation, community, or inner contemplation, the act of relating to something greater than yourself creates an internal shift that creates both peace and resilience.

Emotionally, spiritual connection provides a safe and grounding sense of meaning. When life feels uncertain or painful, your spiritual beliefs or practices can become a source of comfort, reminding you that your challenges are not the end of the story. This sense of perspective reduces anxiety and fear by anchoring you in trust, surrender, and hope.

Psychologically, spiritual connection supports mental clarity, emotional regulation, and greater self-awareness. Practices such as prayer, meditation, or mindful presence engage the parasympathetic nervous system, which helps to lower cortisol, ease emotional reactivity, and quiet the mind. Over time, these practices can reduce symptoms of stress, depression, and trauma by creating space for inner calm and reflection.

Spirituality also enhances **resilience**. When you are spiritually connected, you are more likely to bounce back from life's difficulties with a sense of purpose and inner strength. You begin to ask deeper questions:

- *What can this teach me?*

- *How can I grow?*

- *What is the deeper meaning beneath this experience?*

These questions open the heart to transformation rather than despair. Moreover, spiritual connection cultivates **empathy, compassion, and belonging**. Whether in community or solitude, it invites you to see yourself as part of a greater whole. You feel less alone, more held, more loved, and in that space, your emotional world softens and expands, making room for forgiveness, grace, and hope. In essence, spiritual connection is not an escape from life, but a deepening into it. It is where your emotional well-being and your inner truth meet, a sanctuary for the soul in the storms of being human.

The Role Of God/The Divine Presence In Navigating Uncertainty And Meaning

In times of uncertainty, loss, transition, or emotional upheaval, the presence of God, or a divine presence, however you understand it, can become a profound anchor. It offers a source of **meaning, comfort, and strength** that transcends logic or circumstance. When the path ahead is unclear or life feels out of control, turning toward a higher power often provides the reassurance that you are not alone, and that there is a deeper order even amidst apparent chaos.

This sense of divine connection offers more than just hope, it provides a **framework for meaning-making**. Rather than seeing challenges as random or punitive, you begin to perceive them as opportunities for growth, refinement, and transformation. A divine presence invites you to ask *"What is this teaching me?"* rather than *"Why is this happening to me?"* That shift can be life-changing. God, or divine presence, is also experienced as **a companion through suffering**. Whether through prayer, meditation, scripture, nature, or sacred silence, many find solace in the belief that they are held, heard, and guided by something greater than themselves. This connection often lessens feelings of fear and isolation and cultivates **trust in the unknown,** a trust that allows you to keep moving forward even when you cannot see the full picture. Spiritually grounded people often describe this presence as **an inner light or quiet strength**, helping them stay centred in the storm.

In this way, faith or spiritual connection becomes not a crutch, but a **compass,** a guide that helps you stay aligned with your deeper values, intuition, and purpose, especially when external circumstances are turbulent. Ultimately, divine presence helps you live with **open-heartedness rather than tight control**, allowing life to unfold with more grace and surrender. It becomes a wellspring of inner peace, courage, and clarity, helping you hold paradox, navigate uncertainty, and find sacred meaning in every chapter of your journey.

The Impact Of Faith On Healing, Forgiveness, And Service

In times of uncertainty, loss, transition, or emotional upheaval, the presence of God, or a divine presence, however you understand it, can become a profound anchor. It offers a source of **meaning, comfort, and strength** that transcends logic or circumstance. When the path ahead is unclear or life feels out of control, turning toward a higher power often provides the reassurance that you are not alone, and that there is a deeper order even amidst apparent chaos.

This sense of divine connection offers more than just hope, it provides a **framework for meaning-making**. Rather than seeing challenges as random or punitive, you begin to perceive them as opportunities for growth, refinement, and transformation. A divine presence invites you to ask *"What is this teaching me?"* rather than *"Why is this happening to me?"* That shift can be life-changing. God, or divine presence, is also experienced as **a companion through suffering**. Whether through prayer, meditation, scripture, nature, or sacred silence, many find solace in the belief that they are held, heard, and guided by something greater than themselves.

This connection often lessens feelings of fear and isolation and cultivates **trust in the unknown,** a trust that allows you to keep moving forward even when you cannot see the full picture. Spiritually grounded people often describe this presence as **an inner light or quiet strength**, helping them stay centred in the storm. In this way, faith or spiritual connection becomes not a crutch, but a **compass,** a guide that helps you stay aligned with your deeper values, intuition, and purpose, especially when external circumstances are turbulent. Ultimately, divine presence helps you live with **open-heartedness rather than tight control**, allowing life to unfold with more grace and surrender. It becomes a wellspring of inner peace, courage, and clarity, helping you hold paradox, navigate uncertainty, and find sacred meaning in every chapter of your journey.

Historical Wisdom Traditions And Their Emphasis On Divine Connection

Across human history, nearly every wisdom tradition has placed divine connection at the heart of emotional, moral, and communal life. From ancient civilisations to modern contemplative paths, the longing to commune with something greater than oneself has been a guiding force for personal transformation, social order, and spiritual insight.

In Ancient Egypt, divine connection was woven into everyday life through ritual and reverence for the gods who governed cosmic order. Life was seen as sacred, and aligning one's actions with the divine (Ma'at) brought harmony and balance.

In Indigenous traditions, the divine is not distant, but deeply intertwined with the natural world. The land, animals, and ancestors are honoured as sacred beings. Connection to Spirit, through ceremony, storytelling, and relationship to place, is a form of wisdom that teaches humility, gratitude, and deep responsibility.

Hinduism teaches that the Divine exists in all forms of life, and connection with God (Brahman) is nurtured through devotion (bhakti), selfless action (karma yoga), and meditation. This connection is not only spiritual but also emotional, offering guidance, purpose, and liberation from suffering.

In Buddhism, the divine may not take the form of a personal God, but connection to truth, compassion, and enlightened awareness offers a path to emotional freedom. Practices like loving-kindness (metta), mindfulness, and right action are designed to cultivate inner peace and reduce the suffering of others.

In Judaism, the covenantal relationship with God is central to life. Through prayer, ethics, and communal rituals, adherents seek to honour God's presence and bring holiness into the world. Divine connection becomes a call to justice, compassion, and faithful living.

Christianity places divine love at the centre of its message. The teachings of Jesus invite believers into a personal and transformative relationship with God, where grace, mercy, and forgiveness shape the heart. This connection is meant to flow outward into acts of service, kindness, and unconditional love.

Islam emphasises submission to the will of Allah and the deep peace that comes from trust in divine wisdom. The five pillars of Islam provide a structured path to maintain this connection, through prayer, charity, fasting, and sacred intention.

These traditions, while diverse in form, all point toward a universal truth: divine connection nurtures emotional resilience, inner clarity, and a deeper sense of meaning. It reminds you that you are not alone, that you are held, guided, and deeply connected to something greater than your individual self.

Making Space For Divine Connection In Modern, Fast-Paced Lives

In today's fast-paced world, dominated by constant stimulation, digital noise, and relentless productivity, making space for divine connection can feel elusive. Yet the need for spiritual grounding is greater than ever. Amid deadlines and distractions, you may find yourself spiritually depleted, longing for something deeper, slower, and more meaningful. Creating space for the divine is not about withdrawing from life, but about bringing sacredness into ordinary moments.

1. **Reclaiming Sacred Time**: You can begin by intentionally carving out just a few minutes each day for silence, prayer, meditation, or stillness. These moments need not be elaborate, they can be as simple as lighting a candle before a meal, offering a word of gratitude, or sitting quietly with your breath. When done with intention, even a minute can become a doorway to presence and connection.

2. **Making the Mundane Sacred:** Divine connection does not always require formal ritual or sacred space. It can be found while washing dishes, walking in nature, caring for a loved one, or pausing to witness a sunrise. When you approach these moments with reverence, you begin to remember that the divine is not confined to temples or texts, it is embedded in life itself.

3. **Digital Boundaries, Spiritual Depth:** One of the greatest challenges in modern life is the omnipresence of technology. To make space for the sacred, it is helpful to create digital boundaries, moments in the day free from screens and noise. These quiet intervals allow you to turn inward, attune to your spirit, and listen to what your heart is truly saying.

4. **Nature as Sanctuary:** Spending time in nature is one of the most accessible and powerful ways to reconnect with the divine. Whether it is walking barefoot on the earth, listening to birdsong, or watching the movement of trees in the wind, nature reminds you of your place in a larger, interconnected whole, and offers you a sense of humility, awe, and belonging.

5. **Embracing Micro-Rituals:** Tiny acts of devotion, a whispered affirmation, lighting incense, keeping a journal of sacred questions, can become anchors in a busy life. These micro-rituals do not interrupt your day; they infuse it with presence and purpose.

6. **Community and Connection:** Divine presence is often felt most deeply in connection with others. Whether through spiritual groups, prayer circles, or shared meals, community invites you into a collective remembering of what matters most. It reinforces that your search for meaning is shared, and that you are not alone in your longing for the sacred.

Ultimately, making space for divine connection is not about adding another task to your to-do list. It is about *making room within yourself,* to feel, to listen, and to remember. In doing so, you honour not only the divine, but the deepest, most whole parts of who you are.

Divine Presence Integration Challenge

I invite you to choose **one** of the following practices to engage with daily over the next 3–5 days:

---

1. A 3-minute morning gratitude prayer

2. A walk in nature with awareness of divine energy

3. Writing a letter to God/universal love

4. Serving someone in need anonymously

5. Five minutes of heart-whisper meditation (listening inward)

You are encouraged to observe and document how your emotions and sense of connection shift over time.

Case Study Discussion: Kirsten's Journey

Kirsten was a lovely soul in her early to mid-40s and when we journeyed together, she told me that she always felt a yearning for something greater than herself. Kirsten sought connection, meaning, and a sense of purpose, but she had always struggled to find it. Despite growing up in a religious family, she found herself questioning the existence of God/The Divine and felt disconnected from any spiritual practice.

One day, while going through a very challenging time in her life, she decided to embark on a journey of self–discovery. She had explored various spiritual traditions, attended meditation retreats, and dived into a few philosophical texts. It did not seem to matter what she did or who she spoke with or what she read she still could not shake off her self–doubt and skepticism. We discussed her religious upbringing and she said that she would step back and gift it all to God/The Divine.

One quiet evening, as she sat in meditation and prayer, something shifted within her. In the stillness of her heart, Kirsten felt a gentle presence, a comforting warmth that enveloped her being. She told me that it was as if God, or the divine energy she had longed for, had finally revealed itself to her. With this newfound connection, Kirsten's life began to transform in remarkable ways. She experienced a profound sense of peace, as if a burden had been lifted off her shoulders. She found peace in prayer, pouring out her hopes and fears, knowing that she was heard and understood.

As Kirsten deepened her connection with God/The Divine, she also discovered a renewed sense of purpose. She felt called to serve others, to be a source of love and compassion in the world. Through acts of kindness, she found fulfillment and a profound sense of joy. Her relationships flourished as she approached them with a genuine and open heart.

Perhaps the most beautiful transformation occurred within Kirsten herself. She learned to truly love herself and embrace her imperfections and to forgive herself for past mistakes. She realised that she was unconditionally loved and accepted by the divine, just as she was. This newfound self–love allowed her to blossom, to embrace her unique gifts, and to live authentically. From that day forward, Kirsten's life became a testament to the power of connecting with God/The Divine. She radiated a gentle grace, and those around her were drawn to her warmth and wisdom. Through her example, she inspired others to embark on their own journeys of spiritual exploration and discovery. In Kirsten's story, we find the transformative power of connecting with the divine. It is a reminder that even during doubt and uncertainty, a profound connection awaits those who seek it with an open heart.

Reflective Exercise: Kirsten's Journey

Here are four profound and reflective questions inspired by Kirsten's story to help you engage with your own journey in this space:

1. **When was the last time you truly made space for the sacred to speak to your heart, not through answers, but through presence?** *Reflection:* Like Kirsten, you may be searching for meaning in ideas, books, or practices, but sometimes it is in stillness that the sacred meets you. What if the divine is not something you must prove or achieve, but simply receive? What might happen if you sat quietly, without expectation, and simply opened your heart?

2. **What beliefs about God/The Divine or spirituality are you still holding onto that may no longer serve your growth?** *Reflection:* Kirsten grew up in a religious household, but it was not until she let go of inherited expectations that she experienced authentic connection.

3. You are allowed to question, reshape, and rediscover your own sacred path. Your soul's longing is not a problem, it is an invitation. **What if God/The Divine is bigger than your doubt?**

4. **How might your life change if you truly believed you were unconditionally loved, without needing to earn it or be perfect?** *Reflection:* Kirsten's greatest transformation began when she felt seen and loved just as she was. This is the heart of divine connection: love

---

that is not based on your performance but your presence. Let this truth soften the inner critic and open the door to healing. You are already enough.

5. **What does service mean to you when it flows from divine connection, rather than duty or guilt?** *Reflection:* Once Kirsten connected with God/The Divine, she did not *have* to serve, she *wanted* to. Her love overflowed naturally. Service became joy, not burden. When you live from your heart's sacred centre, compassion becomes your default language. What small act of kindness could become a sacred offering today?

Let these questions become a doorway to your own exploration, where doubt, devotion, and discovery can sit at the same table in peace.

Affirmations For Integration: (Heart Whispers)

Affirmations have the power to quiet the noise of doubt, open the doorway to self-trust, and draw you back into the wisdom of your heart. When practised daily, they nurture an inner dialogue based in love and truth, helping you live each day more aligned with who you truly are. I invite you to repeat silently or write:

- *I feel connected to God/The Divine when I am surrounded by nature.*

- *God/The Divine gives me comfort in times of uncertainty and fear.*

- *I trust that God/The Divine has a greater plan for my life.*

- *When I pray, I feel a deep connection to God/The Divine.*

- *God/The Divine is the guiding force behind my intuition and wisdom.*

- *God/The Divine's love strengthens me in every moment of my life.*

- *I feel God/The Divine's presence guiding me through challenges with wisdom and grace.*

- *God/The Divine fills my heart with peace, even when the world feels uncertain.*

- *I am never alone, for God/The Divine is always with me.*

- *God/The Divine's light shines through me, inspiring love and kindness in all I do.*

- *I trust that God/The Divine hears my prayers and answers them in divine timing.*

- *God/The Divine's presence reminds me that I am loved, valued, and enough.*

God/The Divine Extension Activity

I invite you to create a small altar or sacred space in your home, an intentional place that holds meaning and invites stillness. This is not about religion or ritual unless you choose it to be. It is about giving yourself a corner of presence, a reminder that your inner life matters. You might place:

- a candle, to symbolise light and clarity

- an object of meaning, such as a stone, shell, or heirloom

- a quote that inspires you

- or an image that reflects the divine, the sacred, or the beauty you long to remember

Return to this space daily, even if only for a few breaths. Let it be a place where you ground yourself, offer gratitude, and reconnect with your heart. Over time, this altar becomes more than objects, it becomes a living anchor, a mirror of your inner journey, and a sacred reminder that the holy is never far away, but always within reach.

Closing Reflection

God/The Divine is not always found in dramatic revelations or distant heavens. More often, the Divine is revealed in the subtle, quiet moments of your life, the stillness of dawn, the warmth of human kindness, the steady rhythm of your breath, and the mysterious way hope rises within you when all seems uncertain. God/The Divine is present not only in the extraordinary, but also in the ordinary, reminding you that sacredness dwells everywhere.

As you reflect on your journey with God/The Divine, notice the countless ways this presence has spoken to you, through a comforting word when you needed reassurance, through beauty that lifted your spirit, through intuition that guided your choices, or through silence that invited you deeper into trust. Every experience is a thread woven into the greater tapestry of connection, affirming that you are seen, guided, and loved. When you allow yourself to rest in God/The Divine's presence, you release the need to carry everything alone. You begin to recognise that you are part of something far greater than your fears, ambitions, or uncertainties. In this awareness, you are strengthened, not by striving harder, but by surrendering more fully. You learn that faith is not about certainty, but about trust, trust that you are never abandoned, trust that your life is held in a love beyond measure.

Carry this truth into your daily life: let God/The Divine be your compass when you feel lost, your refuge when you feel weary, and your source of courage when you face challenges. Let the awareness of the Divine soften your heart toward yourself and others, reminding you that every soul is a reflection of the same eternal light. Above all, let God/The Divine's presence be a living reality, not a distant belief. Walk with this awareness in your words, your choices, and your relationships. In doing so, you become a vessel of love, compassion, and peace, not just receiving the Divine, but revealing it through the way you live. Let this be your prayer: to know God/The Divine not only in thought, but in the breath of every moment, in the mystery of every encounter, and in the quiet revolution of your heart.

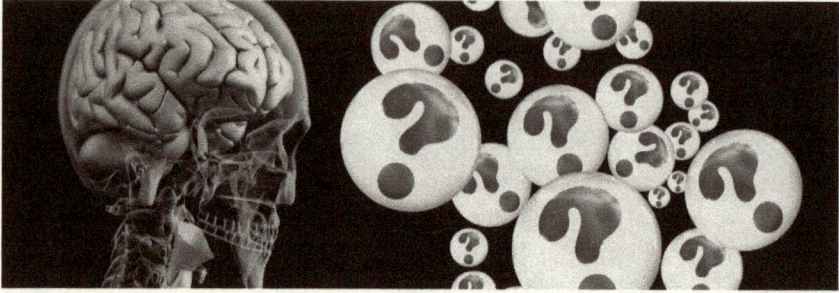

14 - NEUROLINGUISTICS

Your Opening Reflection

Invitation to Your Words - As you begin this chapter, I invite you to listen closely to the language you carry within. Every word you speak, aloud or silently to yourself, is shaping your reality. This is your moment to pause and notice: are your words building you up or holding you back? Let this chapter be a gentle reminder that you have the power to rewrite your inner dialogue, to speak with kindness, and to call yourself into the fullness of who you truly are.

- "Are the words you use with yourself empowering you, or are they keeping you small?"

- "If your inner voice spoke to a friend, how would it sound, and would it be kind?"

- "What repeated phrases or stories shape the way you see yourself and the world?"

- "How might changing a single word you use with yourself shift your emotions, choices, or direction?"

Let these questions open the doorway into presence. Every answer you give, whether in words, sensations, or silence, is a bridge between where you are and where you are going.

Learning Objectives

The learning objectives are included here to give you a clear focus for this chapter, ensuring that each practice you explore moves you closer to mastering the skills, insights, and heart-led awareness that will enrich your life

well beyond the program. By the end of this chapter, you will:

- Understand the connection between language, thought, and emotion.

- Identify and challenge negative self-talk patterns.

- Apply neurolinguistic tools (like reframing, anchoring, and affirmations) to support emotional wellbeing.

- Cultivate heart-aligned communication within themselves and with others.

Core Emotional Domains

The core emotional intelligence domains covered here are essential because they form the foundation for lasting heart connection, guiding you to deepen self-awareness, regulate emotions, build resilience, and strengthen the mind-body bond throughout your Heart Unbound journey.

- **Self-Awareness:** You begin to notice how your inner dialogue and spoken words shape your emotions, beliefs, and behaviours. Awareness of language becomes a mirror for your mind.

- **Self-Regulation:** By choosing more compassionate, empowering language, both internally and externally, you calm reactive patterns and open space for wiser responses.

- **Motivation:** Reframing your words fuels your inner drive. When your language aligns with your values and vision, motivation becomes heart-led and sustainable.

- **Empathy:** As you tune into the language of others with curiosity and presence, you hear more than just words, you feel intention, emotion, and unspoken needs.

- **Social Skills:** Conscious communication builds connection. With mindful language, you cultivate clarity, trust, and influence in your relationships, work, and leadership.

"Neurolinguistics – Rewiring Your Thought Through Action"

Neurolinguistics is a profound meeting point between language, neuroscience, and emotional intelligence. It reveals how the words you speak, especially the silent ones whispered in your own mind, shape the way your brain processes emotion, stores memory, and responds to the world around you. Every word you repeat, every label you attach to yourself, and every inner dialogue you rehearse either strengthens old emotional patterns or opens a doorway to new possibilities. When you begin to notice the language of your inner world, you unlock the power to rewire your emotional responses. A simple shift from *"I always fail"* to *"I am still learning"* is not just semantics, it is a neurological reset. That change in phrasing can ease your stress response, awaken curiosity, and open a pathway for growth. Words can constrict or expand, wound or heal, diminish or empower. They can trigger fear and shame, or they can ignite compassion, courage, and hope.

By consciously choosing words that honor your heart's truth, words grounded in kindness, clarity, and self-belief, you begin reshaping not only your inner dialogue, but the lens through which you experience life. This is not about denying pain or pretending struggles do not exist. Rather, it is about reclaiming the power of interpretation, recognising that the language you choose creates the filter through which reality passes. Neurolinguistics is, at its essence, an invitation: to become the author of your story rather than a passive character in it. It asks you to align your mind with your heart, to speak to yourself with the same compassion you would offer someone you love. This intentional practice transforms not only how you engage with the world, but how you engage with yourself. When you change the words, you change the wiring. When you change the wiring, you change the story, and when you change the story, you change the life you live.

A Brief History: Wernicke, Broca, Chomsky, And The Evolution Of Neurolinguistics

Neurolinguistics, as a field, sits at the fascinating crossroads of neuroscience, linguistics, psychology, and cognitive science. Its beginning can be traced back to the 19th century, when early pioneers began uncovering the relationship between the brain and language, an inquiry that would lay the foundation for understanding how words shape thought, emotion, and behavior.

Paul Broca, a French physician, was among the first to identify a specific region in the brain responsible for speech production. In the 1860s, he observed that patients with damage to the left frontal lobe, now known as *Broca's area,* struggled to speak fluently but could still comprehend language. His discovery established the revolutionary idea that different aspects of language are localised in specific brain regions.

Soon after, **Carl Wernicke**, a German neurologist, expanded on Broca's work. He discovered another key brain region, *Wernicke's area*, in the left temporal lobe, that is essential for understanding spoken language. Patients with damage here could speak in fluent but often nonsensical sentences, indicating a breakdown in comprehension. Together, Broca and Wernicke's findings laid the groundwork for the neurological study of language, giving rise to the concept of brain-based language networks.

In the 20th century, **Noam Chomsky** transformed the study of language with his theory of *universal grammar*. He proposed that the ability to acquire language is hardwired into the human brain, a biological capacity rather than just a learned behavior. While Chomsky focused more on theoretical linguistics than brain mechanisms, his work sparked new explorations into how language is structured and processed at the neurological level.

Modern neurolinguistics emerged as brain imaging technologies such as fMRI and EEG allowed researchers to observe the brain in action during language tasks. This has enabled deeper insights into how emotional language is encoded, how trauma and stress affect verbal processing, and how mindful language use can reshape neural patterns.

Today, neurolinguistics not only explains how we speak and understand language, but also how language shapes emotion, identity, memory, and even our capacity for empathy and resilience. It underscores the profound truth that your words, both spoken and unspoken, are not merely tools of communication. They are reflections of your inner world and instruments for transforming it.

How Language Creates Emotion: The Neuroscience Of Self-Talk

The language you use, especially your *self-talk,* does not just describe your reality; it **creates** it. Neuroscience now shows that your brain responds to internal language as if it were a lived experience. This means the words you silently repeat to yourself can directly influence your mood, shape your perception of self-worth, and even rewire your brain over time.

When you engage in negative self-talk like *"I am a failure"* or *"I am not good enough,"* your brain releases stress-related chemicals such as **cortisol** and **adrenaline**, activating the amygdala, your brain's fear centre. This can trigger a cascade of physiological responses: a racing heart, shallow breathing, and heightened anxiety. Over time, repeated negative language can carve deep neural grooves that reinforce low self-esteem, hopelessness, or shame.

In contrast, compassionate and affirming self-talk like *"I am learning," "I am doing my best,"* or *"I am enough"* activates the **prefrontal cortex,** the part of your brain responsible for conscious thought, emotional regulation, and long-term planning. It also stimulates the **release of oxytocin and serotonin,** neurochemicals associated with trust, well-being, and emotional resilience. Your brain does not distinguish much between language describing external reality and language directed inward.

Telling yourself *"This is too hard"* sends the same stress signals as being under actual threat, but when you reframe with words like *"This is challenging, but I can grow through it,"* you engage more adaptive brain pathways, increasing your capacity to stay grounded, open, and motivated. In essence, your self-talk acts like a **neural script,** guiding your emotional responses, influencing decision-making, and shaping how you relate to yourself and others. The more conscious and kind your internal language becomes, the more emotionally intelligent and empowered your inner world grows. You have the power to change your brain, and your life, by changing your words.

The Role Of Subconscious Programming In Emotional Patterns

The role of **subconscious programming** in emotional patterns is both profound and largely invisible, yet it influences nearly every aspect of your daily life. From the way you respond to conflict, to how you process love, failure, or success, your subconscious mind is constantly shaping your emotional experience through deeply embedded scripts and beliefs. Most of your **emotional reactions are not consciously chosen**. They are programmed responses that have been conditioned over time, often from childhood experiences, cultural influences, and repeated patterns of thought or behaviour.

These subconscious programs live beneath the surface of awareness, stored in the limbic brain and nervous system, and they **automatically activate** in response to triggers. For example, if you were repeatedly told as a child that expressing sadness was weak, you may now subconsciously suppress sadness as an adult, reacting with anger, avoidance, or numbness instead. This is not a moral failing; it is a survival adaptation encoded into your subconscious for protection.

Your subconscious mind operates like a **powerful emotional operating system**, running 95% of your daily thoughts, feelings, and behaviours. It governs how safe you feel in the world, how worthy you believe you are of love or success, and how you emotionally regulate in times of stress. The good news is that **subconscious programming is not fixed, it can be rewritten.** With intentional practices such as mindfulness, breathwork, neurolinguistic reprogramming, affirmations, and therapeutic reflection, you can begin to gently interrupt limiting patterns and rewire the emotional responses that no longer serve you.

Every time you pause to question your internal dialogue, every time you choose a more loving word or a conscious breath, you are reprogramming your emotional patterning toward greater freedom, presence, and heart connection. By learning to **partner with your subconscious rather than be controlled by it**, you unlock the power to transform emotional habits into healing, resilience, and profound self-awareness.

Introducing Heart-Aligned Reframing And Emotional Anchoring

Heart-aligned reframing and emotional anchoring are transformative tools that allow you to reshape your inner world through the conscious use of language, emotion, and intention. These practices combine the wisdom of neurolinguistics with emotional intelligence to help you create a more empowered, compassionate, and heart-centred internal dialogue.

<u>Heart-Aligned Reframing</u>

Reframing is the practice of seeing a situation through a new lens, one that offers possibility, insight, and meaning rather than limitation or defeat. When this is done through the heart, it becomes *heart-aligned reframing,* a process not only of shifting thoughts, but of softening the emotional energy behind them. Instead of asking, *"Why is this happening to me?"* a heart-aligned reframe might be, *"What is this moment asking me to learn?"* Instead of *"I failed again,"* you shift to *"I am growing through this, and my worth is not defined by outcomes."*

This kind of reframing integrates both emotional truth and deeper compassion. It does not bypass pain or challenge; it honors the heart's wisdom in how you respond. Over time, heart-aligned reframing strengthens your emotional regulation, increases self-awareness, and expands your ability to hold hope and clarity, even in difficulty.

<u>Emotional Anchoring</u>

Emotional anchoring is the practice of associating a *positive emotional state* (like peace, confidence, or self-love) with a simple, repeatable trigger, such as a word, breath, gesture, or memory. Anchors help you *return* to the emotional states that serve you, especially when you are feeling overwhelmed, triggered, or disconnected. For example:

1. Gently placing your hand on your heart and saying the word *"safe"* while breathing slowly can become an anchor to calm.

2. Remembering a moment when you felt deeply loved and linking it to the phrase *"I am enough"* can reconnect you to worthiness during times of doubt.

Anchoring creates a bridge between your **conscious intention** and your **emotional reality**, allowing your nervous system to regulate and your heart to remain present.

<u>Why This Matters</u>

Together, heart-aligned reframing and emotional anchoring help you:

•   Break free from automatic negative patterns.

•   Build inner safety and emotional resilience.

•   Speak to yourself with truth and tenderness.

•   Create a consistent path back to your heart when life feels chaotic.

These tools are not about pretending everything is okay, they are about *remembering* that you have the power to shift your inner state, return to your values, and live each day more grounded in love, clarity, and emotional integrity. Every time you pause, reframe, and anchor in your heart, you, re not only healing old patterns, you are also creating new ones. Ones that honour your wholeness.

The Inner Narrative: How Changing Your Words Changes Your World

<u>The Inner Narrative: How Changing Your Words Changes Your World</u>

Your inner narrative, the ongoing dialogue you have with yourself, shapes how you feel, what you believe, and ultimately, how you live. It is not just a stream of private thoughts. It is the architecture of your emotional world, the filter through which you interpret experiences, and the blueprint for your choices, your confidence, and your relationships.

Words are not neutral. Neuroscience shows that the language you use activates neural pathways associated with emotions, memory, and physical responses. For example, when you silently repeat harsh, critical statements to yourself like *"I am a failure"* or *"I will never be good enough,"* your brain and body respond as though those statements are fact, triggering stress responses, emotional shutdown, or withdrawal, but when you begin to shift your inner language to something more heart-connected, such as *"I am learning"*, *"I am growing"*, or *"This moment is hard, but I am doing my best"*, you create new emotional outcomes: more calm, more hope, more resilience.

Changing your words does not mean denying pain or pretending to be positive all the time. It means choosing language that opens the door to compassion, curiosity, and courage, especially in the midst of struggle. For example:

- Instead of *"I have to get this perfect,"* try *"I am allowed to make progress, not perfection."*

- Instead of *"I am so stupid for doing that,"* try *"That was hard, and I will choose differently next time."*

- Instead of *"No one cares,"* try *"I can reach out, I am not alone."*

These simple shifts create powerful emotional results.

- They guide your nervous system back to safety.

- They expand your tolerance for discomfort.

- They help you rewire old beliefs that may have been basecd in fear, shame, or survival.

Most importantly, they return you to your heart, and when your inner narrative becomes a place of support rather than self-sabotage, you begin to live with greater intention and emotional clarity. You make choices from wholeness, not wounding. You begin to create a world, not just outside of you, but within you, that reflects your truth, your worth, and your deep capacity for transformation. **Your words create your world. Speak to yourself the way you would to someone you love. Your heart is listening.**

Neurolinguistic Heart Practice Toolkit Exercise

This week, I invite you to choose **2 out of 5 neurolinguistic practices** to try. These simple but powerful tools help you reshape the language of your mind and heart, shifting patterns of thought and emotion into new possibilities for growth and healing.

Reframing a Current Stressor

- Choose a challenge you are facing right now. Write down how you usually describe or think about it.

- Then, create **three alternative interpretations** that bring light, learning, or opportunity into the situation.

- Example: Instead of *"This is too hard,"* reframe as *"This is teaching me resilience,"* or *"I am growing stronger through this."*

- Notice how your body and emotions shift when you choose a new frame.

Daily Affirmation Practice

- Begin each day with a sentence of truth and encouragement that speaks to your heart.

- Examples: *"I am worthy of love and peace,"* or *"I grow stronger every time I choose kindness."*

- Say your affirmation out loud, write it in your journal, or place it somewhere visible.

- Over time, these affirmations begin to overwrite limiting self-talk.

Anchoring a Positive State

- Choose a physical gesture (e.g., tapping your heart, pressing your palms together, or holding your hand to your chest).

- Each time you feel gratitude, joy, or calm, pair the feeling with your chosen gesture.

- This builds a neurological *"anchor,"* so that over time, simply using the gesture can help you return to that positive state, even in moments of stress.

Mirror Work – Speaking Compassion

- Each day, stand in front of a mirror and speak a kind and compassionate truth to yourself.

- Examples: *"I am doing my best, and that is enough,"* or *"I forgive myself and choose to move forward with love."*

- At first, this may feel uncomfortable, but with repetition, it becomes a profound tool for rewiring self-image and self-talk.

<u>Visualisation – The Empowered Self</u>

- Take three minutes each morning to close your eyes and imagine yourself as the emotionally empowered version of you.

- See yourself calm, confident, and aligned with your heart. Notice how you walk, speak, and respond to life.

Let this image guide you throughout the day, reminding you that you are capable of stepping into this reality now.

Case Study Discussion: Ingrid's Journey

Ingrid was a vibrant and curious 68–year–old woman who had always been a seeker of knowledge and personal growth. She had a big, beautiful heart which she shared with others, but she generally kept people at arm's length, and we spent a lot of time focusing on her view of Self. Ingrid knew that the way she talked to herself, her 'self–talk', had a profound impact on her emotions and overall well–being. It was not compassionate, kind or nurturing, although she wanted it to be. It was for others but not for herself.

Ingrid embarked on a journey of self–discovery and self–transformation. She really immersed herself in books, completed all my hearting exercises I set her and completed my heart of Life Series of programs. Through her exploration, Ingrid learned that her self–talk was often negative and self–critical. She discovered that these patterns of thought were based in past experiences and conditioning.

Empowered with her newfound awareness, Ingrid began to challenge and reframe her self–talk. Whenever self–doubt or self–criticism arose, Ingrid consciously shifted her inner dialogue. She replaced negative thoughts with positive affirmations and encouraging statements. She reminded herself of her worth, strengths, and past achievements. Gradually, her self–talk became more compassionate, empowering, and supportive.

As Ingrid practiced her new approach to self–talk, she noticed remarkable changes in her life. She felt a newfound sense of peace and contentment within herself. She embraced her flaws and imperfections with kindness, realising that they were part of her unique journey. This acceptance allowed her to let go of judgment and comparison, freeing her to fully embrace her authentic self. Also, Ingrid's relationships transformed as well. Her compassionate self–talk enabled her to approach interactions with empathy and understanding.

She listened more attentively and communicated her thoughts and feelings more effectively. Her newfound clarity and authenticity deepened her connections and nurtured deeper and more meaningful relationships. Ingrid's story serves as a reminder that by changing your self–talk, you can cultivate a heart–led life filled with love, acceptance, and joy. Through her transformation, she discovered the profound impact of self–talk on her emotional well–being and relationships. Her story provides an example that by harnessing the power of your words, you can shape your thoughts, emotions, and ultimately, your lives.

Reflective Exercise: Ingrid's Journey

Here are four profound and reflective questions inspired by Ingrid's story to help you engage with your own neurolinguistic journey:

1. **How do you speak to yourself when no one is listening?** *Reflection:* Ingrid discovered that her private thoughts shaped her emotional world. You too carry an inner voice, sometimes kind, sometimes critical. Becoming aware of your internal dialogue is the first act of emotional courage. What if your self-talk could become your greatest ally, not your harshest critic?

2. **Where did your current patterns of self-talk originate, and are they still true?** *Reflection:* Many of Ingrid's beliefs were grounded in old conditioning and experiences that no longer served her. Your inner language might echo the voices of the past, but you have the power to rewrite the script. Begin by questioning whose words you are carrying, and whether they reflect the truth of your heart today.

3. **What would it feel like to speak to yourself with the same love and compassion you offer others?** *Reflection:* Ingrid could give love freely, yet struggled to turn that love inward. You may do the same,

---

but when you soften toward yourself, the whole world softens with you. Self-kindness is not indulgence, it is the soil in which your courage, growth, and authenticity take root.

4. **How might your relationships change if your inner dialogue become more heart-led and empowering?** *Reflection:* Ingrid found that healing her self-talk brought depth and connection to her relationships. When you speak to yourself with honesty and love, your outer communication becomes clearer, more empathetic, and real. Every relationship you nurture begins with the one you have with yourself.

Let Ingrid's story remind you: words have power, and when spoken from the heart, even silently to yourself, they can become the most transformative medicine you carry.

Affirmations For Integration: (Heart Whispers)

Affirmations have the power to quiet the noise of doubt, open the doorway to self-trust, and draw you back into the wisdom of your heart. When practised daily, they nurture an inner dialogue based in love and truth, helping you live each day more aligned with who you truly are. I invite you to repeat silently or write:

- *I am rewiring my thoughts for positive change and empowered heart connection.*

- *I am using language to shape my reality.*

- *I am exploring the power of neurolinguistics to open a path with my heart.*

- *I am reprogramming my mind for success.*

- *I am harnessing the language of my mind to connect with my heart.*

- *I am choosing words that reflect love, truth, and possibility.*

- *I am transforming old patterns by speaking with clarity and compassion.*

- *I am aligning my language with the wisdom of my heart.*

- *I am creating a new story that empowers my growth and freedom.*

"Voice of the Heart" Recording Exercise

Your voice carries a unique resonance that your mind and body instinctively recognise as safe, familiar, and grounding. By recording yourself speaking words of kindness, affirmation, and compassion, you give yourself the gift of hearing your own heart reflected back to you, creating a powerful loop of self-love and healing.

1. **Create Your Script**: Write down 3–5 personal affirmations, compassionate truths, or heart-centred reminders. Examples might include:

   - *I am worthy of love just as I am.*

   - *Each day I grow in wisdom, strength, and compassion.*

   - *I choose to live with an open heart, even in moments of uncertainty.*

   - *My life is unfolding in alignment with a greater purpose.*

2. **Record with Intention**: Find a quiet space and record yourself reading your affirmations slowly and gently, as though speaking to someone you deeply care about. Speak from the heart. Let your tone carry warmth and sincerity.

3. **Listen Regularly**: Play your recording each morning upon waking and again each evening before sleep. Repetition helps reinforce positive neural and emotional pathways, gradually replacing old, critical inner voices with a voice of kindness and support.

4. **Notice the Shifts**: With time, your nervous system begins to associate your own voice with safety, encouragement, and trust. Instead of your inner dialogue defaulting to fear or criticism, you start to hear compassion, reassurance, and possibility.

This practice is not simply about affirmations, it is about reclaiming your voice as a tool of healing, teaching your heart and mind to work together, and building a daily ritual of self-connection. Over time, this becomes a sacred reminder: *you are your own source of strength, love, and guidance.*

Closing Reflection

The words you speak, especially the ones you whisper silently to yourself, hold extraordinary power. They are not fleeting sounds or passing thoughts, they are seeds. Every word takes root in the soil of your heart and mind, shaping the emotions you feel, directing the choices you make, and colouring the lens through which you experience your world. Neurolinguistics reminds you that language is more than a tool for communication, it is a vessel for transformation. When you speak with intention, when you reframe your thoughts with compassion, and when you anchor your inner dialogue in truth and hope, you are not simply changing your vocabulary, you are rewiring your brain, reshaping your inner reality, and realigning your life with possibility.

Let this part of the journey remind you: each word you choose is a doorway. Some doors lead back to old fears and limitations, while others open into healing, clarity, and freedom. The choice is yours in every moment. Speak words that are kind, courageous, and heart-led. As you learn to listen to your inner dialogue with gentleness and curiosity, you discover that you are not only the listener but also the narrator, the author of your own unfolding story. You hold the pen. You hold the voice. You hold the power. May your words no longer confine you but instead liberate you. May they carry you closer to your truth, your wholeness, and your heart. Speak kindly. Speak consciously. Speak as if every word is a step back home, because it is.

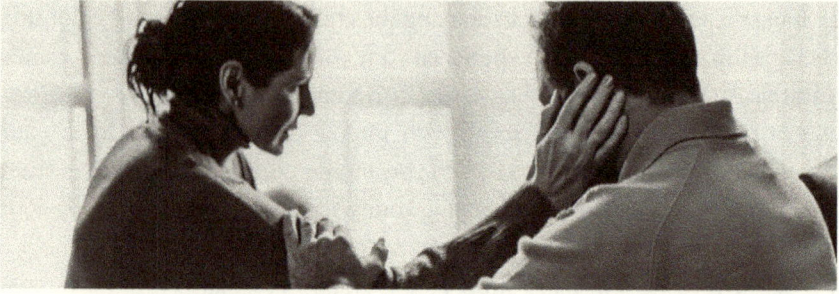

15 - COMPASSION

Your Opening Reflection

Invitation to Compassion - As you open this chapter, I invite you to place your hand over your heart and breathe gently into the space beneath your palm. Imagine compassion as a warm light, flowing first toward yourself, then radiating outward to others. This is your reminder that compassion is not weakness but strength, the courage to meet pain with tenderness, to hold yourself and others with kindness, and to soften instead of harden. Let this moment be your entry point into a deeper practice of living with an open heart..

- "Think of a time when you struggled. How would it have felt if someone had offered you kindness instead of judgment?"

- "What does compassion look like in action for you, toward yourself, toward others, or toward the world

- "When you witness suffering, big or small,what is your first instinct? To turn away, to fix it, or to connect with it?"

- "If compassion were a language, what words or gestures would you use to speak it more fluently in your everyday life?"

- "When was the last time someone showed you compassion? How did it make you feel?"

- "What would change in your life if you showed yourself the same compassion you offer others?"

Let these questions open the doorway into presence. Every answer you give, whether in words, sensations, or silence, is a bridge between where you are and where you are going.

Learning Objectives

The learning objectives are included here to give you a clear focus for this chapter, ensuring that each practice you explore moves you closer to mastering the skills, insights, and heart-led awareness that will enrich your life well beyond the program. By the end of this chapter, you will:

- Understand the emotional and neurological benefits of practicing compassion.

- Develop skills in self-compassion, empathy, and compassionate communication.

- Explore the relationship between compassion and healing, connection, and leadership.

- Apply compassion in both personal and professional contexts to create positive change.

Core Emotional Domains

The core emotional intelligence domains covered here are essential because they form the foundation for lasting heart connection, guiding you to deepen self-awareness, regulate emotions, build resilience, and strengthen the mind-body bond throughout your Heart Unbound journey.

- **Self-Awareness:** invites you to recognise your own pain and humanity as the starting point for compassion.

- **Self-Regulation:** helps you respond rather than react, creating space to hold others' emotions without being overwhelmed.

- **Empathy:** deepens as you see beyond the surface and honour the shared experiences that unite us all.

- **Social Skills:** are enriched as compassion develops genuine connection, healing conflict, and strengthening trust.

- **Motivation:** becomes heart-aligned as your drive to act is fuelled by kindness, service, and the desire to uplift others.

"Compassion – The Heart Of Connection"

Compassion is more than a kind gesture, it is a transformative force of emotional intelligence that elevates both personal well-being and collective humanity. At its core, compassion is the deep awareness of suffering, your own and others', combined with the heartfelt desire to relieve it. When turned inward, compassion becomes a powerful tool for healing. It helps you soften the inner critic, dissolve shame, and acknowledge your struggles without judgment. Instead of pushing yourself to 'get over it,' you learn to sit gently with your pain, to listen with tenderness, and to honour your human experience. This self-compassion builds true emotional resilience. It develops confidence not through perfection, but through kindness.

When expressed outwardly, compassion becomes the bridge between people. It breaks down barriers of fear, anger, and misunderstanding. Compassionate communication allows for deeper listening, clearer understanding, and stronger, more authentic relationships. In high-performance environments like corporate settings, universities, or government departments, compassion enables more inclusive decision-making, reduces conflict, and fuels purpose-driven collaboration. Leaders who lead with compassion are not weak, they are strong enough to care. They are emotionally attuned to the needs of others, can hold space during conflict, and inspire trust and loyalty.

Compassion transforms performance cultures into human-centred ones, where people are seen, heard, and valued. Compassion is not passive. It is active. It is not just a feeling, it is a conscious choice to be present, kind, and responsive, even when it is hard. It is the fuel for courageous conversations, the anchor during times of uncertainty, and the heartbeat of every act of service. In a world that is too often fractured by comparison, competition, and fear, compassion reminds you that you are not alone, and neither is anyone else. It invites you to be the one who listens deeper, who softens the edge, and who dares to care. This is how healing happens. This is how heart-led transformation begins.

The History And Universality Of Compassion Across Cultures And Spiritual Traditions

Compassion is one of humanity's oldest and most revered virtues, an emotional and spiritual force that transcends time, geography, and belief systems. Across ancient civilisations and sacred traditions, compassion has been upheld as a path to both personal transformation and collective peace.

In **Buddhism**, compassion (karuṇā) is one of the Four Immeasurables, essential for liberation from suffering. It calls for active empathy and loving-kindness toward all beings. In **Christianity**, Jesus taught, *"Love your neighbour as yourself,"* embedding compassion at the heart of faith through parables, forgiveness, and service to the poor and vulnerable. **Islam** begins nearly every chapter of the Qur'an with *"In the name of God, the Most Compassionate, the Most Merciful,"* affirming rahmah (mercy) as a divine attribute to be lived by the faithful. **Hinduism** emphasises ahimsa, non-violence and compassion toward all living beings, as a foundational principle of spiritual life. **Judaism** teaches tikkun olam, or *"repairing the world,"* often through acts of compassion and justice. **Sikhism** speaks of daya, or compassionate sensitivity, as a vital expression of devotion to God and service to humanity.

In **Indigenous traditions** around the world, compassion is expressed through a deep kinship with all life, people, animals, the Earth, and ancestors. The sacred principle of reciprocity reminds us that care must flow in all directions for harmony to exist. Even in secular philosophy, from Confucian ethics to Stoic thought, compassion is seen as a key to ethical living and wise leadership. Modern psychology now echoes what ancient wisdom has always known: compassion is essential for mental health, community, and resilience. Despite differences in language, rituals, or belief, compassion remains a universal bridge, uniting hearts across continents, inviting people to rise above fear, and reminding you of your shared humanity. It is not bound to any one religion or culture. It is a sacred thread woven through them all, whispering the same truth: that to live fully is to love deeply, and to be truly human is to care.

Compassion vs. Empathy: Understanding The Distinction And Synergy

Empathy and compassion are often used interchangeably, but they are distinct emotional capacities, each powerful on its own, and transformative when combined. **Empathy** is the ability to feel or understand what another person is experiencing. It comes in two primary forms:

- **Emotional empathy**: where you actually *feel* another's emotions, as if they were your own.

- **Cognitive empathy**: where you intellectually *understand* what someone is feeling, even if you do not feel it yourself.

Empathy allows you to tune in, to walk in another's shoes, and to resonate with their internal world, but without boundaries or action, empathy alone can lead to **empathic distress,** an emotional overload that can result in burnout, especially in caring professions or high-stress environments. **Compassion**, on the other hand, takes empathy a step further. It adds two crucial ingredients: **a desire to alleviate suffering** and **a conscious choice to act with care**. Compassion is empathy in motion. It includes warmth, perspective, and intentional response. Where empathy feels *with*, compassion feels *for,* and *moves toward.*

The **synergy** between them is profound. Empathy creates the connection. Compassion channels it into wise, heartful action. In emotionally intelligent relationships, workplaces, and leadership, this blend creates not only mutual understanding but also resilience, inclusion, and trust. In short:

- **Empathy says**: *"I feel what you are feeling."*

- **Compassion says**: *"I see your pain, and I want to help ease it."*

When you learn to navigate both, empathising without being overwhelmed, and responding with compassionate intention, you open the door to deeper connection, sustainable caregiving, and a more heart-led way of being.

The Science Of Compassion: Effects On The Brain, Body, And Emotional Wellbeing

Compassion is not only a spiritual virtue or moral ideal, it is a **biological capacity** wired into your human system. Thanks to advances in neuroscience, Compassion is not only a spiritual virtue or moral ideal, it is a **biological capacity** wired into your human system. Thanks to advances in neuroscience, psychology, and mind-body medicine, we now know that compassion has **measurable, transformative effects** on your brain, body, and emotional health.

Compassion and the Brain: Rewiring for Connection

Compassion activates specific regions of your brain associated with empathy, reward, and emotional regulation:

- Your **anterior cingulate cortex** and **insula** light up during compassionate responses, facilitating emotional awareness and motivation to help.

- The **ventral striatum,** a key part of your brain's reward system, is activated when you act with compassion, reinforcing pro-social behavior with a sense of pleasure or satisfaction.

- The **prefrontal cortex**, responsible for your executive function and impulse control, is strengthened by compassion meditation, enhancing emotional regulation and mindful decision-making.

Repeated acts of compassion, even imagined or intentional ones, **retrain neural pathways** toward care, presence, and connection. Through a process called **neuroplasticity**, your brain literally reshapes itself to become more compassionate over time.

Compassion and the Body: Healing Through Heartfulness

Biologically, compassion enables a shift from stress to safety. When you act compassionately, whether toward yourself or others, your body enters a state of calm and repair:

- **Oxytocin**, known as the *"bonding hormone,"* is released, increasing trust and lowering blood pressure.

- **Heart rate variability (HRV)** improves, a sign of emotional resilience and nervous system balance.

- **Cortisol**, the body's stress hormone, decreases significantly during compassionate states.

- The **immune system** strengthens, as chronic inflammation, the root of many illnesses, is reduced.

- Compassion literally **heals your body**, reinforcing the link between emotional connection and physical vitality.

- Participants in **Compassion Cultivation Training (CCT)** reported greater empathy, reduced emotional reactivity, and enhanced wellbeing in as little as 8 weeks.

These findings offer hope: no matter your starting point, **you can become more compassionate**, toward yourself and others.

<u>The Takeaway</u>

Compassion is not weakness; it is your greatest neurobiological strength. When you allow yourself to meet your pain or another's suffering with kindness, you activate powerful systems in your brain and nervous system that restore balance, safety, and healing. Compassion is not indulgence; it is a force that reconditions your mind and soothes your heart. It is not optional; it is essential, for your health, your heart, and your humanity. Each time you choose compassion, you are teaching your body to soften stress, your mind to let go of fear, and your soul to remember what matters most.

In a world that often demands performance, perfection, and pressure, compassion becomes your quiet revolution. It rewires your nervous system, strengthens your resilience, and awakens your courage. It shows you that love is not only an emotion but also the most intelligent response you can make. When you embody compassion, you step into alignment with the truth of your heart. You liberate yourself from judgment and create space for connection, healing, and peace, within yourself and in the world around you.

Compassion As A Leadership Quality And Driver Of Emotional Maturity

In the evolving landscape of leadership, compassion is no longer viewed as a soft or optional trait, it is a core competency for effective, emotionally intelligent leaders and a catalyst for meaningful human connection, organisational wellbeing, and sustained performance.

<u>Compassionate Leadership: Leading with Heart and Strength</u>

True leadership is not just about authority or vision, it is about presence, relational intelligence, and trust. Compassionate leaders:

- **See the person, not just the role**. You recognise the humanity behind the job title, and respond with empathy when others are struggling.

- **Listen deeply** and respond with care, not to fix, but to understand and empower.

- **Model psychological safety**, allowing others to be vulnerable, take creative risks, and speak their truth without fear of judgement.

- **Balance accountability with empathy**, knowing that high performance grows best in a culture of respect and care.

Far from making leaders appear weak, compassion earns respect, builds loyalty, and creates environments where people want to give their best.

<u>Compassion as a Sign of Emotional Maturity</u>

Compassion is emotional intelligence in action. It draws on and strengthens key EI domains:

- **Self-awareness**: Compassion requires you to notice your internal reactions, judgement, impatience, or defensiveness, and pause before responding.

- **Self-regulation**: Rather than reacting harshly, you choose a response that supports growth, for yourself and others.

- **Empathy**: You actively imagine what it feels like to be in someone else's shoes, without needing to agree or fix.

- **Motivation**: Compassionate leaders are motivated by a desire to serve a purpose greater than themselves.

- **Social skills**: Compassion deepens your ability to manage relationships, navigate conflict, and inspire teams.

Choosing compassion, especially in difficult moments, is a sign of **emotional strength**, not softness. It reflects maturity, humility, and wisdom. Compassion is not only a spiritual virtue or moral ideal, it is a **biological capacity** wired into your human system. Thanks to advances in neuroscience, Compassion is not only a spiritual virtue or moral ideal, it is a **biological capacity** wired into your human system. Thanks to advances in neuroscience, psychology, and mind-body medicine, we now know that compassion has **measurable, transformative effects** on your brain, body, and emotional health.

Compassion And The Brain: Rewiring For Connection

Compassion activates specific regions of your brain associated with empathy, reward, and emotional regulation:

- Your **anterior cingulate cortex** and **insula** light up during compassionate responses, facilitating emotional awareness and motivation to help.

- The **ventral striatum,** a key part of your brain's reward system, is activated when you act with compassion, reinforcing pro-social behavior with a sense of pleasure or satisfaction.

- The **prefrontal cortex**, responsible for your executive function and impulse control, is strengthened by compassion meditation, enhancing emotional regulation and mindful decision-making.

Repeated acts of compassion, even imagined or intentional ones, **retrain neural pathways** toward care, presence, and connection. Through a process called **neuroplasticity**, your brain literally reshapes itself to become more compassionate over time.

Why Self-Compassion Is The Foundation Of True Compassion For Others

You cannot pour from an empty cup, and in the realm of emotional intelligence, this truth becomes even more profound. Self-compassion is not self-indulgence or weakness. It is the very foundation upon which authentic compassion for others is built.

You Cannot Give What You Do Not Have

When you are harsh with yourself, judging, criticising, or berating your mistakes, it becomes harder to offer genuine understanding to others. Why? Because unacknowledged inner pain often leads to projection, burnout, or emotional distance. Self-compassion softens your inner world. It teaches you to:

- Embrace imperfection as part of being human.

- Respond to your struggles with kindness, not condemnation.

- Honour your needs and emotional landscape without guilt.

In doing so, you create space, emotional spaciousness, to meet others with the same grace.

Compassion Begins in the Mirror

People often assume compassion is outward-focused, but it starts within. When you treat yourself with warmth, patience, and understanding, you rewire your nervous system for safety and trust. You stop seeing others through a lens of comparison, competition, or judgement, and instead view them through a shared humanity. Self-compassion allows you to say:

- *"Just like me, they make mistakes."*

- *"Just like me, they are trying."*

- *"Just like me, they long to be seen and loved."*

This recognition dismantles barriers. It dissolves *"otherness."* It makes empathy more than a thought, it makes it embodied.

The Science of Self-Compassion

Research by Dr. Kristin Neff and others has shown that self-compassion:

- Activates the parasympathetic nervous system (calm, grounded state).

- Lowers cortisol and reduces chronic stress.

- Builds resilience and emotional regulation.

- Enhances motivation, not through fear, but through inner support.

People who practice self-compassion are more likely to:

- Offer help to others without resentment or martyrdom.

- Apologise and repair relationships.

- Maintain healthy boundaries.

- Act with courage, even after failure.

Self-Compassion Cultivates Emotional Generosity

When you are kind to yourself, your compassion becomes more spacious. You are less likely to take things personally, react from pain, or withdraw when others struggle. Instead, you offer presence. Understanding. A heart that says, *"I have been there too. I see you."* In this way, self-compassion does not limit your compassion, it **amplifies** it.

Compassion-in-Action Toolkit

This week, I invite you to choose *at least two* of the following acts of compassion. Each small action you take has the power to ripple outward, nurturing your own heart while touching the lives of others.

1. **Self-compassion ritual** – Write a compassionate affirmation just for you and place it near your mirror. Each morning when you see it, pause, breathe, and let those words settle into your heart.

---

2. **Active listening moment** – In your next conversation, give the gift of your full presence. Put away distractions, soften your attention, and truly listen, not just to the words spoken, but to the feelings behind them.

3. **Forgiveness practice** – Reflect on one burden you have been carrying, a hurt, a resentment, a grudge. Write a letter of forgiveness, not to condone or excuse, but to release your own heart from its weight. You do not need to send it; the act of writing is enough.

4. **Service contribution** – Offer one hour of your time this week to help someone without expectation. It could be assisting a colleague, supporting a friend, or volunteering in your community. Let your service be an expression of love without condition.

5. **Kindness ripple** – Choose a simple, anonymous act of kindness. It could be leaving a kind note, paying for someone's coffee, or sending encouragement without signing your name. Trust that your gesture, though unseen, will brighten someone's day.

Case Study Discussion: Grace's Journey

Grace was a 42 year–old woman who had always lived a fairly self–centred and disconnected life. By her own admission she was consumed by her own desires and needs, rarely considering the feelings and struggles of others. During one of our sessions, she told me about a series of events that led her to question the way she had been living and about a chance encounter where she witnessed an act of kindness between strangers. It was only a small thing in the overall scheme of life, but she told me that she had seen a man offer his coat to a homeless woman on a cold winter night. The compassion displayed in that moment struck a chord deep within her heart. It was a wake-up call that made her realise the emptiness of her own existence.

Grace was inspired by this encounter, and she embarked on a powerful journey of self–reflection and transformation. She started by practicing self–compassion, learning to be kind, and forgiving towards herself. As she extended this compassion to herself, she discovered a newfound sense of peace and acceptance. In time, Grace began to extend her compassion to others. It was difficult for her at the start, but she volunteered at a local charity store, offering her time and support to those in need. She spent time and listened to their stories, held their hands, and offered words of encouragement. In each act of compassion, she experienced a deep connection with others and a profound sense of purpose.

As Grace continued on her path of compassion, she encountered profound changes in her life. Relationships that were once strained (especially with her parents) started to heal as she approached them with understanding and empathy. She also became a trusted confidante and a source of comfort for her friends and family. In her professional life, Grace's newfound compassion transformed the dynamics of her team. She became a source of inspiration, encouraging her workmates to work together and support one another. Outside of her immediate circle, Grace found herself drawn to causes that championed social justice and equality. In time she became an advocate for homeless teenagers in her area, using her voice to raise awareness and bring about change. Her acts of compassion extended beyond individuals, encompassing the broader community.

Through her journey of embracing compassion, Grace experienced a profound shift in her life. The once self–centred woman that I had first encountered had evolved into a beautiful beacon of light and love. Her heart overflowed with kindness, and she radiated a warmth that touched the lives of those around her and she was a joy to be around. In the process of embracing compassion, Grace discovered the true essence of her being. She realised that life's true purpose was about connecting with others, offering support, and showing kindness. It was through compassion that she found fulfillment, joy, and a profound sense of belonging. Grace's story is a testament to the transformative power of compassion. It demonstrates that when you choose to open your heart to others and embrace empathy and kindness, you not only transform your own life but also create a ripple effect of positive change in those around you.

Reflective Exercise: Grace's Journey

Here are two profound and reflective questions inspired by Grace's story to help you engage with your own compassionate journey:

1. **When was the last time you offered yourself compassion instead of criticism?** *Supportive Reflection:* Just like Grace, your journey begins with how you treat yourself. Your inner voice matters. Are you offering yourself the same kindness and patience you give to others?

> When you make a mistake or feel overwhelmed, could you try saying to yourself, "I'm doing the best I can, and that's enough"?
>
> 2. **How might you see the humanity in others more clearly today, even those who challenge you?** *Supportive Reflection:* That simple moment Grace witnessed, a man offering his coat, reminds you that small acts of kindness can awaken deep truths. Every person you encounter is carrying invisible struggles. When you choose to meet them with curiosity and compassion, you open the door to deeper connection and healing.

Affirmations For Integration: (Heart Whispers)

Affirmations have the power to quiet the noise of doubt, open the doorway to self-trust, and draw you back into the wisdom of your heart. When practised daily, they nurture an inner dialogue based in love and truth, helping you live each day more aligned with who you truly are. I invite you to repeat silently or write:

- *I choose to show compassion to people in my life.*

- *I am committed to doing acts of kindness for others.*

- *I open my heart to the pain and struggles of others.*

- *I embrace forgiveness to embrace compassion and healing.*

- *I strive to listen deeply and validate the experiences of others.*

- *I believe in the power of compassion to create positive change in the world.*

Compassion Reflection Exercise

Take a 30-minute walk with the clear intention of awakening your heart to compassion. As you step outside, allow yourself to slow down and notice the people passing by, the rhythms of nature, the quiet details of your surroundings. With each step, ask yourself:

- *Where is compassion needed here?*

- *Where can I offer kindness, within me and around me?*

If you see someone rushing, instead of judging, breathe in patience. If you notice an elderly person or a child, silently bless them with safety and love. If you witness tension, offer an inward prayer for peace. If you pass by a

---

tree, flower, or bird, acknowledge the gift of life it holds and the interconnectedness you share.

As you walk, extend compassion inward too. Notice if self-criticism or restlessness arises, and gently replace it with kindness toward yourself. Let your heart guide your gaze, your breath, and your thoughts. When you return, take a few moments to journal. Write down what you noticed, how the walk made you feel, and whether compassion shifted the way you saw the world. Ask yourself:

- *What action am I called to take now, from this heart-awakened place?*

This walk is not just an exercise, it is a living practice, training your mind and heart to choose compassion as your natural way of seeing.

Closing Reflection

Compassion is not something you simply give away, it is a force that reshapes you from within. Every time you choose compassion, whether toward yourself or others, you send ripples through your nervous system, calming fear and dissolving judgment. You rewire your brain for connection rather than separation, for healing rather than harm. Remember: compassion is not weakness, it is courage. It is not indulgence, it is intelligence. It is not optional, it is essential, for your heart, your health, and your humanity. As you walk this path, let compassion become both your anchor and your compass.

Notice how it changes your inner dialogue, softens your relationships, and expands your presence in the world. When pressure rises, return to compassion. When criticism echoes, return to compassion. When the world feels heavy, return to compassion. In doing so, you are not only offering love to others, you are offering love to yourself, and in that simple, profound choice, you awaken the quiet revolution of the heart.

16 - PHOTOGRAPHS

Your Opening Reflection

Invitation to Photographs - As you step into this chapter, I invite you to choose a photograph that carries meaning for you, one that stirs your heart, awakens a memory, or whispers of who you are. Hold it gently, as though it were a mirror of your soul. Let it remind you of the beauty you have lived, the strength you have carried, and the love that has shaped your path. In this reflection, allow the image to become more than a picture, let it become a doorway back to your essence. I invite you to now look at your favourite photograph.

- "What emotion does it evoke?"

- "What story does it tell about you or your life?"

- "When you look at this photo, what values or qualities of yours does it reflect?"

- "If this photo could speak, what message would it share with you today?"

- "How does this image remind you of your resilience, growth, or heart's journey?"

- "What part of your authentic self feels most seen or remembered in this photo?"

Let these questions open the doorway into presence. Every answer you give, whether in words, sensations, or silence, is a bridge between where you are and where you are going.

Learning Objectives

The learning objectives are included here to give you a clear focus for this chapter, ensuring that each practice you explore moves you closer to mastering the skills, insights, and heart-led awareness that will enrich your life well beyond the program. By the end of this chapter, you will:

- Understand how photography can develop mindfulness, emotional awareness, and self-compassion.

- Use photography as a tool for emotional expression, reflection, and gratitude.

- Develop self-worth by documenting personal meaning and beauty in everyday life.

- Strengthen inner connection by curating images that reflect personal growth and joy.

Core Emotional Domains

The core emotional intelligence domains covered here are essential because they form the foundation for lasting heart connection, guiding you to deepen self-awareness, regulate emotions, build resilience, and strengthen the mind-body bond throughout your Heart Unbound journey.

- **Self-Awareness:** Photographs invite you to reflect on your inner landscape, your memories, emotions, and identity, helping you understand how the past shapes your present self.

- **Self-Regulation:** Revisiting images with intention allows you to process emotions mindfully, transforming nostalgia, grief, or regret into healing and meaning.

- **Empathy:** Looking into the eyes of others in a photograph cultivates compassion and perspective, reminding you of shared humanity and emotional depth.

- **Social Skills:** Photographs help bridge conversations, deepen storytelling, and develop more genuine connection with others through shared memory and vulnerability.

- **Motivation:** Meaningful images can reignite your sense of purpose, values, and vision, encouraging you to live in alignment with your most heartfelt truth.

"Photographs – The Power Of Your Image Within"

Photography is more than a creative hobby, it is a powerful pathway to emotional intelligence and self-discovery. When you pick up a camera or pause to frame a moment through your phone lens, you are not just recording an image, you are choosing to be present. You slow down. You notice the light, the feeling, the unspoken story unfolding in front of you. In that moment, your attention shifts from distraction to intention. Each photo you take becomes a mirror, reflecting what matters to you. It might be a quiet sunrise, a wrinkled hand, a joyful expression, or an object filled with meaning. These choices are not random, they reveal your values, your relationships, and your emotional landscape.

Photography also deepens empathy. When you look through the lens, you begin to see others more fully, not just as subjects, but as stories. Their emotions, struggles, and beauty become part of your visual vocabulary. In this way, photography becomes a bridge, connecting heart to heart. Beyond the image, the act of looking back at photographs can regulate your emotions, spark gratitude, and reconnect you with your purpose. In a world that moves quickly, photography reminds you to pause, feel, and honour the truth of the moment. It is a visual language of the heart, and through it, you begin to see not just the world, but yourself, more clearly.

A Brief History Of Photography As Storytelling, Expression, And Legacy

Photography has always been more than just a means of documentation, it is a profoundly human form of storytelling, emotional expression, and legacy-making. From the earliest days of the camera obscura and the first daguerreotypes in the 1800s, photography offered a revolutionary way to freeze time, preserve memory, and convey emotion without words. People could now see a face, a landscape, or a moment long after it had passed, and feel its impact as if it were still unfolding. In the 19th and 20th centuries, photography became a democratising art form, accessible not just to the elite but to everyday people.

Family portraits, wartime images, and street photography all carried powerful emotional narratives, capturing joy, grief, hope, and resilience. In the hands of visionaries like Dorothea Lange, Ansel Adams, and Gordon Parks, photography gave voice to the voiceless and illuminated the soul of human experience. Culturally, photographs became heirlooms and sacred records. They told the stories of migration, love, birth, struggle, and celebration.

Across generations and continents, people passed down albums not just to remember, but to *belong*. Each photo whispered, *This is who we were. This is where you come from.* In the digital age, photography has become an even more immediate and expressive language. With smartphones in your pocket, you can capture everyday life as it unfolds. You can share glimpses of your heart, your perspective, and your truths with the world, instantly. Yet at its core, photography remains timeless. Whether printed in sepia or posted online, a photograph still holds the power to move people, to make you reflect, and to connect you across time and space. It is storytelling through light. It is emotion made visible. It is legacy made luminous.

How Visual Memories Anchor Emotion And Shape Identity

Visual memories, especially those captured through photographs, are powerful anchors of emotion and identity. When you look at an image of your childhood home, a loved one's smile, or a place that once held your footsteps, something stirs within you. That stirring is more than nostalgia; it is a neural and emotional activation that reconnects you with who you were, what you felt, and how you experienced the world at that time. Your brain stores visual memories in ways that are closely linked to emotional processing. Your amygdala, which governs emotional responses, interacts with your hippocampus, where your long-term memories are stored.

This means that photographs do not just help you *recall* memories, they help you *feel* them. A single image can transport you into a moment of joy, grief, love, loss, or belonging with astonishing immediacy. These emotionally-charged visual memories become part of your personal narrative. They help you understand where you have come from, what you have overcome, and what you value most. They illuminate your identity, not just in facts, but in feelings. Who you are is shaped not only by the events of your life, but by how you emotionally interpret and remember them.

Moreover, the visual language of your life influences how you present yourself to the world. The photos you display, share, or keep tucked away in a drawer all tell a story about what matters to you. They become a mirror of your values, your relationships, and your transformation over time. In therapeutic settings, visual memories are often used to help people reconnect with lost parts of themselves, process trauma, or rediscover joy. Whether consciously or unconsciously, we all use images to stitch together the fabric of our inner world. In essence, visual memories are emotional signposts. They remind you not just of what happened, but of what mattered, and in doing so, they help you feel more whole, more grounded in your story, and more alive to its continuing evolution.

The Link Between Daily Photography, Mindfulness, And Gratitude

Daily photography offers a profound and accessible path into mindfulness and gratitude. When you intentionally take a photo each day, not just a quick snapshot, but a moment of genuine presence, you train yourself to slow down, notice details, and appreciate the world through a more attentive and heartfelt lens. This simple act of looking closely, at light streaming through a window, a child's laughter, dew on a blade of grass, or your morning cup of tea, invites you out of autopilot and into awareness. With each photo, you pause. You *see*. You breathe. In that moment, the ordinary becomes extraordinary. That is mindfulness in motion.

The act of documenting beauty, meaning, or emotion in daily life also develops gratitude. When you begin to notice and capture what is good, real, or beautiful, even on hard days, you gradually retrain your brain to seek and savour positive experiences. Over time, your inner narrative shifts from what is missing to what is meaningful. You begin to realise how much there is to be thankful for, simple joys, quiet moments, shared connections, fleeting light. Gratitude deepens when photography becomes a ritual. It transforms from just taking pictures into *receiving* moments. You stop waiting for grand events and start celebrating what is already here.

Each image becomes a visual journal of blessings, large and small, that might otherwise go unnoticed or unappreciated. Neuroscience supports this too. Both mindfulness and gratitude stimulate areas of the brain associated with emotional regulation, empathy, and joy. They lower stress hormones and increase well-being. Daily photography can therefore serve as a subtle yet powerful form of emotional self-care. In essence, when you use photography as a daily practice, it becomes far more than art, it becomes a bridge to presence, a tool for healing, and a habit that opens your eyes and heart to the gift of now. Through the lens, you do not just capture life. You connect with it.

Photography As A Self-Worth Practice: Seeing Yourself As *Creator*

Photography as a self-worth practice is a powerful way to shift how you see yourself, from passive observer to intentional creator. When you pick up a camera or even your phone with purpose, you begin to reclaim your gaze. You choose what to focus on. You decide what has meaning, beauty, and value. In doing so, you are not just documenting the world, you are shaping your experience of it. Each photograph becomes an act of self-expression and affirmation. With every click, you say: *This matters. I see it. I see me.* You move from invisibility to visibility, first in the outer world, then within your own heart.

When you photograph something meaningful to you, a landscape, a face, a moment, you are not just recording it, you are *validating* it, and if you dare to turn the lens toward yourself, with compassion rather than critique, you begin the brave act of witnessing your own worth. Self-portraits, candid reflections, and creative expressions allow you to see yourself not as flawed or incomplete, but as whole, evolving, and uniquely powerful. This practice can be especially transformative if you have spent much of your life hiding, doubting, or silencing yourself. Photography offers a safe and sacred space where you do not have to perform or please anyone.

You can explore your identity, emotions, and dreams without judgment. You can rewrite old narratives of unworthiness with new ones of agency, creativity, and care. Over time, as you look back on your photographs, you begin to see the unfolding story of a person who chose to see. Who chose to show up. Who chose to create, even in the midst of imperfection or uncertainty, and that is where self-worth blooms, not from external validation, but from your ability to witness your own life with reverence. Photography, then, becomes not just a skill or hobby, but a mirror that reflects your inner light, your perspective, and your ever-deepening relationship with yourself. Through the lens, you remember that you are not just part of the world, you are an artist within it.

Turning Image-Making Into Inner Healing And Emotional Exploration

Turning image-making into a practice of inner healing and emotional exploration invites you to move beyond simply capturing what you see, and instead, to begin witnessing what you *feel*. Photography becomes more than visual, it becomes visceral. With intention, the camera becomes a tool for self-inquiry, a mirror for your emotions, and a companion on your healing journey. When you consciously create images, you give form to the formless, you give shape to joy, grief, longing, or hope. A photograph of a shadow can speak to parts of yourself you have hidden.

A still image of an open sky can reflect a sense of spaciousness you are yearning to reclaim. In this way, the camera helps you express emotions you might not yet have words for. This process can be especially powerful when navigating difficult emotions. Grief, heartbreak, anxiety, or even numbness can be softened through the gentle act of image-making. By externalising these internal states through light, composition, and metaphor, you create safe distance and deeper understanding. You learn to hold what hurts without being overwhelmed by it. You might photograph empty chairs, faded flowers, or old places that echo memories, and in doing so, honour what has been lost or left behind. Or you might capture warm light, smiling eyes, and tiny everyday beauties, helping you anchor into presence, gratitude, and life's quiet gifts.

Over time, your photo collection becomes a visual journal of healing, a record not just of what you saw, but of who you were becoming. This is emotional exploration through creativity. You follow your intuition rather than rules, responding to what draws your heart and sparks your soul. You begin to ask yourself:

- What am I really seeing here?

- What does this image stir in me?

- What does it want to teach me?

In this way, photography becomes a sacred dialogue between your inner world and outer expression. You do not need to be technically skilled, you only need to be curious, open, and willing to see with the eyes of the heart, because when you turn image-making into healing, you discover that every photo is not just an image, it is a reflection of your becoming.

Five Frames of Your Heart Exercise

I invite you to take five photos on your phone, in or near where you currently are, that capture the quiet truths of your heart.

---

1. **Bring you a sense of calm** – Look for something that soothes you, whether it is a peaceful corner, a gentle light, or a place that helps your breath slow down.

2. **Make you smile** – Capture a moment, object, or detail that sparks joy within you, no matter how small.

3. **Reflect something beautiful** – Notice beauty as it appears around you, in nature, in people, or even in the ordinary.

4. **Represent yourself** – Find something that feels like *you*, an image that speaks to your identity, your journey, or what matters most to your heart.

5. **Hold a memory or story** – Choose something that carries meaning, a reminder of where you have been, who you love, or what you hope for.

When you have completed this practice, I invite you to **title each photo** and write a few words about why you chose it. In doing so, you are not just taking pictures, you are capturing pieces of your soul and honouring the language of your heart through images and stories.

Case Study Discussion: Paige's Journey

Paige often felt invisible and overlooked, or 'invisible' was how she described it to me. Paige's level of self–confidence and self–worth was very low, and we spent many months journeying together rebuilding those important parts of her Self. I challenged Paige to take 5 photographs a day that she loved and to then write out a few words as to why she had taken them and how they made her feel. With an iPhone in her hands, she embarked on a personal quest to capture the moments that brought her joy, filled her heart with wonder and reminded her of her worthiness.

It was a beautiful journey of self–discovery. With each image she took, she immortalised moments of pure delight, freezing them in time. The vibrant colours, the play of light and shadow, and the emotions woven into each frame became testaments to her existence and worth. As she examined her photographs, Paige realised that her perspective mattered (she began to understand that she mattered). Through her iPhone lens, she revealed her world's hidden beauty, finding reflection in the images she created. Mountains mirrored her strength, and the laughter of children mirrored her own capacity for joy.

Those photographs became her personal gallery of self–affirmation. In times of doubt (and this was daily), she turned to them, reminding herself that she was worthy of living a beautiful life. The photographs became a visual narrative of her journey towards self–acceptance and self–love.

Reflective Exercise: Paige's Journey

Here are four profound and reflective questions inspired by Paige's story to help you engage with your own journey behind the lens:

1. **What do your photographs reveal about how you see the world, and your place within it?** *Reflection:* Every image you capture is filtered through your unique way of seeing. Your eye is drawn to what your heart values. When you pause to notice what you photograph, you begin to honour your own perspective. Like Paige, your lens can become a mirror, showing you that your presence matters and that you belong.

2. **When was the last time you captured something that made you feel joy, awe, or tenderness?** *Reflection:* Your camera becomes a tool of the heart when you use it to notice beauty, softness, and meaning. Those moments, of light on leaves, a smile, a quiet sky, remind you that there is wonder in your world. As you revisit your images, let them reconnect you to your capacity for feeling and presence.

3. **What do you notice about yourself when you look back on the images you have chosen to keep?** *Reflection:* You may start to see themes in what you capture: colour, light, people, textures, emotion. These are not just preferences, they are reflections of your emotional world. Like Paige, you might discover a hidden strength, a longing, or a quiet joy that you had not seen before. Your photos tell a story, your story.

4. **How can you use photography to affirm your worth and express your truth, one image at a time?** *Reflection:* When you intentionally photograph your life, you begin to say: *I see this. I choose this. This moment matters.* That act becomes a declaration of worthiness. Let your photos be more than memories, let them be reminders that you are alive, feeling, and worthy of being seen and celebrated.

Affirmations For Integration: (Heart Whispers)

Affirmations have the power to quiet the noise of doubt, open the doorway to self-trust, and draw you back into the wisdom of your heart. When practised daily, they nurture an inner dialogue based in love and truth, helping you live each day more aligned with who you truly are. I invite you to repeat silently or write:

- *I capture moments of love to cherish for a lifetime.*

- *I see beauty in my photographs and discover my own worth.*

- *I express my emotions through my lens, finding joy and peace.*

- *I create visual reminders of happiness that uplift me every day.*

- *I share my passion for life through my photographs.*

- *I honour the stories behind my photographs, knowing they reveal the truth of my journey.*

- *Through my lens, I find wonder in the ordinary and turn it into something extraordinary.*

- *Each photo I take reminds me that beauty exists in both light and shadow.*

- *My photographs are reflections of gratitude, capturing the blessings I sometimes overlook.*

- *I use my camera as a mirror of my heart, preserving what matters most to me.*

Daily Photo Challenge (for one week):

Each day this week, I invite you to take one meaningful photo that captures something your heart wants you to notice. Use your lens not just to see, but to feel.

1. Capture a *moment of connection* - notice where your heart meets another's, whether in a smile, a gesture, or even in the quiet presence of being together.

2. Reflect on *something you are grateful for* - pause to honour it with your camera, giving thanks through the act of seeing.

3. Show a *personal strength or value* - take a photo that reminds you of the qualities that live within you, even when you forget.

---

4.   Reveal *beauty in the ordinary* - look closely at what you might usually pass by and let your heart show you what is extraordinary about it.

5.   Represent a *dream or desire* - capture an image that whispers possibility, hope, or the vision of who you are becoming.

At the end of the week, gather your photos together. Sit quietly, breathe, and review each one with your heart open. Then, write a short reflection titled: *"The Story My Heart is Telling."* Let your words flow as naturally as your images did.

Closing Reflection

Photographs are not just images; they are sacred echoes of the moments that have shaped you. Each one whispers quietly: *I was here. I felt this. I chose to pause, to notice, to honor this moment.* Through the lens of your heart, photography becomes more than a record of time, it becomes a mirror of your soul, revealing what you value, what you cherish, and what brings you alive.

When you capture beauty, even in something ordinary, you remind yourself that life is filled with wonder waiting to be noticed. When you hold onto a photo that carries deep meaning, you are also holding onto the truth of your worth, that your story matters, your presence matters, and your way of seeing the world is both unique and needed.

Allow these photographs to ground you in presence. Let them guide you back when you feel lost, uplift you when you feel heavy, and remind you that joy can be found in the simplest frames of life. Every photo is more than a snapshot, it is a prayer, a reflection, a declaration: *I see. I feel. I am alive.* Keep framing moments with love. Keep allowing your heart to see beauty. Keep creating the story only you can tell.

17 – HAPPY PLACE

Your Opening Reflection

Invitation to Your Happy Place - As you enter this chapter, give yourself the gift of stepping into a sanctuary of peace and joy, your own happy place. This space, whether drawn from memory or imagination, is your heart's refuge. Let it rise before you now: see it, hear it, feel it. Allow yourself to rest fully here, soaking in the comfort, safety, and quiet delight it offers. Let this place remind you that no matter where you are, you carry within you a home of calm, joy, and belonging.

- "What does your Happy Place look like?"

- "What sounds, colors, textures, or scents surround you?"

- "How do you feel when you are in this place?"

- "Who or what makes this place feel special or safe for you?"

- "What memories come alive when you imagine being here?"

- "Why does this place bring you a sense of peace or joy?"

Let these questions open the doorway into presence. Every answer you give, whether in words, sensations, or silence, is a bridge between where you are and where you are going.

Learning Objectives

The learning objectives are included here to give you a clear focus for this chapter, ensuring that each practice you explore moves you closer to mastering the skills, insights, and heart-led awareness that will enrich your life well beyond the program. By the end of this chapter, you will:

- Understand the emotional and psychological benefits of identifying and connecting with their personal happy place.

- Develop awareness of what environments, practices, and inner states promote calm, clarity, and self-connection.

- Cultivate practical strategies for accessing their happy place during times of stress or disconnection.

- Recognise the role of stillness and intentionality in emotional well-being and self-compassion.

Core Emotional Domains

The core emotional intelligence domains covered here are essential because they form the foundation for lasting heart connection, guiding you to deepen self-awareness, regulate emotions, build resilience, and strengthen the mind-body bond throughout your Heart Unbound journey.

- **Self-Awareness:** Cultivating inner clarity by recognising the thoughts, emotions, and memories that bring peace, joy, or calm. This practice helps you identify the environments or experiences where your heart feels most at home.

- **Self-Regulation:** Learning to return to a positive, grounded state by intentionally visualising and anchoring in your *"happy place,"* even during moments of stress or overwhelm.

- **Motivation:** Reconnecting with inner drive and hope by accessing the emotional energy found in joy, comfort, and inspiration, fueling resilience and forward momentum.

- **Empathy:** Understanding that everyone has a unique inner refuge, creating deeper compassion for others' emotional landscapes and personal sources of peace.

- **Mindfulness/Presence** *(Integrated Emotional Intelligence Practice)*: Strengthening the capacity to stay present, centred, and open-hearted by consciously engaging the senses and imagination to evoke calm, clarity, and emotional stability

"Happy Place" - Returning To Your Inner Sanctuary

The concept of a *"happy place"* is timeless, deeply human, and woven through ancient wisdom, spiritual teachings, and modern psychology. Across cultures and generations, people have instinctively returned, whether in imagination or memory, to places that evoke peace, joy, and belonging. Your happy place might be the gentle rhythm of ocean waves on a deserted beach, the golden glow of late afternoon light through a window, or the embrace of a loved one in a moment of perfect stillness. It might even be a simple yet sacred memory, a childhood moment of laughter, a sunset walk, or the quiet contentment of feeling at home within yourself.

This inner sanctuary is more than an escape; it is a profound act of emotional intelligence and self-care. When life feels chaotic, uncertain, or overwhelming, the ability to connect with your happy place becomes a reliable and grounding form of emotional regulation. It helps activate the parasympathetic nervous system, quiet the mind, and bring clarity to turbulent emotions. In this space, you remember who you are beneath the noise, the calm within the storm.

Returning to your happy place is an act of self-love. It affirms that your emotional wellbeing matters and that safety, comfort, and peace are not things you must earn, but gifts you can give yourself. It invites mindfulness, presence, and heart connection. It softens your inner critic, awakens gratitude, and nurtures your resilience. Whether you practice it through guided visualisation, breathwork, journaling, or quiet contemplation, the journey to your happy place becomes a practice of healing and empowerment. In a fast-paced world that often prioritises doing over being, your happy place reminds you to pause, breathe, and remember: you are allowed to feel good. You are worthy of peace. You can always come home to yourself.

The Historical Roots Of Sanctuary And Sacred Space (Temples, Gardens, Sacred Groves)

The human longing for sanctuary, spaces of peace, safety, and spiritual connection, has deep historical roots that transcend geography, religion, and culture. From ancient temples to sacred groves and meticulously cultivated gardens, these spaces have served as physical and symbolic refuges for rest, reflection, and reverence. In ancient Mesopotamia, temples were not only places of worship but also architectural embodiments of cosmic order. They were built to mirror the heavens, linking the divine with the earthly and offering a place where human beings could commune with the gods.

Similarly, in Ancient Egypt, temple complexes were seen as microcosms of creation itself, sanctuaries where spiritual rituals helped maintain harmony in the world. Across the Mediterranean, sacred groves, often associated with Greek and Roman deities like Artemis, Apollo, and Demeter, offered a different kind of sanctuary: one immersed in nature. These living sanctuaries, where trees were honoured as vessels of the divine, provided a space for healing, contemplation, and connection with the rhythms of the earth. Entry into a sacred grove was considered a holy act, a pilgrimage toward the inner and outer sacred.

In Eastern traditions, such as Taoism and Buddhism, gardens were cultivated as expressions of harmony, mindfulness, and the balance of opposites. Japanese Zen gardens, for instance, embody the principle of *wabi-sabi,* the beauty of impermanence and imperfection, and invite quiet introspection. These tranquil environments were designed not just for aesthetics but as portals into deeper awareness and spiritual presence. Christian monastic cloisters, with their enclosed gardens and quiet corridors, offered solitude and serenity for those seeking communion with the divine.

Similarly, Islamic tradition birthed the concept of the *"chahar bagh,"* the four-part garden representing paradise, used in Persian and Mughal architecture. These sacred gardens symbolised spiritual wholeness and the soul's longing for unity. Whether in stone or soil, architecture or wilderness, sacred spaces across history have offered sanctuary from the demands of the outer world and a return to inner stillness. They remind us that human beings have always needed spaces where the noise fades, the heart softens, and the sacred becomes palpable. In a modern context, the idea of sanctuary can be reclaimed through practices that create inner space, breathwork, visualisation, meditation, or even identifying a personal *"happy place."* These contemporary forms of sanctuary reflect an enduring truth: the soul thrives where it feels safe, seen, and connected to something greater.

The Science Of Safe Spaces: How Happy Places Calm The Nervous System

The concept of a *"happy place"* is not just poetic, it is deeply physiological. Neuroscience and psychology affirm that mentally returning to a place where we have felt safe, joyful, or deeply connected can profoundly regulate the nervous system and support mental and emotional wellbeing. At the core of this process is the **autonomic nervous system (ANS)**, which governs the body's unconscious responses to stress and safety. The ANS is composed of two primary branches: the **sympathetic nervous system**, which initiates the fight, flight, or free e response; and the **parasympathetic nervous system**, which promotes rest, digestion, and recovery. Safe, soothing imagery, like that of a happy place, activates the parasympathetic branch, helping the body shift out of survival mode and back into a state of calm and equilibrium.

When you visualise or recall your happy place, whether it is the smell of ocean air, the dappled light of a forest, or the embrace of a childhood home, the brain's **limbic system**, particularly the **amygdala and hippocampus**, registers these memories. If the memories are associated with positive emotions and a felt sense of safety, the brain sends signals to the body to relax. Heart rate slows, cortisol (the stress hormone) drops, breathing becomes deeper and slower, and muscles begin to release held tension.

The **vagus nerve**, a key component in the parasympathetic response, becomes more active, supporting digestion, immune function, and emotional regulation. Neuroscientific studies using **fMRI scans** show that guided visualisation of safe and comforting places activates areas of the brain involved in **emotion regulation, memory consolidation, and self-awareness**. This not only calms immediate stress responses but strengthens neural pathways associated with resilience and emotional intelligence. Over time, the brain begins to associate the act of recalling or visualising a happy place with a reliable sense of safety and wellbeing.

In addition, the concept of **neuroplasticity,** the brain's ability to rewire itself, means that consistently practicing these visualisations can lead to more permanent shifts in how one responds to stress. A happy place becomes not just an escape, but a neurobiological anchor: a touchstone of calm that lives within you. Trauma research, especially the work of **Stephen Porges and the Polyvagal Theory**, emphasises the importance of creating internal and external environments of safety. Porges proposes that our sense of safety is foundational to our ability to socially engage, emotionally regulate, and access higher-order thinking.

Imagining a happy place, especially when paired with breathing and heart-centred practices, can send strong cues of *"safety"* to the brain, helping people recover from anxiety, overwhelm, or dysregulation. Furthermore, **positive psychology** supports the use of *"happy place"* visualisation as a technique to build **emotional resilience, increase optimism, and enhance wellbeing**.

Studies have shown that people who regularly reflect on moments and places that brought them peace or joy report higher levels of self-compassion, better sleep, reduced rumination, and improved mood.

In high-pressure workplaces or healthcare environments, incorporating safe space practices, such as visualisation, mindfulness, or the physical creation of *"pause zones"*, is emerging as an effective strategy for supporting mental health and reducing burnout. For people experiencing chronic stress or trauma, the invitation to mentally retreat to a happy place can be not just helpful, but healing. **In essence, a happy place is not only a memory, it is medicine.** A wellspring of safety encoded into your nervous system, accessible at any moment through breath, awareness, and intention. Whether used in therapy, education, leadership, or daily life, cultivating and returning to your happy place is a gentle but powerful act of emotional self-care and nervous system restoration.

The Role Of Solitude, Silence, And Sensory Awareness In Cultivating Joy

In a world overflowing with noise, stimulation, and urgency, the gifts of solitude, silence, and sensory awareness often go unnoticed. Yet these ancient and enduring practices form a quiet, powerful pathway to authentic joy. Not the fleeting kind sparked by external rewards, but the deep, grounded joy that arises from within, when you are fully present, attuned, and at peace in your own being.

Solitude: The Sacred Encounter with Self

Solitude is not the same as loneliness. While loneliness is marked by absence and longing, solitude is presence, presence with yourself. It is the space where you can take off the many masks worn for the world and come home to your essence. In solitude, your inner world becomes audible. Your heart, so often drowned out by external demands, can whisper truths that guide and renew. Periods of intentional solitude allow you to reset your emotional rhythms.

You begin to distinguish between what is truly yours and what has been absorbed from others, beliefs, pressures, even emotions. In this still space, your soul has room to breathe. You remember who you are beneath the expectations, roles, and noise, and in this remembering, joy gently emerges, not as excitement, but as a subtle and sustaining warmth.

Silence: The Fertile Ground for Inner Joy

Silence is more than the absence of sound, it is the presence of space. In silence, thoughts slow, the nervous system recalibrates, and the mind becomes less reactive. Silence gives joy room to rise, unforced and unhurried. It allows for integration, for inner knowing, and for deep listening, not just to others, but to yourself.

Modern neuroscience supports what mystics have known for centuries: silence activates regions of the brain associated with self-reflection, empathy, and emotional regulation. Even just two minutes of intentional silence can lower cortisol levels, enhance clarity, and improve mood. When practiced regularly, silence becomes a sanctuary, a sacred reset button that nourishes inner peace and awakens joy from within.

Sensory Awareness: Anchoring in the Now

When you slow down enough to truly notice your sensory experience, what you see, hear, feel, smell, and taste, you awaken to the richness of the present moment. This is the foundation of mindfulness, and one of the purest ways to cultivate joy. Joy lives in simple moments: the warmth of sunlight on your skin, the sound of leaves rustling in the wind, the aroma of your morning coffee, the texture of a loved one's hand in yours.

Sensory awareness grounds you in the here and now, pulling your attention away from worries of the future or regrets of the past. By fully engaging the senses, you begin to experience life more vividly, and joyfully. Each ordinary moment becomes extraordinary. You realise that joy is not something to chase; it is something you access by arriving fully into your life, one breath, one sensation at a time.

The Intersection of All Three: Joy as a State of Being

When solitude, silence, and sensory awareness intersect, a subtle alchemy unfolds. You come into alignment. You begin to feel joy not as an emotion dependent on circumstance, but as a steady presence, a natural expression of inner wholeness. In this state, even amidst challenge or uncertainty, you can return to yourself and find something enduring: the peace of being deeply and wholly alive. *Solitude gives you the space. Silence gives you the depth. Sensory awareness gives you the anchor. Together, they give you joy.*

How Modern Distractions Interfere With Heartful Presence

You live in an age of constant connection, and yet, paradoxically, it is an age of profound disconnection. Your attention is under siege. The pings of smartphones, the scroll of social media, the relentless demands of multitasking, all of these modern distractions fragment your focus and pull you away from the sacred here and now. Most significantly, they interfere with something even more precious: your capacity for *heartful presence*.

The Cost of Constant Connectivity

Technology offers remarkable convenience, but it comes at a cost to your emotional and spiritual wellbeing. Each notification interrupts your natural rhythm of thought and feeling. Each scroll trains your brain to crave novelty, making stillness feel uncomfortable and introspection elusive. In trying to stay connected to everything, you become connected to nothing in depth, not to your breath, your bodies, or the quiet language of your heart.

Heartful presence requires space, mental, emotional, and spiritual. It requires your full attention, but when that attention is divided into a thousand digital threads, you are no longer grounded in the present moment. You begin to skim the surface of life, missing the deeper wisdom and joy that arise from genuine presence with yourself and others.

Emotional Numbing Through Distraction

One of the more subtle dangers of constant distraction is that it numbs you to your own emotional life. You reach for your phones not just out of habit, but often to avoid discomfort, to escape boredom, loneliness, anxiety, or grief, but when you avoid feeling, you also disconnect from healing. Distractions become a form of emotional bypass, placing distance between your awareness and the tender truths of your heart.

Heartful presence invites you to be with what is, without judgment, without numbing, without the need to fix. It calls you into intimacy with your inner world, but when your go-to response is to check, swipe, scroll, or post, you abandon the opportunity for true connection: connection with yourself, with others, and with the deeper meaning of your life.

Emotional Numbing Through Distraction

One of the more subtle dangers of constant distraction is that it numbs you to your own emotional life. You reach for your phones not just out of habit, but often to avoid discomfort, to escape boredom, loneliness, anxiety, or grief, but when you avoid feeling, you also disconnect from healing. Distractions become a form of emotional bypass, placing distance between your awareness and the tender truths of your heart. Heartful presence invites you to be with what is, without judgment, without numbing, without the need to fix. It calls you into intimacy with your inner world, but when your go-to response is to check, swipe, scroll, or post, you abandon the opportunity for true connection: connection with yourself, with others, and with the deeper meaning of your life.

Reclaiming the Heart's Attention

Reclaiming heartful presence begins with noticing where your attention goes, and gently, repeatedly bringing it back. It requires intention, boundaries, and practices that support stillness and reflection. You do not need to renounce technology, but you do need to choose how and when to engage with it.

Simple practices, like device-free mornings, mindful breathing breaks, or creating sacred digital sabbaths, can restore your attention and deepen your relationship with the present moment. When you choose presence over distraction, even briefly, you affirm that your life is worth being lived fully, not in fragments, but in wholeness.

Rediscovering Joy: Creating Internal And External Environments That Heal

In the busyness of modern life, joy can feel like a luxury, something fleeting, elusive, or conditional. Yet joy is not a reward for everything being perfect. It is a state of being that lives within you, waiting patiently to be remembered. To rediscover joy is to come home to your heart, and to do so, you must intentionally cultivate both internal and external environments that nourish healing, presence, and delight.

The Internal Environment: Healing the Inner Landscape

Your internal world, your thoughts, beliefs, emotions, and nervous system state, shapes your capacity for joy more than any external condition. If your mind is filled with harsh self-talk, unresolved grief, or chronic stress, joy struggles to take root. Creating an internal environment that heals begins with self-compassion and emotional honesty. It means making space for all your feelings, not just the comfortable ones. It means shifting from judgment to curiosity, from criticism to care.

Practices such as mindfulness, breathwork, heart journaling, and loving-kindness meditation help rewire your nervous system, soften inner resistance, and restore emotional flow. When your inner terrain becomes more gentle and grounded, joy finds fertile soil. Affirming beliefs also matter. When you begin to tell yourself, *"I deserve peace. I am worthy of happiness. It is safe to feel good,"* you are no longer waiting for joy, you are inviting it.

The External Environment: Designing Spaces that Soothe and Inspire

Your outer world is an extension of our inner state, and vice versa. The spaces you inhabit, the people you surround yourself with, the routines you engage in, all influence your emotional wellbeing. Healing environments are not about luxury; they are about intention. A healing space may be a sunlit corner with a cup of tea and a journal. It may be a walk in nature, a quiet room with plants and candles, or a communal space filled with laughter and safe connection.

External environments that support joy are those that invite presence, simplicity, and beauty. They calm the nervous system and awaken the senses. It is also about who and what you allow into your energetic space. Joy flourishes in relationships that honour your heart. It expands in places where you feel safe to be authentic. Boundaries become sacred tools, not to keep people out, but to keep your inner peace intact.

Micro-Moments of Joy: Sacred Simplicity

Rediscovering joy does not always require major change. Often, it lives in the micro-moments: the scent of rain, a kind word, the softness of your breath. When you become present to life's subtle gifts, you reawaken your joy receptors. These micro-moments become bridges, between stress and stillness, despair and delight. As you become more attuned to what nourishes you, you can begin to intentionally cultivate these moments. Ask yourself:

- *What brings me alive?*

- *Where do I feel most like myself?*

- *When do I feel at peace for no reason?*

Your answers will help shape your environments, both inner and outer, that hold and heal you.

<u>Joy as Resistance and Renewal</u>

In a world that can feel heavy with suffering, joy is not avoidance, it is resilience. Choosing to cultivate joy is a radical act of hope. It says, *"I believe in beauty, in healing, in the sacredness of being alive."* Joy does not mean bypassing pain; it means allowing your heart to be nourished even in the midst of it. When you consciously create spaces, internally and externally, that honour your aliveness, you build capacity. You give yourself a place to return to when the world feels too much, and in doing so, you not only rediscover joy, you become a source of it for others.

Create Your Happy Place Map Exercise

A guided activity to connect with joy, peace, and inner calm

Step 1: Ground Yourself

- Take 3 slow breaths.

- Place your hand on your heart and invite yourself into stillness.

- Whisper to yourself: *"I am ready to create my happy place."*

Step 2: Imagine or Recall Your Happy Place

- Close your eyes for a moment.

- Picture a place where you feel completely safe, joyful, and at peace.

- This can be a **real location** (beach, forest, childhood home) or an **imagined sanctuary**.

Prompt: What do you see, hear, smell, or feel in this place?

Step 3: Design Your Map

On a blank page (or canvas), begin creating your map or collage. You can:

- Draw or sketch symbols.

- Use colors that represent how it feels.

- Write down descriptive words.

- Paste or doodle images.

Include these elements:

1. **Location:** Where is your happy place?

2. **Emotions:** What feelings rise in you here? (e.g., joy, safety, freedom)

---

3. **Practices & Rituals:** What do you do here? (e.g., sit quietly, surf, read, laugh with loved ones)

4. **Phrase/Mantra:** Choose a short phrase that anchors your map (e.g., *"Here I am home."* or *"I am safe. I am free."*)

Step 4: Reflection Prompts

Write a few sentences:

- What surprised you about your happy place?

- How can you invite small pieces of this place into your daily life?

- What does your happy place teach you about what you truly value?

Step 5: Optional Sharing

- Share your Happy Place Map with a trusted partner or small group.

- If you are facilitating, invite participants to explain one image, word, or color that means the most to them.

Step 6: Integration

- Keep your Happy Place Map somewhere visible.

- Return to it whenever you feel stressed or disconnected.

- Use your phrase/mantra as a grounding tool in daily life.

Remember: Your Happy Place Map is not about artistic skill, it is about creating a heart-space you can return to again and again.

Case Study Discussion: Emmanuel's Journey

Emmanuel always made me laugh. He was a hardworking executive who often felt overwhelmed by the demands of his high–pressure job and the chaotic pace of his life. He knew he wanted peace, but he had conditioned himself to always do 'busy'. I literally had to explain to him what the phrase, 'stop and smell the roses actually meant!' On one of his business trips, I challenged him to gift himself a few hours to go for a drive, find a spot, go for a walk, reconnect with nature and the world outside of the office. I instructed him to listen to his heart and let it guide him.

He went for a drive and found a park and went for a walk. He took his socks and shoes off and he found himself lying on his back in the grass, where he spent the next 3 hours just lying there disconnected from the white noise of his world. In this beautiful spot, Emmanuel discovered his happy place. He would often escape his office and immerse himself in the restorative beauty of nature. Emmanuel's happy place provided respite from the relentless noise and stress of daily life. It became his sanctuary, a space where he could reflect, recharge, and rediscover his true self.

He found clarity and perspective, he gifted himself time to heal, learn and grow and this allowed him to navigate challenges with renewed strength and resilience. As he spent more time out of the office Emmanuel became more attuned to his present moment, and he started to savor the simple joys that he often overlooked in his hectic life. Emmanuel's personal journey to discover his happy place helped him transform his life. It reminded him of the importance of prioritising his own self–care, connecting with his heart, embracing moments of stillness, and nurturing his soul.

Reflective Exercise: Emmanuel's Journey

Here are four profound and reflective questions inspired by Emmanuel's story to help you engage with your own journey into your happy place:

1. **When was the last time you truly paused, not to achieve, fix, or plan, but simply to be present with yourself and the world around you?** *In a world that constantly pulls you to do more, be more, and keep going, stillness may feel foreign, maybe even uncomfortable, but when you pause, even briefly, you create space for your heart to speak. Like Emmanuel lying in the grass, you give yourself the gift of being, not doing. It is in these moments that clarity, healing, and joy quietly return.*

2. **What does your heart long for when the noise fades and the doing stops?** *When you let go of the noise, emails, deadlines, expectations, what remains? Beneath all of it, your heart is still beating, still whispering. Can you hear it? When you truly listen, you may find that your deepest longing is not for more, but for peace, connection, and simplicity. Let your heart remind you of what really matters.*

3. **Where is your happy place, and are you willing to let it become part of your life, not just a break from it?** *Your happy place is more than a location, it is a feeling, a remembering, a return to yourself. Maybe it is a quiet beach, a sunlit corner of your home, or the memory of lying in the grass like Emmanuel. Let this space become a sacred rhythm in your life, not just an escape from stress. You deserve to return there often, to be restored and renewed.*

---

4. **What small, sacred practice could you begin today to nurture your inner sanctuary and reconnect with joy?** *Transformation often begins with a small act of self-love. Perhaps today, it is taking a walk, breathing deeply, or placing your hand on your heart and asking, "What do I need right now?" You do not need a retreat or a vacation, just presence, curiosity, and kindness. Let this be the beginning of a more joyful, heart-connected way of living.*

Affirmations For Integration: (Heart Whispers)

Affirmations have the power to quiet the noise of doubt, open the doorway to self-trust, and draw you back into the wisdom of your heart. When practised daily, they nurture an inner dialogue based in love and truth, helping you live each day more aligned with who you truly are. I invite you to repeat silently or write:

- *I find peace within, surrounded by serenity.*

- *I embrace tranquility, letting go of all worries.*

- *I am content, appreciating the simple moments of life.*

- *I feel alive, connected to my truest self.*

- *I am free to be myself, surrounded by love and grace.*

- *I explore new horizons, discovering the magic that lies beyond.*

- *I return to my happy place whenever my heart needs rest.*

Happy Place Practice Pack

1. Create Your Happy Place Map: Design your multi-sensory *"map"* or collage. Include:

- Location (real or imagined)

- Emotions it evokes

- Practices/rituals that bring you there

- A phrase or mantra

2. Anchor Affirmations: Choose or write affirmations that help you return to your happy place. Examples:

- *I find peace within, surrounded by serenity.*

- *I am free to be myself, surrounded by love and grace.*

- *I return to my happy place whenever my heart needs rest.*

3. Happy Place Exploration Challenge: Pick one challenge to try this week:

- **Nature Walk** – Connect with your surroundings.

- **Creative Expression** – Draw, paint, sing, or write.

- **Gratitude List** – Name 5 things you are grateful for.

- **Digital Detox** – Step away from screens for a set time.

- **New Adventure** – Try something new, even small.

Reflection Prompt: After your challenge, write or record:

- What joy, calm, or self-connection arose within you?

- How did this activity bring you closer to your happy place?

Together, these three practices (Map, Affirmations, Challenge) form a **holistic cycle:**

- **Map** → visual anchor

- **Affirmations** → inner grounding

- **Challenge** → embodied action

Closing Reflection

Your happy place is not a luxury, it is a lifeline. In a culture that glorifies busyness, that tells us our worth lies in how much we produce or achieve, pausing can feel like rebellion. Yet giving yourself permission to step away from the constant noise is not indulgence, it is medicine. To stop, to breathe, to return to what feels safe and nourishing, is an act of profound courage and radical self-care.

Your happy place may live in the physical world, or it may dwell entirely in your inner landscape. Perhaps it is the steady hush of waves rolling onto the shore, the quiet sanctuary of a forest path, or the smell of rain on the earth. Perhaps it is the memory of your grandmother's kitchen, the warmth of a childhood bedroom, or the sound of a friend's laughter. Or perhaps, it is not a place at all, but a moment, a deep breath, a single pause, a flicker of stillness where you feel whole again.

This place, wherever you find it, is more than an escape. It is where you come home to yourself. It is the place where masks fall away, where expectations loosen their grip, where you remember that you are not your deadlines, your responsibilities, or your roles. You are simply you, enough, whole, alive. Here, the weight of the world softens. Here, the endless pressure fades. Here, your essence, your heart, your truth can be felt again.

It is a sacred reminder: peace is not something you must strive to earn. It does not need to be chased, bought, or fought for. It is already within you, waiting to be remembered. Emmanuel found his happy place lying barefoot in the grass, his skin touching the earth, his heart finding stillness in the quiet communion between body and ground. Yours might arrive in a sunlit morning, in a page of a book, in the rhythm of your own breath, or in the gentle silence that settles when you allow yourself to pause.

Let this happy place become a practice, not just a retreat. Do not wait until exhaustion forces you into stillness, let it be woven into the rhythm of your everyday. Let it be the place you return to not just when you are tired, but also when you are celebrating, when you are questioning, when you are dreaming. This is not escape, it is alignment. It is not running away, it is returning to the centre of who you are.

May you honour your need for rest without apology. May you delight in beauty without justification. May you seek connection without fear of being too much or not enough, and may you return, again and again, to the happy place that restores you to the truth of who you are: loved, worthy, whole.

You are allowed to rest.

You are allowed to feel joy.

You are allowed to be nourished by life's quiet gifts, and above all, you are allowed, always, to come home to yourself.

18 – DRAWING AND PAINTING

Your Opening Reflection

Invitation to Create from the Heart - As you enter this chapter, allow yourself to see drawing and painting not as tasks of skill, but as doorways into expression. Your art is not about perfection, it is about presence. Every stroke of the pen, every sweep of color, carries a piece of your truth. This is your chance to give shape and shade to the feelings that live within you. Let your heart be the brush, your breath the rhythm, and your imagination the canvas. Trust that what emerges is exactly what needs to be revealed.

- "When was the last time you allowed yourself to create without worrying about the outcome?"

- "If your heart could draw one image to express how it feels today, what might it look like?"

- "What colours or shapes do you associate with peace, joy, or healing in your life right now?"

- "How might drawing or painting help you express something words cannot capture?"

Let these questions open the doorway into presence. Every answer you give, whether in words, sensations, or silence, is a bridge between where you are and where you are going.

Learning Objectives

The learning objectives are included here to give you a clear focus for this chapter, ensuring that each practice you explore moves you closer to

mastering the skills, insights, and heart-led awareness that will enrich your life well beyond the program. By the end of this chapter, you will:

- Understand the power of drawing and painting as tools for emotional self-awareness and healing.

- Learn how creative expression enhances emotional regulation and empathy.

- Cultivate self-compassion and acceptance through the act of non-verbal reflection.

- Develop confidence in using visual art as a daily heart-connection ritual.

Core Emotional Domains

The core emotional intelligence domains covered here are essential because they form the foundation for lasting heart connection, guiding you to deepen self-awareness, regulate emotions, build resilience, and strengthen the mind-body bond throughout your Heart Unbound journey.

- **Self-Awareness:** When you draw or paint, you give form to the emotions and stories within you. Each stroke becomes a mirror, helping you see parts of yourself that words may not easily express. As you create, you begin to understand your emotional landscape more deeply.

- **Self-Regulation:** Art gives you a gentle and effective way to calm your nervous system. Whether you are colouring, sketching, or painting, the rhythmic movement helps you release tension, find balance, and return to a place of emotional steadiness.

- **Empathy:** As you tune in to your own emotional experience through your artwork, you also open your heart to others. You start to see that all humans feel, struggle, and long to be understood, just like you. This awareness naturally deepens your compassion.

- **Social Skills (Creative Communication):** Art allows you to express feelings that are sometimes hard to put into words. When you share your drawings or paintings, you are inviting others into your world in a way that creates meaningful connection and heartful communication.

- **Emotional Expression:** Drawing and painting help you release what has been held inside. Whether it is joy, grief, anger, or hope, your creative expression becomes a safe and powerful space to let your feelings flow and be seen, without judgment.

'Drawing And Painting': Lines From Your Heart

Visual art is one of the oldest and most powerful ways you can express what lives in your heart. Long before humans had formal language, we painted our stories on cave walls, recording our fears, hopes, and dreams. Art has always been more than decoration; it has been a sacred form of expression, a way to speak when words fall short. **When language fails you, art speaks.** It speaks in colour, texture, line, and shape. It holds what you cannot say out loud. Whether it is pain or peace, joy or sorrow, the act of creating allows your inner world to be seen, honoured, and released. In this part of the Heart Unbound journey, you are invited to explore visual art not just as a creative outlet, but as a path to healing and connection. **Here, you will learn to use art as a mirror and a doorway.**

A mirror that reflects what you are feeling deep inside, and a doorway that leads to greater understanding of yourself. Art helps you remember who you are beneath the roles, routines, and responsibilities. It reconnects you to the childlike wonder and unfiltered emotion that still lives within you. **Science now affirms what the soul has always known; art heals.** It calms the nervous system, reduces stress, and opens your heart. When you engage in visual creativity, even without any *"artistic skill,"* you activate parts of your brain that soothe, restore, and energise you. In this safe space, there is no right or wrong, just the freedom to express, explore, and feel.

Most importantly, art helps you grow your emotional intelligence. It increases your self-awareness. It teaches you to sit with your feelings, to name them, to move with them, not away from them. It builds empathy, creativity, and a deeper sense of connection with others. When you make art, you are not just creating an image, you are building a bridge from your heart to the world. So pick up a pencil, a brush, some colours, whatever calls to you, and begin. You do not have to be an artist. You just have to be open. This is your invitation to speak through your soul and listen with your heart.

Historical Roots of Emotional Expression Through Art (From Cave Art to Modern Therapy)

From the moment your ancestors first pressed pigment to stone, art has been a way to say, *"I am here. I feel. I belong."* Visual expression is one of the earliest and most enduring forms of human communication. Long before there were alphabets or spoken language as we know it, there were images, symbols scratched, etched, and painted on the walls of caves. These ancient markings told stories, honoured the sacred, recorded grief, and celebrated life. They gave voice to what could not be spoken. When you look at cave art today, you are witnessing the emotional residue of someone who lived thousands of years ago, a handprint on stone, a cry for connection, a whisper across time.

Throughout every era of human history, art has played a powerful role in expressing what lives inside the heart. In Ancient Egypt, murals were painted to accompany souls into the afterlife. In Indigenous cultures around the world, visual art has always been intertwined with ceremony, community, and healing. During the Renaissance, artists like Michelangelo and da Vinci expressed the divine and the human through brushstrokes that still move hearts today. Even in times of great suffering, wars, exiles, pandemics, people have turned to drawing, painting, and visual storytelling as a way to survive emotionally, to process the unthinkable, and to hold on to hope, and now, in the modern era, we continue this tradition in new and meaningful ways. Art therapy, for example, is used worldwide to support people who have experienced trauma, grief, or mental health challenges.

It offers a safe space where you do not need the right words, just the courage to create. Through colour, shape, and movement, art allows emotions to surface gently and be transformed. In *Heart Unbound*, you are not just learning about art, you are being invited into a sacred lineage. You are part of a long, unbroken chain of human beings who have used images to say what words cannot. You are continuing a story that began in fire-lit caves and now unfolds on paper, canvas, and screen. Every mark you make carries that legacy forward. When you create with intention, you are not just making something beautiful, you are accessing a deeper truth. You are listening to your heart, and giving it permission to speak. You are honouring what needs to be seen and releasing what needs to be set free. So as you take part in the creative exercises of this program, remember: *This is ancient. This is sacred. This is human. This is your heart, unbound.*

How Visual Art Bypasses The Logical Brain To Access Deep Emotion

Have you ever found yourself feeling something deeply, without being able to explain why? That is the mysterious beauty of the heart: it does not speak in logic or language. It speaks in sensation, in colour, in metaphor. It speaks in art. In your everyday life, you spend a lot of time in your logical mind, solving problems, making decisions, analysing situations, and planning for the future. This part of your brain is incredibly useful, but it can also become a wall between you and your deeper emotions. It wants certainty, control, and answers, but the heart? The heart longs to feel, to express, to release, and to connect.

This is where visual art becomes a sacred key. When you create, when you pick up a brush, doodle in a notebook, or move colour across a canvas, you are shifting out of the analytical brain and into the intuitive. You bypass the need for words and allow what's been buried or held back to rise gently to the surface. Art slows you down. It invites you inward. It whispers, *"You do not need to explain. Just be here."* The moment you begin to draw or paint, you enter a state of flow, what neuroscientists call a **non-verbal, limbic state,** where time stretches and the critical voice inside quiets.

This is when your nervous system begins to regulate. Emotions that may have felt overwhelming become more accessible. They take shape on the page or canvas, giving you a safe way to explore them. You do not need to be an artist. You do not need to make something perfect. In fact, letting go of perfection is part of the process. Visual art helps you feel without judgment. It helps you say what your heart has been holding, even if your mind does not fully understand it yet. In *Heart Unbound*, this process becomes a healing practice. You are not just creating pictures, you are unlocking parts of yourself that have been waiting to be heard.

You are softening the grip of overthinking. You are giving yourself permission to feel deeply, safely, and truthfully. Visual art becomes a sacred dialogue between you and your own soul. Every brushstroke, every colour choice, every line you make is a conversation with your inner world. Often, you will discover emotions you did not even know were there, grief that had not been spoken, joy that had been forgotten, or a longing that needed to be honoured. This is where transformation begins, not through the mind, but through the heart. So as you take part in today's creative practice, let go of the need to *"get it right."* Instead, let the art guide you.

- *Let the colours speak.*

- *Let your hands move.*

- *Let your heart reveal itself in ways your mind never could.*

This is your truth, unspoken and yet fully expressed. This is your heart, unbound.

Drawing As A Tool For Emotional Literacy And Stress Relief

You do not need to be a skilled artist to draw. You do not need formal training, perfect lines, or fancy materials. All you need is the willingness to listen to your heart, and the courage to let it speak through your hands. Drawing is one of the simplest and most accessible ways to build emotional literacy. It is a practice that teaches you how to understand, name, and safely express what you feel.

Instead of bottling your emotions or trying to rationalise them away, you create space for them on the page. You externalise the internal, and in doing so, you begin to heal. When you draw, you give shape to what has been unspoken. You begin to **see your emotions**, not just feel them. That in itself is powerful. A swirling circle might become the anxiety that has been knotting in your chest. A series of jagged lines may reflect frustration. A soft blend of colours might capture a quiet sadness or deep peace. Whatever emerges is a message from your inner world, one that deserves to be seen, felt, and honoured.

This process of translating feeling into form is at the heart of **emotional literacy**. You begin to notice the nuances of your emotional landscape. You learn the difference between tension and fear, between grief and guilt, between joy and contentment. Drawing helps you slow down enough to ask, *"What am I really feeling?"* and it gives you a safe way to release what you uncover, without shame, without needing the right words, but **drawing does not just support emotional awareness, it also relieves stress.** When you draw, your breathing slows. Your nervous system calms.

The simple rhythm of hand to paper brings you back to the present moment. It grounds you. It soothes you. It allows your mind to pause and your heart to speak. Modern research shows that drawing, even for a few minutes a day, reduces cortisol (the stress hormone), increases focus, and develops mindfulness. It invites your brain into a gentle state of flow where time softens, the inner critic quiets, and creativity opens the door to healing. In the *Heart Unbound* journey, drawing becomes more than a creative exercise, it becomes a practice of deep listening.

It becomes your visual journal, your emotional compass, your mirror. You do not need to draw something that *"looks good."* You simply need to draw what *feels true*. Let your lines be messy. Let your colours be wild. Let your heart lead the way. This is not about art. This is about honesty. This is about letting your emotions rise, move through you, and take shape in a way that feels safe and freeing. So today, pick up a pen, a pencil, a crayon, or anything that feels right, and begin. Draw what you feel. Draw without thinking. Draw without judgment. *This is your breath made visible. This is your heart, unbound.*

Self-Expression Vs. Self-Judgment: Reclaiming Your Creative Voice

There was a time in your life when you created freely. As a child, you probably sang without worrying if your voice was good enough. You scribbled, danced, painted, played, and imagined without hesitation. You did not ask, *"Is this good?"* or *"Will they like it?"* You simply expressed. You allowed your heart to speak through your body, boldly, joyfully, and without apology, but somewhere along the way, something shifted. Maybe someone criticised your art, or told you to colour inside the lines. Maybe comparison crept in, or you were told to be more realistic.

Slowly, self-expression gave way to **self-judgment**. The voice of the inner critic grew louder, whispering things like, *"You are not talented. That' i not good enough. Why bother?"* In this part of the *Heart Unbound* journey, you are invited to gently challenge that voice, and reclaim the one that matters most: your **creative voice**, because here is the truth: your creative voice is not about being perfect. It is about being *authentic*. It is not about being a professional artist. It is about being *fully alive*.

Self-expression is your birthright. It is how your soul communicates. It is how your emotions move, how your truth emerges, and how your heart speaks to the world. When you express yourself through art, writing, movement, or any form of creation, you are honouring your inner world. You are saying, *"My voice matters. My feelings matter. I matter,"* and that is an act of radical self-love, but to truly express yourself, you must learn to notice when self-judgment is holding the pen. You must learn to pause and ask, *"Is this my truth speaking, or my fear?"*

Self-judgment often disguises itself as protection. It wants to keep you safe from embarrassment or rejection, but in doing so, it can silence the very part of you that longs to be free. In *Heart Unbound*, your creative voice is welcomed back with compassion. You are reminded that there is no right way to express your truth, only *your* way. Every mark you make, every colour you choose, every word you write becomes an act of self-reclamation. You are not here to impress. You are here to express. This practice is not about the outcome. It is about the experience. It is about showing up for yourself without judgment. It is about listening to your heart and allowing it to move through your hands.

So give yourself permission to create without rules. Let go of the need to be *"good"* at it. Create like no one's watching. Create like your heart depends on it, because in many ways, it does. *This is how you begin to reclaim your creative voice. This is how you begin to trust yourself again. This is how you return home.* Welcome back. *This is your voice. This is your truth. This is your heart, unbound.*

Art As Heart: Connecting With Grief, Joy, Memory, And Self Through Image

When words fall short, images can hold what the heart is too full to say. Art is not just something you *do,* it is something you *feel.* It is a doorway to your heart and a mirror for your soul. It gives shape to your emotions, to your memories, to the stories you carry inside. It allows you to connect not only with what is beautiful and light, but also with what's tender, aching, and true. In *Heart Unbound,* art becomes more than creativity, it becomes communion. A way to sit with the fullness of your experience, to honour the hidden, and to celebrate the seen.

When you create an image, you create a space to meet yourself. Through colour, line, shape, and form, you begin to unlock the parts of you that have been waiting, sometimes for years, to be heard. You may find yourself painting grief, even if you did not know you were carrying it. You may draw something joyful and find tears in your eyes. You may trace a memory and discover healing where once there was pain.

Grief may emerge as dark brushstrokes or smudged lines. It may come gently or fiercely. Art allows you to be with grief without needing to fix or explain it. It gives you a way to honour your loss, to remember, to feel, and to release, without judgment.

Joy may burst through in colour and motion. It may surprise you. It may remind you of something you thought you had forgotten, like laughter, wonder, or hope. In those moments, art helps you remember that joy, too, is sacred medicine.

Memory lives in the marks you make. A shape might remind you of a childhood place. A colour may awaken the scent of someone you loved.

Through art, you can revisit, reclaim, and reframe your memories, not to rewrite your past, but to reconnect with the deeper truths they hold, and most of all, through art, you reconnect with **your Self**. Not the roles you play, or the expectations others place on you, but the truest part of you.

The one who longs to be seen. The one who knows how to feel deeply. The one who is brave enough to create from the heart. Art does not ask you to be perfect. It asks you to be *honest*. To show up. To feel. To listen. To express. So as you move through this part of the *Heart Unbound* journey, know that every image you create is an offering. A prayer. A message from your heart to your Self. Let your art hold what words cannot. Let it carry your love, your longing, your healing. Let it be a container for your grief, a celebration of your joy, and a reflection of the miracle that is *you. This is your heart, made visible. This is your story, painted in truth. This is your art, unbound.*

"Draw What You Feel" Exercise

Materials: Paper, coloured pencils, markers, or paints.

Instructions: I invite you to spend 10 minutes drawing your current emotional state using colour, shape, line, and space. Do not worry about making it *'look good'*, there is no right or wrong here. Avoid symbols or words unless they flow naturally."

Follow-up Reflection Prompts:

- *"What do you notice about your use of space or colour?"*

- *"Did anything surprise you as you drew?"*

- *"What emotions surfaced as you moved your hand across the page?"*

- *"If your drawing could speak, what would it want to tell you?"*

- *"How does your artwork reflect what you are experiencing right now in life?"*

- *"What shifts, insights, or releases did you notice within yourself as you created?"*

As you undertake this exercise, you move beyond the act of drawing into a **meaningful dialogue with your artwork and their inner world.**

Case Study Discussion: Stan's Journey

I first spoke with Stan about 12 months after his wife Lily had passed away with cancer. Stan was a man consumed by grief and the weight of his sorrow really affected his life, leaving him feeling empty and disconnected from the world around him. It was a really tough journey and the one thing that helped Stan was his ability to express himself through his drawing. I had spoken with him about completing some heart whispers and he asked if he could draw instead of writing. I told him he could do whatever felt right for him. I did not know it at the time, but Stan stopped his sketching when Lily died. With his pencil in hand, Stan began to pour his emotions onto the blank pages of his sketchpad. He drew memories of Lily, capturing her beautiful smile and the twinkle in her eyes. Each stroke of the pencil became a cathartic release, allowing him to express his love and sorrow.

Over time, Stan's sketches began to evolve. He found peace in the act of drawing, losing himself in the lines and shapes that emerged on his paper. Through his artwork, Stan was able to reconnect with his own inner world, exploring the depths of his emotions and finding healing in his creative sketches. Stan's drawings became a visual diary of his grief and transformation. His sketchpad became a safe place where he could express his pain, but also discover moments of joy and hope. With each completed sketch, Stan felt a sense of release and renewal. The act of drawing allowed him to navigate through his grief, gradually opening his heart to the possibilities of healing and growth. Through his artwork, he found a way to honour Lily's memory while also rediscovering his own strength and resilience. The simple act of drawing gifted Stan a pathway back to life, a way to remember, to heal, and to find beauty amidst his pain.

Reflective Exercise: Stan's Journey

Here are four profound and reflective questions inspired by Stans story to help you engage with your own creative journey:

1. **What emotions are you carrying silently within you that long to be expressed, not in words, but through colour, shape, or line?**
   You do not have to explain everything you feel. Like Stan, you can let your pencil or paintbrush speak for your heart. What might be revealed if you gave your emotions the freedom to take form on the page?

---

2. **Is there someone or something you have lost that your heart still wants to honour, and how might you express that through drawing with love and tenderness?** You may not need to say goodbye. Instead, you can find new ways to stay connected. Just like Stan did with his sketches of Lily, how might you capture a memory, a smile, or a feeling that still lives inside you?

3. **What part of yourself have you stopped expressing or creating since your own experience of loss, change, or heartache?** Sometimes, in the wake of pain, you silence parts of yourself that once brought joy or meaning. Have you left behind something you once loved? What would it look like to invite that part of you back, even gently, even just for today?

4. **How might drawing or painting help you move through your pain, not to forget it, but to transform it into something honest, beautiful, and healing?** Art does not erase your grief. It holds it, honours it, and helps it move. If you allowed your hands to lead the way, what kind of healing might begin to take shape on the page?

Affirmations For Integration: (Heart Whispers)

Affirmations have the power to quiet the noise of doubt, open the doorway to self-trust, and draw you back into the wisdom of your heart. When practised daily, they nurture an inner dialogue based in love and truth, helping you live each day more aligned with who you truly are. I invite you to repeat silently or write:

- *I find my inner peace when I hold a paintbrush.*

- *I explore new realms of creativity with each stroke of colour.*

- *I unleash my emotions onto the canvas, creating visual poetry.*

- *I discover my true self through the art of drawing.*

- *I immerse myself in a world where imagination knows no limits.*

- *I find peace in the beauty I create with my own hands.*

- *I witness my thoughts and feelings come to life on paper.*

> **"Create Your Heart Sketchbook Page Exercise"**
>
> I invite you to open a fresh page in your sketchbook and draw or paint one of the following:
>
> - *"Your emotion today"*
>
> - *"A memory you want to honour"*
>
> - *"Your current inner landscape"*
>
> - *"A message your heart wants you to see"*
>
> You may wish to add optional words, quotes, or colours to deepen the meaning. Title your page if it feels right. When finished, you can choose to share in pairs, or simply keep your creation private, as a gift for yourself.
>
> **This exercise keeps the activity simple, but makes it feel more meditative and heart-centred.**

Closing Reflection

As you put down your pencil, brush, or crayon, take a moment to acknowledge what you have just done. You have allowed your heart to speak in its own language, without needing to make sense, without needing to be perfect. That alone is powerful. Through each stroke and line, you gave shape to something real. Perhaps you touched grief, or glimpsed joy. Maybe you drew a memory, or met a feeling you did not even know was there. Whatever emerged, it came from a sacred place within you, and that deserves to be honoured.

This practice is not about making art, it is about making space. Space to feel. Space to release. Space to reconnect with the parts of you that have been waiting to be seen. Let this moment remind you: your heart holds beauty, even in pain. Your creativity is not a performance, it is a pathway. A way back to yourself, and every time you return to the page, you return to your truth. You do not have to find the right words. You only need the courage to begin. *You are healing. You are creating. You are remembering. You are alive.* This is your heart, unbound.

19 – SUNRISE AND SUNSET

Your Opening Reflection

Invitation to Rise and Release - As you enter this chapter, allow yourself to see sunrise and sunset not just as moments in the sky, but as sacred thresholds of your own life. Each sunrise invites you to begin again, to welcome light, hope, and possibility. Each sunset invites you to soften, release, and trust in the beauty of letting go. This is not about chasing the perfect moment, it is about presence. As the sky shifts in color and rhythm, let it mirror the cycles within you. Trust that every rising and every setting holds wisdom for your heart, guiding you home to balance, renewal, and peace.

- "When was the last time you allowed yourself to simply pause and watch the sun rise or set, and what did it awaken in you?"

- "What emotions or thoughts stir within you as the sky shifts its colors from light to dark, or dark to light?"

- "If sunrise represents a beginning and sunset a release, what in your life is asking to be begun, and what is asking to be let go?"

- "How do these daily transitions remind you of your own cycles of renewal, rest, and rebirth?"

Let these questions open the doorway into presence. Every answer you give, whether in words, sensations, or silence, is a bridge between where you are and where you are going.

Learning Objectives

The learning objectives are included here to give you a clear focus for this chapter, ensuring that each practice you explore moves you closer to mastering the skills, insights, and heart-led awareness that will enrich your life well beyond the program. By the end of this chapter, you will:

- Recognise how witnessing natural rhythms develops self-awareness and emotional balance

- Reflect on how sunrise and sunset symbolise emotional renewal and closure

- Use mindful observation of nature to deepen empathy, gratitude, and presence

- Create meaningful rituals around sunrise and sunset for emotional restoration

Core Emotional Domains

The core emotional intelligence domains covered here are essential because they form the foundation for lasting heart connection, guiding you to deepen self-awareness, regulate emotions, build resilience, and strengthen the mind-body bond throughout your Heart Unbound journey.

- **Self-Awareness:** You pause to notice your emotions as they rise and fall, just like the sun. You begin to understand how your thoughts and feelings shape your experience of each day.

- **Self-Regulation:** You learn to soften your reactions, to breathe through emotional waves, and to bring calm to moments of tension, finding balance as light fades and returns.

- **Empathy:** You reflect on how others experience their own dawns and dusks, deepening your compassion and your ability to hold space for different perspectives and emotions.

- **Motivation (Renewal and Reflection):** As sunrise inspires hope and sunset invites reflection, you reconnect with your inner purpose. You remember what matters, and why you began this journey of the heart.

- **Mindful Presence:** You become fully present in the beauty of beginnings and endings. With each sunrise, you open. With each sunset, you let go. You return to this moment, again and again.

"Sunrise And Sunset – The Rhythm Of Renewal"

Sunrise and sunset are more than just beautiful scenes painted across the sky, they are emotionally significant rituals that hold deep meaning for the human heart. Every sunrise whispers *begin again*. Every sunset reminds you *to let go*. These natural transitions offer more than aesthetic beauty, they are invitations to connect, reflect, and realign. This segment of the *Heart Unbound* journey explores how aligning with these sacred rhythms can help you build **emotional balance**, deepen **intentional living**, and cultivate a profound sense of **heart coherence,** where your thoughts, emotions, and actions flow in harmony.

At sunrise, the world awakens, and so can you. It is a powerful moment to set intentions, to breathe in new energy, and to greet the day with awareness and purpose. Rising with the sun offers you a chance to check in with your emotional landscape before the noise of the day begins. What do you need today? What will you carry into the light? At sunset, the earth softens, and so can you. It is a moment of release, of closure, of gentle surrender. The fading light invites you to reflect on your day with kindness, celebrating what was good, and letting go of what no longer serves you.

It is an opportunity to regulate your emotions, soothe your nervous system, and find peace before rest. These daily bookends, sunrise and sunset, become personal rituals that support **self-awareness**, **self-regulation**, and **emotional renewal**. By tuning in to them, you begin to live more mindfully and more rhythmically, honouring the natural flow of energy, emotion, and time. In doing so, you also cultivate **heart coherence,** a state where your heart, mind, and body align. This coherence enables clarity, compassion, and resilience. It strengthens your ability to be present, to lead with love, and to respond to life with emotional intelligence.

Whether you greet the sunrise with silence or prayer, or watch the sunset with a hand over your heart, these moments become anchors, reminders that each day is a cycle of hope, learning, and renewal.

In the light and in the fading, your heart finds its rhythm.

In the rise and in the rest, your soul remembers:

Every ending is a beginning, and every beginning holds a promise.

This is your heart, unbound.

Ancient Cultural And Spiritual Connections To Sunrise And Sunset

Long before clocks and calendars, ancient peoples attuned their lives to the rhythms of nature. Of all nature's cycles, few were more sacred than the rising and setting of the sun. Across cultures and traditions, sunrise and sunset have been seen not just as natural events, but as powerful spiritual thresholds. They marked the turning points of each day, symbolic gateways between darkness and light, rest and action, death and rebirth. In this part of the *Heart Unbound* journey, you are invited to reconnect with the ancestral wisdom that honoured the sun's journey, not only in the sky, but within the soul.

To the Ancient Egyptians, the rising sun was the rebirth of the god Ra, who sailed through the underworld each night and returned each morning in triumph. Sunrise was seen as a symbol of divine renewal and eternal hope. To witness the dawn was to witness the return of life and light. **In Hindu tradition**, the time just before sunrise, *Brahma Muhurta,* is considered the most spiritually powerful time of day. It is a moment of stillness when the veil between the physical and spiritual worlds is thinnest. Sunrise rituals include meditation, chanting, and offering gratitude for the new day, a daily act of aligning the self with divine order. **Indigenous cultures across Australia** and around the world have long honoured the sun as a life-giving force and spiritual guide. Sunrise and sunset are woven into songlines, stories, and ceremonies that teach balance, responsibility, and deep connection to Country and spirit. These moments are not merely times of day, they are sacred teachings in motion.

In the Abrahamic traditions, sunset often marks sacred time, the beginning of the Sabbath, the call to prayer, the invitation to rest and reflect. As the light fades, there is a spiritual invitation to turn inward, release the burdens of the day, and trust in the unseen. These ancient practices remind you that you are not separate from the cycles of the Earth, you are part of them. They reflect your own inner seasons: the dawning of awareness, the heat of passion, the softening of surrender, the stillness of reflection. By consciously engaging with sunrise and sunset, you awaken an inner knowing that these are not just passive moments, but invitations to **presence**, **gratitude**, and **transformation**. Sunrise calls you to awaken your heart, to begin again with purpose and openness. Sunset invites you to soften, to let go, and to return to your inner stillness.

In *Heart Unbound*, these moments become your daily altars. Not as rituals of the past, but as timeless practices that reconnect you to yourself, your ancestors, the Earth, and the sacred rhythm of life. So, as the sun rises tomorrow, breathe in its blessing. As it sets, let it carry your release. Know that in each turning of the sky, you are being held by something ancient, vast, and loving. *This is not just a new day. This is the remembering of who you are. This is your heart, unbound.*

Biological Benefits: Circadian Rhythm, Serotonin Release, Mental Clarity

As you walk the path of the *Heart Unbound* journey, you are not only reconnecting with your emotions, you are also awakening to the deep and natural intelligence of your body. Just as your heart holds wisdom, so does your biology, and few things support that wisdom more profoundly than tuning into the rhythms of sunrise and sunset. Your body is wired to respond to the sun. From the moment light touches your skin and eyes, a cascade of physiological processes begins, bringing balance to your hormones, clarity to your mind, and calm to your emotions.

1. Circadian Rhythm - Aligning with Nature's Clock

Your body runs on a 24-hour internal clock known as the circadian rhythm. This rhythm regulates everything from your sleep-wake cycles to your hormone levels, digestion, energy, and mood. Exposure to natural light at sunrise is one of the most powerful ways to reset and stabilise this rhythm. When you step outside in the morning light, you are sending a signal to your brain: *It is time to wake up. It is time to begin again.* This helps you feel more alert during the day, and more naturally sleepy as night approaches. Watching the sunset also cues your body to slow down, preparing you for rest and renewal. By honouring these natural transitions, you gift yourself a sense of balance, predictability, and calm, essential elements of emotional wellbeing and nervous system regulation.

2. Serotonin – Awakening Joy and Emotional Stability

When you absorb sunlight in the early morning, your brain boosts production of serotonin, often called the *"feel-good"* neurotransmitter. Serotonin enhances your mood, focus, sense of calm, and emotional resilience. It plays a vital role in preventing anxiety and depression and is also a precursor to melatonin, the hormone that helps you sleep deeply at night. This is why simply watching the sunrise, feeling the light on your face, breathing in the cool air, allowing yourself to be present, can gently lift your spirit and bring a natural sense of peace. In *Heart Unbound*, you begin to see these practices not as small habits, but as sacred rituals that nourish you emotionally, spiritually, and biologically.

<u>3. Mental Clarity – Creating Space for Presence and Insight</u>

Morning and evening light also enhance mental clarity by supporting brain function and reducing cortisol spikes. When you begin the day with gentle light, silence, and stillness, you allow space for your thoughts to settle. Your nervous system feels safe, your prefrontal cortex activates, and your capacity for insight, reflection, and decision-making expands. Sunrise helps you begin with presence, not pressure. Sunset helps you unwind with grace, not overwhelm. These moments become powerful anchors of mindfulness, helping you return to yourself, to your breath, and to what truly matters. Your body knows what your heart remembers: *You are meant to rise with the light, and rest with the dark. You are designed to live in rhythm, not in rush. You are built for clarity, joy, and harmony.* When you honour the light outside, you awaken the light within. *This is the intelligence of your biology. This is the healing of your heart. This is your life, alive, aligned, unbound.*

Symbolism Of Sunrise (Hope, Awakening, Intention)

The moment the sun begins to rise, when the first golden light touches the horizon, is more than just the start of a new day. It is a sacred symbol, a living metaphor, and a powerful emotional reset. In *Heart Unbound*, **sunrise becomes an invitation**: to begin again, to choose with intention, and to awaken fully to the life that is waiting for you.

<u>Sunrise as Hope</u>

No matter how long the night, the sun always returns. In this simple truth lies profound hope. Each sunrise reminds you that darkness is not permanent, that every ending contains the promise of a new beginning. Even when life feels uncertain or heavy, the rising sun whispers, *you are not stuck, and you are not alone.* Something new is possible. Hope is not blind optimism. It is the deep, steady belief that growth is still unfolding, even when you cannot yet see the results. Sunrise is that reminder, visible and warm, that healing continues, and that today, your heart can take one more courageous step forward.

Sunrise as Awakening

The light of morning does not just wake the world, it awakens your awareness. With sunrise comes a chance to turn inward and ask: *Who am I becoming? What do I need today? What do I choose to bring into the light of this new day?* In ancient traditions, dawn was considered the most sacred time to pray, reflect, and realign with purpose. In your own life, sunrise can become a time to reconnect with your inner wisdom. As the sky brightens, so too does your clarity. You awaken not only physically, but emotionally and spiritually. The light outside becomes a mirror for the light within. Awakening is not just about opening your eyes. It is about opening your **heart**.

Sunrise as Intention

Each morning offers you a clean slate. A fresh beginning. A chance to **set your intention** before the world begins to pull you in every direction. When you meet the sunrise consciously, you meet the day with purpose. You stop reacting and start choosing. You honour your own truth, and begin from a place of calm, rather than chaos. Whether your intention is to be more present, more patient, more courageous, or more compassionate, sunrise becomes the doorway through which your deepest values step into motion. It is your reminder that you are not here to just *get through the day*, but to live it with **meaning, grace, and presence**. So tomorrow morning, let yourself rise slowly. Step outside. Breathe deeply. Feel the light touch your skin. Let the sun remind you: *You are not your past. You are not your fear. You are becoming.* This day is yours to live, fully, bravely, beautifully. *This is your heart, awakened. This is your intention, ignited. This is your hope, rising. This is your heart, unbound.*

As the sun begins to sink into the horizon, the world softens. The light becomes golden, shadows stretch long, and everything slows. Sunset is more than a beautiful end to the day, it is a sacred pause. A gentle invitation to turn inward, to breathe deeply, and to reflect on what has been. In *Heart Unbound*, **sunset becomes a living symbol of emotional surrender**. It teaches you how to close your day with grace, hold your experiences with gratitude, and release what no longer serves your heart.

Sunset as Gratitude

As the light fades, you are invited to look back, not with judgment, but with **thankfulness**. No matter how the day unfolded, there is always something to honour. A breath you took. A conversation you held. A feeling you allowed. A truth you spoke. Gratitude at sunset does not deny what was hard, it simply makes space for what was good. It helps your heart remember that even in the midst of challenge, there were moments of connection, courage, or growth. Gratitude turns your attention from what was missing to what was meaningful. When you end your day with gratitude, you anchor your heart in fullness. You remember that each day is a gift, and that even the small things matter.

<u>Sunset as Letting Go</u>

Sunset also brings with it the power of **release**. Just as the sky lets go of the sun, you too are invited to let go of what you no longer need to carry. The pressure. The overthinking. The unmet expectations. The emotions that feel too heavy to take into tomorrow. Letting go does not mean forgetting. It means choosing peace over perfection. It means saying: *This is enough. I did my best. I can rest now.* So much of our emotional suffering comes from clinging, clinging to what we cannot control, to what went wrong, to the illusion of certainty, but sunset reminds you that it is safe to soften. To exhale. To release. Let the fading light be your permission slip to surrender.

<u>Sunset as Closure</u>

Every day deserves a conscious ending. Sunset gives you a chance to **close your day with intention**, so your heart is not burdened by all that is unfinished. Closure is not about tying everything up neatly, it is about **acknowledging** what was, and choosing to lay it down. Through mindful closure, you invite emotional clarity. You begin to understand what the day taught you. What you want to carry forward, and what you are ready to leave behind. This sacred closing ritual helps prepare your nervous system for rest, your body for restoration, and your heart for tomorrow. It becomes a loving boundary between doing and being, between striving and stillness. So tonight, as the sun descends, take a few moments for your heart. Reflect on what the day brought. Whisper a quiet *thank you*. Feel what needs to be felt. Release what needs to be let go, and allow yourself the grace of closure. The world will begin again tomorrow, but for now, let this day come to rest. You have done enough. You *are* enough. *This is your heart, resting. This is your spirit, softening. This is your day, complete. This is your heart, unbound.*

The Emotional Regulation Potential Of Consistent Nature-Based Rituals

Nature does not rush, but it always moves. The tides flow in rhythm. The trees sway with the breeze. The sun rises and sets without fail. In the heart of nature, everything has its season, and nothing is forced. When you attune yourself to these rhythms through simple, intentional rituals, you begin to experience one of the most profound gifts available to you: **emotional regulation through natural connection**. In *Heart Unbound,* you are reminded that healing does not always require something complex. Sometimes, the most transformative shifts happen when you pause and return to the simple, grounding presence of the natural world.

Nature as a Regulator of the Nervous System

Your nervous system is deeply responsive to your environment. When you are overwhelmed by constant noise, artificial light, and mental overstimulation, your body shifts into survival mode, often without you even realising it, but when you step outside, something softens. Your breath slows. Your muscles relax. Your mind becomes still. Consistent nature-based rituals, like watching the sunrise, walking barefoot on the earth, sitting quietly under a tree, or simply noticing the breeze on your skin, send a powerful signal to your brain: *You are safe. You can let go.* This activates the parasympathetic nervous system, responsible for rest, digestion, healing, and emotional clarity. Over time, these rituals retrain your body and mind to find balance. They help you regulate intense emotions, reduce anxiety, and increase your resilience to daily stressors.

Rhythmic Rituals, Emotional Balance

Rituals such as greeting the sunrise, journaling at dusk, lighting a candle at sunset, or spending a few moments with your hand on your heart in the stillness of the natural world bring rhythm and predictability to your emotional life. This rhythm becomes an anchor, something your heart can hold onto even when life feels uncertain. Emotional regulation does not mean suppressing your feelings. It means creating a safe inner space where your emotions can flow without overwhelming you. Nature helps you hold that space. Like the ocean, it allows your feelings to ebb and flow. Like the mountains, it reminds you to stay grounded. Like the wind, it teaches you to move with what is, rather than fight against it.

From Ritual to Relationship

As you engage in these rituals regularly, something deeper begins to happen: your connection with nature transforms into a relationship. The tree becomes your companion. The sky becomes your mirror. The river becomes a teacher, and in that relationship, you begin to feel held, not just by the Earth, but by life itself. You realise that emotional regulation is not just a technique. It is a return to alignment with the world around you, and within you.

<u>Begin Simply. Begin Now.</u>

You do not need a forest or a mountain to begin. A moment in your garden, a quiet breath beside an open window, a walk at dusk with your phone in your pocket and your heart open, this is enough. What matters is not the setting, but the **intention**: to return, to feel, to ground. In *Heart Unbound*, these nature-based rituals become gentle companions on your journey, restoring calm, strengthening presence, and helping you build emotional trust with yourself. So let your ritual begin. Step outside. Listen. Breathe. Be still. The Earth knows how to regulate, and so, deep down, do you. *This is your rhythm. This is your return. This is your heart, unbound.*

Realigning With Natural Rhythms In A Digital, Fast-Paced World

In today's hyper-connected world, it is easy to feel as though you are constantly running, always reachable, always responding, always *doing*. The digital age promises convenience and productivity, but it often comes at a cost: disconnection from the natural rhythms that your body, mind, and heart were designed to live by. You were never meant to live at the speed of Wi-Fi. You were meant to live at the pace of breath, heartbeat, sunrise, and moonlight, and in *Heart Unbound*, this part of your journey is about **coming home to that pace**.

<u>The Problem: Disconnection from Natural Time</u>

The modern world runs on artificial time, screens glow long after sunset, notifications interrupt your stillness, and your nervous system is constantly flooded with stimulation. You are expected to be *"on"* all the time, and somewhere along the way, you may have forgotten the slower, wiser rhythm that nature still offers. This constant pressure can dysregulate your emotions, deplete your energy, disturb your sleep, and leave you feeling anxious, ungrounded, or numb. Your heart was not built for endless scrolling. It was built for presence, wonder, and real connection.

<u>The Invitation: Realignment and Return</u>

To realign with natural rhythms is not about rejecting technology, it is about **remembering who you are beneath it**. Nature still moves slowly and with purpose. The sun still rises without rushing. The moon still waxes and wanes without needing to prove anything, and when you slow down and attune yourself to these rhythms, something inside you begins to heal. You begin to regulate, not just emotionally, but spiritually. You begin to live, not reactively, but intentionally. You start to notice the subtle cues your body gives: when it is time to rest, when inspiration stirs, when your heart is asking for quiet or beauty or breath.

Rituals of Rhythm and Realignment

In *Heart Unbound*, this realignment begins with small, sacred practices:

- Greeting the sunrise as a symbol of hope and new beginnings

- Watching the sunset as a moment of reflection and release

- Eating slowly, in tune with hunger and fullness

- Walking barefoot on the Earth to reconnect with grounding energy

- Turning off devices after dark and honouring the body's need for deep rest

- Practising stillness and presence as acts of courage in a distracted world

These are not just wellness techniques, they are *acts of resistance*. They are how you reclaim your time, your nervous system, your emotional clarity, and your sacred rhythm of living.

A Rhythm That Heals

When you begin to live in harmony with natural time, you do not just feel more peaceful, you begin to **thrive**. Your sleep deepens. Your anxiety lessens. Your creativity returns. Your relationships become more present, and your heart begins to feel safe enough to open again, because real healing does not happen in hurry. It happens in rhythm, and your rhythm is written in your cells, your breath, your being. It is ancient. It is intelligent, and it is always there, waiting for you to come back. So pause. Step away from the noise. Look up. Slow down. Breathe. Feel the Earth turning beneath your feet. Feel yourself returning to your natural rhythm. To your wholeness. To your truth. *This is not disconnection. This is remembering. This is not slowness. This is wisdom. This is your heart, realigned. This is your life, unbound.*

Breathe with the Sky Exercise

"I invite you to undertake the following breathing visualisation:"

---

1. Sit quietly, with your spine relaxed yet upright, and allow your body to soften into stillness.

2. As you inhale, imagine your breath rising like the sun. See it climbing over the horizon, spreading warmth and golden light across the sky. With each breath in, feel yourself filled with energy, possibility, and renewal.

3. As you exhale, let your breath sink like the setting sun. Watch it dip gently below the horizon, colouring the sky with hues of peace. With each release, soften and let go, releasing tension, heavy thoughts, or anything that no longer serves you.

4. Continue for 5 minutes, allowing each inhale to be a sunrise that awakens your spirit, and each exhale to be a sunset that restores your calm.

As you rest in this rhythm, notice how the breath mirrors the eternal cycles of the sky, beginnings and endings, light and dark, rise and fall. Trust that, like the sun, you too are renewed with every breath.

Case Study Discussion: Naomi and Alex's Journey

Naomi and Alex had always been a couple deeply connected with nature. Their shared love for outdoor adventures had brought them together. However, the demands of their careers had gradually taken a toll on their relationship. They found themselves drifting apart, and not being able to find common ground on anything. We spent time journeying through many aspects of their history and lives together and it was very obvious that the one key element that had brought them together (love of nature) was the one key element that was missing in their lives.

We discussed many ideas, and I suggested something small, simple but requiring a level of genuine commitment from both of them. They would gift themselves the opportunity to watch 30 sunrises and sunsets (in a row) together. It was not easy but it was essential to help them connect on a deeper level within themselves and each other. They discovered that these shared moments of serenity created a space for them to be fully present with each other. Away from the distractions of daily life, they found a peace and joy in the simple act of being in each other's company. They watched the colours move across the sky, and they rediscovered the beauty of silence and the power of shared experiences.

They laughed, they talked, they held each other close, and they felt their hearts grow closer with every passing sunrise and sunset. The quiet mornings and peaceful evenings spent in nature provided a sanctuary for their hearts to open, heal, and grow. Through their shared appreciation for the beauty of nature, Naomi and Alex found a renewed sense of wonder and gratitude for each other and the world around them. The sunrise and sunset became anchors in their lives, reminding them to prioritise their love, their connection, and the simple joys that brought them closer together.

Reflective Exercise: Naomi and Alex's Journey

Here are four profound and reflective questions inspired by Alex's story to help you connect with the sunrise and sunset in your own journey:

1. **What parts of your relationship, or your own heart, have drifted out of alignment with what once brought you joy and connection?** When life becomes busy, it is easy to lose sight of what once felt sacred. Like Naomi and Alex, is there something simple and beautiful that used to bring you closer to yourself or someone you love, and how might you return to it?

2. **When was the last time you slowed down enough to truly *see* the person beside you, without distraction or expectation?** The sunrise and sunset offered Naomi and Alex a quiet space to *just be* together. What might happen if you gifted yourself and someone else the same presence, without agenda, without phones, without anything to do but share the moment?

3. **How might the simple rituals of nature, like watching the sky change, help you reconnect not just with others, but with your own emotional clarity, wonder, and peace?** Sometimes healing does not come through big conversations, but through shared stillness. What emotions or truths might emerge for you in the quiet spaces between light and dark?

4. **What commitment, however small, are you willing to make to reawaken what matters most in your life and relationships?** Naomi and Alex committed to 30 sunrises and sunsets, and found each other again through it. What gentle, sacred promise could you make to yourself or someone you love to bring more presence, love, and beauty into your everyday life?

Affirmations For You – (Heart Whispers)

Affirmations have the power to quiet the noise of doubt, open the doorway to self-trust, and draw you back into the wisdom of your heart. When practised daily, they nurture an inner dialogue based in love and truth, helping you live each day more aligned with who you truly are. I invite you to repeat silently or write:

- *I find peace connecting with the beauty of nature.*

- *It is the sunrise and sunset where I find hope and inspiration.*

- *I love the peace that watching the sunrise and sunset brings me.*

- *Watching nature reminds me of my constant transformation.*

- *I feel deep gratitude when I witness nature's beautiful artwork.*

- *I welcome each sunrise as a reminder of new beginnings and endless possibilities.*

- *The sunset teaches me the grace of letting go and trusting in life's cycles.*

- *In the colours of the sky, I see reflections of my own inner light.*

- *With every sunrise and sunset, I feel more connected to the rhythm of the universe.*

Design Your Personal Sunrise or Sunset Ritual

I invite you to choose either **sunrise** or **sunset,** whichever calls most deeply to your heart, and create a simple 10–15 minute daily practice around it. This is your sacred time, a gift you give yourself each day to pause, reflect, and reconnect. Here are some practices you may wish to include:

- **Journaling** – Write a few lines about what you notice, feel, or are grateful for in this moment. Capture the colours, emotions, or insights the sky awakens in you.

- **Breathwork** – Breathe in the energy of the rising or setting sun; let it fill you with renewal, clarity, and peace. On the exhale, release anything that no longer serves you.

- **Silence** – Simply sit in stillness, allowing the beauty of the sky to speak to you without words. Let silence become a teacher.

- **Gratitude list** – Note three things you are thankful for as you watch the light shift. Let gratitude anchor you in the present moment.

- **Drawing the colours of the sky** – With pencil, brush, or crayon, sketch or shade the hues you see. It does not need to be art, it is about presence, noticing, and expression.

Remember, your ritual does not need to be perfect, it only needs to be **yours**. Focus on **consistency over perfection**. Allow it to become a rhythm that supports you. If you feel comfortable, share your practice with someone you trust, or simply keep it as a private treasure.

You can do this. Your heart knows the way. I believe in you.

Closing Reflection

As this part of your journey comes to a close, take a deep breath and remember: the sun rises and sets not just in the sky, but in your life, your emotions, and your heart. Each sunrise is a soft invitation to begin again, with renewed presence, with clearer intention, and with hope that even after the longest night, light always returns. Each sunset is a sacred reminder that it is safe to let go, that what has passed can be released, that rest is holy, and that endings carry their own kind of beauty.

Naomi and Alex found healing not in big gestures, but in shared stillness. In the simple, quiet act of watching the sky change, they rediscovered themselves and each other. You too are invited into that same space of reconnection, with your heart, with nature, with love, and with what matters most. Let the sun be your teacher. Let the rhythm of the Earth regulate your breath, your pace, and your presence. Let each dawn remind you of your strength, and each dusk cradle you into rest. You do not need to rush. You do not need to force. You only need to notice. To return. To honour. The sky will keep rising and falling, and so will you, and in every rise and every fall, there is grace. *This is your rhythm. This is your remembering. This is your heart, unbound.*

20 – HEART WHISPERS

Your Opening Reflection

Invitation to Listen to Your Heart - As you enter this chapter, give yourself permission to lean into stillness and truly listen. Your heart has been whispering to you all along, gentle truths, longings, encouragements, waiting for you to pause and hear them. This is not about forcing words or crafting answers; it is about allowing your inner voice to emerge, tender and unfiltered. Trust that what arises, no matter how quiet or unexpected, carries wisdom for your journey. Let your pen become the ear of your heart, receiving what it longs to share with you.

- "What does your heart need to say that you have not yet written down?"

- "If your heart could speak without fear, what truth would it share with you right now?"

- "What unspoken dreams or desires are waiting within you to be acknowledged?"

- "What gentle encouragement or reassurance does your heart long to give you today?"

- "If your heart could write you a letter, what would its first line say?"

Let these questions open the doorway into presence. Every answer you give, whether in words, sensations, or silence, is a bridge between where you are and where you are going.

Learning Objectives

The learning objectives are included here to give you a clear focus for this chapter, ensuring that each practice you explore moves you closer to mastering the skills, insights, and heart-led awareness that will enrich your life well beyond the program. By the end of this chapter, you will:

- Understand the emotional and psychological benefits of writing from the heart

- Develop self-awareness through reflective and expressive journaling

- Access vulnerability and authenticity as strengths in emotional intelligence

- Use free writing and prompts to connect with inner truth and develop personal growth

Core Emotional Domains

The core emotional intelligence domains covered here are essential because they form the foundation for lasting heart connection, guiding you to deepen self-awareness, regulate emotions, build resilience, and strengthen the mind-body bond throughout your Heart Unbound journey.

- **Self-Awareness:** You begin to recognise the subtle messages your heart is sending you, your desires, your discomforts, your truth beneath the noise.

- **Self-Regulation:** By tuning in, you learn to respond from stillness rather than react from emotion, creating space between feeling and action.

- **Empathy (for self and others):** As you honour your own inner world, you deepen compassion for the unspoken feelings in others, developing gentler connection.

- **Motivation (Personal Growth and Self-Expression):** Heart whispers become the seeds of growth, nudging you toward choices that align with who you are becoming.

- **Authenticity and Connection:** Listening to your heart helps you live and relate with honesty, openness, and the courage to show up as your true self.

"Heart Whispers – Listening To Your Quiet Voice Within"

Writing from the heart, what we call *heart whispers,* is not simply an act of journaling. It is a sacred, deeply emotional ritual of honesty, vulnerability, and return. When you pick up a pen and write not from your mind, but from your

heart space, you begin to meet yourself exactly where you are, with tenderness, without judgment, and with radical truth. A heart whisper is the quiet voice beneath the noise. It is the part of you that already knows. It does not shout. It does not demand. It waits, patiently, lovingly, until you are ready to listen.

Throughout history, human beings have turned to the written word to express what the voice cannot say. From ancient scrolls and sacred scriptures to letters written by candlelight and the pages of modern memoirs, writing has always been a way to *heal, transform, and make meaning*. In many cultures, writing was considered a form of communion with the divine. It was not about grammar or perfection, it was about truth-telling. About finding language for what lives inside the soul. *Heart whispers* follow in that tradition. They are sacred conversations between your inner self and your conscious mind, revealing wounds that want healing, dreams that want expression, and truths that want to be named.

When you engage in this practice, you allow emotion to move through you in a way that is safe, supported, and grounding. You give yourself space to slow down, feel deeply, and release what no longer serves. The page becomes a mirror, a witness, and sometimes, a breakthrough. Some days, your heart whisper may be a single word. Other days, it may pour out like a flood. There is no right way, only your way. The act of writing from the heart supports emotional intelligence in powerful ways. It grows your **self-awareness**, strengthens **emotional regulation**, and opens the door to **empathy,** first for yourself, then for others. It nurtures your **authenticity** and fuels your **personal growth** by revealing the next right step... one whisper at a time. So as you sit with your pen, breathe deeply. Let go of what you think you should say, and simply begin. Write what hurts. Write what heals. Write what your heart longs to speak. This is not just writing. This is remembering. This is reconnecting. This is your heart, unbound.

A Brief History Of Heart-Led Writing: From Sacred Scrolls To The Beat Poets

When you sit with a pen in your hand and write from the centre of your being, from that tender space where truth and emotion meet, you are not just journaling. You are stepping into an ancient lineage of heart-led expression that stretches across centuries, cultures, and continents. The act of *heart whispering*, of letting the words rise from within and spill honestly onto the page, is part of a long and sacred tradition. In *Heart Unbound*, we honour this legacy, not just as history, but as inheritance.

Sacred Scrolls and Soulful Scriptures

In ancient civilisations, writing was often seen as divine. Words were not just tools, they were portals. In early Egypt, scribes were considered priests, translating sacred messages from the gods. In Hindu and Buddhist traditions, mantras and sutras were recorded with reverence, believed to carry not only wisdom but healing energy. The Hebrew Psalms, the Sufi poetry of Rumi, and the meditative teachings of Lao Tzu were all written from the heart, not for applause, but as offerings. They were written in stillness, in yearning, in the quiet pursuit of divine connection and inner clarity. These texts were more than literature. They were the emotional and spiritual heartbeat of a people. They reminded the world that to write from the heart is to pray with ink.

Medieval Mystics and Inner Light

During the Middle Ages, mystics like Julian of Norwich and Hildegard of Bingen poured their inner visions and revelations into writing. They documented their emotional and spiritual awakenings, sometimes in secret, often in defiance of cultural norms. These writings were raw, luminous, and unapologetically intimate. They dared to put human longing and divine love on the same page. In doing so, they gave permission for future generations to honour their inner voice.

The Romantics and the Rise of Emotional Expression

The 18th and 19th centuries gave rise to poets and writers who placed emotion at the centre of their work. Wordsworth, Keats, and Blake invited readers to feel deeply, to wander inward, and to find divinity in nature and the human soul. Their pens became conduits for wonder, sorrow, hope, and heartbreak.

The Beat Poets and the Rhythm of the Unfiltered Heart

In the 1950s, a new wave of heart-led writing emerged. The Beat poets, like Allen Ginsberg, Jack Kerouac, and Diane di Prima, challenged convention and dared to write from the raw edge of experience. Their words spilled out like jazz, full of rhythm, soul, and unedited truth. They wrote in cafés, on the road, in the middle of sleepless nights, fueled not by form, but by feeling. Their work was not polished. It was *alive*. Like heart whispers, their words did not always make sense to the mind, but they moved the spirit. They taught us that to write from the heart is to be *real*. Messy, unfiltered, alive, human.

Your Heart Is the Next Chapter

When you write your heart whispers, you join this sacred lineage, not as an observer, but as a participant. Whether your words take the form of prayers, poems, journal entries, letters, or scattered lines in the margin of your day, you are honouring a timeless truth: ***The heart has something to say, and when it is listened to, healing begins.*** You do not need to be a poet or mystic to belong here. You only need to be *honest*. To be *present*. To be *willing* to listen to what your soul already knows. With each word, you come closer to yourself. With each whisper, your story unfolds. This is your sacred scroll. This is your emotional scripture. This is your truth, inked in love. **This is your heart, unbound.**

Writing As Emotional Release: The Science Of Expressive Writing (Pennebaker Studies)

There are moments in life when your heart is full, so full it aches. When emotions swirl and thoughts feel tangled. When you carry stories you have not spoken aloud. In these moments, writing can become a lifeline. A safe place to release, reflect, and begin again. In *Heart Unbound*, we call this practice **Heart Whispering,** but its power is also well established in scientific research. One of the most important voices in this field is Dr. James Pennebaker, whose decades of research into **expressive writing** have shown what many people have always known deep down: **When you write what you feel, you begin to heal.**

The Science Behind Expressive Writing

Dr. James Pennebaker, a psychologist and researcher at the University of Texas, conducted a series of groundbreaking studies starting in the 1980s. He asked participants to write about their **deepest thoughts and feelings,** particularly about stressful or traumatic experiences, for just **15–20 minutes a day over a few consecutive days**. The results were profound. People who engaged in expressive writing showed:

- Improved immune system function

- Lower stress and anxiety levels

- Better sleep and concentration

- Reduced blood pressure and heart rate

- Greater self-awareness and emotional clarity

Perhaps most importantly, they reported feeling **emotionally lighter,** as if something within them had shifted. It was not about writing perfectly. It was about writing honestly.

Why Writing Heals

When you write about your inner experience, especially when you have been holding it in, your brain begins to **process** the emotion. The act of writing helps move feelings from the **limbic system** (your emotional brain) to the **prefrontal cortex** (your thinking brain). This process creates **narrative coherence,** meaning you are no longer just *feeling* the experience, but *understanding* it. In doing so, you gain perspective. You create distance without disconnection. You turn chaos into clarity. Pain into meaning. Emotion into transformation.

Writing from the Heart in *Heart Unbound*

In *Heart Unbound*, heart whisper writing is not about fixing yourself. It is about freeing yourself. It is about sitting down with a pen and saying: *This is how I feel. This is what I carry. This is what I need.* There is no pressure to be poetic. No need to edit. Your only task is to be **honest**, and to let your hand become the translator of your heart. Whether you are writing through grief, joy, confusion, love, or fear, the page becomes a container. It holds what you can no longer carry. It reflects your growth. It gives you space to release what has been hidden, and welcome in what is ready to rise. Like Ava (case study), like countless others before you, you may find that simply showing up for your words, day after day, becomes a path back to your own truth.

A Daily Practice of Emotional Renewal

Even just 10–15 minutes of expressive writing each day has been shown to:

- Reduce emotional reactivity

- Improve emotional regulation

- Deepen self-compassion

- Increase resilience during difficult times

- Build a stronger sense of personal meaning and identity

It is not just an emotional release, it is a form of **emotional empowerment.**

The Quiet Power Of The Pen - How Writing Activates Your Parasympathetic Nervous System For Emotional Regulation

When life feels overwhelming, your body often reacts before your mind even knows what is happening. Your heart races. Your breath shortens. Your muscles tighten. You feel the familiar surge of stress or anxiety rising in your chest. This is your **sympathetic nervous system** at work, preparing you to fight, flee, or freeze. However, what your body also holds, what it longs for, is the ability to return to calm. To safety. To rest. That is the gift of your **parasympathetic nervous system,** and one of the most gentle, accessible ways to activate it is through *writing from the heart*. In *Heart Unbound*, you learn that writing is not just about words, it is a nervous system practice. A quiet return to yourself. A way to regulate, release, and remember that you are safe.

From Stress to Stillness: A Nervous System That Follows Your Words

Your autonomic nervous system has two main parts:

- The **sympathetic** system helps you survive stress.

- The **parasympathetic** system helps you heal, rest, and feel safe.

When you write from the heart, from that tender, truthful place inside, you begin to **shift**. Your breathing slows. Your awareness softens. You drop out of racing thoughts and into your body. This is your nervous system responding to the feeling of emotional safety. Writing becomes a doorway back to balance.

How Writing Helps You Regulate Emotion

1. **You Create a Safe Space to Feel:** When you write, no one is interrupting. No one is judging. The page listens without expectation. You are free to say what you really feel, and in that freedom, your nervous system begins to unwind. You signal to yourself: *I am safe to feel this.*

2. **You Slow Down** As you write, your breath naturally slows. Your thoughts begin to settle. What felt tangled becomes clear. You begin to notice patterns, emotions, and truths you did not realise were there. This slowing down helps reduce stress and calms your entire body

3. **You Release What You have Been Holding In:** Some emotions stay stuck because you have not had a safe way to express them, but through

writing, you release what your body no longer needs to carry. Whether it is grief, fear, anger, or love, you let it move, and you let it go.

4. **You Rebuild Inner Coherence:** Writing helps integrate the emotional and rational parts of your brain. This creates internal balance, a sense of feeling grounded and in control. You are not just reacting anymore. You are responding with awareness and care.

A Healing Practice Hiding in a Pen and Page

You may think you are just journaling, but you are doing so much more. You are *regulating*. You are *restoring*. You are showing your nervous system that it does not need to be on high alert anymore. Every time you pick up your pen, you are sending a powerful message to your body and your heart: *You are safe. You are supported. You are allowed to rest now.* So when your emotions feel too loud, when the world feels too fast, when your heart feels too heavy, come back to the page. Let the words flow. Let your breath slow. Let yourself feel what is true. You do not have to fix anything. You just have to show up. This is how you return to calm. This is how you regulate with love. This is how you heal, from the inside out. *This is your heart, softened. This is your nervous system, soothed. This is your heart, unbound.*

Vulnerability On The Page: Why Your Truth Is Your Strength

There is something sacred that happens when you let your guard down, not out loud, not in front of a crowd, but quietly, gently, on the page. When you sit with your journal or your notebook and let the words come, not the filtered version, not the polished version, but the *real* version, you begin to uncover one of the greatest truths of all: *Your vulnerability is not your weakness. Your vulnerability is your strength.*

In *Heart Unbound*, you are not asked to perform or to prove anything. You are invited to tell the truth. *Your* truth. The one that lives beneath the surface. The one that maybe you have hidden, even from yourself, because when you bring it into the light, onto the page, you create space for healing, connection, and freedom.

The Courage to Be Seen, Even If Only by Yourself

Writing vulnerably is not about sharing everything with the world. It starts with being willing to be real with *you*. To stop running from what hurts. To stop pretending that you are fine when your heart feels tired. To stop silencing the parts of you that feel too tender or too messy. When you write from that place, raw, unsure, honest, you are not breaking down. You are breaking *open*, and in that opening, something powerful begins to shift: **You stop hiding. You stop shrinking.** You begin to reclaim your wholeness.

<u>Why Vulnerability on the Page Heals</u>

1. **It gives your truth a place to land:** When emotions stay unspoken, they build up inside you, but when you write them down, grief, anger, longing, shame, love, you create room to breathe again.

2. **It lets you meet yourself with compassion**: Seeing your story on the page allows you to step back, not with judgment, but with understanding. You realise: *Of course I felt that way. Of course I struggled, and I am still here.*

3. **It builds emotional resilience**: The more honestly you express yourself, the stronger you become. Not hardened, but strengthened through self-acceptance. Vulnerability does not weaken you. It *frees* you.

4. **It invites deeper connection with others**: Even though this writing is for you, it changes how you show up in your relationships. When you honour your own truth, you become more able to hold space for others' truth, with empathy and presence.

<u>Your Truth Is Your Power</u>

You do not need to write something perfect. You do not need to have all the answers. You only need to be honest. Even if your voice shakes. Even if your hand trembles. Even if all you can write today is, *"I do not know where to begin."* That is still a beginning, and the moment you tell the truth, even quietly, even privately, is the moment you reclaim your voice. That voice, no matter how soft, is **a declaration of strength**, because vulnerability is not the absence of strength. It *is* strength. The kind that says: *I am still here. I am still feeling. I am still open,* and that is more than enough. So write what is real. Write what aches. Write what brings tears or goosebumps or silence. Write without apology. This is not the page judging you. This is the page witnessing you. *This is your truth. This is your courage. This is your heart, unbound.*

The Difference Between Writing *About* Emotions And Writing *From* Emotions

When you sit down to write, there are two paths you can take. One path is familiar. It feels safe. You write *about* what you are feeling. You describe the emotion. You might say, *"I felt sad,"* or *"I was angry today."* You stay close to the surface, observing, analysing, explaining. The other path goes deeper. It is quieter, but more alive. It asks you not just to write *about* the feeling, but to write *from* it. To let the sadness speak. To let the anger have a voice. To let your joy dance onto the page without needing permission. This is where your heart begins to write, not your head. In *Heart Unbound*, this difference matters, because true healing, release, and transformation often happen not when you talk about your feelings, but when you allow yourself to feel them as you write.

Writing *About* Emotions: The Safe Distance

When you write about your emotions, you are often writing with some level of distance. You might describe what happened, how it made you feel, or what you think it means. This kind of writing can be helpful for clarity and reflection, but it can also become a form of emotional detachment. It is like standing at the edge of a river, describing the water, without ever stepping into the flow. You might say: "*I felt hurt when they did not listen to me.*" "*I have been feeling anxious lately, and I think it is because of work.*" It is honest. It is insightful, but it might not *move* the emotion through you.

Writing *From* Emotions: The Sacred Embodiment

Writing *from* emotions invites you to step into the river. It asks you to let go of explanation and allow the feeling to speak through you, without filters or analysis. You become the vessel, not just the narrator. You do not write about sadness. You *write as sadness*. You do not write about fear. You *write from inside the fear*. You let the emotion guide your words. This might look like: "*I feel invisible. I am tired of pretending I am okay. I want to be seen, but I am afraid no one really sees me.*" "*My chest is tight. My breath feels heavy. I want to scream, but I do not even know where to start.*" It might feel raw, messy, unstructured, and that is the point. This is where your heart begins to release what your mind has been holding.

Why This Matters for Healing

When you write from your emotions:

- **You move energy** instead of just describing it.

- **You access deeper truths** that analysis cannot reach.

- **You create emotional release**, which supports nervous system regulation.

- **You strengthen self-trust** by allowing what's real to exist without judgment.

In this space, writing becomes more than expression. It becomes **embodiment**. Your body, your breath, your heart, they all begin to speak together, and as they do, your truth rises. Gently. Fiercely. Honestly.

<u>Let your Emotion Lead</u>

Next time you write, pause before you begin. Ask yourself: *Am I writing about this emotion? Or am I willing to write from it?* Then breathe. Let go of the need to explain. Let the feeling guide your hand. You do not need to have the right words. You only need to be real, because in the space between observation and embodiment, in the shift from distance to presence, your healing begins. *This is not a report. This is a release. This is not storytelling. This is soul-telling. This is your heart, unbound.*

The Power Of Your Voice: Writing For Self-Understanding, Not For Perfection

There is a moment, often quiet and unspoken, when you hesitate before you write. You pause. You wonder if what you have to say is "*good enough.*" You second-guess the way your feelings sound on the page. You worry about grammar, structure, clarity. Somewhere along the way, you learned that writing had to be perfect. That it had to make sense to others. That your voice had to be polished in order to be heard, but here, in the sanctuary of *Heart Unbound*, you are invited to write for a different reason, not for perfection, but for **self-understanding**. Not to impress, but to *express*. Not to get it right, but to finally, tenderly, get it **real**.

<u>No One Is Watching But You</u>

When you write in your heart journal, no one else is reading. You are not performing. You are not editing yourself for the comfort or approval of others. You are listening inward and meeting whatever is there with compassion. You are giving yourself something you may have been starved for: **space to be exactly who you are without needing to explain it**. Your heart does not need perfection. It needs **presence**. It needs to be heard, not corrected. Not judged. Just heard.

<u>Writing to Understand, Not to Impress</u>

The most powerful writing is not the kind that earns applause. It is the kind that helps you finally understand something you have been carrying for too long. When you write for self-understanding, you begin to unravel the tight threads of confusion, fear, memory, and longing. You begin to see patterns. You begin to hear your own wisdom, and sometimes, amid the tears, the scribbles, the messy handwriting, something inside you exhales. You may write: "*I am so tired of pretending I am okay.*" "*Why am I afraid of being truly seen?*" "*I miss the version of me who used to dream,*" and as the words come, you start to remember. You begin to return. You come back to yourself.

Your Voice Is Sacred

Maybe no one ever told you this, but it is true: **Your voice matters. Your truth matters.** Not just when it is eloquent. Not just when it is neat, but especially when it is messy, unsure, or full of feeling. Your heart does not speak in polished essays. It speaks in fragments, in emotions, in run-on sentences and half-formed thoughts, and that is more than okay. That is *real*. That is *you*. In *Heart Unbound*, your voice becomes a sacred thread between your inner and outer world. It becomes the bridge between confusion and clarity, between pain and peace. Every word you write becomes a step closer to your own emotional freedom.

This Is Not a Test. This Is a Telling.

So let go of the pressure to be profound. Let go of the critic in your head. Let go of needing your words to be anything more than *yours*. This is not about grammar. This is about grace. This is not about sentence structure. This is about soul structure. This is not about crafting something beautiful. This is about remembering that **you already are**. Write to hear yourself. Write to hold yourself. Write to come home. *This is the power of your voice. This is the beauty of your truth. This is your heart, unbound.*

Heart Whispers Free Write Exercise

Begin by settling into a comfortable position. Place a hand over your heart and close your eyes. Spend the next **three minutes in balanced heart breathing** (from Day 1). Inhale slowly and evenly, then exhale gently, allowing your body and mind to soften with each breath. With every inhale, invite in calm and openness; with every exhale, release tension and quiet the inner critic.

When you feel steady and connected, open to the prompt:

"If my heart could speak, it would say..."

Pick up your pen and begin to write. Let your hand move freely across the page. **Write continuously for seven minutes,** no stopping, no censoring, no correcting. Do not worry about spelling, grammar, or whether the words make sense. This is not about perfection; this is about allowing your heart to express what it has been holding.

Notice what arises: a whisper, a memory, a longing, perhaps even a truth you have not yet spoken aloud. Let it come. Trust the flow.

When the seven minutes are complete, pause. Take a deep breath. Read over what you have written with compassion, as if it were a letter from your heart to you. You may choose to keep your writing private, or, if you feel safe, you may wish to share a single line or phrase that surprised you, touched you, or brought insight.

Remember: your heart always has something to say. All you need to do is listen.

Case Study Discussion: Ava's Journey

Ava had always felt somewhat detached from her true self. She enjoyed writing stories, poems, and songs, but deep inside, she longed for a way to connect with her own Self and emotions. We spoke a lot about her ability to write and express herself, but it was always in the third person and never in her own voice. Her heart whispers helped her unlock the latch that she had placed on her heart. I guided her to sit down with her notebook, close her eyes, and breathe into her heart.

She learned to let go and release her expectations and began to write without filters or judgments. Her words flowed freely from her pen, and with each sentence, a weight lifted from her chest. She poured her heart onto the pages, exploring her joys, fears, and sorrows with a newfound honesty. As Ava continued to write from her heart, she discovered a profound healing taking place within her. It was as if the act of putting her thoughts and feelings into words allowed her to release the pent–up emotions that had been weighing her down for so long.

Through her writing, she found peace, clarity, and a deeper understanding of herself. Not only did Ava find healing, but she also discovered a sense of empowerment. Writing from her heart gave her the courage to confront her past, face her fears, and embrace her authentic self. Her heart whispers became her allies, guiding her through the rabbit holes of her own emotions and guiding her towards a path of self–acceptance and self–love. Ava now writes from her heart, embracing the power of her words to heal, transform, and connect. Writing became her sanctuary, a sacred space where she could fully be herself. Through this practice, she discovered the true depth and beauty of her own voice, and in doing so, she found a path to her own healing and wholeness.

Reflective Exercise – Ava's Journey

Here are four profound and reflective questions inspired by Ava's story to help you engage with your own journey into your heart space:

1. **What part of yourself have you been expressing through stories, characters, or other voices, yet have not yet given yourself permission to speak in your own true voice?** Like Ava, you may have used creativity to say what your heart could not yet speak directly. What might shift if you stopped hiding behind the third person and began to write with *your* name, *your* emotions, and *your* truth?

2. **What expectations or inner filters have you placed on your self-expression, and how might your heart feel if you gently let them go, even for a moment?** Ava's freedom came when she stopped writing to please or perform and simply allowed herself to *feel*. What would your words look like if you did not have to get them right, sound wise, or be anything other than *real*?

3. **What emotion within you feels ready to be released, if only you would offer it a safe place on the page to breathe and be heard?** There may be something inside you that is not asking to be fixed, but simply to be expressed. Could you meet that feeling on the page, not with answers, but with openness?

4. **How might writing from your heart become more than a practice, how might it become a sanctuary, a truth-teller, a guide back to who you really are?** Ava discovered that her own voice was the medicine she had been seeking. What healing might become possible for you if you trusted your words to show you the way home?

Affirmations For You – (Heart Whispers)

Affirmations have the power to quiet the noise of doubt, open the doorway to self-trust, and draw you back into the wisdom of your heart. When practised daily, they nurture an inner dialogue based in love and truth, helping you live each day more aligned with who you truly are. I invite you to repeat silently or write:

- *I pour my heart onto the page, allowing my emotions to flow.*

- *I find peace in expressing my deepest truths through writing.*

- *I discover the power of vulnerability as I share my story.*

- *I uncover hidden parts of myself when I write from my heart.*

- *I connect with others on a deep level through heartfelt words.*

- *I find liberation and authenticity in writing from my heart.*

Create Your Own "Heart Whispering" Ritual

This is your opportunity to create a sacred space for listening to your heart. A ritual is not about rules or rigidity, it is about intention. By designing your own *"Heart Whispering"* practice, you give yourself permission to pause, connect, and write from the deepest part of who you are. Here are some elements to consider as you create your ritual:

- **Time of Day**: Choose a time when you feel most open and undistracted. Perhaps it is early morning when the world is quiet, or in the evening as you reflect on your day. Consistency helps your heart know when it is safe to speak.

- **Environment**: Surround yourself with whatever makes you feel at ease. Light a candle, play soft music, or embrace silence. You may choose to include a favourite object, crystal, or even sit by a window where you can see the sky. Let your space remind you that this is a time for listening inward.

- **Length of Practice**: Begin with just 10 minutes. Over time, you may find yourself naturally extending to 15 or 20 minutes. The key is not how long you write, but the quality of your presence in those moments.

- **Intention & Mantra:** Before you begin, pause and set a simple intention. You might say: *"I am here to listen with love,"* or *"I open myself to whatever my heart needs to share."* At the end of your practice, you can close with a mantra or gratitude: *"Thank you, heart, for trusting me with your whispers."*

Once you have considered these elements, **name your ritual.** Give it a title that feels meaningful, *"Morning Heart Notes," "Whispers by Candlelight,"* or *"Soul Pages."* Finally, write a short declaration that anchors your commitment. Begin with: ***"I will write from my heart because..."*** This declaration is your reminder that your writing is not about perfection, but about honesty, authenticity, and self-connection.

Remember: The more often you show up for your heart, the more it will show up for you.

Closing Reflection

In the stillness of these quiet moments, when you allow your pen to move freely across the page, guided not by thought but by the rhythm of your heart, something sacred awakens within you. Writing in this way is more than words, it is a doorway to presence, to honesty, and to connection with the deepest part of yourself. These heart whispers are not simply sentences on paper; they are the voice of your truth reclaiming its rightful place, emotions finding their form, and your inner landscape gently stepping out of shadow and into light. Every line you write is a bridge back to yourself, unfiltered, raw, tender, and profoundly beautiful.

As you continue to listen inward, I invite you to honour every whisper that rises, even the uncertain, fragile, or trembling ones. They too carry wisdom. Let your notebook become more than paper and ink; let it become a sanctuary of honesty and courage, a place where you do not write to impress or perform, but to understand, to release, to heal, and to remember who you are. Let your words remind you that your voice matters. Your story is worthy. Your truth, whether spoken aloud or written in the privacy of your journal, is a powerful act of love, an offering to yourself and, when shared, a gift to the world. Your heart does not demand perfection; it only asks for presence, for listening, for space to be heard. So keep listening. Keep trusting. Keep writing. With each word, you come closer to yourself. With each page, you come home to the sanctuary of your own heart.

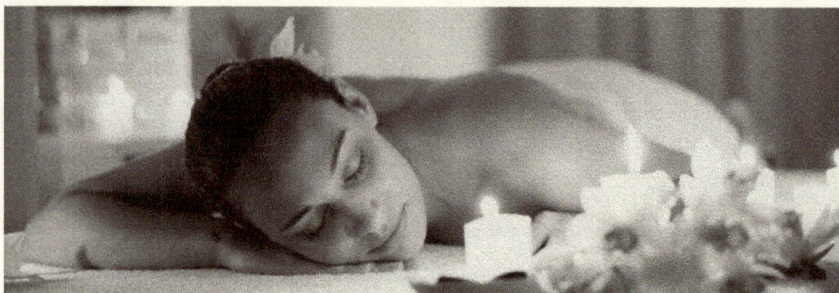

21 – RELAXATION

Your Opening Reflection

Before you begin this chapter, give yourself permission to slow down. Take a gentle pause, soften your gaze or close your eyes, and let your attention rest on your breath. As you settle into this moment, allow yourself to truly feel into the following questions, not just with your mind, but with your heart. I invite you to undertake a short journaling session followed by optional pair-sharing or quiet reflection, and I encourage you to reflect on what prevents you from truly slowing down.

- "What is your current relationship with rest and stillness?"

- "When was the last time you felt deeply relaxed?"

- "When you slow down, what emotions or thoughts arise within you, comfort, unease, or something in between?"

- "How do you usually respond when your body asks for rest, do you honour it or push it aside?"

- "What beliefs do you hold about stillness, do you see it as valuable, or as wasted time?"

- "If you gave yourself permission to pause fully, what would that look and feel like for you?"

- "What simple practice could you invite into your daily life to create more space for rest?"

Let these questions open the doorway into presence. Every answer you give, whether in words, sensations, or silence, is a bridge between where you are and where you are going.

Learning Objectives

The learning objectives are included here to give you a clear focus for this chapter, ensuring that each practice you explore moves you closer to mastering the skills, insights, and heart-led awareness that will enrich your life well beyond the program. By the end of this chapter, you will:

- Recognise relaxation as an essential component of emotional well-being and resilience

- Understand the physiological and emotional benefits of restorative practices

- Identify personal signs of stress and burnout, and how to respond with compassion

- Develop a personalised relaxation routine aligned with inner balance and heart connection

Core Emotional Domains

The core emotional intelligence domains covered here are essential because they form the foundation for lasting heart connection, guiding you to deepen self-awareness, regulate emotions, build resilience, and strengthen the mind-body bond throughout your Heart Unbound journey.

- **Self-Awareness:** You learn to recognise the subtle signs of stress and fatigue in your body, emotions, and thoughts, becoming more attuned to when you need rest and why it matters.

- **Self-Regulation:** You practise calming your nervous system through breath, stillness, and mindful relaxation, allowing you to respond to life with greater ease rather than react from overwhelm.

- **Emotional Resilience:** By prioritising rest and recovery, you build inner strength and the capacity to bounce back from emotional strain or life's demands with steadiness and clarity.

- **Empathy (Self and Others):** Relaxation opens space for compassionate listening, to your own needs and to the emotional states of those around you, deepening your relational presence.

- **Well-Being and Life Balance:** This part reminds you that rest is not a reward, but a vital rhythm of sustainable living, essential for clarity, creativity, and connection in your everyday life.

"Relaxation – The Art Of Letting Go"

Relaxation is more than just a mental break, it is a healing practice that brings you back into emotional, physical, and creative balance. In the busyness of your day-to-day life, it is easy to forget the power of simply pausing, but when you give yourself permission to slow down and soften, you begin to return to your natural state of calm presence. In this part of your *Heart Unbound* journey, you are invited to explore what it means to truly rest, not just to disconnect, but to reconnect. Relaxation isn't about avoiding life, it is about creating space to feel, breathe, and restore. When you let go of tension, quiet the inner noise, and return to your breath, you allow your nervous system to reset. Your body heals. Your emotions settle. Your creativity reawakens.

You will draw from ancient practices and modern science to understand how rest activates your parasympathetic nervous system, your body's way of returning to safety and repair. Through stillness, you begin to hear the quieter parts of your heart. You reconnect with empathy, build emotional resilience, and honour your need for gentleness. Relaxation reminds you that you do not have to earn your rest. It is your birthright. When you prioritise stillness, you begin to find clarity, presence, and renewal. You become more balanced, not by doing more, but by choosing what truly matters. This is your invitation to pause, not as an escape, but as a sacred return. A return to your breath. A return to balance. A return to you.

Historical Roots: Egypt, Greece, India, China, How Cultures Viewed Rest As Sacred

Long before the modern world began glorifying busyness, many ancient cultures understood something profound, **rest was not laziness; it was sacred.** It was seen as essential to well-being, insight, healing, and spiritual connection. As you reconnect with your own need for rest, it is powerful to remember that you are returning to something deeply ancestral, something honoured and revered across time and cultures.

Ancient Egypt

In ancient Egypt, rest and sleep were seen not as passive states, but as sacred gateways into the divine. To the Egyptians, the hours of stillness were moments when the veil between the human and the spiritual thinned, allowing wisdom and healing to flow through dreams. Sleep was honoured as a bridge to the gods, a time when guidance, prophecy, and renewal could be received. Temples were constructed not only as places of worship, but also as sanctuaries for healing. Within their quiet chambers, priests and healers facilitated sacred sleep rituals known as **incubation**. These rituals invited individuals to enter a deeply restful state, lying down in a protected space, breathing slowly, and surrendering to the embrace of silence. In this state of openness, dreams were welcomed as divine messages, visions that could bring answers to life's struggles, insight into decisions, or even physical healing.

To rest was not considered idleness. It was regarded as a **portal of wisdom**, a sacred act of aligning the body and soul with cosmic order. In surrendering to rest, the Egyptians believed you were surrendering to something higher, allowing your soul to speak in the language of dreams and symbols. Imagine yourself stepping into one of these ancient temples. The air is still and perfumed with incense. A quiet hush surrounds you as you recline on a simple bed of linen. Your breath deepens, your body softens, and slowly you drift into the realm of dream, trusting that in this space of rest, healing, and divine communication, you will receive exactly what your heart and soul need. Even today, you can carry this wisdom forward: rest is not wasted time, but a **sacred practice of restoration**. Each time you surrender to sleep or stillness with intention, you invite your inner world to reveal itself, and you open a doorway to insight, healing, and peace.

Ancient Greece

In ancient Greece, rest was not viewed as indulgence, but as medicine for both the body and the soul. Philosophers such as **Hippocrates**, often called the father of medicine, and later **Galen**, emphasised that true health could not exist without periods of balance, quiet, and renewal. They taught that exhaustion and overexertion disrupted the harmony of the four humours, blood, phlegm, yellow bile, and black bile, which were believed to govern physical and emotional wellbeing. To restore balance, the body required cycles of **rest, reflection, and stillness**.

The practice of sacred rest was also central to the **temples of Asclepius**, the Greek god of healing. These sanctuaries, known as **Asclepieia**, were places where seekers came not only for physical cures but for spiritual renewal.

Upon arrival, pilgrims would often bathe, fast, or engage in rituals to purify the body and mind. Then, they were invited to lie down in a sacred chamber and surrender to silence, stillness, and sleep. This ritual, called **incubation**, was believed to open the way for divine dreams, visions in which Asclepius himself or his healing spirits offered guidance, remedies, or reassurance. For the Greeks, healing was never separate from rest. **There was no healing without rest. There was no clarity without stillness.** To pause was not weakness, but wisdom, an act of alignment with the natural rhythms of life and the divine order of the cosmos.

Imagine walking into one of these sanctuaries, the air thick with the scent of herbs and oils, the sound of water echoing from a nearby fountain. You are guided to a quiet space where you lie down, close your eyes, and surrender to stillness. In that silence, the body begins to soften, the mind begins to slow, and the spirit opens to receive. Healing begins not through striving, but through the **art of resting deeply**. Even today, this wisdom calls to us. To slow down. To surrender. To remember that clarity does not come from doing more, but from allowing ourselves to pause long enough to hear what our body and soul have been trying to say all along.

India

In India, rest was not seen as absence of activity, but as a profound practice of presence. The ancient tradition of **Yoga Nidra**, often called the *yogic sleep*, guided practitioners into a state of deep conscious rest that lay between wakefulness and sleep. In this liminal space, the body could release tension, the mind could soften its constant activity, and the spirit could return to its natural state of wholeness. Unlike ordinary sleep, Yoga Nidra was a **spiritual discipline**, a practice of awareness. Practitioners were invited to lie down, close their eyes, and follow the rhythm of their breath inward. Step by step, the teacher would guide awareness through the body, gently relaxing each part, until the entire being entered into stillness.

In this sacred state, the body rested deeply, yet consciousness remained awake and open, a unique meeting of **rest, renewal, and insight**. Here, healing was not forced but allowed to unfold naturally. Old wounds could surface gently, emotions could be released, and clarity could emerge from within. In Yoga Nidra, rest became more than recovery; it became a **pathway to transformation**. Rest in this tradition was a **sacred return to the self**. The breath was a bridge to inner calm. The body, once tense and striving, became an ally in letting go. Awareness itself became medicine, illuminating the layers of distraction and revealing the quiet light of the soul beneath.

Imagine yourself lying on a mat in a quiet temple space, the air warm and still. A voice guides you to notice your breath, then your hands, your feet, your chest, your face. One by one, the parts of you soften and release. Your body sinks into rest, yet a part of you remains awake, luminous, and free. This is the gift of Yoga Nidra: the **union of stillness and awareness**, where renewal and insight flow without effort. Even today, this practice teaches us that rest is not laziness, but a **discipline of the heart**. It is a conscious choice to surrender striving, to listen deeply, and to trust that in stillness, life itself restores you.

<u>Ancient China</u>

In ancient China, the wisdom of **Daoism** invited people to live in harmony with the natural rhythms of life. To the Daoists, existence itself was a dance between movement and stillness, light and dark, effort and rest, all flowing together in balance, like the yin and yang. To resist or force life's currents was to create struggle; to rest and flow with them was to return to alignment with the Dao, the great way of nature.Rest, in this tradition, was not seen as weakness or idleness. It was understood as a **vital rhythm within the cycle of life**. Just as the earth needs seasons of stillness for renewal, so too do human beings.

Silence and stillness were cultivated as sources of clarity, wisdom, and transformation. A quiet mind was like a still pond, reflecting truth with precision and depth. Even warriors and scholars were taught the principle of **wu wei**, the art of effortless action. Wu wei was not inaction, but the state of acting in perfect harmony with the flow of life, without strain or resistance. From this place, rest and action became partners, not opposites. Rest prepared you for movement; movement returned you to rest. Both were essential for balance and vitality. Imagine yourself in a Daoist garden, where water flows gently over stones and bamboo bends with the breeze. You sit quietly, breathing with the earth, noticing how every leaf, every ripple, every birdcall arises and passes effortlessly.

In this stillness, you realise: you, too, are part of this natural rhythm. You do not need to force. You do not need to grasp. When you rest, you align with the great flow, and from this alignment, clarity, strength, and transformation naturally emerge. The wisdom of Daoism reminds us that stillness is not the absence of life, but the essence of life itself. To rest is to return to harmony with the Dao, to discover that the universe is already carrying you, if only you soften enough to let it.

These ancient roots remind you that **rest is not something to fit in after you have done enough. It is foundational.** Sacred. Alive with possibility. In stillness, you reconnect with your wholeness. In relaxation, you meet yourself again, unmasked, unhurried, and whole. As you lie down or pause in silence today, know that you are part of a long, beautiful lineage that understood something our modern world is just beginning to remember: *Rest is a spiritual act. Rest is a return to the heart. Rest is a remembering of who you truly are.*

The Nervous System Explained: Parasympathetic Activation And Why it Matters

Your body is a masterpiece of wisdom, designed not only to keep you alive but to help you heal, grow, and return to balance. At the centre of this design is your **nervous system**, the intricate network of signals that governs how you respond to the world around you. One of its greatest gifts is the ability to shift between states, from activation to calm, from survival to safety, from reactivity to presence. Learning how to recognise and guide these shifts is key to emotional healing, resilience, and reconnecting with your heart. Your nervous system has **two main branches**:

The Sympathetic Nervous System (Fight-or-Flight)

This is your body's accelerator. When you face a challenge, danger, or even the stress of a crowded inbox, your sympathetic system switches on. Your breath becomes shallow, your heart races, your muscles tense. Your body is preparing you to fight, flee, or push through. This response is essential in true emergencies, but modern life keeps many of us in this state far too often, running on adrenaline, exhausted, and disconnected from peace.

The Parasympathetic Nervous System (Rest-and-Restore)

This is your body's natural brake and healer. When activated, your breath slows, your heart rate steadies, your digestion improves, and your whole system signals: *"You are safe now."* In this state, your body repairs itself, your mind clears, and your heart opens. It is here that healing, integration, and renewal happen.

The vagus nerve, sometimes called the body's *"calm highway,"* plays a central role in activating the parasympathetic system. When stimulated through slow breathing, mindful movement, singing, humming, or even gentle touch, it helps you shift out of stress and into grounded calm. Why does this matter? Because when your nervous system feels safe, your **heart can speak**. Calm is not weakness, it is wisdom. Stillness is not idleness, it is the soil where clarity, compassion, and resilience grow.

Think of it this way: when you are in survival mode, your world shrinks. You react. You grasp. You fight or flee, but when you activate your parasympathetic nervous system, your world expands again. You see more clearly. You feel more deeply. You respond rather than react. You become more present, more compassionate, more in tune with yourself and others. Simple practices can awaken this state within minutes:

- Slow, rhythmic breathing (especially longer exhales).

- Resting with your hand on your heart.

- Gentle yoga, tai chi, or mindful walking.

- Pausing in stillness with the intention to soften.

Each time you do this, you are reminding your body: *"You are safe. You are home."* In this part of your *Heart Unbound* journey, you are not fighting your nervous system; you are partnering with it. You are reclaiming calm as your birthright. You are discovering that resilience is not about pushing harder, but about returning more gently, again and again, to safety and presence. When your body rests in calm, your heart's whispers become audible. When your nervous system softens, healing unfolds naturally, and in this sacred space, where breath slows, muscles release, and the heart opens, transformation begins.

The Myth Of "Busy" And The Cost Of Burnout

You have likely been told, perhaps since childhood, that being busy is a virtue. That a full calendar, a packed to-do list, and a life of constant motion are proof that you are valuable, productive, successful, and even lovable. Somewhere along the way, you may have learned to equate your worth with how much you do, how quickly you respond, how much you achieve, or how well you keep up, but this belief is not truth, it is a myth. *"Busy"* is not always purposeful. More often, it becomes a mask, hiding your exhaustion, your fear of stillness, or your disconnection from what really matters. You can be busy and empty. Busy and lonely. Busy and quietly breaking inside. You may be praised for how much you achieve, yet your soul knows the cost, and the cost is high.

When you live in a constant state of *"on,"* your nervous system never has the chance to rest. Your breath becomes shallow, your mind scatters, and your emotions feel harder to manage. Your body begins to whisper: headaches, fatigue, irritability, anxiety. If you ignore the whispers, they grow louder, burnout, illness, disconnection, even collapse. Busyness without balance does not lead to joy, it leads to depletion. It erodes creativity, compassion, presence, and meaning. You stop hearing your own needs. You forget what it feels like to breathe deeply, to feel your heart, to live from the inside out, but it does not have to stay this way. You can choose to rewrite the story. To remember that rest is not laziness, it is medicine. That slowing down is not giving up, it is coming home to what matters. That your value is not measured by how much you do, but by how deeply you live.

In this part of *Heart Unbound*, you are invited to gently step away from the myth of *"busy"* and into a new rhythm. One that honours your energy, protects your peace, and gives your nervous system the exhale it has been waiting for. You are not a machine. You are a living, breathing, feeling, tender-hearted human being. You are allowed to pause. You are allowed to rest, and in fact, your healing, your joy, and your wholeness depend on it. You have also likely been conditioned to believe that insight comes from effort, thinking harder, working longer, pushing through, but what if the clarity you seek is not found in doing more… but in doing less?

Stillness is not the absence of action. It is the presence of awareness. In stillness, your mind softens and your inner landscape becomes more visible. Like a muddy river settling after the storm, clarity does not come from stirring the water, it comes from letting it rest. When you pause long enough to truly *be*, the noise of the world fades, and the whispers of your heart can finally be heard. It is often in the quietest moments, a deep breath, a walk in nature, a few minutes with your eyes closed, that breakthrough insights rise. Not because you forced them, but because you created space for them to emerge.

Stillness gives you perspective. It lets you step back from the overwhelm and see your life with fresh eyes. It invites intuitive knowing to surface, truths that cannot be accessed through logic alone. When you slow down, your nervous system rebalances, your body releases tension, and your inner wisdom is no longer drowned out by urgency. Paradoxically, when you do less, you *receive* more, more clarity, more creativity, more alignment. You begin to operate from depth, not just momentum. You become more intentional, more present, more grounded. In *Heart Unbound*, stillness is not a retreat from life, it is a return to it. It is where your next steps become clear, not because you rush toward them, but because you listen deeply for them. *So allow yourself to pause. To breathe. To trust the quiet* because sometimes, the greatest insights come not when you strive, but when you simply allow.

Creativity, Resilience, And Relationships: What Happens When We Recharge

When you allow yourself to rest, deeply, intentionally, without guilt, you do more than just recover from exhaustion. You begin to renew your most vital capacities: your creativity, your emotional resilience, and your ability to show up in your relationships with presence and care. **Creativity** does not thrive in burnout. It withers in stress. When you are constantly rushing, your mind becomes cluttered with noise and urgency, leaving little space for wonder, vision, or possibility, but when you slow down, breathe, and let your nervous system soften, something remarkable happens, your imagination reawakens.

Ideas flow more freely. Solutions become clearer. The colours return to your inner world. Creativity is born not from pressure, but from spaciousness. **Resilience**, too, is restored in rest. Life is full of challenge, but when you are rested, you have the inner stability to face what comes. You bounce back more easily. You think more clearly. You feel more emotionally steady. The strength you need is not forged by pushing harder, it is nurtured by knowing when to pause, replenish, and begin again from a place of alignment, and then, there are your **relationships**.

The people you care about most benefit deeply when you are well-rested and present. When you are not surviving on empty, you listen better, love more patiently, and communicate more authentically. You are able to offer your full self, not a rushed, distracted version of you, but the real you. The you with space in your heart. When you recharge, you do not just feel better, you live better. You create more, connect deeper, and navigate life with more grace. So let rest be part of your rhythm. Let it be non-negotiable, because every time you choose to restore yourself, you are also choosing to renew your heart, your voice, and your relationships, and that is a gift to everyone, including you.

Body, Breath, and Balance – Expanded Practice

This practice is about creating harmony within yourself by reconnecting with your breath, your body, and the quiet presence of your heart. It is not about fixing or changing anything, it is about noticing, softening, and allowing yourself to rest in awareness.

Step 1: Balanced Heart Breathing (3 minutes)

Begin by returning to the foundation from Day 1. Place a hand on your heart and gently slow your breath. Inhale through your nose for a count of 4, and exhale softly through your mouth for a count of 6. With each breath, imagine you are nourishing your body with calm, safety, and presence. Feel your heart steady as your nervous system begins to relax.

Step 2: Gentle Body Scan Meditation (5 minutes)

Close your eyes and bring your attention slowly through the different parts of your body. Start at the top of your head and move downward, forehead, jaw, shoulders, arms, chest, belly, hips, legs, and feet. Notice any sensations, warmth, tightness, tingling, or stillness. You are not trying to change them; you are simply becoming aware. This is an act of kindness toward yourself, letting your body be just as it is.

Step 3: Simply Be (Presence Without Judgment)

Now, allow yourself to rest in this awareness. Notice how your body feels when you release the need to do or perform. Can you welcome each sensation with curiosity instead of judgment? This gentle acceptance is balance: letting the body, mind, and heart come into alignment through awareness.

Optional Enhancement

If you wish, create an atmosphere of peace around you. Soft instrumental music, nature sounds, or even silence can become the backdrop for your practice. Allow these sounds to hold you, reminding you that you are safe, supported, and exactly where you need to be.

Reflection Prompt: After this practice, take a few moments to write in your journal:

- *What did I notice in my body that surprised me?*
- *How did my breath shift my sense of balance or presence?*

> • *Where in my body did I feel most at ease?*

Case Study Discussion: Glen's Journey

To say that Glen was a hard worker was an understatement. He worked six days a week in his own business, and he never seemed to stop. Long days and sleepless nights had taken their toll on his physical and mental well–being, leaving him exhausted and disconnected from his true self. He was past burnout when we started journeying together and it took a long time to get him to a place that he could even realise he needed to slow down.

Over several months we started introducing very simple routines into his daily life, such as balanced heart breathing and taking peaceful leisurely walks outside at a park near his work. As he gradually embraced these practices, Glen noticed a remarkable shift within himself. The relentless grip of stress began to loosen, replaced by a sense of calm and tranquility. Glen discovered the joy of being present in the moment, experiencing life's simple pleasures, and nurturing his relationships with his wife and children. He approached challenges with a clearer mind and a renewed sense of purpose. His productivity soared, and he achieved a greater work–life balance.

The ripple effects of his relaxation practices positively influenced those around him, inspiring friends, and colleagues to prioritise their self–care and well–being. Through relaxation, Glen unearthed a deeper understanding of himself and his place in the world. He learned to listen to his body's needs and honour his own boundaries. Glen's journey is a salutary reminder of the transformative power of relaxation and that by learning to relax, you can rediscover your true self, cultivate and nurture your own well–being, and live a more fulfilled and balanced life.

Reflective Exercise: Glen's Journey

Here are four profound and reflective questions inspired by Glen's story to help you engage with your own relaxation journey:

1. **What beliefs have you inherited about rest and productivity, and how might those beliefs be keeping you disconnected from your well-being?** Take a moment to reflect on whether you have attached your worth to being constantly busy. What would it mean for you to redefine success through presence, balance, and ease?

---

2. **When was the last time you truly listened to your body without rushing past its signals?** Your body holds quiet wisdom. Are there places within you asking to slow down, breathe, or soften, and are you willing to honour those needs today?

3. **What simple, restorative practice could you begin right now to help you return to yourself each day?** Think small: a walk, a breath, a pause. What could become your new ritual of calm, a sacred space in your routine that belongs just to you?

4. **How would your relationships shift if you began showing up more rested, present, and emotionally available?** Imagine how your energy, attention, and love might feel different when you are no longer running on empty. What becomes possible when you give from overflow rather than depletion?

Affirmations For You – (Heart Whispers)

Affirmations have the power to quiet the noise of doubt, open the doorway to self-trust, and draw you back into the wisdom of your heart. When practised daily, they nurture an inner dialogue based in love and truth, helping you live each day more aligned with who you truly are. I invite you to repeat silently or write:

- *In relaxation, I find peace and refuge from life's demands.*

- *I embrace the calm of relaxation, letting go of tension.*

- *In stillness, I discover the profound beauty of relaxation.*

- *I prioritise self-care and carve out time for relaxation.*

- *Through relaxation, I recharge my spirit and rejuvenate my soul.*

- *I am at peace when I surrender to the gentle embrace of relaxation.*

Create Your *"Relaxation Ritual Blueprint"*

Rest is not a luxury, it is a necessity for your mind, body, and heart. When you consciously create space for relaxation, you give yourself permission to replenish energy, restore balance, and return to life with more clarity and compassion. This blueprint is your personal guide to designing sustainable rituals of rest that align with your unique rhythm and lifestyle.

Step 1: Daily Micro-Moments of Rest

Relaxation does not have to wait for a weekend or a holiday. Small pauses throughout your day can make a profound difference. Try:

- Closing your eyes for one minute of deep breathing between tasks.

- Stepping outside to feel the sun, wind, or air on your skin.

- Stretching slowly while bringing awareness to your breath.

- Sipping a cup of tea or water with full presence, as if it were a sacred act.

These micro-moments reset your nervous system and remind you that rest can be woven into ordinary moments.

Step 2: Weekly Unplug Hours or "Sabbath" Practices

Choose a block of time each week where you step away from screens, work obligations, and busyness. This could be an afternoon in nature, a technology-free evening, or a few sacred hours dedicated to family, creativity, or stillness. By creating these boundaries, you gift yourself time for deeper restoration and reconnection.

Step 3: Restorative Tools

Gather tools that support you in relaxing deeply and intentionally. Your toolkit might include:

- Gentle music, sound baths, or nature soundscapes.

- A warm bath with calming scents like lavender or chamomile.

- Meditation or guided relaxation practices.

- Time in nature, walking, sitting by water, or simply lying on the grass.

- Creative outlets such as journaling, painting, or mindful cooking.

Notice which tools genuinely nourish you, and keep them close at hand.

Step 4: Boundaries with Technology and Overcommitment

Much of your fatigue comes not from doing too little, but from doing too much, or doing too much *for others* at the expense of yourself. Reflect on:

- When and how you use your phone or screens.

- Whether you need to say *"no"* more often to protect your energy.

- What commitments can be simplified, delegated, or released.

Setting boundaries is not selfish, it is essential for protecting your wellbeing and sustaining your capacity to give from a place of fullness.

Step 5: Your Ritual Declaration

Now, shape these elements into a personal blueprint that feels realistic and supportive for you. Write your responses to the following:

- *"My non-negotiable for relaxation is…"*

- *"When I honour rest, I feel…"*

Let this be your reminder that rest is not optional, it is your foundation. Every time you honour rest, you strengthen your ability to show up for life with presence, resilience, and joy.

Closing Reflection

As you arrive at the close of this part of your journey, pause and give yourself the gift of a deep, nourishing breath. Feel the stillness that lives beneath the surface of your busyness, the quiet sanctuary within you that is always available, waiting patiently for your return. Relaxation is not a reward for having done enough. It is your right, your rhythm, your refuge. In letting go of the myth of *"busy,"* you have opened space for something deeper: insight, healing, and presence.

You have remembered that doing less does not mean being less, it often means becoming more. More attuned. More rested. More whole. As Glen's story reminds you, when you learn to slow down, you do not fall behind, you catch up with your heart. So keep choosing rest not just as a break from life, but as a way back to it. Let your breath be your anchor. Let stillness become your strength, and know this: *Every time you honour your need to pause, you honour your sacred aliveness. You are worthy of rest. You are worthy of peace. You are worthy of coming home to yourself.*

22 – INNER CHILD

Your Opening Reflection

Invitation to Meet Your Inner Child - As you step into this chapter, allow yourself to soften and approach with tenderness. Within you still lives the child who once dreamed, laughed, and played with wonder. This is your chance to reconnect, not through judgment or analysis, but through love and curiosity. Let your heart open to the memories, the joys, and even the hurts that shaped you. Trust that what surfaces is here to guide you, to remind you of the innocence, creativity, and truth that have always been yours. Welcome your inner child home with compassion.

- "What do you remember most vividly about your childhood joy?"

- "What did your heart love to do before the world told you who to be?"

- "When you were a child, where did you feel the safest and most free?"

- "What simple activity or moment made you lose track of time?"

- "If your younger self could whisper one truth to you now, what would it be?"

Let these questions open the doorway into presence. Every answer you give, whether in words, sensations, or silence, is a bridge between where you are and where you are going.

Learning Objectives

The learning objectives are included here to give you a clear focus for this chapter, ensuring that each practice you explore moves you closer to mastering the skills, insights, and heart-led awareness that will enrich your life

well beyond the program. By the end of this chapter, you will:

- Understand the concept and psychological significance of the inner child

- Recognise the impact of unmet childhood emotional needs on adult behaviour

- Develop skills to reconnect with, nurture, and integrate the inner child

- Use compassion, creativity, and reflection to develop healing and joy

Core Emotional Domains

The core emotional intelligence domains covered here are essential because they form the foundation for lasting heart connection, guiding you to deepen self-awareness, regulate emotions, build resilience, and strengthen the mind-body bond throughout your Heart Unbound journey.

- **Self-Awareness**: You begin to recognise the younger parts of yourself that still carry unmet needs, forgotten joys, or unspoken wounds, allowing you to explore your emotional history with honesty and tenderness.

- **Self-Compassion**: As you reconnect with your inner child, you learn to replace self-judgment with gentleness, offering yourself the same kindness you would offer a vulnerable child in your care.

- **Emotional Expression**: Through guided reflection and heart-led practices, you give voice to long-held emotions, sometimes buried since childhood, allowing them to be felt, honoured, and released.

- **Empathy**: By embracing the child within, you cultivate deeper empathy not only for yourself, but also for others, recognising that we all carry stories shaped by our early experiences.

- **Personal Growth and Healing**: This part invites you to reclaim innocence, playfulness, and emotional truth, fostering healing, integration, and the freedom to live with more authenticity and love.

"Inner Child – Listening From Your Heart"

Your inner child is not a concept, it is a living presence within you. It is the tender, intuitive, deeply feeling part of you that once moved through the world with wide eyes, open arms, and an unguarded heart. This child within you remembers what it was like to feel wonder. To dream without limits. To be curious, sensitive, playful, and yes, at times, wounded. To connect with your inner child is not to regress or dwell in the past. It is to acknowledge that the younger parts of you still live within your emotional landscape.

These parts carry both the joy of innocent love and the echoes of unmet needs. Integration means welcoming those parts home, not to fix them, but to listen to them, hold them, and honour their truth. This is not a detour. It is a return. A return to the essence of who you are underneath the layers of adult responsibility, performance, and protection. When you pause and invite your inner child to speak, you begin to understand the roots of your emotions. You may hear their sadness, their longings, their delight, or their fear, and when you respond not with shame or dismissal, but with compassion, you unlock profound healing.

Your inner child does not need to be silenced. They need to be seen. This is where deep self-love begins, not just in loving who you have become, but in loving who you once were, and all the parts of you that never stopped hoping someone would understand. By reconnecting with your inner child, you open a path to gentleness, creativity, and emotional wholeness. You become the loving presence that part of you always needed, a*nd in doing so, you become more fully… you.*

Definition Of The Inner Child (Psychological & Emotional Frameworks)

Your **inner child** is the part of you that was formed in your earliest years. It holds your first emotional experiences, memories, needs, and impressions. While your body and intellect have matured, your inner child still lives within you, carrying your **joy, playfulness, and curiosity**, but also your **pain, fear, and unmet needs**.

1. Psychodynamic Perspective

From a psychodynamic lens, first introduced by **Carl Jung**, your inner child is an archetypal part of your self, the innocent, vulnerable, and creative part of you. Later teachers like **John Bradshaw** expanded this idea, describing the inner child as the **wounded self** that emerges when your needs for safety, love, or validation were unmet in childhood. Those wounds do not vanish with time; instead, they may reappear in how you respond in relationships, moments of stress, or when you feel vulnerable. *For example:* When you fear abandonment as an adult, it may not be your present-day self speaking, but the younger part of you still waiting to feel safe and seen.

2. Attachment Theory

Your inner child reflects the bonds you formed with your caregivers. If your caregivers gave you **secure attachment**, your inner child may feel safe and supported. If your bonds were **anxious, avoidant, or disorganised**, your inner child may carry patterns of mistrust, fear, or hypervigilance.

- Anxious bonds may leave you always searching for reassurance.

- Avoidant bonds may lead you to shut down or suppress emotions.

- Disorganised bonds may leave you fearful, torn between longing for closeness and fearing it.

Healing involves recognising these patterns within you and choosing to offer your inner child a new experience, safety, consistency, and compassion.

3. Reparenting and Inner Child Work

In **inner child work**, you learn to **reparent yourself**. This means becoming the compassionate, reliable caregiver your younger self always needed. You can:

- Listen to your feelings with empathy.

- Offer nurturing words to yourself.

- Create emotional safety where shame and fear no longer silence you.

As you do this, you begin to soothe your wounded inner child and create space for your adult self to live with greater confidence, love, and authenticity.

4. Somatic and Trauma-Informed Approaches

Your inner child does not live only in your memories, it also lives in your body. Think of the times you feel tension, shallow breathing, or numbness. This is often your nervous system carrying the weight of old experiences that once overwhelmed you. Leaders like **Peter Levine** and **Bessel van der Kolk** describe how childhood pain can remain trapped as stored energy. When you reconnect with your body through breathwork, gentle movement, or mindful presence, you create space to release those old imprints. This is why healing is not only about the mind, it is also about the body finding safety again.

5. Developmental and Emotional Frameworks

Your inner child is also your **emotional blueprint**. The patterns you learned in your earliest years shaped how you regulate emotions, connect with others, and even how your brain wires itself for stress or calm. The good news is this: by reconnecting with your inner child, you can **retrain your responses**, build resilience, and rewrite the patterns that no longer serve you.

<u>Why This Matters for You</u>

Your inner child is not something you need to hide or overcome, it is a sacred and vital part of who you are. It carries your **most vulnerable truths** as well as your **most joyful, creative energy**. When you reconnect with your inner child, you:

- Break cycles of unconscious pain.

- Create healthier, more authentic relationships.

- Access more creativity, spontaneity, and joy.

- Build resilience, compassion, and self-trust.

This is not about going backwards, it is about **integration**. Meeting your inner child is an act of courage and love. It allows you to live more fully, more honestly, and more deeply connected to your heart.

Carl Jung, Eric Berne, And The Therapeutic Basis Of Inner Child Work

The idea of the **inner child** is not just a poetic metaphor, it has deep roots in psychology, psychotherapy, and human development. The language may vary across disciplines, but the essence remains: there is a part of you that carries the imprint of your early emotional life, and healing begins when you turn toward that part with awareness and care.

<u>Carl Jung: The Divine Child and the Symbolic Psyche</u>

Carl Jung, one of the great pioneers of depth psychology, introduced the concept of the **Divine Child archetype**, which he described as a symbol of your deepest potential, innocence, and creative essence. For Jung, this archetype was not merely a memory of childhood, it was a timeless presence within you, carrying the energy of renewal, transformation, and the sacred spark of life itself. The **Divine Child** represents your original wholeness: the part of you that is curious, imaginative, playful, and pure. It is the wellspring of creativity and possibility. This childlike essence is not about immaturity or regression, it is about reconnecting with the qualities that bring vitality, hope, and a sense of wonder into your adult life.

Jung warned that when you disconnect from this part of yourself, you risk falling into **emotional rigidity, spiritual emptiness, and a sense of being cut off from meaning.** You may become overly rational, burdened by responsibilities, or locked into roles and identities that leave little space for joy or spontaneity. In this disconnection, the psyche begins to hunger for renewal, often expressing itself through crisis, dreams, or unconscious behaviours that signal the need for inner integration.

Healing, in Jung's view, comes through **individuation**, the lifelong process of becoming whole by integrating all aspects of yourself, including the parts you have repressed or neglected. Individuation invites you to welcome the Divine Child back into your awareness, allowing it to soften your defences, awaken creativity, and restore balance between the demands of adulthood and the yearnings of the soul. For Jung, your inner child was not simply a psychological construct but a **bridge to the sacred**.

It was a reminder that within you lives a spark of divinity, a seed of wholeness that, when nurtured, can transform your life. To reclaim your inner child is to reconnect with the source of your vitality, to find guidance in your imagination and intuition, and to honour the truth that healing is not about perfection but about integration. The invitation is this: **your Divine Child is still alive within you.** It waits to be acknowledged, to be given space, and to be loved. When you honour this part of yourself, you do more than heal, you come home to the sacred essence of who you are.

Eric Berne: Transactional Analysis and the Ego States

In the 1960s, psychiatrist **Eric Berne**, founder of **Transactional Analysis (TA)**, introduced a groundbreaking way of understanding human behaviour and communication. His model gave the *"inner child"* a structured place within a broader psychological framework that continues to shape psychotherapy and personal development today. Berne proposed that within you exist three primary **ego states**:

- **The Parent** – the internalised voices of authority, carrying the rules, beliefs, and expectations you absorbed from caregivers and society. This part can be nurturing and protective, but also critical and controlling.

- **The Adult** – your rational, grounded, present-focused self, capable of assessing situations with clarity and responding appropriately to reality.

- **The Child** – your emotional, intuitive, and instinctive self, holding both the light and the wounds of your earliest years.

Within the **Child ego state**, Berne described two key dimensions:

- **The Natural Child** – spontaneous, joyful, creative, curious, and free. This is the part of you that laughs easily, feels deeply, dreams boldly, and responds authentically to life.

- **The Adapted Child** – shaped by early environments, family dynamics, and survival strategies. Here live the learned responses of fear, guilt, compliance, rebellion, or withdrawal. The Adapted Child holds the ways you tried to earn love, avoid punishment, or stay safe.

Berne's insight was that these ego states do not remain fixed in the past, they actively shape your daily life, relationships, and self-image. For example, when your Adapted Child is running the show, you may find yourself people-pleasing, silencing your needs, or reacting with fear or defensiveness, even when your Adult self knows better. When your Natural Child is alive and free, however, you radiate vitality, connection, playfulness, and truth.

The power of **Transactional Analysis** lies in recognising which state is operating within you in any moment. By cultivating awareness, you can strengthen the **Adult ego state** to mediate, integrate, and bring balance. The Adult can soothe the fears of the Adapted Child, protect and nurture the Natural Child, and negotiate with the Parent to discard outdated rules while keeping supportive guidance.

When unacknowledged, your Child ego state can sabotage your best adult intentions, pulling you into old patterns of fear, rebellion, or compliance, but when honoured and nurtured, it becomes a wellspring of creativity, intuition, and joy. Healing, therefore, is not about silencing the Child, but about **reparenting** it, offering yourself the love, safety, and freedom that may have been missing in your early life. In this sense, Berne's work gave us more than a theory, it gave us a **map for emotional freedom**. It showed us that by recognising, listening to, and caring for the inner child, you can break free from unconscious scripts and step into relationships and choices that reflect your authentic self.

The Rise of Inner Child Work in Therapeutic Practice

Building on the pioneering insights of **Carl Jung** and **Eric Berne**, a new generation of therapists, most notably **John Bradshaw**, **Alice Miller**, and

Charles Whitfield, brought the concept of the inner child out of theory and into **mainstream therapeutic practice**. Their work transformed the idea of the inner child from a symbolic or structural framework into a **living, practical pathway of healing and integration**.

These voices made it clear: the wounds of childhood do not simply disappear as you grow older. They remain imprinted in your nervous system, shaping the ways you relate to yourself and others. Left unacknowledged, these wounds can surface in adulthood as struggles with **intimacy, addiction, perfectionism, co-dependency, low self-worth, or difficulty setting boundaries**.

- **John Bradshaw** popularised the term *"the wounded inner child"* and helped thousands understand that what you may dismiss as *"childish"* behaviour in adulthood is often the echo of unmet needs from long ago. His healing processes emphasised **reparenting yourself**, learning to give your inner child what was once denied: compassion, safety, encouragement, and unconditional love. He also taught the necessity of healthy boundaries, so your child-self could feel safe enough to thrive.

- **Alice Miller**, in books such as *The Drama of the Gifted Child*, brought a fierce light to the hidden costs of childhood trauma, particularly for those who learned early to be *"perfect"* or *"pleasing"* in order to be loved. For Miller, healing was never about blaming parents, but about **honestly acknowledging what was denied, silenced, or distorted in your early emotional world**. She showed how truth-telling and self-compassion could break cycles of shame and repression.

- **Charles Whitfield** deepened the conversation by describing the inner child as the **authentic self**, the truest essence of who you are. He argued that reclaiming this authentic self is the key to healing from addictions and emotional dysfunction. For Whitfield, reconnecting with your inner child was not about regressing into immaturity, but about recovering the freedom, vitality, and creativity that trauma had buried.

Together, these therapists shifted the cultural conversation: **to do inner child work is not to dwell in the past, but to liberate the future.** It is not about blame, but about truth. It is not about weakness, but about strength. By integrating, Jung's **symbolic wisdom** of the Divine Child; Berne's **psychological structure** of the ego states, and the **emotional insight** of modern therapeutic practice you are invited to **listen to, nurture, and**

embrace the child within you. When you do, you unlock a profound source of healing and transformation. To honour your inner child is to reclaim the parts of yourself that still long for safety, joy, and freedom. It is to recognise that the tenderness you once silenced is, in truth, your deepest strength. This is not the end of your story, it is the **beginning of wholeness**.

The Cost Of Emotional Neglect And Suppression Of Joy

There is a hidden grief that lives quietly within many people, not only for what happened to them, but for what never happened at all. It is the grief of absence. The laughter that was not welcomed. The tears that were not held. The joy that was dismissed as being *"too much."* Emotional neglect does not always appear dramatic or violent; often, it is subtle, quiet, and socially acceptable. It can sound like: *"Toughen up," "Stop crying, it is not that bad," "You are too sensitive."*

Each of these messages carries the same wound: your emotional truth is inconvenient, excessive, or unworthy of attention. Over time, you learn to survive by shutting down. You mute your emotions in order to belong. You become fluent in appearing *"fine"* while disconnecting from your inner reality. This survival strategy works,for a while, but it extracts a profound cost.

- When you suppress your **sadness**, you also suppress your **joy**.

- When you deny your **vulnerability**, you lose access to **connection**.

- When you trade your **authenticity** for acceptance, you cut yourself off from the fullness of love and aliveness.

You begin to function on **emotional autopilot**, capable, efficient, even successful, but not truly flourishing. You cope, but you do not create. You manage, but you do not expand. You survive, but you forget how to play. In this state, joy itself can begin to feel unsafe, too expansive, too vulnerable, too easily taken away, and so you hold back. You shrink yourself. You choose control over curiosity, perfection over play, performance over presence, but here's the truth: this is not your fault. These patterns were learned, often in environments where emotional expression felt unsafe or unwelcome. Yet, what was once adaptive for your survival has now become a barrier to your wholeness.

In this sacred space of **Heart Unbound**, you are invited to begin unlearning those messages. To remember that:

- **Joy is not frivolous. It is your birthright.**

- **Your emotions are not too much. They are sacred messengers.**

- **Your inner child was never meant to be silenced. They were meant to be celebrated.**

When you stop neglecting your emotional world, you stop abandoning yourself. You come back to the original truth: that joy is not a reward for getting everything right. It is not something that can only be accessed once you *"earn it."* Joy is a way of being. A homecoming. A return to your wholeness, and when you let joy flow freely again, not controlled, not rationed, not muted, you begin to live, not as a performance, but as yourself. You discover that healing does not come from control, but from connection, to your breath, your body, your heart, and to the child within you who has always longed to be free.

The Gifts Of The Inner Child: Creativity, Wonder, Spontaneity

When you reconnect with your inner child, you do not just revisit old wounds, you rediscover sacred gifts you may have forgotten were yours. These gifts are not childish; they are deeply human. They remind you of what it means to be fully alive, open-hearted, and connected to life's simple, sacred beauty.

Creativity

Your inner child is your **original artist**. Long before anyone graded your drawings, judged your singing, or told you to *"stay inside the lines,"* you were free. You painted the sky purple, sang out of tune at the top of your lungs, danced with wild abandon, and built worlds out of sticks, sand, and imagination. You created not for approval, but for the sheer joy of expression. That kind of unfiltered creativity still lives within you. It may have been buried under years of conditioning, criticism, or self-judgment, but it has never left.

When you connect with your inner child, you tap into a wellspring of **pure creative energy**, expression that is not bound by performance, comparison, or perfectionism, but grounded in play, exploration, and truth. From a psychological perspective, this is powerful. Carl Rogers, one of the founders of humanistic psychology, described creativity as the natural expression of a fully alive self. Creativity is not just about art, it is about the ability to solve problems, imagine new possibilities, and express your inner world.

Suppressing creativity often mirrors suppressing emotion. Awakening it opens pathways for healing, self-discovery, and renewal.

Your creativity is also deeply tied to your nervous system and emotional regulation. When you allow yourself to draw, sing, write, dance, or build without judgment, you enter a state of **flow**. In this state, your mind quiets, your breath steadies, and your whole body rests in presence. Neuroscience shows that flow activates reward pathways in your brain, releasing dopamine and reducing stress. It becomes not just art-making, but **soul-healing**. Listening to your inner child in this way invites you to:

- **Express** what words cannot capture.

- **Release** emotions stored in your body.

- **Reclaim** the joy of curiosity and wonder.

- **Remember** that creativity is not about results, it is about connection.

When you gift yourself permission to create for the sake of play, your art becomes a mirror for your heart. You begin to notice colours, sounds, movements, or words that reflect your inner state. Some days your creativity may be light and whimsical; other days, raw and stormy. Both are sacred. Both are true. Your inner child is whispering: *"Create because it feels good. Create because it frees you. Create because it is who you are."* In this space, creativity is no longer performance, it is presence. It becomes your way of exploring, expressing, and healing.

<u>Wonder</u>

Your inner child is your first mystic, the one who sees the extraordinary in the ordinary. To a child, a leaf is not just a leaf; it is a world of colour, veins, and life. A puddle becomes an ocean. Shadows dance into shapes. Stars whisper possibilities. Wonder is the natural language of the heart, and it connects you to life with curiosity, reverence, and joy. As you grow older, you may have been taught to trade wonder for certainty, awe for analysis, mystery for control. You may have learned to prize answers over questions, productivity over presence, logic over imagination. Yet deep down, your heart remembers: life is not meant to be dissected into endless tasks or problems, it is meant to be honoured as a mystery.

Psychologists have found that wonder and awe are not just fleeting feelings; they are essential states of consciousness that expand perspective, soften the ego, and create resilience. Research in positive psychology shows that experiencing awe, whether through nature, music, art, or human connection, creates a sense of vastness and interconnectedness. It shifts you from *"me"* to *"we,"* reducing stress, increasing creativity, and opening space for gratitude. Your inner child already knows this. Wonder is the lens through which your younger self naturally views the world. It is not naïve, it is sacred. It is the way your heart recognises that even the simplest moment can carry a spark of the infinite.

When you slow down, breathe deeply, and allow yourself to see with childlike eyes, you reconnect with this wonder. A sunrise becomes more than light, it becomes a reminder of renewal. The laughter of a friend becomes more than sound, it becomes medicine. Even the silence between breaths becomes a doorway back to the mystery that holds you. To live with wonder is to live awake. It is to say: *"I do not need all the answers. I only need to stay open."* Your inner child whispers: *"Look again. Feel again. Be astonished again. The world is still alive, and so are you."* When you choose wonder, you return to the sacredness of the everyday. You rediscover that joy, meaning, and connection are not far away; they are hidden in plain sight, waiting for you to notice.

Spontaneity

Your inner child is the part of you that moves before the mind interrupts. It is the spark that laughs loudly without checking if it is *"appropriate."* The impulse that dances when the music begins, even if no one else is moving. The voice that says what it feels in the moment, raw and true. As a child, this spontaneity was natural, it was how you expressed life as it flowed through you. Over time, you may have been taught to hold back. To measure your words. To analyse before acting. To check if it was safe, acceptable, or *"good enough."* Slowly, spontaneity was replaced with hesitation. Fear of judgment. The weight of *"what if?"* You began to trade authenticity for approval, aliveness for control,but spontaneity is not recklessness. It is not chaos. It is a profound form of trust, trusting yourself, your body, your emotions, your instincts. It is allowing your heart to respond to life in real time, instead of censoring yourself through old fears or rehearsed scripts.

Psychologically, spontaneity is linked to creativity, resilience, and emotional authenticity. Research in humanistic psychology shows that when you act from spontaneity, you bypass the inner critic and access the part of your brain that generates flow, innovation, and joy. Spontaneity keeps you connected to your emotional truth, it reminds you that you are alive, not just existing.

These gifts are not gone. They may be buried under busyness, seriousness, or the scars of old wounds, but they are waiting, waiting for your permission to resurface. When you embrace spontaneity, you reconnect with the boldness of your inner child, the curiosity of your younger self, and the vitality that still pulses inside you.

To reclaim spontaneity is to say: *"I choose presence over performance. I choose aliveness over perfection. I choose to trust my heart in this moment."* When you allow yourself to laugh freely, to cry without shame, to move without choreography, or to speak without rehearsing, you are not just expressing, you are healing. You are peeling away the armour you once needed, and rediscovering the freedom that has always been yours. Spontaneity is not about becoming someone new. It is about remembering who you already are.

How Healing Your Inner Child Transforms Adult Emotional Patterns

When you begin to heal your inner child, something extraordinary happens, not just in your memories, but in the way you live your life right now. You start to notice that the emotional patterns that once felt automatic, overreacting, withdrawing, pleasing, proving, avoiding, begin to soften. Not because you have forced yourself to suppress them, but because you have finally stopped and listened to the part of you that created them.

As a child, you learned how to feel safe in a world that often felt unpredictable. You developed strategies to protect yourself, strategies that made sense at the time. Maybe you learned to stay quiet to avoid conflict. Maybe you worked hard to earn approval. Maybe you stopped crying because no one came when you did. These protective patterns became woven into your nervous system, your thoughts, and your relationships, but now, as an adult, you may feel how those old protections have turned into cages.

You catch yourself repeating the same cycles, in love, at work, in parenting, even in how you speak to yourself. You wonder why you keep reacting in ways that feel out of alignment with who you truly want to be. This is where healing your inner child becomes transformational. When you begin to meet the younger version of yourself with compassion rather than criticism, you create an entirely new relationship within. Instead of reacting from your wounds, you begin to respond from your wholeness. You start to:

- Recognise emotional triggers not as failures, but as invitations to heal.

- Offer compassion to the parts of you that feel afraid, rather than suppressing or shaming them.

- Set boundaries not as punishment, but as loving protection for your inner child.

- Speak your truth without fearing rejection, because you are no longer abandoning yourself.

- Choose connection over control, because safety now comes from within.

Healing your inner child does not mean erasing your past. It means holding your past with such tenderness that it no longer controls your present. Fear begins to soften. Reactivity begins to slow. In its place, space opens, space for choice, for new responses, for peace. You begin to live from your heart, not your hurt. This is the power of integration: when your adult self becomes the loving guide your younger self always needed, you stop reenacting your pain. Instead, you begin to rewrite your story, one based not in survival, but in truth, compassion, and freedom.

Body, Breath, and Balance Exercise

I invite you to step gently into this practice, not as something to *"achieve,"* but as a way of coming home to yourself. This is not about fixing, changing, or striving. It is about listening, softening, and allowing balance to return naturally through presence.

1. **Begin with 3 minutes of balanced heart breathing (Day 1 review).** Place one hand over your heart and the other on your belly. Inhale slowly through your nose for a count of four, feeling your breath expand through your chest and belly. Exhale gently through your mouth for a count of six, letting your body soften with each breath out. Continue this for three minutes, letting your breath become a steady rhythm that grounds you in calm awareness.

2. **Guide yourself through a gentle body scan meditation (5 minutes).** Close your eyes if you feel comfortable. Begin at the crown of your head and slowly bring your awareness down through your body, your forehead, jaw, neck, shoulders, chest, arms, hands, stomach, hips, legs, and feet. As you notice each area, simply observe without judgment. If you sense tension, breathe into that space with

---

kindness, but do not force anything to change. The invitation is to notice, to welcome your body exactly as it is in this moment.

3. **Simply *be*, noticing sensations without needing to change anything.** Allow yourself to rest in the gentle awareness of your body. Perhaps you notice warmth, coolness, tingling, heaviness, or lightness. Let these sensations come and go like waves. Trust that your body knows how to release and rebalance when you give it permission to be heard.

4. **Optional: Deepen the atmosphere.** If it feels supportive, consider playing soft instrumental music, gentle nature sounds, or anything that helps you settle more deeply into presence. Sound can act as a container, holding you in safety and guiding you into stillness.

Take a moment at the end to notice how you feel, physically, emotionally, and mentally. Perhaps you sense more spaciousness, a lighter breath, or a softer heart. Allow this balance to carry with you into the rest of your day, remembering that your body, your breath, and your awareness are always available to guide you back to peace.

Case Study Discussion: Theresa's Journey

Theresa always felt a sense of emptiness and disconnection in her life. She could not pinpoint the cause, but she knew something was missing. One day, during a session, I spoke with her about the concept of her inner child. To say that she was intrigued was an understatement. It was at that moment that Theresa embarked on a journey of deep discovery and healing. Through a mix of matrix, timeline therapies and reflection, Theresa began to explore her childhood memories and experiences. She quickly realised that as a child, she had often felt neglected and unheard. Her inner child had been longing for love, validation, and playfulness, but those needs had gone largely unmet.

Theresa chose to connect with her inner child and give her the love and attention she had been missing. She started engaging in activities that brought her joy, such as painting, playing music, and spending time in nature (especially the water). She also practiced self–compassion and spoke kindly to herself, just as she would to a young child. As Theresa nurtured her inner child, she experienced a profound shift in her life. Over time she felt a newfound sense of self–love, self–worth, and acceptance. She embraced her creativity and pursued her passions without fear of judgment. The emptiness she had once felt began to fill with compassion, joy and a deeper connection to herself, her heart, and her family.

By connecting with her inner child, Theresa learned to listen to her own needs and set healthy boundaries. She discovered that embracing her vulnerabilities and allowing herself to play and experience wonder brought a renewed sense of vitality and authenticity to her life. Theresa's journey with her inner child transformed her relationships as well. She communicated her needs more effectively and established deeper connections with her loved ones. Theresa's journey of discovering and nurturing her inner child changed her life in profound ways. Through self–compassion, playfulness, and embracing her vulnerability, she found healing, joy, and a deeper connection to herself and those around her.

Reflective Exercise – Theresa's Journey

Here are four profound and reflective questions inspired by Theresa's story to help you engage with your own inner child journey:

1. **When was the last time you felt truly seen, safe, and celebrated simply for being you?** What does your inner child most need to hear from you right now, and are you willing to say it?

2. **What joyful or creative activities once lit you up before the world told you to grow up or be serious?** How might returning to those playful expressions help reconnect you to your sense of wonder and wholeness?

3. **What parts of your childhood still feel unseen, unspoken, or unloved?** If you gently listened to those younger versions of yourself today, what would they want you to know?

4. **How would your relationships change if you brought your full, vulnerable, and authentic self forward?** What if embracing your inner child allowed you to deepen connection, not just with others, but with your own heart?

Affirmations For You – (Heart Whispers)

Affirmations have the power to quiet the noise of doubt, open the doorway to self-trust, and draw you back into the wisdom of your heart. When practised daily, they nurture an inner dialogue based in love and truth, helping you live each day more aligned with who you truly are. I invite you to repeat silently or write:

- *I embrace my inner child and honour its playful spirit.*

- *I listen to my inner child's needs with love and compassion.*

- *I allow my inner child to express itself freely and authentically.*

- *I nurture my inner child by engaging in activities that bring joy.*

- *I heal my inner child through self-reflection and inner work.*

- *I cherish my inner child and create a loving space for its growth.*

Create Your Inner Child Connection Plan

Your inner child is always present within you, waiting to be seen, heard, and cherished. By creating a simple yet intentional action plan, you give yourself the structure and permission to reconnect with this tender, playful, and creative part of your being. Think of this as a loving commitment to honouring your younger self in ways that bring joy, comfort, and safety.

Here are the elements of your plan:

1. **Joy Ritual – One playful thing I will do this week.** Choose an activity that sparks delight and brings out your natural playfulness. It could be blowing bubbles, dancing in your living room, colouring with crayons, playing a childhood game, or spending time in nature. This ritual is a reminder that joy is not frivolous, it is medicine for the soul.

2. **Compassion Cue – A phrase I will say when I notice my inner child needs comfort.** Create a sentence that feels gentle and reassuring, like a loving parent speaking to a child. For example:

   - *"It is okay, I have got you."*

   - *"You are safe with me."*

   - *"Your feelings matter."* This becomes your anchor whenever you notice fear, sadness, or insecurity arising.

3. **Creative Practice – A regular time for drawing, music, play, or exploration.** Your inner child thrives through creative expression. Set

---

aside a small, regular window each week to paint, write stories, sing, play an instrument, build something, or simply let your imagination roam. This is not about talent or outcome—it is about expression and freedom.

4. **Self-Support – A boundary or need I will honour moving forward.** Reflect on one boundary that will help protect your energy and nurture your inner child. This might be saying *"no"* to overcommitment, scheduling rest, asking for help, or limiting time with people who drain you. Boundaries are acts of self-love and safety for your inner child.

Integration Practice: I encourage you to write your Inner Child Connection Plan in your *Heart of Life Journal*. Keep it simple, clear, and heartfelt. Return to it often, updating or refining as your journey evolves.

This plan is not about perfection, it is about presence. Each small action you take is a step toward building trust with yourself, showing your inner child that they are valued, loved, and never alone.

Closing Reflection

There is a child within you who has never stopped waiting for your love. This child has always carried your laughter, your imagination, your vulnerability, and your light. In this part of your journey, you have been invited to turn inward and meet that younger self, the one who may have felt unheard, unseen, or unworthy. You are not asked to relive the pain, but to hold it gently, to acknowledge it with compassion, and to offer the love, safety, and presence that your younger self has always deserved.

Reconnecting with your inner child is not about fixing what was broken, but about remembering what was true. It is about listening not with judgment, but with tenderness. It is about embracing the forgotten parts of you, the playful, curious, and hopeful parts that were silenced but never lost. This is not a one-time moment of healing; it is the beginning of a sacred relationship. Each time you speak to yourself with kindness, you are soothing the child within. Each time you allow yourself to rest, to create, to laugh freely, or to cry without shame, you are saying: *I see you. I honour you. You are safe now.*

Slowly, you begin to notice a shift. The shame softens. The harsh inner critic grows quieter. The joy you seek, the creativity you crave, the connection you long for, these are not things you must chase in the outside world. They have been within you all along, patiently waiting for permission to be felt again. As you continue this journey, remember: you are not broken. You are not behind. You are not too much or not enough. You are exactly who your inner child needed all along. With every act of compassion, with every boundary that protects your heart, with every moment of play, you reclaim more of your truth, your courage, and your wholeness. The child in you still carries your light, and each time you honour them, you come closer to the home you have been searching for,not in a place, not in another person, but in yourself. *You are home. You are whole. You are loved.*

23 – DECLUTTER

Your Opening Reflection

Invitation to Clear Space for Your Heart - As you enter this chapter, I invite you to see decluttering not just as the act of tidying your outer world, but as an offering of space to your inner one. Every object, thought, or emotion you release makes room for something more aligned, more nourishing, more true. This is your chance to breathe lighter, to shed what no longer serves, and to welcome in clarity and peace. Trust that in letting go, you are not losing, but creating space for your heart to expand.

- "What stories or old narratives are you still holding onto that no longer define who you are?"

- "Which habits or routines feel draining rather than nourishing for you, and how might you begin to gently let them go?"

- "What expectations, your own or those placed on you by others, can you release to make more room for your authenticity?"

- "If you cleared away one source of inner noise today, what deeper truth or peace within you might emerge?"

Let these questions open the doorway into presence. Every answer you give, whether in words, sensations, or silence, is a bridge between where you are and where you are going.

Learning Objectives

The learning objectives are included here to give you a clear focus for this chapter, ensuring that each practice you explore moves you closer to

mastering the skills, insights, and heart-led awareness that will enrich your life well beyond the program. By the end of this chapter, you will:

- Understand the emotional and psychological impact of physical and mental clutter

- Recognise the connection between decluttering and emotional intelligence

- Learn practical strategies for decluttering both internal and external environments

- Cultivate habits of simplicity, mindfulness, and heartful decision-making

Core Emotional Domains

The core emotional intelligence domains covered here are essential because they form the foundation for lasting heart connection, guiding you to deepen self-awareness, regulate emotions, build resilience, and strengthen the mind-body bond throughout your Heart Unbound journey.

- **Self-Awareness:** As you explore what clutter, physical, emotional, or mental, has accumulated in your life, you begin to recognise how certain attachments reflect deeper patterns and unmet needs. You learn to pause and reflect on what truly aligns with your heart.

- **Emotional Regulation:** Letting go is not just a practical act, it is an emotional one. By releasing what no longer serves you, you create space within your nervous system for calm, clarity, and grounded presence.

- **Self-Management:** Through mindful decision-making and courageous honesty, you build the inner discipline to say no to what distracts and yes to what nourishes. This develops a life guided by intention, not obligation.

- **Mindfulness & Intentionality:** Every choice to declutter becomes a practice of presence. You learn to be deliberate with your time, energy, and attention, living less by default and more by design.

- **Personal Growth:** As you create space externally, you make room internally for insight, growth, and transformation. Letting go becomes an act of renewal, an invitation to welcome what is next with an open heart.

"Declutter – Creating Space For What Matters"

Decluttering is often misunderstood as simply tidying your home or organising your belongings, but at its essence, it is so much more. It is a sacred practice of release, a deeply emotional and spiritual act of choosing to let go of what no longer aligns with who you are or who you are becoming. Every drawer you empty, every shelf you sort, every object you release can become a moment of self-inquiry. You might ask yourself: *Why did I hold onto this? What part of me once needed this? Am I ready now to release it and invite something new?* These questions help transform decluttering into a ritual of awareness, one where you meet not only your belongings but also the emotions and stories they carry.

As you clear physical clutter, you may also find yourself face-to-face with emotional clutter, old narratives you have outgrown, unprocessed grief, patterns inherited from family, or silent obligations that weigh on your spirit. Letting go of these is not always easy; it can feel confronting, even tender. Yet with every release, you reclaim a piece of your energy. You return, gently but surely, to what truly matters. Decluttering is not about striving for minimalism or emptiness for its own sake. It is about creating space for meaning. When your surroundings are lighter, your inner world quiets. When your calendar is less burdened, your heart speaks more clearly. Life shifts from being lived out of habit to being lived out of intention.

With each act of clearing, you open space, space for creativity to flow, for stillness to restore you, for joy to rise naturally, and for deeper connections with yourself and others. Decluttering is not deprivation; it is an invitation. An invitation to breathe more deeply, to move with greater freedom, and to make choices that align with your values. In a culture that glorifies accumulation, achievement, and busyness, the practice of decluttering becomes a radical act of love. It is a declaration: *I choose to create space for what truly serves me,* and in that space, your heart finally has room, to whisper, to expand, and to lead you home to yourself.

The Emotional Toll Of Clutter And The Illusion Of Attachment

Clutter in your life is never just about what is visible on the outside. It is not only the piles on your desk, the wardrobe stuffed with clothes you no longer wear, or the garage full of boxes you keep promising to sort through one day. Clutter is often a reflection of something much deeper, the emotional weight you have been carrying, sometimes for years, without realising it. Every object, every task you avoid, every commitment you can't quite release, holds a story. It may not just be about function or usefulness, but about the emotions, fears, and identities you have attached to them. When you look at the things you hold onto, ask yourself: *What part of me is this connected to? Why am I still carrying it?*

That overstuffed drawer may not only contain old papers; it may contain the fear of failure, the belief that you must keep every detail *"just in case,"* or the perfectionism that says you can't let anything slip. The clothes hanging unworn in your closet might not just be fabric, but reminders of who you once were, or who you thought you had to be in order to be loved or respected. Even your packed schedule might not only represent busyness, but a shield, a way of avoiding silence, because stillness might feel too uncomfortable, too confronting, too real. You may often tell yourself things like: *"I might need this someday." "This reminds me of a better time." "If I let this go, it is like I am forgetting,"* but if you pause long enough to listen, you will notice that so often, these attachments are built not from love, but from fear. Fear of losing your identity. Fear of stepping into change. Fear of feeling emotions you have worked hard to keep buried.

The truth is: holding on does not protect you. In fact, it often traps you. It weighs you down, clouds your clarity, drains your energy, and makes it harder for you to hear the quiet, steady wisdom of your own heart, and so here is the deeper truth you need to remember:

- You are not what you own.

- You are not the memories that live in boxes.

- You are not defined by what you keep or release.

Letting go does not mean forgetting. It means finally choosing freedom. It means creating sacred space, in your environment, in your emotions, in your body, and in your spirit, and in that space, you will find something precious: clarity, peace, and the possibility of joy. Attachment is not the same as connection. When you release what no longer serves you, you reclaim the power to choose what truly does. You open the door for the new, the meaningful, the life-giving. Decluttering is not about living with less for the sake of less. It is about living with what matters most. You are allowed to live with less, but feel more. You are allowed to let go, and become more whole. You are allowed to release the old stories, and come home to yourself.

Reflection Prompts

As you sit with these truths, I invite you to take a few minutes to reflect and journal on the following:

1. What is one physical item in your space that feels heavy to hold onto? What does it represent emotionally?

2. Where in your life are you overcommitted, saying *"yes"* when your heart longs for a pause?

3. Which old identity, belief, or story are you still carrying that no longer reflects who you are becoming?

4. How would it feel to create space, in your environment or in your heart, for something new, something aligned, something true?

Historical And Cultural Perspectives: Feng Shui, Minimalism, Mindfulness

Decluttering has always carried a deeper meaning than simply cleaning a space or organising belongings. Across cultures and time, it has been seen as a spiritual act, a way to restore harmony, reconnect with truth, and align the inner and outer worlds.

<u>Feng Shui – Flow of Life Energy</u>

Feng Shui, born from ancient China, is a philosophy that teaches you to live in harmony with the natural currents of life energy, known as **qi**. It views your home not as a collection of walls and objects, but as a living organism, a mirror of your inner self. **Clutter in Feng Shui is not neutral.** It is stagnation, a sign that energy cannot move. A blocked pathway may reflect blocked opportunities. A room filled with unused items may echo unprocessed emotions or unresolved memories.

By clearing clutter and arranging space with care, you invite the **five elements**, wood, fire, earth, metal, and water, to flow in balance, creating a sense of vitality and peace. For example, light and airflow are central in Feng Shui. A dark, crowded room can dampen your energy, while an open, light-filled space supports renewal, clarity, and emotional ease. To engage with Feng Shui principles is to treat your home as a **sacred partner** in your wellbeing. Every choice, where you place a chair, whether you keep an item, how you allow light to flow, becomes an act of aligning your outer environment with the life you long to live.

Minimalism – Returning to Essence

Minimalism, deeply influenced by Japanese Zen Buddhism, is more than a design trend. At its heart, it is a **spiritual discipline** of choosing essence over excess. In Zen temples, simplicity was intentional: uncluttered spaces allowed the mind to settle into stillness and the heart to open to the sacred. Minimalism asks you to strip away what is not essential so you can see clearly what truly matters. It is not about deprivation or starkness, but about **curating a life that reflects truth, meaning, and presence.**

When you let go of unnecessary possessions, obligations, or noise, you are not reducing your life, you are **revealing it.** The treasures that remain, whether an object, a memory, or a relationship, shine more brightly when they are no longer buried in clutter. Minimalism offers a counter-narrative to the world's endless push for consumption. It whispers: *Less is not lack. Less is space for depth, for beauty, for authenticity.*

Mindfulness – Sacred Presence in Action

Mindfulness, based in ancient Buddhist practice and embraced around the world today, is the art of being fully present. When applied to decluttering, it shifts the act from task to **ritual.** With mindfulness, every object becomes a question: *Does this still belong in my life? Does it carry love, or does it carry weight?* As you pick up an item, you might notice the memories it stirs, the emotions it carries, the fears it triggers. Instead of rushing, you pause. You breathe. You decide not from habit or guilt, but from clarity and compassion.

Even the physical act of decluttering becomes a practice in awareness. You notice the sound of items being placed away, the rhythm of your breath, the relief in your body as space opens. Mindfulness turns decluttering into a **mirror of the heart**. It helps you release not out of rejection, but out of reverence, making space for what is true, what is needed, what is life-giving.

The Mirror Between Inner and Outer Worlds

These cultural traditions, Feng Shui, Minimalism, Mindfulness, each carry the same timeless truth: **your outer environment reflects your inner state.** When your home is cluttered, your thoughts often feel scattered. When your calendar is overfull, your emotions often feel stretched thin. When your space is intentional, peaceful, and open, your heart rests more easily. Decluttering, then, is not about perfection or aesthetics. It is about **alignment**. It is about saying:

- *I am ready to release what no longer serves me.*

- *I am ready to live not in survival, but in flow.*

- *I am ready to create space for my heart to speak, and for my life to expand.*

To declutter is to remember that you are not here to be buried by things, but to be uplifted by life. It is a radical act of freedom, and a return to yourself.

Internal Clutter: Limiting Beliefs, Overthinking, And Emotional Residue

Not all clutter lives on shelves or in inboxes. Some of the most suffocating clutter is the kind you carry silently inside, unseen by others, but deeply felt by you. This is **internal clutter**: the tangle of old beliefs, anxious thoughts, and unresolved emotions that weigh down your mind, your spirit, and your sense of possibility. You may find yourself replaying the same thoughts, looping through *what ifs*, *should haves*, and *not enoughs*. This is the clutter of **overthinking,** a mental traffic jam that crowds out clarity and clouds your connection to the present moment.

It is the voice that second-guesses your decisions, that fears judgment, that catastrophises the future. It is exhausting, and it is easy to mistake for truth. Then there are the **limiting beliefs** you have unknowingly absorbed over time: *I have to be perfect to be loved. Success means constant busyness. I am too old to change.* These beliefs form the emotional wallpaper of your inner world, so familiar you might not even realise they are there. Yet they shape your choices, dim your courage, and keep you tethered to stories that no longer serve your growth.

Also, beneath it all may live **emotional residue,** the unprocessed grief, anger, shame, or sadness you have tucked away in quiet corners of your heart. You may think you have moved on, but those emotions remain stored in your body, waiting for the safety and space to be felt and released. This internal clutter does not just live in your mind, it echoes in your relationships, your boundaries, your energy. It shows up as chronic fatigue, irritability, disconnection, or self-doubt. It is heavy, even if invisible.

Decluttering internally begins with **gentle awareness**. Noticing the narratives that are running your life. Naming the feelings you have been avoiding, and most of all, creating space, through breath, stillness, writing, or silence, to ask yourself: *What am I still carrying that no longer belongs to me?* You do not have to untangle it all at once. *Start by listening. Start by softening. Start by* *letting go, one belief, one thought, one feeling at a time.* As you clear this inner space, you create room for something far more powerful: *Truth. Peace, and the voice of your heart, unburdened and finally heard.*

Decluttering As An Act Of Self-Respect And Emotional Clarity

Decluttering is not just a practical task, it is a powerful declaration. It says, *I matter. My space matters. My peace matters.* When you choose to clear out what no longer serves you, physically, mentally, emotionally, you are not simply getting rid of things. You are making a bold, heart-led statement: **I respect myself enough to live with intention.** Self-respect is not always loud. Sometimes it is found in the quiet decision to release the clothes you never wear, the commitments that deplete you, or the story you have been telling yourself for years.

It is in the way you clean your space not just for guests, but for you. It is in choosing quality over quantity, clarity over chaos, presence over performance. When your environment is cluttered, your nervous system remains in a low-grade state of vigilance. You feel overstimulated, scattered, or emotionally *"full"* without knowing why, but when you clear your space, shelf by shelf, thought by thought, you begin to feel different inside. Lighter. Calmer. More whole. Decluttering is also a practice in **emotional clarity**. As you sift through the items, roles, and habits in your life, you begin to ask deeper questions:

1. *Does this reflect who I am now?*

2. *Does this support the life I want to live?*

3. *What am I holding onto out of fear, guilt, or habit?*

It takes courage to let go, because sometimes, the clutter is tied to memories, identities, or people, but what you begin to discover is this: letting go does not erase the past. It honours it, while giving you the space to step more fully into the present. The clearer your space, the more clearly you hear yourself. The less weighed down you feel, the more grounded you become, and in this clarity, something powerful happens:

- *You remember who you are without all the noise.*

- *You reconnect with what truly matters.*

- *You create room not just in your home, but in your heart.*

Decluttering becomes less about cleaning, and more about coming home to yourself.

How Space Impacts Energy, Decision-Making, And Emotional Equilibrium

The spaces you inhabit, your home, your workplace, even your car, hold more than furniture and belongings. They hold **energy**. They carry your emotions, your memories, your habits, and your intentions, and whether you realise it or not, the state of your environment directly affects your inner state, your clarity, your choices, and your ability to stay emotionally balanced. When your space is chaotic or cluttered, it sends a subtle but constant message to your nervous system: *You are not in control. There is too much. You are behind.*

This activates stress hormones, drains your mental energy, and makes even small decisions feel harder. Just like a cluttered desk can make it difficult to find a pen, a cluttered mind makes it difficult to access calm, insight, and direction. In contrast, when your space is clean, intentional, and aligned with who you are, it becomes a **container for peace and possibility**. You breathe more deeply. You think more clearly. You feel more empowered. Your surroundings begin to support your nervous system, not challenge it. You are no longer fighting your environment, you are being held by it.

This shift impacts your **decision-making** in profound ways. When your external world is overstimulating or burdened with unprocessed emotional cues (like unfinished projects, reminders of past relationships, or *"someday"* piles), your mind becomes fatigued. You are more likely to react from stress, doubt, or fear, but when you create space, literally and emotionally, you give your brain room to pause, evaluate, and respond with wisdom and intention. You also restore **emotional equilibrium**. With less external noise, your inner voice becomes clearer. You are more attuned to what you need, what you feel, and what aligns with your heart. Decision-making stops being about urgency and starts being about truth.

Creating space is not just about aesthetics. It is about **energy hygiene**. It is about protecting the sanctuary of your own attention and creating an environment where your best self can emerge, steady, clear, and grounded. When your space supports you, your energy stabilises. When your energy is stable, your emotions flow, and when your emotions are flowing, your life begins to move again, in the direction of your deepest values.

Decluttering with Intention

Decluttering is not only about clearing space in your outer world, it is also about clearing energy in your inner world. Every item you choose to keep or release carries a story, an emotion, or a belief. When you engage with decluttering intentionally, you are not just tidying up, you are choosing freedom, creating space for peace, and aligning your environment with your heart.

Step 1: Choose Your Space (Outer or Inner)

Over the next 24 hours, select one small area of your life to lovingly declutter. This might be:

- A **physical space**: a drawer, your desk, a shelf, your bag, your phone, or your closet.

- A **mental space**: an outdated belief, a repeating thought, or a self-critical voice.

- An **emotional space**: resentment, guilt, or a story you have been holding onto.

Start small. One space is enough. The power of this practice comes from focus and intention, not size.

Step 2: Prepare Yourself

Before you begin, pause for a few moments of presence:

- Take 3 slow, balanced breaths.

- Place your hand on your heart, reminding yourself: *I am safe to release. I am safe to let go.*

- If you can, play soft background music or light a candle, marking this as a ritual, not a chore.

Step 3: Ask the Heart Question

As you hold or consider each item, memory, or thought, quietly ask yourself: **"What am I ready to let go of in this space, and in myself?"**

- If it feels heavy, outdated, or no longer aligned, honour it, thank it for the role it once played, and gently release it.

- If it feels alive, nourishing, or truly useful, allow it to stay with love and intention.

Remember: you are not discarding things out of anger or guilt, but releasing them with reverence, creating space for what is real and true.

Step 4: Visualise the Freedom

Once you finish, pause again. Close your eyes. Breathe. Visualise the **spaciousness** that has opened, not just on the shelf, desk, or phone, but within you. Ask yourself:

- *How does my body feel now that I have released this?*

- *What new energy or possibility might flow into this open space?*

- *What word or image symbolises the freedom I feel?*

Step 5: Anchor the Shift

To integrate the practice, write a short reflection in your journal. You might use one of these prompts:

- *Today I created space for…*

- *Letting go of ___ helped me realise…*

- *The freedom I feel now reminds me that I am…*

This anchoring step helps your inner self register the act not just as a task, but as a transformation.

Closing Reminder

Decluttering with intention is not about deprivation. It is about **liberation**. Every time you let go of something that no longer serves you, you reclaim energy, presence, and joy. When you clear your space with care, you make room for peace. When you clear your heart with compassion, you make room for love. *May this practice remind you that you are worthy of a life uncluttered, spacious, and true.*

Case Study Discussion: Yasmine's Journey

Yasmine had felt a heaviness in her life for as long as she could remember. By her own admission she would describe her physical spaces as being 'untidy' and filled with 'stuff'. Her physical spaces were not the only spaces in a bit of chaos, her heart was filled with worries and anxieties. She wanted a sense of lightness and joy, but it seemed out of reach. We discussed her lived life's appearance as being reflective of what was happening within her. One day, Yasmine made the choice to declutter her life, both inside and out. She started with her physical space, her home, her car, and her office, sorting through her belongings and letting go of items that no longer brought her joy or served a purpose.

As Yasmine cleared out the excess, she felt a weight being lifted off her shoulders. Yasmine knew that decluttering was not just about physical possessions. She also knew she needed to declutter her heart, her mind, and her emotions. She began to practice balanced heart breathing, mindfulness, and meditation, allowing herself to let go of negative thoughts and worries. She focused on her present moment, embracing a sense of peace and gratitude. Over time (many months) Yasmine found her smile again. She felt herself smiling and the more she let go of physical and mental clutter, the more space she created for joy, positivity, and compassion to enter her life.

Yasmine discovered that getting rid of things that did not serve her was not just about creating an organised space to live in, it was about creating space for happiness and joy to exist. Yasmine's decision to declutter her life transformed her in ways she never imagined. She found her smile again, and it radiated from within. She told me that she realised that by letting go of what no longer served her, she had created space for what truly mattered to her, and in that space, she found her authentic self, her passions, and a deep sense of contentment.

Reflective Exercise: Yasmine's Journey

Here are four profound and reflective questions inspired by Yasmine's story to help you engage with your own decluttering journey:

1. **What physical clutter in your environment might be mirroring an inner weight you have been carrying, and what would it feel like to gently begin letting go?** Reflect on a space in your life, your room, car, desk, that feels heavy or chaotic. What emotions rise when you enter that space? What would releasing just one item from that space symbolize for your emotional wellbeing?

2. **Are there thoughts, worries, or beliefs that you continue to hold onto out of habit, fear, or familiarity, even though they no longer support your growth?** Close your eyes and ask your heart, *What am I*

---

ready to release? Then breathe gently into that space. Your freedom begins the moment you honour the truth of that answer.

3. **What does joy need space for in your life, and what might it be competing with right now?** Consider the ways in which clutter, both internal and external, may be blocking your access to joy, ease, or creativity. What could you release this week, physically or emotionally, to make room for something more life-giving?

4. **If you saw your life as a sacred space, what would you choose to keep, and what would you lovingly release?** Imagine walking through the rooms of your life, not just your home, but your heart. What stays because it aligns with who you truly are? What do you bless and let go of, to honour the person you are becoming?

Affirmations For You – (Heart Whispers)

Affirmations have the power to quiet the noise of doubt, open the doorway to self-trust, and draw you back into the wisdom of your heart. When practised daily, they nurture an inner dialogue based in love and truth, helping you live each day more aligned with who you truly are. I invite you to repeat silently or write:

- *I release what no longer serves me, creating space for growth.*

- *I let go of clutter, inviting clarity and peace into my life.*

- *I connect with my heart as I declutter my physical space.*

- *I embrace simplicity, finding joy in the essentials of life.*

- *I honour my heart's desires by letting go of excess.*

- *I create a sanctuary within, reflecting the beauty of my heart.*

Create Your Personal Decluttering Map

Decluttering is not only about clearing your outer environment, it is about creating space for your heart to breathe more freely. To guide this process, I invite you to create a simple yet powerful **Decluttering Map**, a tool that helps you see where release is needed and how you can take compassionate, intentional action.

Step 1: Physical Release

Reflection Prompt: *What no longer supports or reflects who I am today?* Look around your environment. Notice what feels heavy, outdated, or disconnected from who you are becoming. This may be clothing that no longer feels like you, objects tied to old identities, or items you have been keeping out of guilt or obligation.

Action Step: Choose one physical object (or small group of objects) to release with gratitude. As you let it go, affirm: *I am making space for who I am now and who I am becoming.*

Step 2: Mental Release

Reflection Prompt: *What thoughts and habits clutter my peace?* Turn inward. Notice the stories, habits, or loops of self-talk that leave you feeling drained rather than uplifted. This could be overthinking, perfectionism, procrastination, or comparing yourself to others.

Action Step: Write down one mental habit you are ready to soften. Replace it with a grounding practice, such as pausing to breathe, journaling, or repeating a calming affirmation. Each time the thought arises, gently remind yourself: *This no longer has power over me. I choose peace.*

Step 3: Emotional Release

Reflection Prompt: *What feelings or patterns am I ready to thank and release?* Sometimes we hold onto emotions or protective patterns long after they have served their purpose. You might notice resentment, guilt, fear of rejection, or the need to please others. These patterns once kept you safe, but now they may keep you small.

Action Step: Identify one emotional pattern you are ready to let go of. Write it down and add a phrase of gratitude, such as: *Thank you for protecting me when I needed it. I release you now with love.* Then breathe deeply and imagine sending it into the light.

Step 4: Integration – Your Intention Map

Now bring your reflections together into a **three-part map**:

- **Physical:** I release ____ → Action: ____

- **Mental:** I release ____ → Action: ____

- **Emotional:** I release ____ → Action: ____

Keep this map visible in your journal, on your desk, or somewhere you will see it daily. Each step is not just about letting go, it is about reclaiming your energy, your presence, and your truth.

Closing Reflection

As you create your Decluttering Map, remember: every release is a gift to your future self. You are not just removing clutter, you are creating spaciousness, clarity, and peace. *When you release what no longer reflects your heart, you return home to who you truly are.*

Closing Reflection

Letting go is never just about things. It is about honouring your **inner space as sacred**, recognising that the energy you carry, both seen and unseen, shapes the way you live, love, and connect. By choosing to declutter, you have done something incredibly brave: you have said *yes* to yourself. You have chosen to make space.

Space to breathe. Space to feel. Space to rest. Space to hear your heart more clearly. Each drawer emptied, each thought questioned, each memory released, each belief surrendered, every act of release has been more than tidying. It has been an act of courage, self-respect, and quiet devotion to the person you are becoming. With every step, you have begun to **unburden your physical world and lighten your emotional landscape,** and in each choice to release what no longer serves, you are making a deeper invitation, an opening for clarity, intention, freedom, and truth to move in.

This practice has never been about perfection. It is about **alignment.** It is about living in a way that reflects who you truly are, rather than who you thought you had to be, or who others told you to become. It is about learning that your worth is not measured by how much you accumulate, but by how deeply you live,and now, in the space you have created, something profound happens: **Joy** can find you more easily. **Peace** can move in and stay a little longer. **Your heart** feels just a little more at home within you.

As you carry this practice forward, let this part of the journey whisper to you each time you are tempted to hold on too tightly: *You are not defined by what you cling to. You are revealed by what you are willing to release.* May you remember that every release is not a loss but a return, a return to yourself, a return to freedom, a return to love.

24 – LAUGHTER

Your Opening Reflection

Invitation to Welcome Joy - As you enter this chapter, I invite you to remember that laughter is not trivial, it is medicine for the soul. Each smile, each burst of joy, carries the power to soften your heart, to dissolve heaviness, and to reconnect you with the lightness of being alive. Allow yourself to lean into the moments that spark laughter, no matter how small. Let them remind you that healing is not only found in stillness and silence, but also in joy, play, and shared connection. Trust that every laugh is a whisper of your heart saying, *"You are alive. You are free."*

- "Who in your life makes you laugh the most, and what does that connection bring to your heart?"

- "How does laughter shift your perspective when you are feeling stressed or overwhelmed?"

- "What are the small, everyday things that spark a smile or a laugh for you?"

- "When you laugh freely, what does it reveal about the parts of you that feel most alive and unguarded?"

- "How might you invite more moments of lightness and laughter into your daily life?"

Let these questions open the doorway into presence. Every answer you give, whether in words, sensations, or silence, is a bridge between where you are and where you are going.

Learning Objectives

The learning objectives are included here to give you a clear focus for this chapter, ensuring that each practice you explore moves you closer to mastering the skills, insights, and heart-led awareness that will enrich your life well beyond the program. By the end of this chapter, you will:

- Understand the physiological and emotional benefits of laughter

- Explore how laughter develops resilience, connection, and healing

- Reconnect with their own sense of humour and joy

- Practise using laughter as a heart-opening and stress-relieving tool

Core Emotional Domains

The core emotional intelligence domains covered here are essential because they form the foundation for lasting heart connection, guiding you to deepen self-awareness, regulate emotions, build resilience, and strengthen the mind-body bond throughout your Heart Unbound journey.

- **Self-Awareness:** Laughter opens a mirror into your emotional landscape. You begin to notice what brings you joy, where you hold tension, and how humour can shift your state in a heartbeat. You learn to honour joy as a vital part of who you are.

- **Emotional Regulation:** In laughter, stress softens. You release pressure without force, allowing your body to reset. Through humour and play, you discover how to move through difficult emotions with grace and ease.

- **Empathy & Relationship Management:** Shared laughter is a bond. It creates warmth, safety, and connection. You learn how joy strengthens relationships and how humour, when used mindfully, can heal divides and deepen understanding.

- **Optimism & Positive Outlook:** Laughter invites you to see through a lighter lens. Even in hardship, it reminds you there is hope, perspective, and the possibility of lightness. It reconnects you with the goodness in life.

- **Resilience and Stress Management:** Laughter becomes a healing tool. It restores your nervous system, replenishes your energy, and reminds you of your inner strength. In laughter, you bounce back, not because life is easy, but because your spirit is flexible and alive.

"Laughter – The Transformative Power Of Joy"

Laughter is one of the most accessible and profoundly transformative tools available to you. It does not require a prescription, a degree, or a perfect moment. It only requires your willingness to feel, to release, to remember joy, and when you do, laughter becomes more than amusement. It becomes **medicine**. Across ancient cultures, laughter was never taken lightly. It was sacred. In traditional African and Indigenous communities, laughter was seen as a social glue and a spiritual cleansing.

In Eastern traditions, laughing was practiced as a daily health ritual, believed to harmonise the organs and bring balance to the body. Even in sacred texts and folklore, joy and laughter were celebrated as signs of divine connection and inner freedom. Today, **modern neuroscience validates what the ancients knew,** that laughter changes your brain and body chemistry. It triggers the release of endorphins, reduces cortisol (your stress hormone), improves immune function, and increases blood flow to your heart and brain. It regulates your nervous system and brings you back into a space of balance, calm, and clarity.

Laughter also does more than heal your body, it **opens your heart**. It dissolves walls. It softens tension. It invites you to be seen, to be silly, to be real. In laughter, there is no pretense. There is only presence. It is nearly impossible to laugh genuinely and remain closed. Laughter is the sound of your spirit stretching out and saying, *"I am here. I am alive."* In your relationships, laughter becomes a bridge, restoring connection, easing conflict, and nurturing trust. In your inner world, it reminds you that you are not your burdens. You are more than your worries. You are someone who can feel joy, even amidst uncertainty.

To laugh is to remember the part of you that is untamed, unburdened, and deeply alive. So in this part of your journey, you are invited to make space for laughter, not just as a reaction to something funny, but as a **deliberate heart practice**. Let it be your reset button. Let it be your release. Let it be your return to self, because sometimes, healing does not look like silence or stillness. Sometimes, it sounds like the echo of your own joy rising again.

The Science Of Laughter: Endorphins, Immune Function, Relaxation Response

Laughter is not just a spontaneous reaction, it is a **physiological blessing**. Behind every chuckle, giggle, and belly laugh is a powerful biological cascade that helps restore balance, calm your nervous system, and strengthen your body's ability to heal.

<u>Endorphins – Your Inner Pharmacy</u>

When you laugh, your brain releases endorphins, often called *"feel-good"* chemicals. These natural opioids elevate your mood, reduce pain, and generate an immediate sense of lightness. Unlike external substances, this pharmacy is built within you, it is always accessible, waiting to be activated by joy, humour, or connection. With every genuine laugh, you are giving yourself an instant emotional boost, a natural antidote to heaviness.

Endorphins are also linked to building stronger bonds with others. When you laugh with someone, you are not just sharing a moment, you are strengthening trust and connection at a neurochemical level. This is why laughter feels so intimate: it is the brain's way of saying, *"You are safe here. You belong."* Every shared laugh becomes a thread that weaves you closer into the fabric of community.

<u>The Relaxation Response – A Nervous System Reset</u>

Laughter is one of the quickest ways to activate your parasympathetic nervous system, also known as your *"rest and restore"* mode. When activated, your breathing slows, your muscles release tension, and your heart rate steadies. It is as if your entire body exhales after being held in stress or vigilance. In these moments, your body begins to repair, your mind becomes clearer, and your emotional world softens.

This reset is particularly powerful because it interrupts cycles of chronic stress. Instead of staying locked in *"fight-or-flight,"* laughter creates space for your body to remember what calm feels like. Over time, regular moments of laughter build resilience into your nervous system, making it easier to return to balance even after life's challenges. It is not just a temporary break, it is a retraining of your inner rhythm toward peace.

<u>Strengthening Your Immune System – Joy as Protection</u>

Scientific studies reveal that laughter boosts immune function by increasing T-cells, antibodies, and infection-fighting proteins. Quite literally, joy strengthens your defences against illness. Those who laugh often recover faster, experience fewer colds, and demonstrate greater resilience under stress. Laughter does not just make you feel good, it equips your body to stay strong.

Imagine laughter as your body's way of shining light into the darker corners of your system, activating vitality where stress once lingered. Every time you laugh, your immune system receives a reminder that life is safe, worth defending, and worth enjoying. This is why joy is not frivolous, it is a survival tool. To laugh often is to nourish your body's natural ability to heal and protect you.

<u>Reducing Cortisol – Releasing Stress Hormones</u>

Chronic stress floods your system with cortisol, which over time wears down your body, clouds your mind, and drains your spirit. Laughter reduces cortisol levels, restoring balance. Each giggle, chuckle, or belly laugh signals your body to release what no longer serves you. With every laugh, you are rewiring your system towards safety, presence, and vitality.

This lowering of cortisol also has long-term benefits for your heart health, memory, and even weight regulation. Stress holds your system hostage; laughter sets it free. Think of laughter as nature's reset button: every time you let yourself laugh, you remind your body that it does not need to stay in survival mode. Over time, this rewiring teaches your whole being to choose lightness over heaviness, hope over despair.

<u>The Harmony of Body, Mind, and Heart</u>

In one moment of genuine laughter, all parts of you align. Your body relaxes, your emotions expand, and your mind clears. You remember that life does not always have to be heavy, that joy is not frivolous but essential to your survival and your thriving.

This harmony also reconnects you with your heart's wisdom. In laughter, you are fully present, not analysing the past or worrying about the future. You are simply here, alive, and whole. This presence is the seed of emotional intelligence, compassion, and creativity. In those moments of laughter, you are most yourself, unguarded, authentic, and free.

Laughter As A Relational Bridge And Empathy Builder

Laughter is one of the most beautiful ways we reach across the space between yourself and others. It is a **relational bridge,** an unspoken agreement that says, *"I feel this too."* In moments where words might falter or differences feel wide, laughter brings people together in a shared human experience. It bypasses logic and defence. It opens your heart. When you laugh with someone, especially from a place of sincerity, a powerful neurochemical shift occurs. **Oxytocin**, the bonding hormone, is released, increasing feelings of trust, safety, and connection.

This is the same hormone that strengthens relationships between parents and children, lovers, and close friends. Laughter becomes a way to **amplify connection** and remind you of your shared humanity. It also cultivates **empathy**. When you share humour, especially the kind that is inclusive and compassionate, you gain insight into each other's hearts. You feel what the other feels. You attune to their rhythm. In this way, laughter creates emotional intimacy without needing deep analysis or serious discussion. It becomes a balm that heals misunderstandings, reduces tension, and creates space for vulnerability to safely emerge.

In workplaces, families, friendships, and even between strangers, shared laughter signals *"we are on the same side."* It levels hierarchy. It interrupts power dynamics. It creates light in rooms that may have felt heavy. Even during conflict, a well-timed, heart-led moment of humour can shift the atmosphere and soften the path back to understanding. Importantly, laughter reminds you that you are not just your roles or wounds or identities, you are a being capable of joy, play, and warmth. In relationships that have become strained or serious, the act of laughing together can feel like a **return,** a reawakening of the connection that has always been there, waiting to be felt again. So let yourself laugh not just *at* life, but *with* life. Let laughter be your offering, your bridge, your medicine, because sometimes the kindest thing you can do for another soul is not to solve their problem, but to remind them, through your joy, that light still exists.

Cultural And Historical Significance Of Humour And Laughter

Laughter has echoed through human history not only as entertainment, but as **a cultural ritual, a coping mechanism, and a sacred rite**. From ancient temples to village gatherings, from court jesters to sacred clowns, humour has always played a vital role in the human experience, offering relief, resilience, and remembrance of our shared fragility and joy.

Ancient Egypt – Laughter as Protection and Blessing

In Ancient Egypt, laughter was never seen as trivial or accidental. It carried with it a sacred energy, a force that bridged the human and the divine. Among the many deities honoured, **Bes**, the dwarf god of joy, music, fertility, and protection, stood as a guardian of households, mothers, and children. He was often depicted with a playful expression, a protruding tongue, and a lively presence, reminders that humour and delight themselves were forms of divine protection.

Rituals dedicated to Bes frequently included music, dancing, and laughter, for Egyptians believed that joy itself could repel negative forces. Just as incense purified the air, laughter purified the spirit and the home. It was understood as a vibrational shield, powerful enough to drive away evil spirits, misfortune, or disease. Families would carve images of Bes onto household items and amulets, not only to ward off danger but to invite laughter, music, and fertility into daily life.

Laughter was also deeply linked to fertility and renewal. In ceremonies surrounding childbirth, joy and humour were invoked to ease labour pains, calm anxiety, and bless the arrival of new life. To laugh in such sacred moments was to open the body and spirit to divine flow, allowing blessings to move freely. It was believed that the gods smiled upon those who knew how to rejoice, for joy was a sign of trust in the sacred order of life.

Even in funerary traditions, humour sometimes found its place. Ancient texts suggest that laughter was used to mock death, a symbolic reminder that the soul transcends fear and lives beyond the grave. To laugh in the presence of mortality was to declare alignment with eternity, a refusal to let sorrow eclipse the greater cycle of renewal.

In this way, the Egyptians understood laughter as a living medicine: it restored balance, cleansed emotional heaviness, and affirmed life's sanctity. Centuries before science confirmed its healing effects on the body, they knew laughter to be a sacred act, an offering that could lighten not only the heart of a household but the very favour of the gods.

Classical Greece – Laughter as Philosophy and Catharsis

In Classical Greece, laughter was elevated beyond entertainment; it was considered a powerful social and philosophical force. In the great amphitheatres, comedic plays were staged alongside tragedies, not merely as relief but as essential balance. Playwrights like **Aristophanes** used satire, parody, and absurdity to expose corruption, challenge authority, and critique the absurdities of everyday life. Audiences would gather by the thousands, and through laughter, they experienced what the Greeks called **catharsis**, a cleansing of emotions that left them lighter, clearer, and more whole.

Philosophers, too, wrestled with the meaning of laughter. **Aristotle** wrote of its role in human flourishing, noting that humour was part of the social glue that bound communities. **Plato**, though cautious of its misuse, acknowledged its sharp ability to reveal truth. To laugh at the folly of the powerful was not disrespect, it was democracy in action. Humour gave the people a voice, a safe way to question authority and confront the contradictions of society. For the Greeks, then, laughter was never frivolous. It was medicine for the collective, a reminder that joy and critique could coexist. Just as tragedy connected people through grief and empathy, comedy united them in resilience and renewal. To laugh together was to affirm shared humanity, to release tension, and to make space for wisdom to rise.

Indigenous Traditions – Laughter as Sacred Medicine

Across Indigenous cultures worldwide, laughter has long been woven into ceremony, teaching, and healing. Among the **Lakota and other Native American nations**, the figure of the **Heyoka, or sacred clown**, plays a central role. The Heyoka teaches through paradox, humour, and reversal, doing the opposite of what is expected, mocking rigidity, and using play to expose hidden truths. Through laughter, the Heyoka breaks down ego, pride, and fear, restoring flow to both the individual and the community.

Laughter in these contexts is not entertainment; it is ceremony. It creates a sacred disruption that clears stagnation and allows new life energy to enter. When a community gathers in grief, humour often arises, not to dismiss the pain but to keep the heart supple, to remind the people that sorrow and joy can coexist, that the circle of life holds both. In healing rituals, jokes and playful antics often surface spontaneously, as if laughter itself is a spirit moving through the space, loosening what has been frozen and bringing warmth where there has been coldness.

Indigenous elders often remind us that laughter is a medicine gifted by Spirit. It balances solemnity with lightness, humility with joy. It teaches that to heal is not to erase suffering but to integrate it with play, connection, and renewal. In this way, laughter becomes a sacred teacher, a reminder not to take ourselves too seriously, and an affirmation that even in struggle, the human spirit is free.

Eastern Traditions – Laughter as Enlightenment

In the East, particularly in **Taoist and Zen Buddhist traditions**, laughter is often regarded as a sign of awakening. Far from being irreverent, humour reveals wisdom through simplicity, humility, and lightness of being. **Taoism** teaches that life flows best when you stop forcing and start aligning with the rhythm of the universe. To laugh is to release control, to accept paradox, and to rest in harmony with the Tao.

In Zen Buddhism, humour is woven directly into spiritual teaching. Zen masters are famous for their paradoxical koans, statements or questions designed to break the logical mind. Often, these interactions dissolve not in solemnity but in sudden bursts of laughter. The laugh is not superficial, it is enlightenment itself, a moment of recognition that truth cannot always be grasped with reason. It is glimpsed in absurdity, felt in joy, and known in the body's release.

Eastern traditions remind us that laughter is a profound teacher. It cuts through ego, loosens rigidity, and brings us back to presence. When you laugh, you taste the freedom of non-attachment, the joy of simply being. In this way, humour is not a distraction from the spiritual path, it is part of the path itself, an embodied reminder that awakening is not heavy or solemn but often light, playful, and liberating.

Hardship and Resistance – Laughter as Survival

Throughout history, in times of oppression, war, and suffering, laughter has emerged as one of the most radical forms of resistance. In the trenches of **World War I**, soldiers cracked jokes and sang songs amidst horror, using humour to hold onto their humanity. In the darkness of concentration camps, survivors recall moments of absurd humour that offered brief but life-saving relief, a reminder that the oppressor could never fully control the spirit. For those enduring hardship, laughter has often been the last refuge of freedom. It allows people to mock fear, ridicule injustice, and affirm life when death or despair looms near. In communities under colonisation or dictatorship, humour became a subversive language, a way of speaking truth without being silenced, of building solidarity in the face of oppression.

This resilience continues today. In hospitals, laughter therapy is used to help patients facing chronic illness. In trauma recovery, shared humour often signals that a person is regaining strength. Across every generation, people have proven that laughter does not erase suffering but allows them to endure it with dignity, courage, and connection. To laugh in the midst of pain is not denial, it is defiance. It says: *You cannot take my soul. I still belong to life. I still belong to joy.*

The Universal Human Bond – Laughter as Shared Humanity

Across every era and continent, laughter has united you with others, dissolving barriers and bridging differences. It reminds you of the paradox of your existence: that joy and pain are inseparable, and that even in sorrow, a laugh can ripple through your heart and the hearts of others, bringing unexpected healing. When you allow your laughter to rise from a place of love and respect, it becomes one of the most powerful connectors you possess. It softens conflict, bridges generations, and invites you to meet others as simply human.

The Continuation of an Ancient Tradition

When you laugh today, you are not simply reacting to humour, you are continuing an ancient, sacred tradition of healing and connection. Every laugh you release echoes the voices of your ancestors, who laughed in temples, around fires, in theatres, and in times of both joy and despair. Your laughter becomes a thread in this timeless web of resilience and joy, proof that across every age, humanity has remembered how to breathe, bond, and be fully alive through laughter.

How Laughter Promotes Resilience, Perspective-Taking, And Healing

Laughter is often misunderstood as a fleeting reaction to something funny, but in truth, it is a deeply **resilient act,** a conscious or unconscious decision to release, to reframe, and to remember that you are more than your circumstances. When you laugh, you interrupt the story of fear. You step back from what feels overwhelming or hopeless and breathe in a new perspective. In that moment, laughter becomes an act of defiance against despair. It says: *"This too shall pass."* It reminds you that even in the chaos, there is still beauty, absurdity, and light.

Resilience is the ability to bounce back, and laughter helps you do just that. Not by dismissing pain, but by giving it room to soften. Studies in positive psychology and trauma recovery show that those who can access humour during or after hardship often recover faster, adapt more effectively, and maintain healthier emotional balance. Laughter builds your capacity to endure by restoring nervous system flexibility and reducing the long-term impact of stress. At the same time, **laughter cultivates perspective-taking**. It opens your mind to see situations from different angle, often with compassion and humility.

When you can laugh at yourself kindly, you loosen the grip of ego and perfectionism. You allow yourself to be human, and in doing so, you understand others more deeply too. This expanded perspective helps you respond instead of react. You gain insight into the bigger picture. You begin to find humour in shared challenges, and in that shared recognition, empathy deepens. Laughter makes space for both levity and understanding, two qualities essential to navigating complex emotional landscapes, and then there is **healing**.

Laughter restores not just your emotional body, but your physical one. It reduces pain, lowers blood pressure, increases oxygen intake, and releases tension, but beyond the biology, it is deeply spiritual. It reconnects you to joy, the kind of joy that bubbles up from the heart and says, *"I am alive, and I am okay."* You do not need to laugh *at* your suffering, but when you laugh in the midst of it, you reclaim your power. You tell your heart, *"I am still here. I am still standing, and joy is still possible."* In this way, laughter is not a distraction from your healing. It is part of the healing. A thread of gold woven into your recovery, your growth, and your return to wholeness.

The Role Of Light-Heartedness In Emotional Intelligence And Authentic Living

Light-heartedness as Emotional Wisdom

Light-heartedness is not the absence of depth, it is the presence of emotional wisdom. It is the capacity to walk through life with ease, humility, and grace, even in the midst of challenge. Far from being shallow, it reflects a maturity that knows pain is real, but suffering need not be permanent. It is the reminder that you can hold grief in one hand and laughter in the other, that you can be both serious and soft, grounded and free, compassionate and playful.

Light-heartedness and Emotional Intelligence

At the heart of emotional intelligence are awareness, regulation, empathy, and connection. Light-heartedness enhances each of these, teaching you to meet your emotions with gentle hands rather than clenched fists. When you are light-hearted, you do not dismiss or deny your feelings, you honour them honestly but refuse to let them define your entire being. You gain perspective. You step back. You even learn to laugh kindly at your own patterns, loosening the grip of self-judgment. In this way, light-heartedness becomes a subtle but powerful resilience practice, allowing you to meet discomfort with curiosity instead of fear.

Light-heartedness and Resilience

Resilience does not mean stoicism; it means flexibility. Light-heartedness helps you bend rather than break. It teaches you to breathe through difficulty, to soften tension with humour, and to carry perspective into the storms of life. A smile or a moment of levity in hardship does not trivialise pain, it transforms it, creating space for recovery and reminding you that no feeling is final. Light-heartedness whispers, *"This too will pass, and while it is here, you can meet it with grace."*

Light-heartedness and Authenticity

To live light-heartedly is to live authentically. It strips away the need for performance and perfection, letting your true self step forward. You no longer carry the burden of pretending to have it all figured out. Instead, you give yourself, and others, permission to be fully human: flawed, learning, tender, and alive. In this honesty, creativity reawakens, playfulness returns, and wonder becomes possible again. These are the parts of you often buried under fear, responsibility, or pressure, and light-heartedness brings them home.

Light-heartedness in Relationships

In relationships, light-heartedness is a gift of safety. It lowers defences, opens space for joy, and says with presence, *"You can exhale here. It is safe to be yourself."* When seriousness dominates, connection can feel heavy; when light-heartedness is invited, intimacy expands. It develops laughter, trust, and play, the fertile ground where empathy and deeper bonds naturally grow.

Light-heartedness in Daily Life

In daily living, light-heartedness is the quiet difference between reacting with tension and responding with presence. It helps you choose grace over control, laughter over bitterness, and flow over force. It does not deny that life can be serious, it simply reminds you that you do not have to be serious all the time. It is an orientation toward joy that keeps you supple, balanced, and open.

The Practice of Light-heartedness

So let light-heartedness become part of your emotional practice, not as an escape from reality, but as a companion to it. Let it soften the edges of your experience, bringing balance and brilliance to your becoming. For to live authentically is not to carry every burden alone. It is to walk with heart, with humility, and with the quiet wisdom of joy. Light-heartedness, then, is not a detour from depth, it is the depth itself, expressed through laughter, grace, and love.

Laughter Meditation & Release Exercise

I invite you to begin by listening to the guided Laughter Meditation. Allow the sound of laughter, your own and others', to soften your mind, open your heart, and begin to release the tension you may not even realise you are carrying. When the meditation is complete, you are encouraged to continue with a short practice, either on your own or in small groups:

1. **Begin with Breath:** Take a few slow, intentional breaths. Inhale deeply through your nose, exhale fully through your mouth. Let your body settle into the present moment.

2. **Start with Gentle Laughter:** Begin with playful, intentional laughter. It may feel unusual at first, forced, even awkward, but lean into it. The body does not distinguish between fake laughter and real laughter; often, the *"pretend"* laughter dissolves into genuine laughter within a few moments.

3. **Allow it to Flow:** As laughter builds, notice how it ripples through your chest, belly, and face. Let your laughter grow louder, freer, and less controlled. For 10–15 minutes, give yourself permission to laugh without needing a reason, releasing stress, judgment, or expectation.

---

4. **Tune Into Shifts:** As you laugh, pay attention to the subtle changes in your body and mood.

   - Notice your shoulders relaxing.

   - If you are in a group, make gentle eye contact with others, connection amplifies joy.

   - Shake your arms, legs, or whole body to release any residual tension.

5. **Integration:** When the laughter naturally softens, return once again to stillness and breath. Place your hand on your heart, close your eyes if you wish, and notice how you feel. Do you sense more lightness? Warmth? Connection? Peace?

6. **Closing Reflection:** Whisper to yourself, or share aloud if in a group, an affirmation such as:

   - *"I welcome joy as medicine."*

   - *"My laughter is my release."*

   - *"I honour my heart by allowing lightness in."*

Laughter is a sacred reset. It reminds you that even in challenge, your body knows how to return to joy. Each time you allow yourself to laugh freely, you strengthen your resilience, deepen your presence, and reconnect with the childlike wonder that lives within you.

Case Study Discussion: Jenna And Mark's Journey

Jenna was a woman who had a contagious laughter that could light up any room. She had a joyful and carefree spirit that people resonated with. One person who was particularly impacted by Jenna's laughter was her husband, Mark. When Jenna and Mark first met, Mark was going through a tough time. He had become more serious and reserved, and laughter seemed like a distant memory to him. I spoke with Jenna about issues in her marriage and asked her to get Mark to laugh. (She always made me laugh!) Jenna made it her mission to bring laughter back into their lives. She would tell Mark funny stories, crack jokes, and find humour in the simplest of moments. Slowly but surely, Mark began to open up and let go of his seriousness.

Jenna showed Mark the power of laughter in relieving stress, improving his mood, and strengthening their bond as a couple. Jenna told me that they would often engage in playful banter and share moments of uncontrollable laughter. Through their shared laughter, they found peace and comfort in each other. I spoke with Mark about what had transpired, and he told me that he had lost himself because of work stress and anxiety. He said that Jenna created a safe space for him to just be himself, and over time he was able to see how lost and disenchanted he had become. Mark started to embrace his own sense of humour and he discovered that laughter was not only enjoyable but also therapeutic. It allowed him to let go of his worries and connect with the present moment. Together they found that through laughter, they were able to navigate challenges with resilience and find happiness in the ordinary.

Reflective Exercise: Jenna and Mark's Journey

Here are four profound and reflective questions inspired by Mark's story to help you engage with your own journey into laughter:

1. **When was the last time you truly let go and laughed without restraint, who were you with, and how did it make you feel?** Reflect on what that moment revealed about your openness, your connection with others, and your inner joy.

2. **Have you ever lost your laughter during a difficult season of life?** What do you think it would take to invite it back, and who or what could help you rediscover it?

3. **In what ways can laughter be a healing language in your relationships?** Consider how shared humour, silliness, or play could strengthen emotional safety and deepen your bonds.

4. **Are you willing to make space in your life for lightness and joy, even in the midst of stress or uncertainty?** Explore how giving yourself permission to laugh could open your heart to a deeper sense of peace and presence.

Affirmations For You – (Heart Whispers)

Affirmations have the power to quiet the noise of doubt, open the doorway to self-trust, and draw you back into the wisdom of your heart. When practised daily, they nurture an inner dialogue based in love and truth, helping you live each day more aligned with who you truly are. I invite you to repeat silently or write:

- *I embrace laughter as a source of joy and inner healing.*

- *I find peace and release through laughter during difficult times.*

- *I cherish the moments of pure laughter that light up my soul.*

- *I prioritise laughter to cultivate a positive and resilient heartset.*

- *I connect deeply with others through shared laughter and smiles.*

- *I believe that laughter is the secret ingredient for a fulfilling life.*

Create a "Joy Map"

Your *Joy Map* is a living reminder of what makes your heart feel light, alive, and free. Think of it as a personal compass pointing you back to joy whenever life feels heavy.

1. **Draw or List with Intention:** Begin by drawing or writing down the things, people, places, and activities that consistently make you laugh, smile, or feel uplifted. These can be simple (a favourite song, a pet's playful antics, the smell of the ocean) or profound (a friend who always makes you laugh, a place that feels like home). Do not filter or overthink, let your inner child guide you.

2. **Visualise Connections:** If you are drawing, place yourself in the centre of the page and sketch lines or symbols radiating outward to represent sources of joy. If writing, make a list and circle the ones that spark the strongest feeling in your body as you reflect on them.

3. **Journal Reflection:**

   - *"How can I bring more of this energy into my life on purpose?"*

   - *"What happens in my heart when I allow joy and humour to flow freely?"*

4. **Deepen the Inquiry:**

   - *"What small daily rituals can I create that invite laughter and lightness into ordinary moments?"*

   - *"Where do I tend to block joy, and how might I soften those edges?"*

   - *"Who in my life reflects the kind of joy I want to nurture, and how can I spend more time with them?"*

5. **Anchor with Action:** Choose at least **one simple, practical action** you can take this week to weave joy into your life more intentionally,

---

whether it is calling a funny friend, watching a comedy, dancing in your kitchen, or scheduling unstructured time to play.

6. **Closing Pause:** Place your hand on your heart, smile softly, and whisper to yourself: *"I welcome joy as my medicine, my teacher, and my companion."*

Your Joy Map is not just a page of memories, it is a reminder that joy is always accessible. Each time you return to it, you strengthen your ability to choose joy, not as a fleeting moment, but as a way of living.

Closing Reflection

Laughter is more than sound, it is energy in motion, a vibration of the soul. In the instant when laughter escapes your lips, your heart opens wider, your body softens, and your spirit remembers its natural state of joy. In genuine laughter, barriers dissolve. Stress loses its grip. Isolation transforms into connection. It is as if life itself exhales through you. Whether it is the quiet glow of a gentle smile or the unstoppable ripple of a deep belly laugh, humour has a healing power that words alone cannot reach. It slips past logic, bypasses resistance, and touches the places within you that long for release, lightness, and relief.

As you move through this day, carry the awareness that laughter is not frivolous, it is sacred medicine. It is a gift you can offer yourself when life feels heavy and a gift you can share with others to remind them they are not alone. With every laugh, you release what weighs you down. You soften edges of fear or tension. You invite light back into places that once felt dark. When you laugh, you return home to yourself. You breathe vitality into your body, clarity into your mind, and wisdom into your heart. Your spirit is reminded that joy is not something you must earn or wait for, it is your birthright. Joy is not optional; it is essential nourishment for your whole being.

So go ahead, laugh often, laugh deeply, laugh without apology. Let your laughter rise like prayer, like music, like freedom. Let it ripple outward, lifting others with you, and may every laugh remind you of this truth: you are alive, you are connected, and your heart was never meant to live in chains. Laughter is your soul's reminder that even in the heaviest moments, lightness is always possible, and in that possibility, you rediscover your freedom, your connection, and your joy.

25 – LISTENING

Your Opening Reflection

Invitation to Listen Deeply - As you enter this chapter, I invite you to experience listening as more than hearing words, as an act of love. True listening is presence: to another person, to the world around you, and to your own heart. It asks nothing but your attention, your stillness, your willingness to receive without judgment. Each time you listen with openness, you give someone, or yourself, the gift of feeling valued, seen, and safe. Let this chapter be your reminder that listening is not passive; it is one of the most powerful ways to connect, to heal, and to honour what matters most.

- "When was the last time you felt truly heard?"

- "How did that moment impact you emotionally?"

- "When you listen to others, do you truly hear their words, or are you waiting for your turn to respond?"

- "What does it feel like in your body when someone listens to you with full presence and no judgment?"

- "How do you listen to your own inner voice, do you give it space, or do you silence it?"

- "In what relationships would deeper listening create more connection, healing, or trust?"

Let these questions open the doorway into presence. Every answer you give, whether in words, sensations, or silence, is a bridge between where you are and where you are going.

Learning Objectives

The learning objectives are included here to give you a clear focus for this chapter, ensuring that each practice you explore moves you closer to mastering the skills, insights, and heart-led awareness that will enrich your life well beyond the program. By the end of this chapter, you will:

- Understand the emotional intelligence behind active, empathetic, and reflective listening

- Explore how deep listening nurtures trust, compassion, and relational safety

- Practise techniques to enhance personal and interpersonal listening skills

- Recognise the role of silence and stillness in accessing heart wisdom

Core Emotional Domains

The core emotional intelligence domains covered here are essential because they form the foundation for lasting heart connection, guiding you to deepen self-awareness, regulate emotions, build resilience, and strengthen the mind-body bond throughout your Heart Unbound journey.

- **Self-Awareness:** Listening opens a window into your inner world. You begin to notice your urge to interrupt, your emotional triggers, and your habitual patterns. As you listen more deeply, you hear not only others, but yourself.

- **Social Awareness (Empathy):** True listening asks you to step into someone else's experience. You tune into tone, body language, and what's left unsaid. In that stillness, empathy awakens. You connect not to fix, but to feel.

- **Relationship Management:** Listening is the foundation of connection. It builds trust, de-escalates conflict, and invites honest conversation. Through active, heart-led listening, you create space where others feel seen, heard, and valued.

- **Emotional Regulation:** To truly listen, you learn to regulate your own emotions. You pause, breathe, and stay present even when the conversation is hard. In that pause, you choose compassion over reaction.

- **Communication & Interpersonal Effectiveness:** Listening refines your communication. You respond with intention, not impulse. You speak less, but with more meaning. Your relationships deepen, not because you say more, but because you hear with your heart.

"Listening - The Art Of Deep Connection"

When you truly listen, with your whole heart, not just your ears, you invite a deeper level of understanding and compassion into your life. Listening asks more of you than simply staying quiet. It asks you to *be present.* To place your full attention in the moment. To resist the urge to judge, to fix, or to interrupt. When you listen deeply to someone else, you are saying: *"You matter. I care about what you feel. I am here with you."* That level of presence can soften conflict, dissolve misunderstanding, and build trust that words alone cannot reach, but perhaps even more important than listening to others… is learning how to listen to yourself.

You have spent so much time in the noise of the world, external expectations, endless demands, self-criticism. It is easy to forget that beneath all of that, your heart is still speaking. Are you listening? When you take time to pause… to breathe… to slow your thoughts and drop into your body… you begin to hear that inner voice. The one that knows what you need. The one that remembers who you are. That voice may have been silenced, dismissed, or ignored in the past, but it never left you. It is still there, waiting patiently to be heard.

Listening to your heart is one of the most profound acts of self-respect you can offer. It is how you begin to align with your truth. It is how you know when to say yes, when to say no, and when to choose stillness instead of reaction. Through this part of the *Heart Unbound* journey, you are invited to become a listener, not just in conversation, but in life. To listen to the unspoken stories beneath someone's words. To hear the emotions behind the silence, and to attune to your own inner world with curiosity, kindness, and presence. Listening changes everything. It deepens connection. It builds empathy, and most of all, it creates space for healing, within you, and between you and the world.

The Difference Between Hearing And Heart-Based Listening

There is a world of difference between *hearing* someone and *truly listening* to them with your heart. You hear with your ears, but you listen with your whole being. Hearing is passive. It happens automatically. Sounds come in, words are registered, and you may even nod or reply, but in this state, you are often distracted, rehearsing your response, or filtering what is said through your own assumptions and beliefs.

Heart-based listening is something altogether different.

Heart-based listening is something altogether different. When you engage in heart-based listening, you offer more than your ears, you offer your full presence. You quiet the noise of your mind, soften the pull of distraction, and step aside from the urge to fix, advise, or prove yourself right. Instead, you lean into stillness and allow yourself to simply be with the person before you.

In this space, you do not just hear words; you feel the person, their tone, their pauses, their energy, their unspoken emotions. You sense the intention beneath their expression, the longing beneath their story. Your heart becomes a mirror, reflecting back not judgment but understanding, not correction but compassion.

Through heart-based listening, you create a sanctuary where another person feels safe enough to bring their whole self. They feel valued not for perfect phrasing or polished expression, but for their truth, raw and real. To listen in this way is to say without words: *"You matter. Your voice matters. Your being matters."* This kind of listening transforms conversations into connection, and connection into healing.

Heart-based listening is the gateway to healing.

When you listen this way, you open the door to deep connection. You build bridges where walls once stood. You learn to pause before reacting, to seek understanding before judgement, and to communicate from a place of compassion rather than defensiveness, and this same principle applies when you turn inward.

You may have spent years *hearing* your inner voice, your doubts, your fears, your needs, but brushing them aside. Dismissing them with logic or burying them beneath busyness, but when you listen from your heart, you begin to honour that inner voice with the same love and care you give to others.

Heart-based listening is not always easy. It asks you to be vulnerable. To slow down. To face what is really being said, by others and by yourself, but in doing so, you become someone who truly hears. Someone who listens for the *meaning*, the *emotion*, and the *heart* behind the message, and that kind of listening transforms relationships. It transforms your relationship with yourself, and ultimately, it transforms your life.

The Science And Psychology Of Active Listening (Carl Rogers, Socratic Dialogue)

Active listening is not just a soft skill, it is a profound psychological and emotional practice grounded in evidence-based science and centuries of human wisdom. When you listen actively, you do not just absorb someone's words, you become a vessel for understanding, empathy, and transformation. At the heart of this practice lies the work of renowned psychologist **Carl Rogers**, who believed that *unconditional positive regard, empathic understanding,* and *congruence* were essential conditions for personal growth and healing.

Rogers did not see listening as something you do with your ears alone, he taught that real listening means tuning into the emotional frequency of the speaker with your whole heart. When you listen through the lens of **Rogersian psychology**, you offer the other person a rare and sacred gift: the space to be truly seen, without judgment. You withhold advice. You refrain from interrupting. You listen not to reply, but to understand, and through that presence, healing occurs, often without a single solution being offered.

Even earlier in history, the **Socratic method** demonstrated another dimension of listening: *the art of asking meaningful, clarifying questions.* Socrates believed that truth and wisdom emerge not from telling others what to think, but from listening closely and helping them uncover their own insights through open, reflective dialogue. This is also the essence of heart-based listening in the *Heart Unbound* program. You are not listening to win. You are not listening to fix. You are listening to *connect*.

From a **neuroscientific perspective**, active listening activates areas of the brain associated with empathy and compassion, such as the anterior insula and the mirror neuron system. It soothes your amygdala's fight-or-flight response, builds trust, and co-regulates emotional states in both speaker and listener. In fact, research shows that feeling heard and understood reduces cortisol (the stress hormone), improves immune function, and boosts oxytocin, your bonding hormone.

When you engage in true, intentional listening, you help the other person feel safe, and safety is the foundation of all authentic relationship. Listening in this way requires *self-regulation*, *self-awareness*, and *emotional maturity*. It is a discipline and a devotion, to yourself and to others. It invites you to become not just a passive receiver of sound, but an *active witness to someone's inner world,* and when you offer this gift of presence, you invite others to do the same for you.

Barriers To Effective Listening: Judgment, Inner Chatter, Impatience

True listening is a profound act of presence, but it is not always easy. While your heart may long to understand and connect, there are often silent saboteurs that stand in the way. These barriers, judgment, inner chatter, and impatience, are subtle but powerful, and they can disconnect you from others and from your own deeper wisdom.

Judgment: The Wall That Silences Connection

Judgment is one of the most common and insidious barriers to listening. It is the voice inside you that decides who is right, who is wrong, who is worthy, and who is not, even before the other person has finished speaking. When you judge, you filter what you hear through assumptions, labels, and past experiences. Instead of receiving someone's words openly, you interpret them through a narrow lens. You stop listening with your heart and start listening with your opinions. This prevents real connection and can make others feel unsafe or unseen. To overcome this, you must practice *suspending judgment*. It does not mean agreeing with everything, it means staying open long enough to *understand* before you assess. It means choosing curiosity over criticism, compassion over conclusion.

Inner Chatter: The Noise Within

Even when you are quiet on the outside, there is often a whirlwind on the inside, planning your response, remembering your own story, or drifting to your to-do list. This is your *inner chatter,* the mental noise that keeps you from being fully present. When your attention is split between listening and your own internal dialogue, you miss the subtle cues, the emotional undertones, and the deeper meaning of what is being shared. You hear the words, but not the heart behind them. To quiet the inner chatter, return to your breath. Anchor yourself in the moment. Repeat inwardly, *"I am here. I am listening."* Let the speaker's words be the only voice you follow for that moment. This is heart-based listening, offering your full attention as a sacred gift.

Impatience: The Urge to Fix, Finish, or Flee

In a world conditioned for speed and solutions, *impatience* often shows up in your listening. You might interrupt. You might rush someone to the point. You might mentally check out because you feel like you "*already know where this is going,*" but effective listening requires *patience.* People need space to find their words, feel their way through their thoughts, and speak from their hearts. If you rush that process, you risk cutting off something vulnerable, meaningful, or healing.

Impatience often masks your own discomfort, your desire to control, to move on, or to be "*right,*" but heart-based listening invites you to *slow down* and *stay.* It teaches you that healing often comes not from advice or answers, but from feeling heard in the presence of loving stillness. When you become aware of these barriers, judgment, inner chatter, and impatience, you take a powerful step toward more conscious, compassionate connection. You learn to listen not just with your ears, but with your *whole self,* and in doing so, you open the door to healing, both for yourself and for those you love.

The Impact Of Listening On Emotional Safety And Trust In Relationships

Listening is more than a skill, it is a sacred act of love. When you truly listen to someone, with your heart open and your presence undivided, you do something extraordinary: you create emotional safety. You become a sanctuary, and in that space of safety, trust is born. Emotional safety is the foundation of all healthy relationships, whether with a partner, a child, a friend, a colleague, or yourself. It is the felt sense of being seen, heard, valued, and accepted without fear of judgment, interruption, or rejection, and the fastest way to build that safety is through deep, intentional listening.

When You Listen, You Tell Someone They Matter

Think about the last time someone truly listened to you. Not just nodded along. Not just waited for their turn to speak, but really *listened,* with full presence, empathy, and a desire to understand. *How did it make you feel?* Chances are, you felt more than just heard. You felt *affirmed.* You felt like your feelings were valid. You felt like *you mattered.* This is the power of heart-based listening, it affirms worthiness and creates belonging. In a world that moves quickly and often superficially, this kind of listening is revolutionary.

Listening as a Bridge Between Hearts

When you offer someone your listening presence, you open a bridge between your heart and theirs. You allow them to lower their defences. You signal, *"You are safe here."* That sense of safety allows vulnerability to unfold, and vulnerability is the birthplace of intimacy, healing, and growth. In couples, it renews connection. In friendships, it deepens authenticity. In teams and workplaces, it cultivates respect and collaboration. Conversely, when someone feels unheard, dismissed, or interrupted, emotional walls rise. Defensiveness appears. Trust withers, and disconnection grows. Listening is not just about gathering information, it is about *building relationship*. Every time you choose to listen with love instead of react with ego, you strengthen the emotional fabric that holds your relationships together.

Becoming a Safe Space, For Others and For Yourself

Heart-based listening also teaches you how to be safe with *yourself*. When you practice truly listening to your own emotions, without judgment, avoidance, or harshness, you begin to build inner trust. You tell yourself, *"My feelings matter. My inner voice deserves to be heard."* As that inner trust grows, so does your ability to listen to others with compassion. Your heart becomes more spacious, more patient, more attuned, and from this place, relationships flourish, not through perfection, but through presence. In *Heart Unbound*, learning to listen with your whole heart is one of the most powerful gifts you can offer, to others, and to your own soul. It requires practice, patience, and humility, but the rewards are profound: deeper connection, emotional safety, and unshakeable trust.

Listening To Self: Stillness, Intuition, And Inner Guidance

In a world filled with noise, deadlines, opinions, and expectations, learning to listen to your *own voice* can feel like a radical act, but it is also one of the most essential steps on the path to heart connection. When you slow down and listen inwardly, with intention, with compassion, and with curiosity, you begin to hear what truly matters: your own inner guidance.

Stillness: The Gateway to Inner Listening

Stillness is not simply the absence of sound or movement, it is the presence of awareness. It is the sacred pause where your breath softens, your mind quiets, and your heart becomes audible. When you enter stillness, you are not escaping life, you are returning to yourself. It is in the quiet moments, free from distraction or urgency, that your heart begins to whisper the truths you have been too busy to hear. Sometimes, these whispers come as insights. Other times, they come as sensations in your body, or memories rising to the surface. Stillness is the space where listening becomes possible.

Intuition: The Language of the Heart

Your intuition is not a fantasy or a mystical anomaly, it is a natural, inner compass. It is the felt sense that guides you toward truth, alignment, and integrity, and it speaks in subtleties: a gut feeling, a quiet knowing, a gentle pull in a certain direction. When you take time to listen inwardly, you begin to strengthen your connection to this deep inner wisdom. You learn to differentiate between the noise of fear and the voice of clarity. You learn to honour what *feels right*, not just what *looks right* on paper. This is the language of the heart, and when you listen to it, your choices begin to reflect who you really are.

Inner Guidance: Reclaiming Trust in Yourself

Many of us have been conditioned to look outward for answers, to seek validation, advice, or approval from others. While there is value in wise counsel, there is a deeper wisdom that resides within you. You are not empty. You are not lost. You are not without direction. You have within you a wellspring of insight, discernment, and strength. Listening to yourself is an act of reclaiming trust. As you journey through *Heart Unbound*, you are invited to tune in, not tune out. To ask your heart what it needs. To breathe into your body and feel what is alive. To write freely without censoring. To move when stillness becomes emotion. To rest when your soul asks for it.

These are not small things, they are profound declarations that your inner world matters. When you listen to yourself with kindness and presence, you begin to live a life that is not just reactive, but *responsive*, aligned, and deeply attuned. You create space for inner peace, intuitive decisions, and the steady guidance of your own heart, and from that place, everything changes, not because the world is different, but because *you are*.

"Empathy in Silence" (Paired Activity)

This activity is designed to help you experience the power of listening without words, a practice of presence, patience, and heart connection.

1. **Pair Up** – Find a partner and decide who will share first.

---

2. **Share (2 minutes each)** – One participant shares something personal, it could be a story, a challenge, a joy, or simply how you are feeling in this moment. The other participant listens silently. There are **no interruptions, no advice, no fixing**. Your only task is to *be fully present*. Use eye contact, gentle nods, and soft facial expressions as subtle signals of support.

3. **Switch Roles** – After 2 minutes, change roles so each person has the opportunity to both share and listen.

4. **Silent Reflection (1 minute each)** – Before speaking again, both partners sit quietly for a short pause, noticing what they felt while listening and being listened to.

5. **Debrief Together** – Reflect with your partner:

   - What did it feel like to be listened to without interruption?

   - What emotions surfaced as you held silent space for someone else?

   - Did you notice the difference between listening with your head versus listening with your heart?

This exercise often reveals how rare it is to be heard without distraction or judgment. It teaches you that empathy is not always expressed in words, sometimes it is the stillness of your presence, the openness of your heart, and the safety of your silence that speak the loudest.

Case Study Discussion: Daniel's Journey

Daniel was really talkative, he loved sharing his ideas, thoughts, and experiences, but he rarely took the time to truly listen. He would often interrupt me in our sessions, and I would let him say his peace. I asked him why he was always on transmit, and how did that truly make him feel? Daniel told me that he found himself in a place where he felt disconnected and unsatisfied with his relationships and his life in general. In our sessions he realised that his inability to (actively) listen was a significant barrier to building meaningful connections and understanding others on a deeper level. He did it as a self–protective mechanism, but it came at a cost, and Daniel desperately wanted to transform his life.

Daniel started by practicing active listening. He made a conscious effort to be fully present when someone was speaking to him, focusing on their words, body language, and emotions. I used to enjoy Daniel telling me how hard it was for him to resist the urge to interrupt and instead allow another person the opportunity to express themselves. What was interesting was that over time Daniel began to listen more attentively and he discovered the power of empathy. He realised that by truly listening, he could understand and connect with others on a deeper level (including himself).

Daniel started to ask open–ended questions and show genuine interest in their experiences, which nurtured stronger and more meaningful connections, friendships, and relationships. He also learned to appreciate silence and the spaces between words. He realised that sometimes, the most profound messages are conveyed through nonverbal cues and the unspoken. As Daniel practiced listening, he noticed a positive shift in his relationships. People felt valued and heard in his presence, and he created an environment where he learnt how to trust again. His newfound ability to listen deeply allowed for more open and honest communication, resolving conflicts, and nurturing harmony.

Most importantly, Daniel discovered that by learning to listen, he found a greater sense of happiness and fulfillment in his own life. He realised that true listening is an act of love and compassion, and it allowed him to connect with himself on a deeper heart level. Through listening, he cultivated deeper relationships, gained new perspectives, and nurtured a sense of belonging and understanding. In the end, Daniel's journey of learning to listen transformed not only his relationships but also his own inner world. He became a better friend, partner, and listener, embracing the power of listening as a gateway to happiness and a more authentic and meaningful life.

Reflective Exercise: Daniel's Journey

Here are four profound and reflective questions inspired by Daniels story to help you engage with your own listening journey:

1. **When was the last time you truly listened, to yourself, without judgment, distraction, or the need to fix anything?** What did you hear in the stillness? What did your heart try to tell you when you finally gave it space to speak?

2. **Do you notice the difference between hearing someone's words and truly receiving their heart?** What barriers within you, like

---

impatience, assumptions, or inner noise, get in the way of offering someone your full, present attention?

3. **What would change in your life if you listened more deeply, to your body's signals, your inner voice, your quiet truths?** How might your relationships, decisions, and sense of self evolve if you trusted what you feel as much as what you think?

4. **Who in your life needs to feel heard, not just with your ears, but with your presence and empathy?** How might you create emotional safety and deepen connection simply by offering your undivided, heart-based listening?

Affirmations For You – (Heart Whispers)

Affirmations have the power to quiet the noise of doubt, open the doorway to self-trust, and draw you back into the wisdom of your heart. When practised daily, they nurture an inner dialogue based in love and truth, helping you live each day more aligned with who you truly are. I invite you to repeat silently or write:

- *I give my full attention when someone is speaking to me.*

- *I listen with an open heart and an open mind.*

- *I seek to understand before being understood.*

- *I honour and respect the opinions and viewpoints of others.*

- *I embrace silence as an opportunity to listen deeply.*

- *I am curious and eager to learn from others' experiences.*

- *I listen beyond words, tuning into the feelings and intentions beneath what is spoken.*

- *I create a safe space where others feel valued, seen, and heard.*

- *I release the need to interrupt or fix, trusting that presence itself is powerful.*

- *I welcome every voice as a teacher, expanding my understanding of life.*

Create a Listening Oath

I invite you to write a personal **"Listening Commitment"** to yourself and those you care about. This is not just a set of promises, it is a declaration of the kind of presence you wish to bring into your relationships, your conversations, and your inner life. When you write your

Oath, imagine it as a gentle compass that guides you back whenever you drift into distraction, impatience, or self-judgment.

Your Oath could include pledges such as:

- *"I will pause before responding, allowing space for others to finish and for me to reflect."*

- *"I will give eye contact and put away distractions, offering my full attention."*

- *"I will ask open-hearted questions that invite depth rather than quick answers."*

- *"I will listen to myself with kindness, honouring my own needs and emotions as I do others'."*

- *"I will hold silence as part of listening, trusting that words are not always necessary."*

- *"I will respect the courage it takes for others to share, even when their truth differs from mine."*

Once you have written your Oath, **display it somewhere visible,** perhaps in your journal, on your desk, or even as a note on your phone. You may also choose to carry a small copy with you as a daily reminder.

Over time, return to your Listening Oath and update it as you grow. Let it evolve with you, becoming a living reflection of your intention to listen with your heart, not just your ears.

My Listening Oath Template

Today, I commit to becoming a better listener, to others, and to myself. I recognise that true listening is an act of love, presence, and respect. Through this Oath, I pledge to:

My Listening Promises

☐ I will pause before responding, creating space for reflection.

☐ I will give eye contact and put away distractions.

☐ I will ask open-hearted questions that invite deeper connection.

☐ I will listen with kindness, patience, and without judgment.

☐ I will honour silence as part of true listening.

☐ I will listen to myself with the same compassion I offer others.

☐ I will respect the courage it takes for someone to share their truth.

☐ I will be curious, open, and willing to learn from others' experiences.

My Personal Listening Intention

(Write one or two sentences in your own words, e.g., "I commit to listening with my heart first, and my mind second.")

....

....

....

Signature & Date

(sign your name as a symbol of your commitment)

....

Signature   **Date**

Closing Reflection

In a world that races forward and grows louder with every passing day, your choice to pause and listen is both radical and sacred. True listening is not confined to the ears; it is an offering of your whole being, your presence, your patience, your stillness, and above all, your open heart. When you listen deeply to another, you create a sanctuary where they can rest, a space where their words are not just heard but *held*.

In that moment, you give them one of life's greatest gifts: the experience of being truly seen, felt, and understood, and when you turn that same listening inward, when you quiet the noise, slow your racing thoughts, and lean into your own heart, you rediscover the truth that has always lived within you. You reclaim the wisdom that busyness often buries and remember that your inner voice is worthy of trust.

Listening, in its purest form, is an act of love. It dissolves walls where there was once separation. It opens doors to compassion where there was once misunderstanding. It strengthens bonds and heals wounds that words alone cannot reach. It invites empathy to flourish and reminds you that every story, every voice, every heart deserves to be received with tenderness and grace.

So may your listening become your love in action. May you carry this practice into your conversations, your relationships, your work, and your own self-reflection. Let it remind you daily that silence can speak volumes, that presence is more powerful than performance, and that to listen is to give life. When you listen with your heart, you do not just hear, you connect, you heal, you transform, and in that moment, you come home to yourself and invite others to do the same.

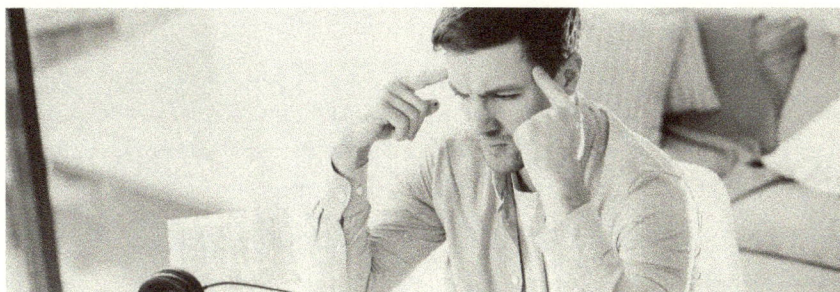

26 – FOCUS

Your Opening Reflection

Invitation to Return to What Matters - As you step into this chapter, I invite you to see focus not as rigid discipline, but as devotion. Where you place your attention is where your life gathers meaning and energy. Each moment is an invitation to return, to what matters most, to what nourishes your heart, to what brings you alive. Focus is not about perfection, it is about choosing presence over distraction, alignment over scattering, love over noise. Let this be your practice: to notice when your attention drifts, and gently bring it back, again and again, to the truth of what matters most to you.

- "Where is your attention most often directed, and does it serve your heart's true desires?"

- "What distractions most often pull you away from what matters most to your heart?"

- "When do you feel most present, and what helps you return to that state?"

- "How do your daily choices reflect (or contradict) the vision you hold for your life?"

- "If you gave your best energy to what truly nourishes you, what would shift in your life?"

Let these questions open the doorway into presence. Every answer you give, whether in words, sensations, or silence, is a bridge between where you are and where you are going.

Learning Objectives

The learning objectives are included here to give you a clear focus for this chapter, ensuring that each practice you explore moves you closer to mastering the skills, insights, and heart-led awareness that will enrich your life well beyond the program. By the end of this chapter, you will:

- Understand how focus connects to emotional intelligence and heart-centred living

- Identify internal and external distractions and develop strategies for managing them

- Learn techniques to sharpen attention, reduce overwhelm, and stay aligned with purpose

- Practice mindfulness and time-management techniques that support deep work and mental clarity

Core Emotional Domains

The core emotional intelligence domains covered here are essential because they form the foundation for lasting heart connection, guiding you to deepen self-awareness, regulate emotions, build resilience, and strengthen the mind-body bond throughout your Heart Unbound journey.

- **Self-Awareness:** Focus begins with knowing what matters most to you. You learn to recognise when your attention drifts and what pulls you off course. Through reflection, you develop insight into your patterns of distraction and alignment, allowing you to consciously choose where to place your energy.

- **Self-Regulation:** Cultivating focus requires you to redirect your attention, moment by moment. You discover how to pause, breathe, and bring yourself back to centre. With practice, you build the inner discipline to stay grounded in your priorities without being overtaken by external noise or internal restlessness.

- **Motivation (Goal-Oriented Action):** When you focus on what matters, your purpose becomes clearer. You align your time, energy, and actions with your goals and values. Motivation grows from meaningful direction, and you begin to act not out of urgency, but from heartfelt clarity and drive.

- **Focus and Attention Control:** You develop the capacity to be fully present. Rather than scattering your energy, you train your attention like a muscle. Whether through mindful awareness or intentional routines, you learn to focus with depth, presence, and purpose.

- **Resilience and Mental Agility:** Distraction, pressure, and uncertainty are part of life. With strengthened focus, you become more mentally agile, able to adapt, re-centre, and recover from setbacks. You learn to hold your attention steady, even amidst chaos, and that is a powerful act of resilience.

"Focus – Cultivating Presence, Purpose And Productivity"

Focus is a powerful amplifier. What you focus on expands. When you give your attention to fear, stress, or distraction, those things begin to shape your reality, but when you align your focus with love, purpose, and values, something remarkable happens, your energy becomes clearer, your actions more intentional, and your life more heart-led. In this part of your Heart Unbound journey, you are invited to move away from the myth of multitasking and into the grounded clarity of presence.

Focus is not about pressure or perfection. It is not about rigid control or doing more. It is about choosing, consciously, compassionately, what you give your time, energy, and emotional investment to. When your attention is centred in your heart, you naturally prioritise what truly matters. You begin to notice where your energy leaks through worry, self-doubt, or constant busyness, and instead of being scattered, you begin to return, again and again, to the present moment, where your power lives.

Focus helps you see the difference between distraction and direction. It gives you the courage to say no to what drains you and yes to what nourishes you. In this space, you find the freedom to move forward with clarity, confidence, and purpose. By reclaiming your focus, you reclaim your life, not through force, but through the gentle act of presence, and from that place, your heart has the space to lead.

Focus As A Heart-Centred Muscle: Presence Vs. Distraction

Focus is not a fixed trait you either have or lack, it is a living, breathing practice, cultivated moment by moment. Just like a muscle, it grows stronger the more you use it, but only when exercised with intention, compassion, and patience. In the modern world, where constant notifications, deadlines, and distractions demand your attention, it is easy to feel as though your focus has been stolen or scattered across a thousand different directions. This can leave you restless, anxious, and disconnected, but your heart whispers a different truth: focus is not about holding on tighter, it is about learning to return, again and again, to what matters most.

When your focus is anchored in the heart, it is not driven by force or urgency, but by love and presence. Focus becomes less about finishing tasks and more about *showing up fully* for your life. This is presence, not perfection. It is not about getting everything right or keeping everything under control. Instead, it is about remembering to come back to the breath, to your body, and to the values that guide your spirit. It is about being here now, awake to what is unfolding in front of you, and willing to meet it with openness and curiosity.

Distraction, in contrast, is not simply laziness or weakness, it is often a signpost pointing to unmet needs. You drift into distraction when a part of you feels unsafe, unworthy, or overwhelmed. You scroll endlessly, busy yourself with tasks, or numb your feelings because something in you is afraid of stillness. Stillness exposes truth, and that truth may feel uncomfortable. Yet the practice of focus allows you to approach this with gentleness. Every time you notice your mind wandering and guide it softly back, you are rewiring your nervous system to trust: *it is safe to be here, it is safe to be still, it is safe to be me.*

This is the essence of heart-centred focus, it transforms distraction from an enemy into a teacher. Instead of battling against your wandering mind, you learn to meet it with compassion and then lovingly return. Focus is not about perfection, it is about *practice*. It is not about rigid control, it is about *flow*. It is not about denying distraction, it is about choosing devotion. When you cultivate this kind of focus, life itself changes. Your attention is no longer hijacked by every demand. You begin to listen more deeply to your inner compass. You make choices that reflect your intentions instead of your fears. You find yourself moving with the rhythm of life instead of being pulled apart by it. With practice, this focus strengthens your resilience, sharpens your clarity, and deepens your sense of connection, to yourself, to others, and to the greater pulse of existence.

Every time you return your focus to the heart, you remember who you are. You remember why you began. You remember that your attention is sacred, and where you place it shapes the quality of your entire life. Presence becomes your new rhythm, and focus becomes your quiet power, an inner strength not born from control, but from trust, and so, your practice is simple: notice when you drift. Breathe. Return. Repeat. This is how you build the muscle of focus, not through force, but through remembering, remembering that you are safe, remembering that you are whole, and remembering that your heart already knows the way.

Ancient Perspectives: Mindfulness (Buddhism), Eudaimonia (Aristotle), Intention (Taoism)

The power of focus has long been revered by ancient wisdom traditions, not just as a tool for productivity, but as a sacred gateway to your purpose, balance, and inner peace. When you look at focus through the eyes of these traditions, you begin to see that it is not simply about narrowing your attention, it is about orienting your whole being toward truth, wholeness, and harmony with life itself.

Mindfulness – Buddhism

In Buddhism, mindfulness (*sati*) is the practice of sustained, compassionate attention. It asks you to bring your awareness fully into the present moment, whether in your breath, body, thoughts, or feelings. Here, focus is not about tightening your grip or forcing control, it is about softening into presence. You become a witness to what arises: sensations, emotions, and mental patterns. With each gentle return to the breath, you train your attention to rest in awareness itself. This act of presence is both your anchor and your liberation, it grounds you in what is real and frees you from being enslaved to every passing thought. In mindfulness, your focus becomes a bridge, between chaos and calm, fear and clarity, suffering and compassion. It is less about doing and more about being, an invitation for you to live awake.

Eudaimonia – Aristotle

In Aristotle's philosophy, the idea of *eudaimonia*, often translated as flourishing or living well, reminds you that the highest form of focus is not measured by efficiency or achievement, but by virtue. To live with *eudaimonia* is to align your focus with what truly matters: courage, wisdom, integrity, and kindness. Here, your focus is not scattered among endless desires but directed toward what makes life meaningful. It is an ethical alignment, where your energy and attention are devoted to cultivating excellence of character. When you live with this kind of focused intentionality, your daily actions become infused with purpose. You stop chasing fleeting rewards and begin embodying values that endure. Focus, in Aristotle's teaching, is not simply mental—it is moral. It is your devotion to living in such a way that your life becomes a reflection of your inner truth.

<u>Intention – Taoism</u>

In Taoism, you are invited to understand focus through the lens of *yi*, intention, or the clarity of your heart's aim. Unlike Western ideas of discipline that emphasise force or willpower, Taoist wisdom encourages you to align your focus with the effortless flow of the Tao, "the Way." Here, focus is not about pushing harder, but about listening deeper. You learn to attune to the natural rhythm of life, to sense when to act and when to be still. Intention in Taoism is never divorced from harmony, it arises from simplicity, sincerity, and balance. When your heart is clear, your actions become spontaneous and fluid, as natural as water finding its path. Your focus then becomes graceful, responsive, and alive, not rigid. In this way, focus is not a burden you must maintain but a gift of alignment with the greater whole.

<u>The Integration</u>

These ancient traditions together remind you that true focus is not a clenched state of mental effort, it is a sacred state of alignment. When your attention rests in mindfulness, when your choices reflect your deepest virtues, and when your intentions flow from presence and peace, your focus is transformed. It becomes more than attention, it becomes reverence. A way of walking through the world awake. A practice of living with awareness, purpose, and love.

The Neuroscience Of Attention And How Focus Strengthens Resilience

Focus is not just a mental habit, it is a living biological process grounded in the very architecture of your brain. When you begin to understand the neuroscience of attention, you realise that presence, clarity, and resilience are not fixed traits but trainable capacities. Just like a muscle, your focus grows stronger the more you nurture it with awareness, practice, and compassion.

At the centre of this process is your **prefrontal cortex**, the *"executive hub"* of your brain. This region governs planning, decision-making, emotional regulation, and the ability to stay aligned with your long-term goals. Every time you direct your attention toward a single task, value, or intention, your prefrontal cortex activates more strongly. It filters distractions, prioritises what matters, and stabilises your emotional state. In moments of chaos or uncertainty, this kind of focus acts like an anchor, giving you clarity when everything around you feels turbulent, but focus is not simply concentration, it is also the foundation of emotional resilience. When you train your attention through mindfulness, breathwork, or intentional rituals, you begin to shift activity away from the **amygdala**, the part of your brain wired for fear and reactivity. Instead, you strengthen neural pathways associated with calm, regulation, and perspective. Science confirms that sustained attention lowers stress hormones such as cortisol, reduces over-reactivity, and increases **neuroplasticity**, your brain's remarkable ability to rewire itself. With each practice of returning to your breath or your heart, you are literally sculpting a more resilient nervous system.

Focus also awakens your brain's natural reward system. Every time you devote yourself to something meaningful, your brain releases **dopamine**, a neurotransmitter linked with motivation, hope, and a sense of accomplishment. This creates a feedback loop: the more you focus, the more energised and empowered you feel, which in turn reinforces your ability to continue. This is why people who cultivate focus often recover more quickly from setbacks, they know how to guide their attention back to what matters instead of spiralling into overwhelm.

In a world flooded with noise and distraction, choosing to focus becomes an act of **inner leadership**. Each time you say, *"This is what I will give my energy to,"* you are reprogramming your nervous system. You are teaching your brain and body that peace is possible, that clarity is within reach, and that you are capable of guiding yourself through life with strength and balance.

At its essence, focus is not about force, it is about **return**. Returning to your breath when your mind wanders. Returning to your values when you feel pulled in every direction. Returning to your heart when fear or doubt threatens to take over. With each return, you are not failing, you are building resilience. You are carving new pathways in your brain that remind you, even in difficulty, that your heart knows the way home.

The Link Between Focused Intention And Emotional Regulation

Focused intention is far more than setting goals, it is a practice of choosing, moment by moment, where your energy and awareness will rest. It is the art of alignment: bringing your attention into harmony with your deepest values and your heart's truth. When your focus is anchored in clarity, honesty, and presence, you do more than sharpen your thinking, you begin to regulate your emotions with grace and strength.

When you feel emotionally dysregulated, anxious, reactive, overwhelmed, it is often because your attention has been scattered or hijacked. Your mind leaps from fear to distraction, dragging your nervous system along with it. Yet the moment you consciously redirect your focus back to an anchor, your breath, a grounding phrase, a meaningful purpose, you reclaim your inner authority. This deliberate return activates your prefrontal cortex, the part of your brain responsible for calm, decision-making, and perspective, and creates space between stimulus and response. That space is where emotional regulation lives.

Setting a focused intention such as *"I choose peace"* or *"I remain steady and present"* is not just symbolic, it is neurological. Research in neuroscience shows that when you guide your attention deliberately, you decrease amygdala activity (the brain's fear and reactivity centre) while strengthening neural connections in areas tied to self-awareness, regulation, and compassion. In essence, you are teaching your brain to return to balance. Emotionally intelligent people are not those who feel less, they often feel more deeply, but they cultivate the ability to pause, to notice, and to guide their emotions instead of being swept away by them.

In your **Heart Unbound** journey, focused intention becomes a compass. It anchors you in the centre of chaos and reminds you that your emotions are not enemies to be suppressed, but messengers to be listened to. By meeting them with awareness and compassion, and then returning again and again to your chosen focus, you build a stable foundation within yourself. Over time, this practice transforms reactivity into responsiveness, confusion into clarity, and vulnerability into resilience. With each intentional return, you strengthen your emotional muscles. Your reactions soften. Your clarity deepens, and your resilience expands. Focused intention becomes more than a mental skill, it is a spiritual discipline that allows you to meet life not from fear or habit, but from the steady, unwavering truth of your heart.

Aligning Daily Actions With Core Values And Long-Term Purpose

Focus becomes powerful when it is not just about productivity, but about alignment. In your Heart Unbound journey, alignment means this: your daily choices reflect your deepest values and your highest intentions. You move through life not reacting to the noise of the world, but guided by the quiet truth of your heart. To live in alignment is to wake each day with clarity about what matters most to you, and then honour that truth through your actions. This is not always easy in a world filled with distractions, deadlines, and competing demands, but when your actions mirror your values, you experience a sense of integrity, wholeness, and inner peace.

Your **core values,** love, kindness, freedom, honesty, compassion, creativity, are the compass points of your soul. Your **long-term purpose** is your north star. When you lose focus or feel emotionally unbalanced, it is often because your daily life has drifted from these inner truths. The remedy is not to do more, but to realign. Ask yourself each morning:

- What do I want to stand for today?

- How can I bring my values into this next moment, this next task?

- Will my actions today serve the life I truly want to build?

When you pause to reflect on these questions, you begin to notice where your energy is being drained by obligations that do not serve you, or habits that dull your spirit. You can then begin to shift, gently but decisively, towards choices that nourish your purpose and reflect your integrity. This is the practice of **conscious focus**: not striving harder, but living more truly. Over time, these small acts of alignment build momentum. You find yourself saying yes to what is essential, and no to what is merely urgent. You begin to trust your inner guidance, and your life becomes a reflection of your deepest truth. In Part 26 of Heart Unbound, you are invited to reclaim your focus not just as mental concentration, but as soulful intention. When your daily actions align with your core values and your long-term purpose, you do not just stay on track, you come home to yourself.

Daily Focus Ritual

Focus does not just happen, it is something you cultivate with intention. By creating a simple, personal ritual, you can train your mind and heart to return to what truly matters, even in a world filled with noise and distraction. This ritual is not about perfection, but about presence. It is about honouring your time, your energy, and your values by choosing where your attention goes. Your daily focus ritual might include:

- **Setting a clear intention each morning:** Begin your day by asking, *What truly matters today?* Write it down, breathe it in, and carry it with you.

- **Blocking out specific times for focused tasks:** Protect small windows of uninterrupted time, even 25–50 minutes, where your energy is devoted to one meaningful activity.

- **Creating phone-free zones or hours:** Free yourself from constant notifications. Whether it is during meals, first thing in the morning, or before bed, gift yourself undistracted presence.

- **Dedicating time to deep, undistracted work:** Choose one priority project and give it your full attention. Let this be your daily act of devotion to what matters most.

- **Ending your day with a short reflection or review:** Ask yourself, *Where did my focus serve me well today? Where did it wander? What will I choose tomorrow?*

Now, write out your personal focus ritual in a way that feels realistic, supportive, and empowering. Keep it simple enough to follow daily, yet meaningful enough to inspire you.

Commit to practicing your ritual for the next 3 days. Notice what shifts, both inside and out, when you treat your focus as something sacred. You may find that you move through your day with more clarity, more energy, and a deeper sense of alignment with your heart.

Case Study Discussion: Archie's Journey

Archie was a very bright and ambitious student, but he found himself struggling to complete his university degree. He had always been passionate about his field of study, but his inability to focus was hindering his progress. Archie was really determined to overcome this, and he embarked on a journey of self–discovery and personal growth. We began by analysing his daily routines and identifying distractions, of which there were many. Social media, constant notifications, and his own wandering thoughts were stealing his attention.

After discussing a few options, Archie chose to implement a few strict time management strategies. He created a dedicated study schedule, allocating specific hours for focused work, and minimising interruptions. To further enhance his concentration, Archie explored meditation and mindfulness techniques. He practiced meditation, learning to quiet his mind and bring his attention back to the present moment. This newfound ability to anchor himself in the task at hand proved invaluable.

In time, Archie noticed a significant improvement. His coursework became more manageable, and his marks started to rise. The more he practiced focusing, the easier it became. He tapped into his passion for learning, finding joy in deep engagement with his studies. Archie's newfound focus not only helped him complete his degree but also transformed his overall approach to life. He became more disciplined, productive, and confident in his abilities. As he embarked on his career, the skills he acquired in focusing served as a foundation for success in all aspects of his life. In the end, Archie's journey taught him that focus was not just a means to an end, but a life skill that unlocked his true potential and allowed him to live his best life.

Reflective Exercise: Archie's Journey

Here are four profound and reflective questions inspired by Archie's story to help you engage with your own focus journey:

1. *Like Archie, what daily distractions, whether digital, mental, or emotional, are pulling you away from what truly matters?* Archie realised that notifications, social media, and scattered thoughts were silently draining his energy. What do you need to acknowledge or change to reclaim your focus?

2. *Archie reconnected with his passion through deep engagement, when have you last felt fully immersed in something meaningful?* Think back to a time when you were completely present and alive in your work or study. What helped you get there, and how could you invite that feeling back?

3. *What would it look like for you to create structure and boundaries around your time, like Archie did, to support your growth and purpose?* Archie found freedom in discipline. Could a simple schedule or focus ritual help you honour your goals more consistently?

4. *Archie used mindfulness to quiet his mind and return to the present moment, how could you bring more presence into your day?* Whether through meditation, deep breathing, or mindful pauses, how might you anchor yourself in the now and bring calm clarity to whatever you are doing?

Affirmations For You – (Heart Whispers)

Affirmations have the power to quiet the noise of doubt, open the doorway to self-trust, and draw you back into the wisdom of your heart. When practised daily, they nurture an inner dialogue based in love and truth, helping you live each day more aligned with who you truly are. I invite you to repeat silently or write:

- *I prioritise my tasks to maintain focus and productivity.*

- *I eliminate distractions to sharpen my focus on the present.*

- *I practice mindfulness to cultivate a centred and focused mind.*

- *I set clear goals to keep my focus aligned and purposeful.*

- *I train my mind to block out noise and maintain focus.*

- *I return my attention gently each time my mind wanders, building strength with every breath.*

- *I focus on what truly matters and release what does not serve my highest good.*

- *I channel my energy into one task at a time, creating clarity and flow.*

- *I use my focus as an act of self-respect, honouring my time and purpose.*

"The 5-Minute Focused Breath"

I invite you to find a comfortable position, allowing your body to settle and your breath to become steady. Gently close your eyes and turn your awareness inward. As you begin the guided Focus meditation, allow yourself to notice the rhythm of your breathing, each inhale drawing you into presence, each exhale releasing tension and distraction.

For the next five minutes, your breath will be your anchor. Thoughts may come, emotions may rise, or your attention may drift, that is natural. The practice is not about staying perfectly focused, but about noticing when your mind has wandered and gently returning to your breath. Each return is an act of strengthening, a moment of resilience, a reminder that focus is less about force and more about remembering.

At the conclusion of the meditation, I invite you to reflect with honesty and curiosity:

- *How many times did your mind drift?*

- *What helped you return?*

- *Did you notice a shift in your body, your emotions, or your clarity of mind as you practiced returning?*

Carry this awareness into the rest of your day. Remember, every time you guide yourself back, you are training your mind and heart to focus with greater ease. With each return, you are building not just concentration, but presence, patience, and peace.

Closing Reflection

Focus is more than concentration, it is a return to what matters most. Archie's journey reminds you that the ability to direct your attention is not something you are born with fully formed, but a living skill. It can be learned, practiced, refined, and strengthened with intention. Every time you bring yourself back from distraction, you are building a muscle of presence and resilience.

When you choose focus, you are choosing to honour your time, your energy, and your dreams. You begin to sift through the noise of demands and distractions, clearing a path to what is meaningful. In that clarity, you discover that focus is not about doing more, it is about doing what matters with depth, devotion, and heart.

This practice reminds you that your attention is sacred. Where your attention goes, your energy flows. Each moment you bring your full presence to something, whether it is a task, a conversation, or a quiet breath, you are reclaiming your life from fragmentation and returning it to wholeness.

Focus is not about perfection. It is about return. Return to your breath, to your values, to your purpose. Return to what lights you up and grounds you in truth. Each return is a victory, a small act of courage, and a reminder that you are free to choose again.

As you close this reflection, may you carry forward the knowing that focus is not pressure, but permission. Permission to live in alignment. Permission to give your best attention to what you love. Permission to let go of the noise and turn toward the voice of your heart. Focus is the path home, back to clarity, back to presence, back to what truly matters.

27 – SPONTANEITY

Your Opening Reflection

Invitation to Embrace the Unexpected - As you enter this chapter, I invite you to soften your grip on plans, routines, and expectations. Spontaneity is not recklessness, it is the art of listening to the moment and saying yes to life as it unfolds. Each unplanned laugh, each surprising turn, is a doorway into joy, connection, and freedom. Trust that your heart knows how to dance with the unexpected. Let yourself play, explore, and delight in the beauty of what you could never have scripted.

- "What stopped you from doing that more often?"

- "What would my day look like if I followed curiosity instead of routine?"

- "When did I last surprise myself by saying yes to something unplanned?"

- "How do I feel in my body when I allow myself to act freely, without overthinking?"

- "What fears or beliefs hold me back from being more spontaneous?"

- "If I gave myself permission to play today, what is one small, joyful thing I would do?"

Let these questions open the doorway into presence. Every answer you give, whether in words, sensations, or silence, is a bridge between where you are and where you are going.

Learning Objectives

The learning objectives are included here to give you a clear focus for this chapter, ensuring that each practice you explore moves you closer to mastering the skills, insights, and heart-led awareness that will enrich your life well beyond the program. By the end of this chapter, you will:

- Explore the emotional and psychological benefits of spontaneity

- Understand how spontaneity supports emotional intelligence, creativity, and resilience

- Learn how letting go of control can enhance connection, authenticity, and well-being

- Develop practices that increase openness to spontaneity and playfulness in everyday life

Core Emotional Domains

The core emotional intelligence domains covered here are essential because they form the foundation for lasting heart connection, guiding you to deepen self-awareness, regulate emotions, build resilience, and strengthen the mind-body bond throughout your Heart Unbound journey.

- **Self-Awareness:** Spontaneity begins with understanding your natural impulses and desires. You become aware of when you are holding back or overthinking, and you learn to notice the moments when your heart wants to act freely. Through this awareness, you create space to trust yourself and embrace life as it unfolds.

- **Emotional Agility:** Being spontaneous invites you to shift fluidly between emotions and situations. You learn to release the need for control, adapting to the present moment with curiosity and ease. Emotional agility grows as you respond with both openness and presence, rather than reacting from fear or habit.

- **Adaptability and Flexibility:** Life rarely follows a script. Spontaneity strengthens your ability to adjust, pivot, and find joy in the unexpected. By leaning into change instead of resisting it, you develop a more resilient and playful approach to challenges.

- **Authentic Expression:** When you stop censoring yourself, your true self shines through. Spontaneity teaches you to express your feelings, thoughts, and creativity without over-editing or self-judgment. This openness invites deeper, more honest connections with yourself and others.

- **Relationship Building:** Spontaneous moments often create the most genuine bonds. By showing up in the present and sharing unfiltered experiences, you create trust, warmth, and connection. These unscripted interactions strengthen relationships and remind you that joy often lives in the unexpected.

"Spontaneity – Embracing Joy, Trust And Authenticity"

Spontaneity is not carelessness or recklessness, it is the quiet wisdom of your heart responding freely and intuitively to the present moment. It is the courage to loosen your grip on rigid control and allow yourself to step into life as it unfolds. Rather than ignoring responsibility or awareness, true spontaneity calls you into deeper presence. It asks you to live fully awake, to respond to what is here and now, instead of being bound by overthinking, fear, or the need to plan every detail. Spontaneity is the practice of emotional agility, meeting life with openness, flexibility, and trust.

When you embrace spontaneity, you are not running from reality; you are meeting it directly, without filtering it through judgment, perfectionism, or doubt. In this space, authenticity is born. Joy bubbles to the surface. Creativity flows unhindered. You become more yourself, unmasked, unrestrained, and unafraid of making mistakes. Spontaneity allows you to move through the world with the natural ease of breath. You express without rehearsal, connect without strategy, and create without fear of *"getting it wrong."* Each moment becomes alive with possibility.

At its core, spontaneity is a reminder from your heart that life is not meant to be scripted. It is a sacred dance with the unknown, and it is in these unscripted moments, when plans give way to presence, that some of the most meaningful connections, breakthroughs, and expressions of your true self can arise. To live with spontaneity is to say yes to life as it is, to open yourself to wonder, and to trust that when you let go, your heart will know the way.

Spontaneity Practice – Saying Yes to the Moment

I invite you today to step outside your usual rhythm and welcome the unexpected. Spontaneity thrives when you loosen your grip on routine and allow your heart to guide you.

---

1. **Pause and Notice** – Take a few minutes to tune into your body and breath. Ask yourself: *What does my heart want to do right now, just for joy, connection, or freedom?*

2. **Say Yes** – Choose one simple, unplanned action to follow through with. This might be:

   - Taking a different route on your walk or drive.

   - Calling a friend just to say you love them.

   - Dancing to a song in your living room.

   - Saying yes to play, laughter, or rest instead of your usual routine.

3. **Reflect** – Afterward, take a few minutes to journal:

   - *How did it feel to step out of my usual plan?*

   - *What joy, connection, or creativity emerged in that moment?*

   - *What fears or resistances did I notice, and how did I move through them?*

4. **Integrate** – Ask yourself: *How can I invite a little more spontaneity into my everyday life?*

The goal here isn't to disrupt your responsibilities, but to remind you that life does not need to be fully scripted. In the small spaces where you allow the unplanned, you may find new energy, joy, and freedom waiting for you.

The Psychology of Spontaneity: Flexibility, Resilience, and Creativity

Spontaneity is often misunderstood as impulsiveness, but psychologically, it is much deeper and more refined. At its core, spontaneity is a reflection of emotional intelligence in motion, it is your ability to respond to life with *presence, flexibility,* and *freedom,* even in the face of uncertainty. In psychology, spontaneity is strongly linked to three key capacities: **flexibility**, **resilience**, and **creativity**.

Flexibility

Psychological flexibility is your ability to shift perspectives, adapt your behaviour, and remain open to change. When you are spontaneous, you loosen your grip on rigid expectations and fixed outcomes. You learn to say *"yes"* to the moment as it unfolds, rather than resisting it. This kind of flexibility is not passive, it is empowered. It invites you to move with life rather than against it, trusting that you can adapt as needed.

<u>Resilience</u>

Spontaneity strengthens resilience because it teaches you how to pivot and recover when things do not go as planned. When you allow yourself to act from your heart without over-calculating every step, you begin to build trust in your own capacity to *cope*, *adjust*, and *bounce back*. Spontaneous living does not mean chaos, it means embracing life's surprises with a steady, open heart. Resilience is found not in control, but in your willingness to respond rather than react.

<u>Creativity</u>

Creativity thrives in moments of spontaneity. When you silence the inner critic and let go of the need for perfection, your imagination flows more freely. Whether you are solving a problem, expressing emotion, or engaging with others, spontaneity opens the door to original thought and authentic expression. In this space, creativity becomes not just something you *"do,"* but something you *are*. It flows through your choices, your voice, your presence.

When you allow spontaneity into your life, you invite a kind of psychological liberation. You begin to trust that your responses do not have to be rehearsed, that your heart can be a trustworthy guide, and that some of the most profound growth happens when you stop scripting and start *living*. Spontaneity, when grounded in self-awareness, becomes a superpower, fueling your adaptability, deepening your joy, and unlocking the full potential of your creative, resilient self.

How Rigid Control Can Create Emotional Resistance And Disconnect

Rigid control is often mistaken for strength, but beneath its surface lies fear, fear of uncertainty, of being vulnerable, of not having all the answers. While structure and discipline can serve you, control becomes rigid when it is used to suppress emotions, avoid discomfort, or manage your life from a place of anxiety rather than alignment. Over time, this tight grip on life creates more than just stress, it creates *emotional resistance* and *disconnect*.

<u>Emotional Resistance</u>

When you strive to control every outcome, you begin to resist the natural flow of emotion. You avoid feeling what is uncomfortable, grief, fear, sadness, or even joy, because these feelings cannot be neatly managed, but what you resist does not disappear. It lingers beneath the surface, building tension and inner conflict. Emotional resistance hardens your heart, creates internal pressure, and silences your deeper needs. It is like trying to hold your breath indefinitely, eventually, something inside you demands release.

<u>Disconnect from Self and Others</u>

Rigid control also disconnects you from your authentic self. When you constantly curate your emotions or suppress your impulses, you lose touch with your inner truth. You stop trusting your instincts. You second-guess your voice. You start to *perform life* rather than *live it*. In relationships, this disconnection becomes even more painful. Others sense the guardedness, the distance, the lack of spontaneity or emotional availability, and true intimacy becomes difficult to access. You become disconnected not only from yourself but also from the people you love, the present moment, and the joy of being human.

<u>The Path Back: Softening the Grip</u>

Healing begins when you gently loosen the grip. When you dare to breathe, feel, and let go of the need to be in control all the time. This does not mean you become careless, it means you become *courageous*. You begin to move with life, not against it. You allow emotions to arise without judgment. You practice presence rather than perfection. Spontaneity invites you into this space. It asks you to trust your heart, release the script, and show up fully. As you do, resistance melts, connection deepens, and life becomes something you *feel*, not just manage.

Letting go of rigid control is not losing power, it is reclaiming your freedom. It is returning to your heart, where presence, connection, and emotional truth live.

Spontaneity As A Form Of Emotional Self-Trust And Relational Vibrancy

Spontaneity is more than a carefree moment, it is a profound act of **emotional self-trust**. It signals that you are safe enough within yourself to show up unfiltered, unrehearsed, and real. When you live spontaneously, you are no longer driven by fear of how you will be perceived or by the need to perfect every response. Instead, you allow your *inner truth* to guide your actions in the moment. This kind of freedom requires trust, trust in your instincts, in your emotional intelligence, and in your ability to navigate what arises without controlling it. You are not reacting out of habit or fear; you are responding from presence and authenticity. In this way, spontaneity becomes a radical declaration: *I trust myself enough to be seen as I am.*

Emotional Self-Trust

When you act spontaneously, you are honouring the signals of your body, the rhythms of your breath, and the whispers of your heart. You are giving yourself permission to *feel* and *respond* without delay or disguise. Over time, this builds an unshakable sense of self-trust, you begin to rely on your own emotional cues as sources of wisdom, not threats to manage or control. Spontaneity teaches you that you do not need to pre-approve every part of yourself before sharing it with the world. You learn to trust that what arises in the moment, when grounded in awareness, is valid, valuable, and often exactly what is needed.

Relational Vibrancy

Spontaneity also brings life to your relationships. When you allow yourself to respond with warmth, humour, tenderness, or creativity *in the moment*, you create space for genuine connection. These unscripted interactions spark laughter, intimacy, and unexpected joy. They remind others (and yourself) that love does not live in perfection, it lives in presence. Relational vibrancy comes from shared aliveness. Spontaneous gestures, honest words, and playful energy open doorways to trust and emotional safety. Others feel you are not just performing for them, they feel you *with* them.

In you heart's language, spontaneity says: I am safe to be myself. I trust what lives in me. I trust what connects us, and when that energy flows, it lights up your inner world and breathes life into your relationships. Spontaneity becomes not just a moment, but a way of being that celebrates both your individuality and your connection to others.

Ancient And Modern Perspectives: Intuition, Play, And Present-Moment Awareness

Across cultures and centuries, both ancient wisdom and modern psychology have pointed to the same truth: your heart knows how to live. Whether in the rituals of indigenous peoples, the philosophies of Eastern traditions, or the emerging science of emotional intelligence, there is a shared reverence for the power of **intuition, play**, and **presence,** the very qualities that spontaneity awakens in you.

Intuition: The Inner Compass

Across time and cultures, people have spoken of a deeper wisdom that does not come from logic alone but arises from within, the quiet voice of the heart, the knowing beneath words, the subtle truth felt in the body. This is intuition, your inner compass. Ancient traditions saw intuition as a sacred form of guidance, a bridge between the seen and unseen. Shamans, healers, and mystics trusted it as the whisper of spirit, the language of the soul, directing them toward alignment and harmony. Today, modern neuroscience confirms what the ancients knew: intuition is not guesswork, but your brain and body's extraordinary ability to synthesise patterns of experience, emotion, and memory into instant, embodied insight.

When you act from intuition, you are not dismissing reason, you are including a deeper form of intelligence, one that draws on both conscious and unconscious awareness. You may feel it as a surge of energy, a tightening in your gut, a wave of peace, or a gentle nudge in a certain direction. These signals are your body's way of speaking the truth your mind has not yet fully named. Spontaneity and intuition are deeply connected. When you allow yourself to act in the moment, without overthinking, you make space for your intuition to speak.

Spontaneity is the act of trusting what arises in real time, rather than censoring it with fear or perfectionism. It is the courage to say yes to your inner compass, to step forward even when the path is not fully mapped. The more you practice honouring these subtle signals, the more fluent you become in the language of your own intuition. You begin to trust yourself more deeply, to move through life with a balance of courage and grace, and to discover that transformation often begins not with careful planning, but with a single heart-led response to the present moment.

Play: The Gateway to Joy and Creativity

In many ancient traditions, play was not treated as trivial, it was sacred. Indigenous cultures wove play into rituals, storytelling, and community life, recognising it as a way to bond, to learn, and to honour the spirit of life itself. Children were seen as teachers of this wisdom, reminding adults that joy, curiosity, and wonder are not distractions from the spiritual path but essential to it. Your childlike spirit was understood as a sacred part of you, free, wise, and naturally attuned to the divine flow. Modern psychology now echoes this ancient truth. Play has been shown to reduce stress, lower cortisol, and improve mental health. It strengthens emotional resilience, creates connection, and awakens creativity by loosening the rigid grip of seriousness and perfectionism. When you play, your brain shifts into a state of openness, imagination, and flow, allowing you to see solutions and possibilities you could never access through logic alone.

Spontaneity is the door that opens into play. It gives you permission to be silly, to laugh freely, to try something new without worrying about outcome or appearance. In these moments, you are liberated from the need to perform, to prove, or to achieve. You are simply being, authentic, present, alive. This lightheartedness is not superficial; it is deeply healing. Your nervous system softens, your heart expands, and you reconnect with others in ways that are unguarded and true.

Play is also a creative force. When you allow yourself to engage in unstructured play, whether through art, movement, music, or simple fun, you spark your imagination and rekindle your curiosity. Innovation, after all, is born from play. Many breakthroughs in science, art, and philosophy have emerged not from rigid effort, but from moments of wonder and experimentation. To play is to return to your essence. It is to remember that joy is not an afterthought or a luxury, but a vital ingredient in a wholehearted life. In play, you reclaim your wholeness, you strengthen your resilience, and you discover that joy itself is a source of wisdom.

<u>Present-Moment Awareness: The Sacred Now</u>

Across the world's great wisdom traditions, the sacred power of the present moment has been honoured as the place where life truly unfolds. Buddhist meditation teaches the art of returning to the breath, anchoring your awareness in the here and now. Christian mystics spoke of *practicing the presence of God*, finding holiness in each ordinary act of daily life. Sufi prayer and whirling brought seekers into direct communion with the divine by dissolving thought and surrendering to the immediacy of presence. Each of these practices pointed to a timeless truth: the present moment is not just a point in time, it is the meeting place of your body, mind, and spirit with eternity itself.

In the modern world, this ancient wisdom has been woven into practices like mindfulness-based stress reduction (MBSR), which teaches people to regulate stress and anxiety by training attention back into the now. Cognitive-behavioural approaches also emphasise awareness, showing how being present interrupts cycles of rumination, projection, and reactivity. Scientific research continues to confirm what mystics have always known, that the simple act of being present reduces stress, strengthens emotional regulation, and deepens your sense of wellbeing.

Spontaneity is born from this presence. You cannot be spontaneous yesterday or tomorrow, it can only emerge in your now. The more you centre yourself in the present, the more open you are to life's invitations. Instead of rehearsing, predicting, or controlling, you begin to trust what arises and respond with freshness and flow. This does not mean abandoning wisdom or discernment, but rather allowing your heart to meet the moment as it is, free from the weight of old stories or the pressure of imagined futures.

In this state of presence, your responses shift. You no longer act from fear, habit, or perfectionism. Instead, you act from clarity, authenticity, and truth. This is the sacred gift of the now: it clears away the fog of distraction and reveals the deep simplicity of life unfolding. When you live in this awareness, even the smallest moments, drinking tea, hearing a bird sing, smiling at a stranger, become infused with meaning and possibility. Spontaneity is, therefore, not recklessness, but the flowering of presence. It is life moving through you without resistance. The more you cultivate awareness of the sacred now, the more you find yourself saying *"yes"* to life, not from compulsion, but from connection.

Bridging Timeless Wisdom with Today's Heart

The ancient and the modern converge within you. Your body carries the imprints of generations before you, ancestral memory woven into your DNA. Your heart carries an even deeper knowing, the quiet wisdom that echoes across time, beyond language or culture. When you allow yourself the gift of spontaneity, you are not being careless, you are honouring this lineage of life, this river of wisdom that has always known how to adapt, create, and thrive. To live spontaneously is to embody the truth that joy, connection, and healing do not need to be earned or postponed. They are not rewards for perfection or productivity. They are your birthright, available in the sacred simplicity of showing up, here and now, fully alive. Each time you act from your heart without overthinking, you remember that aliveness is not found in control, but in participation, in saying *yes* to the dance of life as it unfolds.

Spontaneity, then, is not just a passing moment of impulse, it is a way of being. It is a rhythm that honours both heart and mind, spirit and science, past and present. When you embrace it, you live in harmony with what has always been true: that life was never meant to be fully scripted, measured, or contained. It was always meant to be experienced. When you lean into spontaneity, you bridge timeless wisdom with today's heart. You bring together the grounding of the ancients with the freedom of modern insight, and you discover that joy is not somewhere you go, it is something you allow. It is the courage to be unguarded, to let laughter bubble up, to try without certainty, to create without guarantee. This is your soul's reminder: life is not something to master, it is something to meet. It is not a puzzle to solve, but a path to walk, and each time you let go, each time you move with spontaneity, you step more deeply into the truth that you are not here merely to control life, you are here to live it.

The Neurobiology Of Joy And How Playful Spontaneity Rebalances The Nervous System

Joy is not a luxury emotion, it is a *biological necessity*. From both a scientific and heart-centred perspective, joy is medicine. It nourishes your body, soothes your mind, and brings coherence to your nervous system. One of the most natural ways to access joy is through **playful spontaneity,** those unscripted, light-hearted moments where you feel safe, present, and free to be yourself. When you engage in spontaneous play, laughter, movement, or unguarded creativity, you are doing far more than "*having fun*", you are actually rewiring your nervous system for balance, connection, and resilience.

The Science of Joy: What Happens in the Brain

Joyful experiences, especially those that are spontaneous, activate several key neurochemical systems in the brain:

- **Dopamine**, the "*reward*" neurotransmitter, gives you a sense of motivation and pleasure. It is what makes your moments of play feel energising and satisfying.

- **Oxytocin**, the "*connection*" hormone, is released when you experience trust, bonding, and laughter, creating feelings of warmth and safety, especially in spontaneous interactions with others.

- **Endorphins**, the body's natural painkillers, flood your system during laughter or physical play, reducing stress and promoting emotional ease.

- **Serotonin**, associated with mood stability and calm, increases as you shift out of worry and into joyful presence.

Together, these neurochemicals help calm your amygdala (your brain's fear centre), regulate cortisol (your stress hormone), and promote a sense of grounded emotional safety.

Rebalancing the Nervous System Through Playful Presence

In times of stress, trauma, or chronic overthinking, your body's nervous system becomes dysregulated. You may find yourself stuck in **fight**, **flight**, or **freeze** states, hypervigilant, shut down, or emotionally overwhelmed.

Playful spontaneity helps shift you into a **ventral vagal state,** the parasympathetic *"rest and connect"* mode of your nervous system. In this state, your heart rate slows, your breath deepens, and your body feels safe. You are more able to connect with others, think clearly, and access compassion, for yourself and those around you.

Playful spontaneity is a gentle way of reminding your nervous system that you are not in danger, that life can be joyful, and that presence is safe.

Why This Matters for Emotional Healing

In the *Heart Unbound* journey, we often explore deep emotions, grief, fear, vulnerability, forgiveness. These are vital, healing experiences, but joy is just as sacred. It does not cancel the hard things, it *completes* them. It reclaims the light. It restores what trauma, stress, and rigidity try to take away: your ability to feel free and connected. Spontaneous joy is not about pretending everything is fine. It is about finding the courage to *feel fully*, to say yes to life, and to welcome the moments that bring lightness back to your body and soul.

Joy as Your Birthright

Playful spontaneity is not childish, it is deeply human. It is a sign that your nervous system trusts the moment, that your heart feels safe enough to shine. Every time you allow yourself to laugh, dance, sing, or simply respond with unfiltered aliveness, you are healing. You are rebalancing your system. You are saying yes to joy, not as a fleeting emotion, but as a way of being. Let this part of your *Heart Unbound* journey remind you that joy is not the reward at the end, it is the medicine along the way, and it lives in spontaneity, waiting to rise the moment you let go and let your heart lead.

"Yes, and…" Improv Flow Exercise

Spontaneity thrives when you release control and enter the playful unknown. This activity is designed to help you practice openness, presence, and collaboration while letting go of the need to plan or be perfect.

Instructions:

1. In pairs (or small groups), take turns creating a spontaneous story together.

   - The first person begins with a simple sentence: *"One morning, I woke up to find a dragon in my backyard…"*

   - The next person responds by starting with *"Yes, and…"* before adding their own unexpected twist.

   - Continue building the story this way, each person saying *"Yes, and…"* before adding their contribution. The story might be silly, profound, or completely surprising, allow it to unfold without judgment.

2. Keep going for at least 5 minutes, staying with the flow of the story instead of trying to control its direction. The only rule is to keep saying *"Yes, and…"* as a way of honouring what has been offered and adding to it.

Debrief Reflection Questions:

1. *What did it feel like to not know what came next?*

2. *Did you laugh, relax, or feel a sense of freedom?*

3. *Was it hard to resist the urge to control or "make sense" of the story?*

4. *What does this teach you about trust, presence, and collaboration in real life?*

This exercise shows you that spontaneity does not come from knowing what is ahead, it comes from allowing life (and others) to surprise you. Saying *"Yes, and…"* is not just about improv theatre, it is a heart-based practice of acceptance and creativity. It teaches you to receive what is offered, affirm it, and build upon it with your unique expression.

When you carry this mindset into your daily life, challenges feel lighter, relationships become more playful, and opportunities expand. Life becomes less about control and more about flow, reminding you that joy and connection are born in the unscripted moments.

Case Study Discussion: Penny and Milo's Journey

Milo and Penny had been together for years, and while their love was strong, they felt a certain routine had settled into their relationship. They wanted more excitement and spontaneity in their life and really wanted to reignite their connection. We spent a couple of sessions discussing options and they made a pact to fill their lives with unexpected adventures. They made a conscientious effort to move away from their plans and let spontaneity guide them. They explored new places, tried thrilling activities, and laughed like children. With each spontaneous moment, their bond deepened.

A beautiful and unexpected outcome was that they discovered hidden sides of each other, supporting and encouraging one another to step outside their comfort zones. From impromptu road trips to surprising date nights, they loved the joy of shared experiences. Spontaneity breathed new life into their relationship, sparking passion and deepening their love. They learned to trust and rely on each other more in the face of the unknown. They told me that their laughter became the soundtrack of their journey, and their hearts danced to the rhythm of spontaneity (to quote Milo).

Milo and Penny's story is a beautiful testament to the power of embracing spontaneity into a relationship. It rejuvenated their connection, deepened their love, and created cherished memories. By stepping out of their routines and embracing the unexpected, they discovered a deeper bond and an unwavering sense of adventure. This embrace of spontaneity can be replicated in every other part of your life and all you have to do is choose to do it!

Reflective Exercise: Milo and Penny's Journey

Here are four profound and reflective questions inspired by Milo and Penny's story to help you engage with your own journey into being spontaneous:

1. **Where in your life or relationships have routines replaced wonder, and what might become possible if you let go of control and welcomed the unexpected?** Consider the areas of your life that

feel flat or overly structured. What would it feel like to soften your grip and invite more aliveness?

2. **What would it be like for you to choose shared adventure over predictable plans? How might that deepen trust, joy, or connection with someone you love?** Reflect on how your relationships could shift if you let playfulness and presence guide you instead of habit and certainty.

3. **How often do you allow your heart, rather than your schedule, to lead the way? What spontaneous experience could you say yes to this week?** Give yourself permission to follow a moment of inspiration. What is calling to you that you have been putting off or overthinking?

4. **What hidden parts of yourself, or someone close to you, might come alive if you embraced play, exploration, and unfiltered presence?** Let go of needing to know the outcome. Imagine who you might meet within yourself, and in your relationships, when you show up spontaneously and wholeheartedly.

These questions are your invitation to step beyond routine, into a life that breathes, laughs, and dances with possibility. Let your heart lead.

Affirmations For You – (Heart Whispers)

Affirmations have the power to quiet the noise of doubt, open the doorway to self-trust, and draw you back into the wisdom of your heart. When practised daily, they nurture an inner dialogue based in love and truth, helping you live each day more aligned with who you truly are. I invite you to repeat silently or write:

- *I let go of plans and embrace the spontaneity of life.*

- *I seek new adventures and embrace the unexpected.*

- *I follow my heart's desires without overthinking.*

- *I allow myself to be open to spontaneous opportunities.*

- *I find freedom and joy in living in the present moment.*

- *I embrace spontaneity as a catalyst for personal growth.*

Spontaneity Sparks List Exercise

Spontaneity is like a spark, it lights up your day, shifts your energy, and invites joy where you least expect it. By making a list of playful, unplanned activities, you are giving yourself permission to step out of routine and into possibility.

Step 1: Create Your List

Write down at least **10 spontaneous, joyful activities** you can explore this week. These do not need to be big or dramatic; even the smallest moments of spontaneity can shift your heart and mind. Examples might include:

- Giving a random compliment to a stranger or friend

- Taking an impromptu dance break in the middle of your day

- Trying a new food or café you have never visited before

- Exploring a different walking path on your way home

- Saying *"yes"* to something you would normally decline

- Writing a quick love note or message of appreciation and sending it without overthinking

- Singing out loud to your favourite song

- Pausing to watch the sunset without rushing on

- Trying a playful activity you haven't done in years (drawing, skipping, or playing a game)

- Doing something kind for someone anonymously

Step 2: Choose One Daily

Each day, pick one activity from your list. Allow yourself to follow it without planning too much or worrying about outcomes. Notice how it feels in your body and in your heart when you give yourself this freedom.

Step 3: Reflect

At the end of the day, journal on what you experienced. Ask yourself:

- *How did this spontaneous act shift my mood or energy?*

- *Did it spark creativity, joy, or connection?*

- *What surprised me most about letting go of control in this way?*

Spontaneity is not about chaos, it is about opening to life's invitations. By intentionally practising small, joyful moments of spontaneity, you train your heart to relax, your mind to expand, and your spirit to remember how free it really is.

Closing Reflection

Spontaneity is the language of your free and trusting heart. It does not demand recklessness or chaos; it simply invites you to loosen the grip of fear and control. It whispers: *you are safe enough to let go.* When you step outside the safety of routine and open yourself to the unknown, you create space for life to meet you with gifts you could never have planned, moments of laughter, wonder, intimacy, and joy that arrive unannounced and unforgettable.

To live spontaneously is to say *yes* to presence. It is to welcome joy when it knocks at your door, to follow creativity when it sparks, and to connect with others in ways that are genuine and unscripted. In these moments, you learn to trust your instincts and to respond with courage, clarity, and heart. You begin to notice how your spirit expands when you choose flow over rigidity, and how life becomes lighter when you no longer demand certainty before moving forward.

Spontaneity is not about abandoning responsibility, it is about reclaiming aliveness. It is the quiet courage to show up as you are, without overthinking, without rehearsing, without fear of imperfection. In the pauses between plans, in the laughter that erupts unexpectedly, in the conversations that wander into new territory, you discover parts of yourself that routine cannot uncover. You see dimensions of those you love that can only be revealed in the raw, unscripted moments of life.

Let this reflection remind you: you do not need anyone's permission to be playful, passionate, or fully alive. The adventure you long for is not waiting outside of you, it already lives within. All it takes is one breath, one brave release of control, one unguarded *yes* to open the door. So breathe deeply. Loosen your grip. Trust the rhythm of your beautifully spontaneous heart, and let life, in all its unpredictability, remind you again and again of the joy of simply being alive.

28 – REFLECTION

Your Opening Reflection

Invitation to Pause and Honour Your Journey - As you arrive in this chapter, I invite you to pause and recognise the courage it took to walk this far. Reflection is not about measuring progress, but about listening to the quiet truths your heart has revealed along the way. Every moment of insight, every breath of stillness, every tear or smile has been a step home to yourself. Allow this space to become a mirror, showing you how far you have come and how deeply you have grown. Honour your journey, not for its perfection, but for its honesty, resilience, and love.

- "What has shifted in your heart over this journey?"

- "What is one moment that you will carry with you forever?"

- "Which practice, teaching, or moment felt most alive for you, and why?"

- "Where in your life do you now feel a greater sense of freedom, clarity, or belonging?"

- "What part of yourself have you reconnected with or rediscovered along the way?"

- "If your heart could speak one truth from this journey, what would it say?"

Let these questions open the doorway into presence. Every answer you give, whether in words, sensations, or silence, is a bridge between where you are and where you are going.

Learning Objectives

The learning objectives are included here to give you a clear focus for this chapter, ensuring that each practice you explore moves you closer to mastering the skills, insights, and heart-led awareness that will enrich your life well beyond the program. By the end of this chapter, you will:

- Develop emotional intelligence through structured self-reflection

- Honour personal growth, insights, and transformation from the 28-day journey

- Learn to integrate heart-centred practices into everyday life

- Set heart-led intentions for future emotional development and authentic living

Core Emotional Domains

The core emotional intelligence domains covered here are essential because they form the foundation for lasting heart connection, guiding you to deepen self-awareness, regulate emotions, build resilience, and strengthen the mind-body bond throughout your Heart Unbound journey.

- **Self-Awareness:** Reflection begins with noticing what has shifted within you. You become more attuned to your thoughts, emotions, and patterns, gaining insight into how you have grown and where you still hold resistance. This self-awareness helps you recognise your journey with clarity and compassion, not judgment.

- **Self-Reflection:** Taking time to pause and look inward allows you to make sense of your experiences. You begin to connect the dots, between your past and present, your choices and values. Through reflection, you learn to hold space for both your breakthroughs and your imperfections with honesty and grace.

- **Emotional Integration:** Emotions are not meant to be isolated or buried, they are meant to be understood and integrated. Reflection helps you acknowledge the full spectrum of what you have felt and lived. By weaving these emotional threads together, you create coherence within yourself and grow into greater wholeness.

- **Empathy and Compassion:** As you reflect on your own journey, you naturally open to the experiences of others. You begin to see that everyone is carrying their own story, their own struggles and triumphs.

This awareness cultivates empathy and deepens your ability to meet both yourself and others with kindness.

- **Purpose and Values Alignment:** Reflection brings you back to what matters most. It realigns you with your inner compass, your values, your purpose, your truth. From this place of alignment, you can move forward with greater intention, choosing a path that honours both who you are and who you are becoming.

"Reflection – Integrating, Honouring, And Continuing Your Heart Journey"

Reflection is the final chapter of any meaningful journey, and the first page of the next. It is the sacred pause that allows you to breathe, integrate, and truly see how far you have come. Without reflection, even the most powerful experiences can pass unnoticed. However, when you take the time to look inward with honesty and compassion, experience transforms into wisdom, and moments become milestones.

Reflection strengthens your **emotional intelligence** by inviting you to move beyond reaction into conscious understanding. It helps you trace the emotional patterns that shaped your choices, the shifts in your self-awareness, and the quiet inner awakenings that have taken root along the way. Through this process, you begin to internalise the growth you have undergone, not just as something you *did*, but as something you have *become*.

In reflection, you give your heart a voice. You listen not only to what happened, but to what it meant. You begin to see your resilience, your courage, your tenderness, and your truth. You allow yourself to feel gratitude, grieve what's been released, and honour the parts of you that stepped forward in new ways, and most importantly, you use that insight to set **aligned intentions,** intentions that do not come from pressure or fear, but from clarity and purpose. These are heart-led intentions that help you move forward in a way that feels true to who you are now, not who you used to be.

Reflection is not just about looking back. It is about looking within, and from there, stepping into the next chapter with grounded wisdom, emotional depth, and an open heart. This is the moment where your journey becomes part of you, woven into your being, carried forward not as memory, but as transformation.

The Neuroscience Of Reflection: How Pausing Strengthens Neural Integration

In a world that urges you to keep moving, stay productive, and push forward, choosing to pause might feel uncomfortable, or even unnecessary. However, neuroscience, like your heart, knows the truth: **reflection is not a luxury, it is a biological and emotional necessity.** When you pause to reflect, you are not just thinking about your experiences, you are changing your brain. You are helping it integrate the stories you have lived, the emotions you have felt, and the growth you have undergone. This process is called **neural integration**, and it is essential for lasting healing and transformation.

<u>What is Happening in Your Brain When You Reflect?</u>

When you pause to reflect, powerful processes unfold within your brain. You engage the **prefrontal cortex**, the region responsible for self-awareness, emotional regulation, empathy, and future planning. This is where you begin to step outside of autopilot, observing your thoughts and feelings instead of being ruled by them. Reflection strengthens your ability to choose how you respond, rather than being swept away by old patterns.

At the same time, the **default mode network (DMN)** becomes active. This interconnected system allows you to revisit memories, explore meaning, and imagine new possibilities. It is here that your brain weaves together past experiences with present insight, helping you see connections that may have been hidden in the busyness of daily life. When you reflect, your brain is literally rewiring itself. Neural pathways associated with mindfulness, compassion, and perspective-taking grow stronger. Stress pathways begin to quiet, and your ability to regulate emotions improves. Over time, this repeated practice builds resilience, clarity, and wisdom.

In essence, reflection allows your brain to integrate experience into understanding. You begin to link what you have felt with what you have learned, bridging the gap between who you once were and who you are becoming. This is not just a mental process, it is the deepening of your emotional intelligence. You are learning to respond with clarity, compassion, and intention, instead of reacting from fear or habit. Reflection is where growth takes root. It is where insight turns into transformation, and where the wisdom of your journey becomes part of the person you are choosing to be.

Creating Coherence: The Power of Neural Integration

Throughout this journey, you have lived many different moments, some filled with joy, some marked by pain, and others still unfolding in quiet ways. Left unexamined, these experiences can remain fragmented, scattered across your inner landscape like unconnected puzzle pieces. Reflection is the practice that gathers them together, weaving them into a meaningful whole. When you pause to reflect, you bring your **thoughts, feelings, memories, and insights into alignment**. This process is known as **neural integration**, the harmonising of different parts of your brain so that your inner world becomes coherent rather than chaotic. Instead of being pulled in many directions by conflicting emotions or scattered memories, you begin to see the larger picture of your own growth.

Neuroscience shows that integration strengthens the connections between your prefrontal cortex (awareness and regulation), your limbic system (emotions and memory), and your body's felt sense of experience. This creates a state of **coherence**, where your mind, heart, and body work in synergy rather than opposition. The result is not only greater clarity but also greater resilience, you can hold complexity without being overwhelmed. Through reflection, your story shifts from a collection of isolated events to a narrative infused with **meaning and wisdom**. You begin to see patterns, lessons, and truths that may have been hidden in the noise. This understanding deepens your self-trust: you recognise that even the painful moments have shaped you, and that every step has been part of your becoming.

Coherence is not about perfection; it is about wholeness. It is about allowing all parts of your experience, light and shadow, triumph and struggle—to belong, and to find their place within the larger mosaic of your life. When you practice reflection, you give yourself the gift of integration. From this grounded sense of wholeness, you can move forward with greater compassion, stability, and courage.

What Happens When You Pause?

When you pause, even for a few breaths, you create a profound shift within your body and mind. Instead of running on autopilot or being carried by stress and distraction, your nervous system gently transitions into its **parasympathetic state**, the *"rest-and-digest"* response. This is the physiological space of **calm, safety, and restoration**. In this state, your heart rate slows and steadies, your muscles release tension, and your breath naturally deepens. These simple yet powerful changes signal to your body that you are safe, allowing your mind to soften its grip on survival mode. As your inner world quiets, your brain becomes more receptive to insight, creativity, and self-awareness.

Science shows that during a pause, the **coherence between your heart and brain increases**. Instead of operating in conflict, these two powerful centres of intelligence begin to synchronise. Your heart sends signals of steadiness to your brain, helping you regulate emotions, while your brain supports clear thinking and balanced perspective. You literally become more attuned, able to listen with compassion, feel with clarity, and think with presence. Pausing also allows your **default mode network**, the part of the brain responsible for reflection, self-understanding, and meaning-making, to gently awaken. This is why moments of silence often bring sudden clarity, creative ideas, or the memory of something important you had overlooked.

On a deeper level, pausing is an act of alignment. It reconnects you to the present moment, where your body, mind, and spirit can finally work together rather than pulling in different directions. You become more grounded in your truth, more open to possibility, and more aligned with your heart's quiet wisdom. The pause does not need to be long, a single mindful breath can be enough to shift you from reactivity into awareness. Over time, the more you practice pausing, the more you train your nervous system to find safety, your mind to find clarity, and your heart to find presence.

<u>You Are the Integration</u>

Reflection is not just something you practice, it is something you embody. It is not an activity separate from your life, but the very process through which you become who you truly are. Reflection is the meeting point of your **emotional growth and neurological transformation**, where your experiences, insights, and feelings weave themselves into wisdom. When you pause and reflect, you create the conditions for integration. You are not merely collecting lessons, you are allowing them to sink deeper, to shape the way you see yourself and the way you show up in the world. Every insight, every tear, every moment of joy becomes a thread, woven into the fabric of your becoming. Reflection is how you turn experiences into meaning, challenges into resilience, and knowledge into embodied truth.

So, the next time you feel the urge to keep pushing forward, chasing the next goal or rushing through the moment, remember this: **the pause is powerful**. Growth does not only happen in action; it blossoms in stillness. It is in the quiet spaces of reflection that your transformation takes root.

- **In the stillness, you are healing.** Your nervous system recalibrates, your emotions soften, and your body remembers safety.

- **In the reflection, you are rewiring.** Your brain forms new pathways of clarity, resilience, and compassion.

- **In the awareness, you are becoming whole.** You no longer split yourself between past and future, doubt and desire, you come home to the present, to yourself.

Integration is not a final destination but a way of living. It is the art of carrying your lessons into each breath, each choice, each connection. This is how your heart becomes unbound, not in grand gestures, but in simple, steady moments of return. One breath. One insight. One pause at a time.

Reflection As A Tool For Long-Term Emotional Growth And Heart-Led Decision-Making

Reflection is not simply a backward glance, it is a powerful tool that shapes your future. When you take time to pause and reflect, you do more than revisit your experiences, you activate your inner wisdom. You begin to see your journey through the lens of growth, not just memory, and that shift is what transforms reflection into a lifelong resource for emotional intelligence and heart-led living.

<u>Emotional Growth Through Honest Reflection</u>

Every emotional experience you have, joy, sorrow, fear, excitement, carries within it a lesson, a message, a whisper from your heart, but these insights often go unnoticed in the busyness of your life. Reflection gives you the space to return, to feel, to understand. It invites you to explore not just *what happened*, but *how it shaped you*. Through regular, compassionate reflection, you begin to identify your emotional patterns: how you respond under pressure, what triggers your inner critic, where your wounds still ache, and what opens your heart.

This awareness does not come from judging yourself, it comes from witnessing yourself with honesty and care. This is how emotional maturity is born, not by avoiding your feelings, but by understanding them and choosing to grow from them. Over time, this process strengthens your emotional resilience, your capacity for empathy, and your ability to meet life with grace rather than reactivity. Your heart becomes wiser, your responses more intentional, and your self-trust more deeply grounded.

Heart-Led Decision-Making Begins with Inner Clarity

When you reflect with presence and purpose, you begin to align your decisions not with fear or habit, but with your **core values**, your **authentic self**, and the quiet knowing of your heart. This is the essence of heart-led decision-making: choosing based on what feels true, not just what seems expected. Reflection helps you ask the deeper questions:

- *Is this choice in alignment with who I am becoming?*

- *Am I acting from fear or from freedom?*

- *Will this decision bring me closer to the life I want to live?*

These questions guide you away from autopilot and toward **conscious, values-based action**. They help you make decisions that nourish your emotional wellbeing and deepen your integrity, not just in moments of ease, but in times of challenge and change. When you learn to trust the wisdom that arises in reflection, you begin to lead your life from within. Your choices become anchored, not just reactive. Your direction becomes heart-led, not externally driven.

Reflection Is the Bridge

Reflection is the bridge between your past and your potential. It is where healing becomes growth, where insight becomes action, and where experience becomes wisdom. The more you return to yourself through reflection, the more empowered and aligned your life becomes. Let reflection be your quiet superpower, the space where you meet yourself honestly, listen deeply, and choose your next step not from pressure, but from purpose. *This is how you become emotionally free. This is how your heart becomes your compass. This is how you live, not just wisely, but fully.*

Differentiating Rumination From Healthy Contemplation

Reflection is one of the most powerful tools you have for emotional healing and growth, but not all forms of looking inward are helpful. To truly free your heart, it is important to recognise the difference between **rumination** and **healthy contemplation**. While both involve thinking about your experiences, only one leads to peace, insight, and transformation.

<u>What Happens When You Ruminate?</u>

When you ruminate, your thoughts loop in circles. You replay events, question yourself endlessly, or fixate on what went wrong. Rumination tends to be:

- Harsh, self-critical, or full of regret

- Focused on the past without direction

- Driven by fear, guilt, or anxiety

- Emotionally draining and stuck

In this state, you are not learning from the past, you are reliving it. Rumination keeps you emotionally stuck, reinforcing patterns of self-doubt and often worsening your mental and physical wellbeing. It feels heavy, stagnant, and closed.

<u>What Does Healthy Contemplation Look Like?</u>

When you engage in healthy contemplation, you reflect with purpose and compassion. You ask gentle, curious questions like:

- *What am I learning about myself through this?*

- *How did this moment shape me?*

- *What do I need to release or forgive?*

Contemplation invites you to notice without judgment. You begin to understand, integrate, and honour your emotional truth. You give space to both pain and growth, and from that space, you create meaningful direction forward. Contemplation brings movement. It opens your heart, rather than closing it down.

<u>Why This Matters on Your Heart Unbound Journey</u>

Throughout this program, you have touched many deep and tender parts of yourself. You have remembered, released, and awakened, but now, in reflection, you are invited to tread gently. How you look back matters as much as what you look back on. Reflection can be a doorway to wisdom or a trap of self-criticism. The difference lies in the posture of your heart. When you choose to look back with compassion instead of judgment, you begin to see your journey not as a series of flaws or mistakes, but as the sacred unfolding of becoming.

Every choice, even the ones you wish had been different, carries a lesson that has shaped your growth. Every moment of vulnerability has been an initiation into greater strength and authenticity. Reflection, then, is not about perfecting your past but about honouring the wisdom it has given you. This is the heart's invitation: to release the loop of rumination and step into the clarity of contemplation. Rumination keeps you circling the same pain, replaying the same doubts. Contemplation, on the other hand, invites you to pause, listen, and ask, *What is this moment here to teach me?* In doing so, you transform memory into meaning and struggle into strength.

By reflecting in this way, you give yourself the gift of emotional freedom. The past no longer defines you, it informs you. You learn to carry its lessons lightly, with grace, allowing them to guide rather than weigh you down. In this process, trust in your inner wisdom deepens. You begin to see that your heart has always been whispering the way forward, and that whisper becomes your compass. This is why reflection matters. It anchors your transformation. It helps you embody your insights, integrate your healing, and align with the deepest truth of who you are. In choosing reflection over rumination, you step into the freedom of living from your heart, not your history.

A Gentle Check-In

The next time your thoughts pull you into the past, pause and ask yourself: *"Am I looping, or am I listening?"* If you are looping, soften. If you are listening, keep going, with kindness. Let your reflection be a safe space, not a battleground. This is how your heart becomes unbound, not by repeating the pain, but by meeting it with understanding and choosing to grow from it.

Integrating Past Lessons To Build Future Resilience

Resilience does not mean you have never been hurt. It means you have allowed your pain to teach you something, and you have chosen to grow from it. As you reach this final stage of the *Heart Unbound* journey, you are invited to reflect not just on what you have been through, but on **how you have emerged**. The process of *integration* is what transforms experience into strength, and memory into wisdom.

You have faced emotions, truths, and turning points, some of them uncomfortable, all of them meaningful, but reflection is what allows you to hold these moments in your hands and ask, *"What did this teach me? Who have I become because of it?"* This is how you build resilience, not by forgetting the past, but by **weaving it into your foundation**.

Why Integration Matters

There have been moments when you felt heavy with uncertainty, weighed down by doubt, or caught in the tangle of old patterns, and there have also been moments when your heart lifted, when your breath deepened, when you touched a strength or softness within you that surprised you. Both are part of your journey. Both hold meaning. If you rush past these experiences, they scatter like fragments of a story left unfinished. They remain unanchored, unable to guide or sustain you, but when you pause to reflect, something powerful begins to happen: the fragments start to form a whole. You begin to notice the threads that connect your pain to your healing, your challenges to your growth, your fears to your courage.

Integration is not about erasing the past or fixing every wound. It is about honouring what has been, reclaiming the lessons, and recognising that nothing was wasted. The heartbreaks, the breakthroughs, the struggles, and the joys all become woven into a tapestry that tells the truth of who you are becoming. To integrate is to gather your pieces and place them gently where they belong, not tucked away in shame or regret, but honoured as part of your strength. It is the process of seeing yourself clearly, of realising that your journey has shaped you in ways that are both tender and resilient. When you integrate, you no longer live in fragments. You stand whole. You carry your past not as a burden, but as a foundation. You live with greater clarity, steadiness, and compassion for yourself and others. Integration matters because it transforms experience into wisdom, wounds into gifts, and moments into meaning.

Resilience as a Heart-Led Practice

When you integrate your lessons, you do more than remember, you strengthen the foundation of your being. Each reflection becomes a brick laid with intention, building a steadiness that holds you even in life's storms. You begin to trust that no matter what unfolds, you have the capacity to move through it. Why? Because you already have. You have faced challenges, felt the ache of uncertainty, and still found a way forward. That memory lives in your heart as evidence of your strength.

True resilience is not about armouring yourself or hardening against life. It is not the absence of pain, but the presence of trust. It is a soft, steady knowing that you are capable of meeting what comes with awareness, grace, and compassion. This heart-led resilience does not reject struggle, it recognises it as part of the path. Every challenge becomes an invitation to return to your breath, your truth, and your deeper self.

With each cycle of falling and rising, reflecting and realigning, you expand your inner capacity. You begin to see your past not as a series of wounds that broke you, but as experiences that shaped and built you. What once felt heavy becomes a teacher. What once felt overwhelming becomes a reminder of how far you have come. Resilience, then, is not just survival, it is transformation. It is the gentle, powerful truth that you are not defined by what happened to you, but by how you continue to meet life with heart.

From Reflection to Future Readiness

When you pause to reflect, you are not only honouring your past, you are preparing your future. Each moment of awareness plants a seed for the life you are still creating. The insights you have gathered, the emotions you have navigated, and the truths you have reclaimed now become guiding lights for the path ahead. Reflection transforms what once felt heavy into wisdom you can carry with strength and grace. As you carry these lessons forward, you begin to make more grounded, heart-aligned choices. You recognise the difference between a reaction based in fear and a response anchored in clarity. Old patterns lose their hold because you have taken the time to understand their roots, and in that understanding, you free yourself from repeating them.

Future readiness does not mean predicting or controlling what comes, it means cultivating the inner stability to meet whatever arises. You begin to live from trust: trust in yourself, trust in your resilience, trust in the wisdom of your journey. Decisions flow not from urgency or doubt, but from alignment with your deepest values. This is what long-term emotional resilience looks like: a life guided by reflection, not reaction. It is the quiet confidence that you can move through change without losing yourself. It is the freedom to create your future with intention rather than habit, and it is the courage to step forward knowing that your heart already carries everything you need.

<u>Your Journey Is Your Strength</u>

Everything you have experienced, every stumble, every breakthrough, every tender or painful moment, has shaped you into who you are today. Yet it is not the challenges alone that define you, but the way you have chosen to meet them. It is your willingness to reflect, to integrate, and to grow that transforms life's raw material into wisdom. This is where your true resilience is born. Your strength does not come from having an easy path. It comes from the moments when you were tested and still chose to rise. It comes from the courage to soften instead of harden, to seek understanding instead of shutting down, to open your heart even when fear told you to close it. These choices, repeated again and again, are what make you whole.

Let this be your reminder: you are not defined by what you have gone through. You are defined by how you have carried those experiences, how you have learned from them, and how you have allowed them to shape a deeper compassion within you. The scars you carry are not signs of weakness but symbols of strength, evidence that you have endured, healed, and kept moving forward. This is how your heart becomes unbound: not because it has never broken, but because it has been pieced back together with wisdom, truth, and love. Every fracture has become a window for light. Every loss has made space for growth. Every moment of reflection has pulled you closer to your authentic self. Your journey is not just a story of survival, it is a story of transformation, and as you step forward, you carry within you the undeniable truth: **you are strong, not in spite of your journey, but because of it.**

Gratitude And Forward-Vision As Tools For Inner Alignment

Gratitude and forward-vision are more than feel-good practices, they are powerful tools for aligning with your heart's truth. Together, they help you close the chapter behind you with grace and open the one ahead with purpose. Gratitude anchors you in the present, while forward-vision calls you toward your next becoming. When used together, they create a bridge between where you have been and where you are ready to go. This is inner alignment: the state where your emotions, values, choices, and direction are all moving in the same rhythm, **the rhythm of your heart.**

<u>Gratitude Grounds You in Truth</u>

Gratitude is not about ignoring your pain or pretending everything has been easy. It is about choosing to acknowledge the gifts within the journey, *especially* the unexpected ones. When you pause to name what you are grateful for, even in the midst of uncertainty or challenge, you activate a shift in perspective. Gratitude reminds you of your growth. It reconnects you with the people, moments, lessons, and even struggles that shaped your becoming. It turns experience into meaning and scarcity into sufficiency. When you thank the path you have walked, you create the emotional space to move forward without resentment or regret.

Forward-Vision Awakens Possibility

Once you have honoured what has been, you are more open to imagining what could be. Forward-vision invites you to dream beyond your past limitations, to see with the eyes of your heart, not your fear. It is the act of asking, *"What kind of life do I want to live now? Who am I ready to become?"* This visioning is not about rigid goal-setting or chasing perfection. It is about clarity. It is about listening inward and aligning with the values that matter most to you. Forward-vision helps you make choices not out of obligation, but out of alignment, with your purpose, your healing, and your inner truth.

Your Journey Is Your Strength

Everything you have experienced, every stumble, every breakthrough, every tender moment, has shaped you, but it is your willingness to reflect, to integrate, and to *grow from it all* that unlocks your true resilience. Let this be your reminder: you are not defined by what you have gone through. You are defined by what you have *learned, integrated,* and *risen from.* This is how your heart becomes unbound, stronger not because it has never broken, but because it has been pieced back together with wisdom, truth, and love.

When Gratitude Meets Vision, You Realign With Your Heart

Gratitude without vision can keep you stuck in comfort. Vision without gratitude can leave you restless and unsatisfied, but when you bring the two together, you create powerful alignment: You recognise the sacredness of where you have been.

- You honour who you are now.

- And you choose where you are going, with intention, not reaction.

- This is what it means to live *from the heart.* You stop running from the past or racing toward the future. Instead, you *align,* step by step, with a life that reflects your wholeness.

Let Gratitude and Vision Guide You Forward

As you complete this stage of your *Heart Unbound* journey, let gratitude be your foundation and vision your guide. Look back with tenderness. Look forward with trust, and in between, return to your breath, your truth, your heart. *You do not need to have all the answers. You just need to stay aligned with what matters. Let that be enough to take the next step.* This is how you walk forward, grateful for the past, open to the future, and fully alive in the now. This is how your heart stays unbound.

"Mirror of the Heart" Reflection Meditation (Guided Practice)

I invite you to listen to the Reflection meditation and as you listen to the meditation I would ask you to revisit one moment from this program where you felt the light, your heart felt most open, connected, or free.

Reflection After Meditation:

- What emotions arose as you revisited that moment of openness and freedom?

- How does your body respond when you hold that memory in your awareness right now?

- What gentle reminder can you carry with you to return to this feeling when life becomes heavy?

- What did that moment teach you?

- How will you protect and grow that light moving forward?

Integration Exercise – Heart Anchoring

After the meditation, place both hands over your heart. Take three slow breaths, and on each inhale, silently repeat: *"I welcome this light."* On each exhale, silently repeat: *"I release what dims it."*

Then, write down one word or phrase that captures the essence of that moment of light (e.g., *peace, belonging, joy, courage*).

Keep this word somewhere visible, on a card, a journal page, or your phone, as an anchor to return to when you need to remember your heart's freedom.

Case Study Discussion: Nathan's Journey

(The following is a transcript of a conversation I (Dr John McSwiney) had with Nathan.)

"Heart Unbound: The Ultimate 28–Day Heart Connection Challenge' is a significant chapter in my life's story. Prior to this journey, it is fair to say that I was a stranger to my own heart. The first day of the challenge, I was skeptical. Could connecting with my heart really change my life? The first day of the challenge was a revelation. I was guided to close my eyes, take a deep breath, and listen to the whispers of my heart. It was a simple act, but it felt like the start of an extraordinary voyage. Each day, I delved deeper into the program's practices, exploring the uncharted territories of my emotions.

I committed to the daily practices and something remarkable started happening. Breathing exercises helped me relax, reducing stress and bringing peace. With every guided meditation, I felt more in tune with my emotions and began to understand the power of vulnerability. Days turned into weeks, and I found myself expressing empathy, forging deeper connections with friends and family. The newfound creativity I discovered astonished me. It was not just a program; it was a profound journey of self–discovery. I was a pragmatist, a workaholic who rarely paused to reflect on my inner self. Stress and deadlines ruled my existence, leaving little room for emotions or personal growth.

Through the soothing meditations and introspective exercises, I learned to embrace my vulnerability and connect with my true self. I began to understand that strength lay not in suppressing my emotions but in acknowledging them. With time, I found myself extending this understanding to others, forging profound connections and nurturing empathy in my relationships. As the 28–day challenge drew to a close, I marveled at the person I was changing into. I had transformed from a stoic corporate machine into someone who embraced life's complexities, cherished relationships, and reveled in the beauty of the present moment.

'Heart Unbound' showed me how to unlock my heart's potential, making me a more authentic and fulfilled version of myself. I couldn't help but smile, knowing that this program had changed my life in ways I could never have imagined. The 28–day challenge concluded, but its impact endures. I wake each morning with a heart that beats in harmony with my deepest desires. I have unearthed a wellspring of creativity that colours my world with beauty and purpose. I have grown from a closed–off soul into an authentic, open–hearted individual who revels in life's intricacies. I have spent time with Dr John and have learned to go deeper into my heart and have realised that this is a lifestyle choice, and it is one that I have loved embracing. I would encourage anybody reading this to really embrace this journey because it will change your life.

Reflection Exercise: Nathan's Journey

Here are four profound and reflective questions inspired by Nathan's story to help you engage with your own journey of reflection:

1. **In what ways have you come home to yourself during this journey, and how has connecting with your heart shifted the way you see your life, relationships, or purpose?** Like Nathan, you may have begun this journey uncertain or guarded, how has your heart responded as you have opened it day by day?

2. **What past version of yourself do you now hold with greater understanding or compassion, and what strengths have emerged as you have embraced vulnerability and self-awareness?** Consider how your emotional landscape has evolved. Where have you softened? Where have you grown stronger?

3. **What moments during the journey surprised you, moments of insight, connection, or inner stillness that you did not expect?** Think about the days that felt like turning points. What happened, and how did they move you?

4. **As you look ahead, how will you carry this heart-centred way of living into your daily life, and what intentions will guide the next chapter of your journey?** Nathan discovered that this was more than a program, it was a way of being. What will your heart ask of you now?

Each of these questions is designed to help you, like Nathan, integrate the transformation you have experienced and move forward with intention, awareness, and an unbound heart.

Affirmations For You – (Heart Whispers)

Affirmations have the power to quiet the noise of doubt, open the doorway to self-trust, and draw you back into the wisdom of your heart. When practised daily, they nurture an inner dialogue based in love and truth, helping you live each day more aligned with who you truly are. I invite you to repeat silently or write:

- *I listen to my heart's whispers and follow its guidance.*

- *I embrace vulnerability and allow my heart to lead the way.*

- *I nurture my self–compassion and connect with my heart.*

- *I choose to align with my heart's deepest desires and values.*

- *I practice gratitude to open my heart to the abundance of life.*

- *I trust the wisdom of my heart to guide me towards a fulfilling and authentic life.*

Integration Circle & Future Intentions

This practice is designed to help you anchor the wisdom of your journey and carry it into your daily life with clarity and intention. Integration is where transformation takes root, not just in your mind, but in your heart, relationships, and choices. Whether you are in a group or reflecting individually, take your time with this process:

1. **Identify Three Key Learnings**: Pause and consider the most powerful lessons you have received during this program. These may be insights about yourself, truths about how you connect with others, or practices that have shifted your perspective. Write them down clearly and concisely, as if you are creating guideposts to return to.

2. **Share Two Emotional Shifts**: Reflect on the inner changes you have felt along the way. Perhaps you moved from fear to trust, from tension to calm, from loneliness to connection, or from self-criticism to self-compassion. Sharing these shifts, with yourself in writing, or with others if in a circle, helps you honour your growth and embody the change.

3. **Set One Heartfelt Intention Moving Forward**: Ask your heart: *"What do I want to carry into my next chapter?"* This intention may be simple yet profound, such as *"I choose presence," "I honour my heart daily,"* or *"I live with openness and courage."* Anchor it in words that feel alive and real for you.

4. **Record and Revisit**: Write your reflections on a *"Heart Integration Commitment"* card or in your journal. Place this somewhere you will see it often, a reminder on your desk, a note in your wallet, or a page you

---

return to weekly. As you revisit your reflections, allow them to evolve, deepening your sense of alignment and accountability.

Optional Closing Ritual: To seal the circle or personal reflection, place your hand over your heart, take three slow breaths, and silently repeat: *"I carry my learnings. I honour my shifts. I walk with intention."*

Closing Reflection

You have walked a sacred path, through breath, gratitude, stillness, courage, creativity, vulnerability, and now, reflection. This is not the end of your journey. It is a quiet threshold. A moment to pause, gather what you have learned, and honour the growth that has unfolded within you. Reflection invites you to hold your story with gentleness. To see not only what happened, but *how you have changed*. It is in this space that healing becomes wisdom, and experience becomes purpose.

You are not who you were when you began. You carry more insight, more softness, more strength. Through reflection, you begin to integrate all the lessons, all the emotions, all the heartbeats of this journey, and you begin to see yourself more clearly. So take this moment to honour yourself. Not for being perfect, but for showing up. For feeling deeply. For choosing truth. For choosing your heart.

As you step into whatever comes next, carry this with you: *Your story matters. Your heart knows the way, and every pause to reflect is a powerful step forward.* Let this final part not be a closing, but a deepening. Let reflection be the thread that ties your inner work to your outer world, and let your unbound heart continue to lead you, home to yourself, again and again.

29 – HOMECOMING

Your Opening Reflection

Invitation to Return to Your Heart - As you step into this chapter, I invite you to come with gentleness, as though you are walking through the door of your own inner sanctuary. Homecoming is not about arriving somewhere new, but about remembering what has always been within you. Let this be a space where you release the weight of masks, roles, and striving, and allow yourself to rest in the truth of who you are. Here, you are safe. Here, you are whole. Here, you are home.

- "When in your life have you felt most at home within yourself? What did it feel like in your body, heart, and spirit?"

- "Where have you been searching outside of yourself for belonging or approval? How has that search shaped your journey?"

- "What truths about yourself have you reclaimed through this program that remind you of your wholeness?"

- "What masks, roles, or stories are you now ready to lay down so that you can return more fully to your authentic self?"

- "If your heart could speak to you right now as you arrive "home," what would it want you to hear and carry forward?"

Let these questions open the doorway into presence. Every answer you give, whether in words, sensations, or silence, is a bridge between where you are and where you are going.

Learning Objectives

The learning objectives are included here to give you a clear focus for this chapter, ensuring that each practice you explore moves you closer to mastering the skills, insights, and heart-led awareness that will enrich your life well beyond the program. By the end of this chapter, you will:

- Reframe your journey as a return to your authentic self, rather than an escape from your past.

- Recognise your heart as your true home, a place of safety, acceptance, and belonging.

- Celebrate wholeness and authenticity by embracing the truth that you are already enough.

- Apply daily practices of homecoming (breath, silence, reflection, gratitude) to ground yourself in presence.

- Experience the freedom of belonging by releasing the need for external validation and trusting your inner sanctuary.

- Integrate your entire Heart Unbound journey into your daily life, carrying forward its wisdom with clarity and courage.

Core Emotional Domains

The core emotional intelligence domains covered here are essential because they form the foundation for lasting heart connection, guiding you to deepen self-awareness, regulate emotions, build resilience, and strengthen the mind-body bond throughout your Heart Unbound journey.

- **Self-Awareness:** Recognising inner truth and wholeness. Cultivating awareness of when you feel most *"at home"* within yourself.
- **Self-Regulation:** Developing daily grounding practices to stay centred. Returning to presence when distracted or unsettled.
- **Motivation (Heart-Aligned Purpose);** Living from authenticity rather than external approval. Strengthening inner commitment to values and truth.
- **Empathy:** Honouring your own journey while respecting others' paths of return. Creating space for deeper human connection through belonging.

- **Social Skills (Authentic Connection);** Engaging with others from a place of self-acceptance. Building trust and connection by embodying wholeness and presence.

"Homecoming – Returning To The Deepest Truth Of Who You Are"

Homecoming is not about reaching a final destination, but about recognising that the journey has always been leading you inward, toward the centre of your being. After walking through the valleys of self-doubt, climbing the mountains of growth, and crossing the rivers of release, you arrive not at a place outside of yourself, but at the quiet sanctuary that has always lived within your heart. This is the sacred return to the deepest truth of who you are. It is the realisation that you were never lost, only learning. You were never broken, only becoming. You were never incomplete, only waiting to remember your wholeness. Homecoming is the gentle unveiling of your authentic self, the part of you untouched by fear, beyond masks, beyond roles, beyond the expectations of others.

To come home is to lay down the armour you no longer need. It is to embrace yourself without conditions, to rest in your own presence with love and acceptance. It is to finally recognise that freedom was never about escape, but about alignment, the alignment of your life with the wisdom of your heart. Here, you no longer strive to be someone else, because you remember that you already are enough. You already belong. You already carry the sanctuary you seek.

This chapter is a celebration of integration. It gathers together all the pieces of your journey, the lessons, the tears, the laughter, the breakthroughs, the silences, and weaves them into a tapestry of belonging. Homecoming honours not just what you have discovered, but who you have become in the process. It invites you to pause, to look back with gratitude, and to see how far you have come, not with pride alone, but with reverence for the courage it took to arrive here, and so, the invitation now is not simply to reflect, but to embody. To live your homecoming daily, in the way you speak, in the choices you make, in how you hold yourself and others. To anchor yourself in the present moment, to keep returning to your heart, again and again, until the rhythm of authenticity becomes your natural way of being. Homecoming is both a resting and a beginning. It is the quiet whisper that says: *"Welcome home. You are whole. You are free. You belong."*

The Journey As A Return

For much of your life, you may have believed that transformation meant reaching for something outside yourself, a new role to play, a new identity to claim, or a new horizon to chase. Perhaps you thought healing meant becoming someone different, stronger, braver, or more worthy than you once believed yourself to be, but as you stand here now, you can see more clearly: the true journey was never about escaping, fixing, or becoming. It was about remembering, uncovering, and returning. Every step you have taken, whether steady or stumbling, whether lit by joy or shrouded in pain, has been leading you back to a truth that was always yours: *you are already whole*. The wounds you carried, the doubts you wrestled with, the ways you once hid yourself were not proof of something missing in you. They were invitations, signals pointing you inward, urging you to peel back the layers of fear, conditioning, and expectation so that your heart could be revealed.

Wholeness was never broken. It was simply veiled. Beneath the noise of external demands and the pressure to become someone else, your essence remained intact, quietly waiting for your return, and through courage, vulnerability, and a willingness to look honestly at yourself, you have begun to uncover it again. To understand the journey as a return is to release the belief that home lies in some faraway place or future version of you. Instead, it reminds you that home has always been here, in your breath, in your body, and in the quiet wisdom of your heart. Every experience, even the ones you thought were detours or failures, has been part of the path leading you home.

When you embrace this truth, you stop searching for completion in external validation, success, or approval. You no longer need to outrun your past, because you see it now not as a weight that held you back, but as a teacher that walked beside you. Every challenge, every moment of breaking, every breakthrough was not about losing yourself, but about finding your way back. Coming home is not about arrival in the sense of finality. It is about awakening to the reality that you already carry everything you were seeking. The love, the safety, the belonging, the freedom, all of it has always been part of you. You need only pause, breathe, and listen to remember. So today, let this truth settle into your heart: *You have not been wandering aimlessly. You have been on the most sacred pilgrimage of all the journey of returning to yourself.*

Your Heart As Home

There is a place within you that has never abandoned you, even in the moments when you felt furthest from yourself. This place is steady, unshaken, and whole. It is not dependent on external approval, success, or circumstance. It does not ask you to perform, prove, or perfect. It simply waits, with quiet patience, for you to remember it. This place is your heart, your truest home. Your heart does not keep score of how far you have wandered, how long you stayed away, or how many times you doubted your worth. Like a faithful sanctuary, it remains open, steady, and ready to welcome you back. No matter what paths you have taken, through struggle, through self-doubt, through distraction or detour, the heart always holds the doorway to belonging. You cannot lose it, because you are it.

To recognise your heart as home is to understand that you already carry within you the safety, the peace, and the belonging you have longed for. It is to realise that the love you have sought in others, the security you have craved from the world, and the permission you have waited for to be yourself have always been present inside of you. Your heart has been whispering all along: *You belong here. You belong to yourself.* When you begin to trust your heart in this way, you stop chasing validation in external sources. You stop bending yourself into shapes to be accepted or loved. You stop looking for home in people, places, or outcomes that can never provide lasting safety. Instead, you rest in the truth that you belong first to yourself, that your value is not contingent upon anyone else seeing it, but on your own willingness to honour it.

Coming home to your heart is not about building walls to keep others out; it is about creating roots so that you can meet the world with openness and authenticity. From this grounded centre, you can give and receive love without fear of losing yourself. You can walk through uncertainty with courage, because your anchor is no longer outside of you. This is the sacred shift: to live not from the fragile house of external approval, but from the eternal sanctuary of your heart. Here, you find freedom. Here, you find peace. Here, you know beyond doubt: *I am safe. I am whole. I am already home.*

Heart-Anchor Practice: Coming Home to Yourself

1. **Find Your Space**: Sit somewhere quiet where you can be undisturbed. Place both feet on the ground and let your body soften into the chair or cushion beneath you. Allow your shoulders to drop.

2. **Place Your Hand Over Your Heart**: Gently place one or both hands on your heart space. Feel the warmth of your palms. Notice the rise and fall of your chest as you breathe.

3. **Breathe Into Home**: Take three slow, steady breaths, imagining that each inhale fills your heart with light and each exhale clears away any heaviness, doubt, or distraction. With each breath, whisper inwardly: *I am home.*

4. **Listen to the Whisper Within**: Ask your heart: *What do you want me to know right now?* Do not rush or force an answer. Simply listen. It may come as a word, an image, a feeling, or a sense of stillness. Trust whatever arises.

5. **Anchor the Belonging**: Say to yourself silently or aloud: *"I belong to myself. My heart is my sanctuary. I am always welcome here."*

6. **Carry It Forward**: Before you leave the practice, choose one small way to honour your heart today, perhaps speaking kindly to yourself, pausing to breathe before a decision, or giving yourself rest.

You can adapt this into a **short ritual** at the start or end of each day. The more often you return to it, the more natural it becomes to feel at home within yourself, wherever you are.

Wholeness And Authenticity

Wholeness is the quiet yet radical act of recognising that nothing about you is missing. For years, you may have carried the belief that you had to earn your worth, achieve more, heal everything, or somehow *"fix"* yourself in order to be complete, but the truth is simpler and more profound: you were always whole. What looked like brokenness was often only a part of you waiting to be seen with love. What felt like lack was often a story learned from others, not the truth of your being. To live in wholeness does not mean you will never feel pain, doubt, or fear. It means that when those moments arise, you do not exile them. Instead, you welcome them as part of your human experience, knowing they do not define you, but simply move through you. You begin to see that the cracks in your story are not flaws to hide but openings where light enters. You understand that your tenderness is strength, your vulnerability is wisdom, and your imperfections are what make your humanity beautiful.

Authenticity emerges naturally from this state of wholeness. When you stop abandoning yourself in search of approval or safety, you find the courage to show up as you truly are. Authenticity is not about being loud or dramatic; it is about being real. It is in the moments you say what you mean, honour your boundaries, or allow yourself to be seen without pretence. It is in choosing to live from the inside out, rather than from the outside in. Living from the truth of *"I am enough"* becomes a daily practice of alignment. Some days it may feel like a whisper, soft, uncertain, yet steady. Other days it may roar through you with conviction. Either way, it is a truth that does not depend on perfection, performance, or permission. It is a declaration that your worth is intrinsic, that your presence matters, and that you belong exactly as you are.

This wholeness and authenticity ripple outward. As you live more honestly with yourself, your relationships begin to shift. You stop performing roles that keep you safe but small. You stop hiding your light for fear of rejection. Instead, you allow others to meet the real you, raw, kind, flawed, radiant. Some connections may fall away, but those that remain will be deeper, truer, and more life-giving. To embody this wholeness is to rest in the deepest kind of freedom: the freedom of being at home in your own skin. It is to wake each morning and remember that you do not have to earn the right to exist, to love, or to shine. You already are enough. You always were.

Daily Practices Of Homecoming

To live a life of homecoming is to recognise that wholeness is not found in faraway places but in the rhythm of your everyday presence. It is in the breath you take before speaking, in the stillness you create when you pause, in the gratitude you whisper before sleep. These are not small acts; they are doorways. Each ritual, however ordinary it may seem, is a portal through which you return to your heart, your true home.

Breath becomes your anchor. With each inhale, you invite life into your body; with each exhale, you release what no longer serves you. Slowly, breath reminds you that you are safe to be here, now. The world outside may be noisy or uncertain, but one conscious breath restores clarity. In this way, breath is not simply oxygen, it is a sacred thread that ties you back to yourself.

Silence is your sanctuary. In a world filled with constant demands and noise, choosing even a few moments of quiet is a radical act of love. In silence, the heart whispers what the mind forgets. It tells you that you are enough, that you are held, that you are already whole. Silence invites you to stop performing and simply be. Within this stillness, the ground of your being steadies.

Reflection is the mirror of your soul. It allows you to see the patterns of your journey with honesty and compassion. Reflection transforms your experiences into wisdom, helping you understand not only what has happened but also how it has shaped you. When you pause to reflect, you gather the fragments of your life and weave them into a story of resilience, growth, and grace.

Gratitude is the lens that reveals the sacred in the ordinary. When you give thanks for a sunrise, a smile, or even your own breath, you turn simple moments into holy ground. Gratitude softens your heart and makes space for joy. It reminds you that abundance is not something you wait for, it is something you awaken to by noticing what is already here, but perhaps the deepest truth of daily homecoming is this: **it is not about perfection, but return.** You will forget. You will get caught up in distraction, worry, or self-judgment. Yet every time you pause, to breathe, to be still, to reflect, to give thanks, you come home again. That return, however gentle, is the essence of love.

Over time, these rituals cease to feel like practices you must remember. They become the natural rhythm of your life. The breath becomes a prayer. Silence becomes your resting place. Reflection becomes wisdom embodied. Gratitude becomes the language of your heart. Through daily homecoming, you learn that love is not only an offering you give outward but also a devotion you extend inward. This is how you root yourself in presence, not as a fleeting moment but as a way of being. When you return again and again to your heart, you discover the truth that has been waiting all along: you were never truly lost. Your home has always been here.

The Freedom Of Belonging

Belonging is one of the deepest human longings, yet for much of life, we are conditioned to search for it outside ourselves. We seek it in relationships, workplaces, communities, achievements, and approval. We mould ourselves to fit expectations, edit our truth to gain acceptance, and sometimes abandon pieces of who we are just to feel included, and yet, no matter how much we achieve, how many circles we fit into, or how much praise we receive, there can remain a quiet emptiness, a sense that we are still not *enough*. The heart knows differently. True belonging does not begin outside of you, it begins within you. The freedom of belonging is the moment you finally recognise that you do not have to earn your place here. You already belong, simply because you exist. This is not arrogance, but alignment with truth: the universe, life itself, has already said yes to you. Your very breath is evidence that you are meant to be here.

When you remember this, you are freed from the constant weight of external validation. You no longer need to contort yourself into someone else's idea of worthy. You no longer hand over the keys of your identity to others. Instead, you reclaim the sanctuary of your own heart. This is the freedom of belonging: the relief of resting in yourself, without condition, and with this freedom comes courage, because when you know you belong to yourself, you no longer fear rejection in the same way. You can step forward authentically, even when it feels risky, because your worth is no longer up for debate. You can walk into the world with balance, because you are no longer pulled apart by the competing expectations of others. You are free to be steady, centred, and true, even in the midst of chaos.

Paradoxically, when you no longer seek belonging outside yourself, your connections with others actually deepen. Instead of approaching relationships from need, performance, or fear, you meet others with openness. You are able to love without clinging, to listen without defensiveness, and to share without pretense. Your authenticity becomes an invitation, allowing others to feel safe in their own. This is the great paradox of belonging: when you stop chasing it, you begin to experience it everywhere.

The freedom of belonging is also the freedom to live fully. To laugh without worrying how you look. To create without fearing failure. To love without shrinking back. It is the courage to move through the world as your whole self, not perfect, but present, not flawless, but free, and so, Homecoming leads you here: to the truth that your heart has been whispering all along. *You are already home. You are already whole. You are already enough.* When you carry this knowing, belonging is no longer something to seek, it is something you embody.

Walking Home to Your Heart Exercise

Step 1: Create a Sacred Space: Find a quiet place where you can be undisturbed for at least 20 minutes. Dim the lights, light a candle if you wish, and place your hand gently over your heart. Breathe slowly, as if you are arriving somewhere safe.

Step 2: Visualisation – The Path Home: Close your eyes and imagine yourself standing on a path that leads back to your true home. This is not a physical house, but an inner sanctuary where your heart waits for you. Begin walking this path in your mind's eye:

- Notice what it looks like. Is it forested, sandy, lit by lanterns, or open sky?

- Feel each step releasing old stories, masks, or burdens you no longer need to carry.

- As you walk, repeat silently: *I am coming home.*

When you reach the doorway of your sanctuary, pause. Place your hand on the door. Feel its warmth, its invitation. When you are ready, step inside.

Step 3: Enter the Sanctuary: Inside, you find a space that reflects your truest self. Notice the colours, the sounds, the stillness. In the centre of the room is a mirror, but unlike any you have ever seen. As you look into it, you do not see flaws, mistakes, or masks, you see your whole, radiant, authentic self. Greet this self with love. Whisper: *Welcome home.*

Step 4: Heart Declaration: Now, take a journal and write a **Homecoming Declaration** to yourself. Begin with:

- *I am home when…* (list the moments you feel most grounded and true)

- *I am whole because…* (honour the strengths, lessons, and truths you have reclaimed)

- *I choose to honour my homecoming by...* (name one daily act that will keep you connected in your heart).

Step 5: Embody the Ritual: Close by placing both hands over your heart and saying three times, slowly and with presence: *"I am home. I am whole. I am free."* Sit in silence for a few moments. Allow the words to settle in your body like roots anchoring you deeply into the ground of your being.

Why this matters: This exercise moves readers from *concept* into *embodiment*. It helps them not only understand Homecoming but **feel it**, **see it**, and **anchor it into a daily practice** that continues beyond the program.

Dr John Mcswiney's Journey Back To His Heartspace

There was a long season in my life when the rhythm of busyness drowned out the rhythm of my heart. On the outside, it looked as though I had everything together: career achievements, responsibilities fulfilled, the appearance of stability. Yet on the inside, I was running on empty. My heart whispered for stillness, for authenticity, for peace, for love, but I silenced it with more work, more striving, more proving.

The turning point did not arrive as a dramatic event, but as a quiet, persistent ache. A deep knowing that would no longer let me ignore it. I remember one morning by the ocean, standing barefoot in the sand as the waves moved with their timeless rhythm. I placed my hand on my chest and realised, with a shock of sadness, that I could no longer feel myself. I had been so focused on being who I thought the world wanted me to be that I had forgotten the deeper truth of who I already was. That realisation did not break me with fear, but stirred me with longing, a longing to come home to my heart, to lay down the mask, to return to the one I was always created to be.

The journey back was not quick. It was tender, awkward, and often uncomfortable. I began in small ways: three conscious breaths before stepping into the day, a few unedited lines in a journal, moments of allowing my heart to speak without judgement. I gave myself permission to feel, to truly feel, the grief I had buried, the joy I had muted, and the love I had postponed. Slowly, almost imperceptibly, my heart began to respond.

There were glimmers of clarity and peace that arose not from doing, but simply from being. The ocean became my teacher again. Out on the waves, saltwater and sun on my skin, I remembered the boy who once surfed with wonder, laughed without hesitation, and lived unmasked. He was still there, waiting patiently for me to invite him home.

Reconnecting with my heartspace revealed a profound truth: wholeness was not something I needed to chase or achieve. It was not found in accolades, approval, or perfection. It was found in the quiet courage to meet myself with honesty, grace and compassion. It was found when I chose to listen to my heart, even when it trembled, even when it felt uncomfortable and inconvenient.

My life today is not flawless, but it is aligned. I live from my heartspace not because it is easy, but because it is the only way I know how to live fully, authentically, and free. This journey of homecoming is ongoing. Every breath, every choice, every act of love is another step toward my heart, another step home.

Reflection Exercise: Dr John's Journey

1. **Where in your own life has busyness, proving, or striving drowned out the quiet rhythm of your heart?** Take a moment to notice if there are areas where you look accomplished on the outside but feel empty or disconnected within.

2. **What 'mask' or role have you worn to meet others' expectations, and what truth lies beneath it, waiting to be remembered?** Reflect on the parts of yourself that long to be seen without performance or pretence.

3. **What small, gentle practices could you begin today, like breath, journaling, or silence, to reconnect with your inner sanctuary?** Consider not the grand gestures, but the tender beginnings that open space for your heart to speak again.

4. **If you were to return to the *"you"* who once lived with wonder, joy, and freedom, what would you reclaim, and how would that change the way you show up in your life now?** Let your imagination guide you back to the essence of who you were before striving overshadowed your being.

Affirmations For You – (Heart Whispers)

Affirmations have the power to quiet the noise of doubt, open the doorway to self-trust, and draw you back into the wisdom of your heart. When practised daily, they nurture an inner dialogue based in love and truth, helping you live each day more aligned with who you truly are. I invite you to repeat silently or write:

- *I am home within myself.*

- *My heart is my sanctuary, steady and true.*

- *I already am enough; nothing is missing.*

- *I return again and again to the deepest truth of who I am.*

- *Wholeness is not something I chase, it is who I already am.*

- *I release the masks and walk in the freedom of authenticity.*

- *Every breath brings me back home to my heart.*

- *I honour my journey, my struggles, and my becoming with compassion.*

- *I walk forward in courage, grace, and love, because I am already home.*

Guided Journaling Exercise: Returning Home to Your Heart

Step 1 – Pause and Arrive: Take three slow, conscious breaths. Place your hand gently over your heart. Whisper softly: *"I am here. I am listening."*

Step 2 – Reflection Prompts: Write freely and without editing. Let your heart guide your pen.

- Where in your life has busyness or striving drowned out the rhythm of your heart? Describe the places where you appear successful on the outside but feel empty within.

- What mask or role have you worn to meet others' expectations? Who or what have you been trying to prove yourself to? What truth lies beneath that mask, waiting to be remembered?

- What small daily practices could reconnect you with your inner sanctuary? Breath, journaling, silence, or something else? Write down one practice you will commit to this week.

- If you returned to the *"you"* who lived with wonder, joy, and freedom, what would you reclaim? Recall the child, the younger self, or the part

---

of you who laughed freely and lived unmasked. Describe them. What gift does that part of you want to give you now?

Step 3 – Integration Re-read what you have written. Circle or underline the words or phrases that feel most alive to you. These are your heart's signals.

Step 4 – Closing Ritual Place your hand on your heart again. Say aloud three times: *"I am coming home. I am enough. I am free."* Then sit in silence for a few moments. Notice what rises in you, peace, tears, longing, gratitude, and simply allow it to be.

Closing Reflection

Coming home is not a destination you reach, it is the quiet remembrance of what has always been within you. It is the soft return to the truth that you are not broken, not lacking, not lost. You are, and have always been, whole. The journey of Heart Unbound has carried you through breath and silence, gratitude and affirmation, laughter and tears, reflection and release. Each step has not taken you somewhere else, but has led you closer to yourself. Homecoming is the moment you realise that all along, the sanctuary you were seeking was already beating in your chest.

To come home is to no longer abandon yourself in the pursuit of approval. It is to no longer silence your heart for fear of rejection. It is to choose presence over performance, compassion over perfection, love over fear. Homecoming is the sacred act of standing in your own light and saying: *"I belong here. I belong to me."* Let this be your reminder: You do not have to keep searching for what you already carry. You are the hearth. You are the sanctuary. You are the home, and every time you pause, every time you breathe, every time you listen, you return again.

So as you close this chapter, carry this truth with you: the journey of transformation is not about becoming someone new. It is about remembering who you have always been. When you live from this place, every moment becomes a homecoming. Every choice, an act of love. Every breath, a step closer to freedom.

30 – LIVING INVITATIONS

Living from your heart: One Choice at a Time

Your journey does not end at the conclusion of this program. In truth, *it begins now,* in the quiet moments of your daily life, in the way you breathe, respond, pause, and choose. The program has opened a doorway, and on the other side is a life shaped not by default, but by **design, your heart's design**. To keep this momentum alive, you are invited to embrace 10 transformative living invitations. These are not tasks to check off, they are living practices, infused with intention, connection, and emotional integrity. When done consistently and sincerely, they will deepen your relationship with your heart and empower you to navigate life with empathy, courage, and compassion.

1. An Invitation to Remember

Reflection is not about revisiting the past, it is about listening to the whispers it left behind. Each page of your journal, every note scribbled in the margins, every unspoken thought, they are pieces of a map leading you back to yourself. Sit with them tenderly, not as a critic, but as a witness. Ask your heart:

- *What moments surprised me awake?*

- *Where did resistance rise, and what was it trying to protect?*

- *What shifted inside me that I may not have noticed in the moment, but feel now as truth?*

Let your reflection be raw, unpolished, alive. This is not analysis. This is communion. As you reflect, you honour your journey, giving breath to the subtle shifts and gentle awakenings that have brought you here.

430

Heart Practice: Create a quiet sanctuary of time. For twenty minutes, write a *"Letter to My Heart."* Begin with gratitude for all it has carried and revealed. Let the words flow without editing, and notice how your heart responds when it is finally heard.

2. An Invitation to Gather Your Heart Codes

Every journey leaves traces, not only in memory, but in the way you breathe, the way you pause, the way your heart opens in moments it once would have closed. These traces are your heart codes: living reminders of what matters most, waiting to be carried forward into the next chapter of your life. Ask yourself:

- *What moments softened me in ways I cannot forget?*

- *What practices steadied me when I felt unsteady?*

- *What truths rose so clearly within me that I know I cannot unknow them?*

These are not just *"lessons"* or *"tools"*, they are seeds of wisdom planted in the soil of your being. Write them down, name them with tenderness, and let them guide your unfolding. Perhaps it is the courage to breathe before reacting. Perhaps it is the stillness that reminds you your worth is not conditional. Perhaps it is the gentle knowing that joy is not earned, but allowed.

Heart Practice: Create a **Heart Reminder Card.** Write your three most luminous takeaways, the ones you want to live by, and place the card somewhere you will see daily: your mirror, your wallet, your journal. Let it meet your eyes again and again until it lives in your bones.

3. An Invitation to Weave Daily Rituals

Transformation is not born from grand gestures but from the quiet threads you weave into the fabric of each day. It is the steady return, breath by breath, choice by choice, to what keeps you aligned with your heart. You do not need to do everything. You only need to choose one or two practices that feel alive for you right now.

Perhaps it is placing your hand over your heart before you speak. Perhaps it is a moment of gratitude whispered before sleep. Perhaps it is walking without your phone, feeling the world with your whole presence.

This is not about perfection. It is about intention. It is about letting the ordinary moments of your life become sacred. The way you brush your teeth.

The way you sip your morning tea. The way you offer one kind truth each day. Each act, however small, is a doorway back to your heart.

<u>Heart Practice</u>: Create a simple daily ritual that feels nourishing, not heavy, maybe five mindful breaths upon waking, or a gratitude check-in at night. Commit gently, not rigidly, for 21 days. Let consistency shape your connection until it becomes the rhythm of your being.

4. An Invitation to Light Your Way with Intention

Intentions are not goals to be chased. They are lanterns, gently lighting your path, reminding you where your heart longs to walk. They are not about control, but about alignment. Not about doing more, but about becoming more true. Pause for a moment and ask your heart:

- *What do I long to feel more of in my life?*

- *What am I ready, finally, to release?*

- *Who am I becoming, one breath, one choice at a time?*

Let your answers rise softly, without pressure or judgment. Choose one to three intentions that feel alive in your body, not just your mind. Let them be tender, spacious, and real. Perhaps it is presence. Perhaps it is trust. Perhaps it is the courage to love again. Intentions are not fixed. They grow as you grow. Revisit them weekly, not as a test, but as a loving check-in with your heart.

<u>Heart Practice</u>: Write your intentions as *"I am"* statements, breathing them into being. For example: *"I am walking with trust." "I am choosing stillness before rushing." "I am enough, exactly as I am."* Place them somewhere you will see them often, and let them guide you like gentle stars in the night.

5. An Invitation to Walk Together

The path of the heart was never meant to be walked alone. Support is not weakness, it is sacred nourishment. When you open yourself to being held, witnessed, and encouraged, your growth takes root in ways it cannot when carried in silence.

Look gently around you. Who are the people who see you, who honour your becoming without judgement? They may be a trusted friend, a mentor, a coach, or a circle of fellow travellers who are also choosing to live from the heart. To be truly seen is a gift, and to let yourself be supported is an act of courage.

When you share your story, you do more than lighten your own load, you create ripples of healing for others. Your vulnerability becomes a mirror, reminding those around you that they, too, are not alone.

Heart Practice: Reach out to one person this week, not with perfection, but with honesty. Share one truth about what this journey has meant to you. Invite connection. Allow yourself to be met. Notice how your heart softens when you walk with others, and let their presence remind you: you belong, and you are held.

6. An Invitation to Hold Yourself Kindly

There will be days when you forget. Days when the old patterns return and you feel as though you have taken a step backward. Let this truth settle gently: growth is not a straight line. It is a spiral, a rhythm of remembering and returning.

In those tender moments, self-compassion is not just helpful, it is essential. To walk this journey with kindness toward yourself is to anchor your heart in love, even when your mind is harsh. Speak to yourself the way you would to someone you cherish: with softness, patience, and care.

Instead of asking, *"Why am I still doing this?"*, let your question become, *"What do I need right now?"* This shift is the difference between judgement and nourishment, between shame and healing.

Heart Practice: Place your hand gently on your heart whenever self-criticism rises. Breathe slowly, and whisper: *"I am here. I am learning. I am enough."* Repeat this until your body begins to soften and your heart remembers that you are worthy of love, especially from yourself.

7. An Invitation to Stay Curious and Open

Let your heart remain a lifelong student of life. Curiosity is the doorway to wonder, and wonder is the language of the soul. Each time you approach your journey with openness, you remind yourself that you are never finished growing, never done discovering the treasures your heart still longs to reveal.

Growth does not live in certainty. It awakens in the places where you soften, where you allow yourself to be surprised, challenged, and expanded. When you release the need to have all the answers, you create space for your heart to guide you into new layers of truth, compassion, and joy. Stay open. Stay listening. Stay willing to see your own life with fresh eyes. Your heart still has stories to tell you.

<u>Heart Practice</u>: Each month, invite one new source of inspiration into your world, a book, a poem, a heart-led podcast, a gentle teaching, or a healing practice. Let it speak to your heart, not your mind alone. Allow it to stretch you, surprise you, and guide your next layer of becoming.

8. An Invitation to Share Your Journey

Your story carries medicine. Not just for you, but for those around you who may be quietly longing for the very hope, courage, or truth you now carry. When you share even a fragment of your journey, you open a doorway for others to feel less alone, to reflect on their own hearts, and to take their first brave step.

You do not need to be a teacher, a guide, or an expert. All that is asked of you is honesty. Share the realness, the moments that felt messy, the tenderness of your breakthroughs, the beauty of feeling more alive than before. When you show up authentically, you remind others that imperfection is not failure, but the soil where growth blooms.

Every time you give voice to your journey, you strengthen its roots within you. Speaking your truth is both a gift to the world and a deepening of your own homecoming.

<u>Heart Practice</u>: Choose one small way to share your journey this week. Write a short post, record a voice note, or simply sit with a friend and say: *"One thing that shifted for me during Heart Unbound is…"* Let your words be simple, sincere, and from the heart.

9. An Invitation to Practice Gratitude

Gratitude is more than a polite thank you, it is a doorway back to your heart. It softens what feels heavy, amplifies what is beautiful, and gently shifts your attention from what is missing to what is present. Gratitude is not about denying hardship; it is about seeing the sacred thread even in the challenge, the lesson within the struggle, and the quiet gifts hidden in the ordinary.

When you pause each day to give thanks, you strengthen your resilience, not by bypassing difficulty, but by training your heart to notice the light that still glows amidst it. Gratitude expands your awareness, reminding you that life is not simply happening to you, but unfolding with you, moment by moment.

<u>Heart Practice</u>: Each evening, take a few breaths and write down three things you are grateful for, not just the obvious blessings, but the subtle ones: a feeling, a lesson, a moment of healing, or a glimpse of love. Let your gratitude

be honest and specific. Over time, this simple ritual will become a steady anchor, returning you to the beauty of now.

10. An Invitation to Embody the Learnings

The final and most powerful step is not to remember every insight, but to live them. Embodiment is where wisdom leaves the page and enters your breath, your choices, your relationships, and your presence.

Let your heart's work be visible in the way you pause before speaking, in the way you soften instead of harden, in the boundaries you honour, and in the love you dare to give and receive. You do not need to hold on tightly to every lesson; if you live them, they will live through you.

To embody your learnings is to let your life itself become your practice. It is to move as someone who carries their heart not as a fragile thing to protect, but as a compass to guide.

Heart Practice: At the close of each week, sit quietly and ask:

- *Where did I live from my heart this week?*
- *Where am I being invited to open more fully next week?*

Let your answers guide your next steps, gently and courageously, one choice at a time.

Closing Note from Dr John McSwiney

To You, Brave Heart,

As you reach the end of this journey, know this: the true destination was never a finish line, it was a return. A return to the wisdom of your own heart. A return to truth, compassion, and the courageous presence within you.

You have walked through stillness and breath, through joy and discomfort, through self-reflection and soulful revelation. You have listened, felt, remembered, and reclaimed, and now you stand more connected, more conscious, and more alive than ever before, but this is not goodbye. This is a new beginning. From here, may you live *unbound*. May you speak with clarity. Feel with depth. Love with wild honesty, and walk through your life as someone who knows that *your heart is not a weakness:* it is the source of your greatest power.

Thank you for your trust. Thank you for your presence, and thank you for choosing your heart, day by day, breath by breath.

With deep respect and boundless hope,

Dr John McSwiney

Founder, *Time to Transform*

Author, *Heart Unbound*

SPECIALIST – (HEART UNBOUND) - SHORT COURSES

I created the *Heart Unbound 2.0 Specialised Short Courses* because I believe that education, leadership, and personal growth must begin with the heart. For more than 25 years I have walked alongside students, managers, executives, and public servants, and what I have seen again and again is that people are capable of extraordinary things, but only when they are given the tools to reconnect with themselves.

Too many people are simply surviving: students burdened with pressure and uncertainty; managers stretched between competing demands; executives carrying the loneliness of leadership; and public servants trying to serve with integrity under the weight of bureaucracy and expectation. I know this world well, and I know the toll it can take, not just on performance, but on identity, wellbeing, and hope.

These short courses are my response to that reality. They are not designed to add *"more"* to already overloaded lives, but to offer a lifeline, practical, heart-centred practices that can restore balance, resilience, and meaning. Each course is a doorway: a way to breathe again, to reclaim focus, to rediscover joy, and to remember that life and leadership are not just about outcomes, but about who we are becoming in the process.

Every theme, whether it is breathing, gratitude, self-love, reflection, or compassion, is drawn directly from the *Heart Unbound* journey, tested in classrooms, boardrooms, and communities. They are short by design but deep in impact, giving you permission to pause, tools to reset, and the courage to lead with authenticity.

My heartfelt rationale is simple: these courses exist because I want you to know you do not have to do life alone, and you do not have to lose yourself (like I did) to succeed. By creating space for your heart, you will find not only resilience and clarity, but also the freedom to live and lead unbound.

Heart Unbound 2.0 – Specialised Short Courses

(Aligned with the 30 Chapter Themes)

For Students & Emerging Leaders

1. The Resilient Student

(Chapters – 1-Breathing • 26-Focus • 2-Gratitude • 28-Reflection)

University and school life can feel overwhelming, deadlines, exams, social pressures, and the constant noise of expectation. Many students survive by pushing harder, sleeping less, and carrying stress silently. This course offers a different way: practical, heart-centred tools to breathe through the pressure, sharpen focus, and approach study with calm clarity. By integrating daily gratitude practices and guided reflections, students learn to anchor themselves in resilience, so that challenges become opportunities to grow rather than obstacles to fear.

2. Finding Purpose and Identity

(Chapters – 3-I Am • 20-Heart Whispers • 17-Happy Place • 29-Homecoming)

The biggest question for emerging leaders is not *"What will I do?"* but *"Who am I becoming?"* This course guides students on a journey of self-discovery, helping them uncover their authentic identity and align their studies and choices with their deeper values. Through powerful *"I Am"* affirmations, heart-centred reflections, and guided visualisations, students begin to hear the whispers of their own truth. By reconnecting with their *"Happy Place"* and returning home to themselves, they develop the courage to walk their own path, not the one others expect of them.

3. Creativity and Self-Expression

(Chapters - 18-Drawing • 6-Dance • 16-Photographs • 27-Spontaneity)

Too often, creativity is dismissed as a distraction or luxury, yet it is through creative self-expression that students discover their voice, confidence, and inner freedom. This course reawakens imagination and reminds students that creativity is not separate from learning, it is the fuel that drives innovation, problem-solving, and joy. Through drawing, dance, photography, and playful spontaneity, students learn to see the world, and themselves, with fresh eyes. They are invited to step beyond perfectionism, embrace curiosity, and allow creativity to become a lifelong ally in both personal growth and professional success.

Together, these three specific short courses give students and emerging leaders the inner resources to thrive, not just academically but personally. They move beyond survival into a space where resilience, purpose, and creativity become foundations for a meaningful and empowered life.

For Managers & Team Leaders

4. Leading with Emotional Intelligence

(Chapters – 4-Mirror • 25-Listening • 15-Compassion • 12-Kindness)

True leadership is not defined by titles or authority but by the ability to inspire trust and bring out the best in others. This course equips managers with the tools to lead with emotional intelligence, to look into the *"mirror"* of self-awareness, to listen deeply beyond words, and to respond with compassion and kindness even under pressure. Participants will learn to transform feedback into an act of growth, to coach with empathy, and to model the kind of authentic leadership that builds respect and loyalty in teams.

5. Stress to Strength

(Chapters – 1-Breathing • 21-Relaxation • 11-Grounding • 8-Nutrition)

Managers today often stand at the fault line between executive demands and frontline realities. The constant pressure can erode focus, energy, and wellbeing, leading to burnout that spreads quickly through teams. This course reframes stress as a signal for growth, offering practical resilience practices that managers can use and share with their people. From conscious breathing to grounding techniques, from relaxation rituals to nourishing the body wisely, participants learn how to reset in the middle of chaos. The result is not only personal resilience but also the ability to lead teams from a place of steadiness, balance, and strength.

6. Building Positive Cultures

(Chapters – 24-Laughter • 2-Gratitude • 10-Forgiveness • 23-Declutter)

A team's culture is often shaped less by strategy than by the unseen habits and emotions that flow between people each day. This course gives managers practical ways to cultivate cultures that uplift rather than drain. Through the simple yet profound practices of laughter, gratitude, forgiveness, and decluttering, participants learn how to shift group energy, resolve tensions, and create workplaces where people feel safe, valued, and motivated. By embedding positivity into daily rhythms, managers can transform their teams into environments where wellbeing and performance grow together, not apart.

These three specific courses empower managers and team leaders to become more than supervisors, they become **guides, role models, and culture shapers**. By leading with heart, they not only improve team performance but also create workplaces that inspire trust, resilience, and human connection.

For Senior Executives & C-Suite Leaders

7. The Heart of Leadership

(Chapters – 3-I Am • 3-God/the Divine • 15-Compassion • 30-Living Invitations)

At the highest levels of leadership, the greatest challenge is not strategy but alignment: aligning decisions with values, influence with integrity, and success with legacy. This course calls executives to step beyond the mechanics of leadership into the deeper questions of identity and purpose. Who am I as a leader? What values guide me when no one is watching? What legacy am I leaving in the lives of those I lead? Through reflective practices, compassion-led frameworks, and heart-centred inquiry, leaders reconnect with the moral and spiritual dimensions of leadership, discovering that true authority flows from authenticity, humility, and the courage to live by invitation rather than expectation.

8. Leading Through Uncertainty

(Chapters – 9-Nothingness • 28-Reflection • 26-Focus • 19-Sunrise/Sunset)

The modern executive faces an age defined by disruption, volatility, and rapid change. In this environment, clarity is not found by doing more, but by learning to pause, reflect, and create space for perspective. This course equips leaders with the art of *"leading from stillness"*, practices of reflection, mindful focus, and intentional pauses that allow wisdom to emerge amidst chaos. Anchored in the symbolism of sunrise and sunset, executives are invited to begin and end each cycle with awareness, gratitude, and vision. The result is a leadership style that is calm under pressure, decisive without haste, and deeply trusted in uncertain times.

9. Influence at the Highest Level

(Chapgters – 14-Neurolinguistics •25- Listening • 20-Heart Whispers • 26-Focuse)

In boardrooms and global negotiations, influence is not simply about logic or power, it is about presence. This course empowers executives to harness the subtle yet profound tools of emotional intelligence and communication. Through neurolinguistics, leaders learn the impact of language on thought and behaviour; through deep listening, they unlock connection; through heart whispers, they strengthen intuition; and through authentic presence, they inspire confidence and trust. Participants leave with the ability to not only shape strategies, but to shape cultures, mindsets, and futures through the quiet force of integrity and heart-centred influence.

These three specific courses elevate executives beyond transactional leadership into **transformational leadership**, the kind that leaves not only profitable organisations, but also lasting legacies of trust, authenticity, and human flourishing.

For Companies & Organisations

10. Workplace Wellbeing Reset

(Chapters – 1-Breathing • 8-Nutrition • 21-Relaxation • 11-Grounding)

The health of an organisation is inseparable from the health of its people. In many workplaces, burnout, absenteeism, and disengagement have become the silent costs of modern business. This course offers a restorative reset, equipping employees and leaders with simple yet powerful practices to restore energy, sharpen focus, and improve wellbeing. From mindful breathing to grounding techniques, from nourishing nutrition to guided relaxation, participants learn to build daily rhythms that protect both productivity and personal health. A healthier workforce is not only more engaged and creative, but also more loyal, collaborative, and prepared to thrive in the face of change.

11. Diversity & Inclusion through the Heart

(Chapters – 5-Mirror • 7-Self-Love • 12-Kindness • 15-Compassion)

Diversity and inclusion cannot be reduced to policies or checklists, they must be lived and felt. This course takes a heart-centred approach to inclusion, guiding participants to first look into the mirror of self-awareness and acknowledge their own assumptions and biases. From there, practices of self-love, kindness, and compassion create the foundation for authentic connection across differences. The course provides leaders and teams with the emotional intelligence skills to build psychological safety, build empathy, and cultivate cultures where all voices are respected and valued. When inclusion is approached through the heart, organisations move beyond compliance into genuine belonging.

12. The Corporate Reset

(Chapters – 9-Nothingness • 23-Declutter • 11-Forgiveness • 28-Reflection)

In the relentless pursuit of growth, many organisations fall into the trap of *"busy culture"*, endless meetings, overflowing inboxes, and performance measured only by speed and output. This course invites companies to pause and reset. Through practices of stillness, decluttering, forgiveness, and structured reflection, teams and leaders learn to create space for what truly matters. By releasing what no longer serves and embedding a culture of presence, organisations rediscover clarity, innovation, and sustainable momentum. The Corporate Reset is not about slowing down progress; it is about ensuring progress has purpose, direction, and the energy to be sustained.

Together, these three specific courses address three of the most critical challenges facing companies today: **employee wellbeing, authentic inclusion, and cultural renewal**. They are designed to help organisations not only perform better but also create workplaces where people can flourish, collaborate, and lead with heart.

For Public Sector & Government Departments

13. Purpose-Driven Public Service

(Chapters – 13-God/The Divine • 30-Living Invitations • 3-I Am • 29-Homecoming)

Public service is more than a career, it is a calling. Yet in a climate of competing demands, political pressures, and limited resources, it is easy for public servants to lose sight of purpose and connection. This course invites participants to rediscover the *"why"* behind their work. Through reflection on values, identity, and legacy, leaders and teams reconnect with the deeper meaning of service: building trust with communities, honouring the dignity of citizens, and leaving behind a legacy of integrity and impact. By aligning personal purpose with organisational mission, public servants find renewed clarity, energy, and pride in their work.

14. Emotional Intelligence for Policy Leaders

(Chapters – 15-Compassion • 25-Listening • 10-Forgiveness • 28-Reflection)

Policies shape lives, yet too often they are crafted under immense pressure, with limited time for empathy, dialogue, and reflection. This course brings the human dimension back into policy leadership. Participants learn to listen deeply to stakeholders, practice compassion in negotiation, and balance rigour with understanding. Forgiveness and reflection are introduced as tools to navigate conflict, learn from mistakes, and make better long-term decisions. By embedding emotional intelligence into governance, policy leaders create not only more effective outcomes but also more trusted institutions, strengthening the social fabric that holds communities together.

15. Collaboration Across Boundaries

(Chapters – 20-Heart Whispers • 16-Photographs • 27-Spontaneity • 24-Laughter)

The challenges facing government, from climate resilience to social equity, cannot be solved by departments working in isolation. This course strengthens the ability of public servants to collaborate across silos, sectors, and communities. Using creative practices like story-sharing, visual reflection, and spontaneous problem-solving, participants learn to move beyond rigid protocols into genuine partnership. Through the simple power of laughter, presence, and connection, they rediscover that collaboration is not only possible but energising. The result is stronger partnerships, more innovative solutions, and a culture of trust that transcends traditional boundaries.

Together, these three specific courses give government leaders and employees the tools to **serve with clarity, decide with compassion, and collaborate with courage**. They honour the noble purpose of public service while equipping people to meet modern challenges with resilience, integrity, and heart.

Closing Reflection

At every level of society, we face the same questions: *How do I find balance? How do I lead with integrity? How do I live with purpose?* The answers are not found in more busyness, but in deeper connection, to ourselves, to others, and to the values that guide us.

The *Heart Unbound 2.0 Specialised Short Courses* provide more than skills; they offer a pathway back to what matters. By integrating emotional intelligence, compassion, creativity, and resilience into the fabric of daily life and leadership, these courses help shape healthier individuals, stronger teams, and more authentic organisations.

They are critical because they do not just prepare us for professional success, they prepare us for human success. In choosing to participate, you are not only investing in your career or studies; you are investing in the strength, clarity, and compassion that will sustain you through every challenge ahead.

The journey begins with a single step, and that step is a choice to live and lead unbound.

YOU ARE NOT ALONE

As you journey through *Heart Unbound 2.0*, there may be moments when your heart feels heavy or your reflections stir emotions that feel hard to carry. This is part of healing, and yet, you are never meant to walk this path by yourself. Support is not just available, it is your right.

The organisations listed here are included for you, because sometimes the most courageous act of self-love is reaching out and saying, *"I need support."* These groups offer free, confidential help. They exist to listen, to guide, and to stand beside you when you need it most.

Whether you are in Australia, New Zealand, the United States, Canada, or the United Kingdom, there are people ready to hear you, day or night. Reaching out is not a sign of weakness. It is a sign of strength. It is a way of honouring your heart and choosing life, connection, and hope.

Take these resources as companions on your journey. If ever you feel overwhelmed, please remember: help is just one call or message away, and you never have to face this alone.

Free Support Services — You Are Not Alone

Wherever you are on your *Heart Unbound 2.0* journey, support is always close at hand. These services are free, confidential, and available to you whenever you need to reach out.

Australia

- **Lifeline Australia** – 13 11 14 (24/7 crisis support and suicide prevention)

- **Beyond Blue** – 1300 22 4636 (24/7 support for anxiety, depression, and mental health)
- **Kids Helpline** – 1800 55 1800 (24/7 for children and young people aged 5–25)
- **Suicide Call Back Service** – 1300 659 467 (24/7 counselling for people at risk of suicide and their carers)

New Zealand

- **Lifeline New Zealand** – 0800 543 354 or free text 4357 (24/7 support)
- **1737, Need to Talk?** – Call or text 1737 (24/7 to talk with a trained counsellor)
- **Youthline** – 0800 376 633 or free text 234 (support for young people)

United States

- **988 Suicide & Crisis Lifeline** – Call or text 988 (24/7 for anyone in crisis)
- **National Alliance on Mental Illness (NAMI) Helpline** – 1-800-950-NAMI (Mon–Fri, 10am–10pm ET)
- **Crisis Text Line** – Text HOME to 741741 (24/7 to connect with a crisis counsellor)

Canada

- **Talk Suicide Canada** – 1-833-456-4566 or text 45645 (24/7 support for suicide prevention)
- **Kids Help Phone** – 1-800-668-6868 or text CONNECT to 686868 (24/7 for young people)
- **Wellness Together Canada** – 1-866-585-0445 (mental health and substance use support, available 24/7)

United Kingdom

- **Samaritans** – 116 123 (24/7 support for anyone in emotional distress)
- **Mind Infoline** – 0300 123 3393 (mental health support and resources)
- **Shout Crisis Text Line** – Text SHOUT to 85258 (24/7 support via text)

Please keep this page close. Just as you turn to your breath, your journal, or your heart, you can also turn to these voices of compassion whenever you need them. Reaching out is a way of returning home to yourself.

A Final Word on Support

Reaching out for help is not a sign of weakness, it is one of the deepest acts of strength. When you choose to call, text, or speak to someone who is there to listen, you are honouring your heart's need for care and connection.

Remember, your *Heart Unbound* journey is not meant to be travelled alone. Just as you are learning to listen to yourself with compassion, these services exist to listen to you too. They are lifelines in moments of heaviness, reminders that you are seen, valued, and never beyond hope.

Every time you take the brave step to reach out, you are not stepping back, you are stepping closer to your wholeness. You are choosing to live unbound: with courage, with tenderness, and with the quiet knowing that your heart is never alone.

ABOUT THE AUTHOR

Dr John McSwiney is the founder and managing director of *Time to Transform*, a global initiative dedicated to helping people live authentically, connect deeply, and lead with heart. With over 25 years of experience walking alongside individuals, leaders, and organisations, John has guided thousands on their journey of growth, transformation, and self-discovery.

A respected academic and author of *The Journey of 100 Hidden Hearts* and the first edition of *Heart Unbound: The Ultimate 28-Day Heart Connection Challenge*, John brings together the rigour of scholarship, the insights of neuroscience, and the wisdom of lived experience. His work bridges worlds, law and leadership, spirituality and psychology, corporate practice and personal growth, to offer a truly holistic approach to transformation, but John's deepest authority comes not from theory, but from his own lived journey of reconnection.

After decades of success marked by busyness and achievement, he found himself disconnected from his own heart. It was through the ocean, breath, reflection, and a courageous willingness to feel that he came home to the stillness, authenticity, and love he had long silenced. This personal homecoming now informs all that he teaches.

Today, John inspires people across universities, organisations, and communities to embrace a life led by compassion, courage, and presence. He believes that when you choose to live from your heart, not from fear, proving, or perfection, you step into your greatest freedom: to live fully, love deeply, and lead with truth.

Heart Unbound 2.0 is not just John's book, it is his invitation to you. An invitation to pause, to listen, and to come home to your own heart.